Accounting Practice: A Real-World Approach

会计真账实操教程

李婧 佟晨 主 编
[美] Young Kwak 林灵 副主编

东北财经大学出版社
Dongbei University of Finance & Economics Press
大 连

图书在版编目（CIP）数据

会计真账实操教程 / 李婧，佟晨主编．—大连：东北财经大学出版社，2018.5
ISBN 978-7-5654-3148-7

Ⅰ．会…　Ⅱ．①李…②佟…　Ⅲ．会计学-教材　Ⅳ．F230

中国版本图书馆CIP数据核字（2018）第089232号

东北财经大学出版社出版
（大连市黑石礁尖山街217号　邮政编码　116025）
网　　址：http://www.dufep.cn
读者信箱：dufep@dufe.edu.cn

大连美跃彩色印刷有限公司印刷　东北财经大学出版社发行

幅面尺寸：185mm×260mm　字数：602千字　印张：25　插页：1
2018年5月第1版　2018年5月第1次印刷

责任编辑：王　莹　刘晓彤　徐　群　责任校对：贺　贝
高　铭　吴　茜　周　晗
封面设计：张智波　版式设计：钟福建

定价：88.00元

教学支持　售后服务　联系电话：（0411）84710309
版权所有　侵权必究　举报电话：（0411）84710523
如有印装质量问题，请联系营销部：（0411）84710711

序

中美合作办学会计项目是宁波工程学院中外合作办学运行最成熟的项目之一，以国际一流商学院为依托，实行全英文教学，从教学大纲、课程设置、师资聘用到教学模式、教材资料，都全盘引自美方大学的商学院，与其本土专业完全一致。至今，该项目已连续招收七届本科生，培养的毕业生以其专业的实践操作能力、流利的英语水平深受用人单位好评。近年来，随着财务国际化、资本全球化的发展，越来越多的中国本土企业赴美上市，来华投资的美资企业越来越多，对拥有国际视野的会计人才的需求趋势越来越强烈。将本土企业案例与美式会计理论结合起来编写会计实践类配套教材是中外合作办学本土化培养方案实施的重要一环。

《会计真账实操教程》是会计理论教学的实践配套教材，全书以美国会计准则的最新规定为理论依据，采用中国本土企业真实案例，介绍手工会计核算和计算机会计核算，力求实现将美式会计理论与中国本土案例实践密切结合。本教材坚持学以致用的教学理念，融理论分析、方法应用、实践操作为一体，注重对学生综合应用能力的培养；引入本土案例和运用美式思维方式进行案例分析，激发学生的学习兴趣，培养学生发现问题、分析问题、解决问题的实践应用能力；通过理论和方法的实际操作，培养学生运用美式会计理论与方法解决中国企业会计问题的能力，注意培养学生的创新意识。通过本教材的学习，学生既能够掌握会计的基本理论、基本方法和基本分析技能，又能够掌握会计的先进分析方法，还能有针对性地提升运用信息技术解决企业管理决策问题的能力。

在框架设计上，与会计教材通常按会计要素介绍会计知识的方式不同，本教材以企业的业务循环为基础将会计知识与实际业务相结合，按照企业实际经营的先后顺序，依次介绍筹集资金业务、采购业务、生产过程、销售业务、经营成果核算、纳税实务等六大业务循环；将会计原理、会计实务及财务软件的应用三者融为一体；模拟中国本土企业实际会计月度的经济业务，以真实的案例资料再现企业实际经营过程。以美式电子账务系统为平台分步骤演示企业中财务管理信息化的具体实现方式和方法（请扫码阅读），与本教材的会计知识相呼应，让使用者体会到实战带来的收获。

本教材由美国特拉华州立大学和宁波工程学院国际交流学院的教师们共同编写。

编　者

2018年4月

Preface

Accounting cycle is a series of processes for an accountant to follow in order to finish his or her work during a certain period. This is a basic concept in accounting practice and therefore is the first lesson in this book.

Accounting cycle will be involved all the time. The seven steps are necessary to an accountant if he or she intends to prepare financial statements. All steps will be described one by one from Chapter 2 to Chapter 8. Xinle Air-blower Co., Ltd is adopted here as an example to explain each step.

Chapter 2 explains the first step of accounting cycle, which is to make journal entries and record those transactions in T-accounts. Journal entries will be made for all transactions of Xinle Air-blower Co., Ltd. Those transactions will also be recorded in T-accounts book. Chapter 3 explains the second step of accounting cycle, which is to post transactions recorded in journal entries to the ledger. Chapter 4 shows the third step of accounting cycle − to prepare unadjusted trial balance. The purpose of unadjusted trial balance is to make sure that all debits equal to all credits before adjusting entries were made. In Chapter 5, the fourth step of accounting cycle is described, which is to make adjusting journal entries and record those transactions in T-accounts. At this moment, there are no longer two types of journals. Only one journal should be used, which is the general journal. Chapter 6 explains the fifth step of accounting cycle, which is to prepare adjusted trial balance. The sixth step of accounting cycle is described in Chapter 7, which is to make closing entries and record those transactions in T-accounts. Chapter 8 shows the seventh step of accounting cycle, which is to prepare financial statements. There are three types of financial statements. They are income statement, balance sheet and cash flow statement. Statement of owners' equity will also be prepared.

Contents

CHAPTER 1 ACCOUNTING CYCLE

Accounting cycle will be introduced in this section. The seven steps are necessary for an accountant if he or she intends to prepare financial statements. All steps will be described one by one.

STEP 1 RECORD IN JOURNALS AND T-ACCOUNTS

The first step of accounting cycle is to make journal entries and record those transactions in T-accounts. There are two types of journals. They are general journal and special journal. Special journal can be various. Most small and medium companies in the United States will choose to open four kinds of special journals, which are cash receipts journal, cash payments journal, sales journal and purchases journal. Those four types of special journals are illustrated as follows with general journal. Transactions other than cash receipts, cash payments, sales and purchases should be recorded in general journal. When journal entries are posted to the ledger, post reference should be recorded. There are two columns to record the amount of the transaction. They are debit column and credit column.

GENERAL JOURNAL PAGE 1

	DATE		DESCRIPTION	POST. REF.	DEBIT	CREDIT	
1							1
2							2
3							3
4							4
5							5
6							6
7							7
8							8
9							9
10							10

Cash receipts journal is used to record all transactions that receive cash. Adoption of cash receipts journal can save a lot of time for accounting department since this journal has already listed all most frequently used account names. There are two types of cash. They are bank deposit and cash on hand.

CASH RECEIPTS JOURNAL										PAGE 1	
	DATE	DOC. NO.	ACCOUNT NAME	POST. REF.	GENERAL CREDIT	SALES CREDIT	SALES TAX PAYABLE CREDIT	ACCOUNTS RECEIVABLE CREDIT	BANK DEPOSIT DEBIT	CASH ON HAND DEBIT	
1											1
2											2
3											3
4											4
5											5
6											6
7											7
8											8
9											9
10											10

Cash payments journal is used to record all transactions that involve cash expenditure. Adoption of cash payments journal can save a lot of time for accounting department since this journal has already listed all most frequently used account names such as accounts payable, bank deposit and cash on hand. Accountants can also record in accounts that do not appear in this journal.

CASH PAYMENTS JOURNAL										PAGE 1
	DATE	DOC. NO.	ACCOUNT NAME	POST. REF.	GENERAL		ACCOUNTS PAYABLE DEBIT	BANK DEPOSIT CREDIT	CASH ON HAND CREDIT	
					DEBIT	CREDIT				
1										1
2										2
3										3
4										4
5										5
6										6
7										7
8										8
9										9
10										10

Sales journal is used to record all transactions for credit sales. Cash sales are not recorded in this journal. This journal has already listed all frequently used accounts for credit sales, such as sales revenue, sales tax payable and accounts receivable. Accountants should also specify customer's name in this journal.

SALES JOURNAL								PAGE 1
	DATE	SALES SLIP NO.	CUSTOMER'S ACCOUNT DEBITED	POST. REF.	SALES REVENUE CREDIT	SALES TAX PAYABLE CREDIT	ACCOUNTS RECEIVABLE DEBIT	
1								1
2								2
3								3
4								4
5								5
6								6
7								7
8								8
9								9
10								10

Purchases journal is used to record all transactions for credit purchases. Cash purchases are not recorded in this journal. This journal has already listed all frequently used accounts for credit purchases, such as accounts payable, purchases and general accounts. General accounts are used to record transactions in accounts that are not specified in this journal.

PURCHASES JOURNAL										PAGE 1
	DATE	INVOICE NO.	CREDITOR'S ACCOUNT CREDITED	POST. REF.	ACCOUNTS PAYABLE CREDIT	PURCHASES DEBIT	GENERAL			
							ACCOUNT DEBITED	POST. REF.	DEBIT	
1										1
2										2
3										3
4										4
5										5
6										6
7										7
8										8
9										9
10										10

T-accounts book is one of the most widely used tools to collect transactions. It is called T-account because of its shape. At the end of the period, balances of accounts will be calculated by accountants to make adjusting entries and to prepare financial statements.

Debit	Credit

Debit	Credit

Debit	Credit

Debit	Credit

Debit	Credit

Debit	Credit

Debit	Credit

Debit	Credit

Debit	Credit

STEP 2 POST TO THE LEDGER

The second step of accounting cycle is to post transactions recorded in journal entries to the ledger. There are two types of ledgers. They are general ledger and subsidiary ledger. Subsidiary ledger can be various. Most small and medium companies in the United States will choose to open a bunch of subsidiary ledgers. The appearance of general ledger and subsidiary ledger are similar. They are illustrated as following table. The column of POST. REF. will specify the journal type and page. For example, G1 means this transaction is posted from page 1 of general journal. There is also a column called POST. REF. in journal entries. In those columns, accountants need to specify account number of the ledger.

ACCOUNT__________ ACCOUNT NO. 101

	DATE	DESCRIPTION	POST. REF.	DEBIT	CREDIT	BALANCE		
						DEBIT	CREDIT	
1			G1					1
2								2
3								3
4								4
5								5
6								6
7								7
8								8
9								9
10								10

GENERAL JOURNAL PAGE 1

	DATE	DESCRIPTION	POST. REF.	DEBIT	CREDIT	
1			101			1
2						2
3						3
4						4
5						5
6						6
7						7
8						8
9						9
10						10

Account number and account name are necessary for posting. In practice, every company has its own account list book, which lists all account names and corresponding numbers. This can be illustrated in following table.

Control Account #	Sub-account Level 1 #	Sub-account Level 2 #	Sub-account Level 3 #	Account Name
101				Cash on Hand
102				Bank Deposit
103				Bank Draft
104				Notes Receivable
	1041			Notes Receivable-A
	1042			Notes Receivable-B
105				Discounts on Notes Receivable
106				Accounts Receivable
	1061			Accounts Receivable-A
	1062			Accounts Receivable-B
	1063			Accounts Receivable-C
⋮				⋮

STEP 3 PREPARE UNADJUSTED TRIAL BALANCE

The third step of accounting cycle is to prepare unadjusted trial balance. The purpose of worksheet unadjusted trial balance is to make sure that all debits equal to all credits before adjusting entries were made. Unadjusted trial balance reduces the time that accountants spend in searching for errors and therefore this improves the efficiency. This is illustrated in following table.

Unadjusted Trial Balance		
Account Name	Debit	Credit

STEP 4 PREPARE ADJUSTING ENTRIES AND POST TO THE LEDGER

The fourth step of accounting cycle is to make adjusting journal entries and record those transactions in T-accounts. At this moment, there are no longer two types of journals. Only one journal book should be used, which is the general journal. The recording and posting methods are similar to the ones for period transactions. Those entries should also be posted to the ledger. When journal entries are posted to the ledger, post reference should be recorded.

GENERAL JOURNAL						PAGE 1
	DATE	DESCRIPTION	POST. REF.	DEBIT	CREDIT	
1						1
2						2
3						3
4						4
5						5
6						6
7						7
8						8
9						9
10						10

POST TO THE LEDGER

Initial recording of those adjusting entries has been finished. Those entries should be posted to the ledger. Both general ledger and subsidiary ledger should be used at this point.

STEP 5 PREPARE ADJUSTED TRIAL BALANCE

The fifth step of accounting cycle is to prepare adjusted trial balance. The purpose of worksheet adjusted trial balance is to make sure that all debits equal to all credits before income statement was made. Adjusted trial balance reduces the time that accountants spend in searching for errors and therefore this improves the efficiency. This is illustrated in following table.

Adjusted Trial Balance		
Account Name	Debit	Credit

STEP 6 PREPARE CLOSING ENTRIES AND POST TO THE LEDGER

The sixth step of accounting cycle is to make closing entries and record those transactions in T-accounts. At this moment, there are no longer two types of journals. Only one journal book should be used, which is general journal. The recording and posting methods are similar to the ones for period transactions. Those entries should also be posted to the ledger. When journal entries are posted to the ledger, post reference should be recorded.

POST TO THE LEDGER

Initial recording of closing entries has been finished. Those entries should be posted to the ledger. Both general ledger and subsidiary ledger should be used at this point.

STEP 7 PREPARE FINANCIAL STATEMENTS

The seventh step of accounting cycle is to prepare financial statements. There are three types of financial statements. They are income statement, balance sheet and cash flow statement. Statement of owners' equity will also be prepared. The first two types of financial statements are illustrated in following tables.

Income Statement

For Year XXXX

Revenue		**Amount**
XXXXXXXX	$	XXXXXXXX
XXXXXXXX		XXXXXXXX
XXXXXXXX		**XXXXXXXX**
Expense		
XXXXXXXX		XXXXXXXX
XXXXXXXX		XXXXXXXX
XXXXXXXX		XXXXXXXX
Other Revenue & Expense		
XXXXXXXX		XXXXXXXX
XXXXXXXX		XXXXXXXX
XXXXXXXX		**XXXXXXXX**
XXXXXXXX		XXXXXXXX
XXXXXXXX	$	**XXXXXXXX**

Balance Sheet

For the Year Ended on XX XX, XXXX

Assets	XX/XX/XXXX
XXXXXXXX	$ XXXXXXXX
XXXXXXXX	XXXXXXXX
XXXXXXXX	XXXXXXXX
XXXXXXXX	XXXXXXXX
XXXXXXXX	XXXXXXXX
XXXXXXXX	XXXXXXXX
XXXXXXXX	XXXXXXXX
XXXXXXXX	XXXXXXXX
XXXXXXXX	XXXXXXXX
XXXXXXXX	XXXXXXXX
XXXXXXXX	XXXXXXXX
XXXXXXXX	XXXXXXXX
XXXXXXXX	XXXXXXXX
XXXXXXXX	XXXXXXXX
XXXXXXXX	XXXXXXXX
Liabilities	
XXXXXXXX	XXXXXXXX
XXXXXXXX	XXXXXXXX
XXXXXXXX	XXXXXXXX
XXXXXXXX	XXXXXXXX
XXXXXXXX	XXXXXXXX
XXXXXXXX	XXXXXXXX
XXXXXXXX	XXXXXXXX
XXXXXXXX	XXXXXXXX
XXXXXXXX	XXXXXXXX
XXXXXXXX	XXXXXXXX
Owner's Equity	
XXXXXXXX	XXXXXXXX
XXXXXXXX	XXXXXXXX
XXXXXXXX	XXXXXXXX
XXXXXXXX	XXXXXXXX
XXXXXXXX	$ XXXXXXXX

CHAPTER 2 RECORD IN JOURNALS AND T-ACCOUNTS

The first step of accounting cycle is to make journal entries and record those transactions in T-accounts. In the following part of this section, journal entries will be made for all transactions of Xinle Air-blower Co., Ltd. Those transactions will also be recorded in T-accounts book. In the United States, there is no invoice. Source documents in the United States are also different from those in China. These will be illustrated in following transactions.

TRANSACTION 1

On December 1, Xinle issued a check to withdraw $1, 500 for petty cash. The source document is CHECK STUB NO. 029. This source document is converted to same type of document in the United States. All the following source documents are converted version.

$ 1,500.00 CHECK STUB NO. 029

Date December 1 2016

To Xinle Air-blower Co., Ltd.

For Petty Cash

	Dollars	Cents
Balance brought forward	2,352,000	00
Add deposits		
Total	2,352,000	00
Less this check	1,500	00
Balance carried forward	2,350,500	00

WHAT TO DO?

Step 1 Analyze Transaction

Accounts Affected:

There are two accounts affected by this transaction. They are **Petty Cash** and **Bank Deposit.**

Increase/Decrease:

Petty Cash is increased by $1,500. **Bank Deposit** is decreased by $1,500.

Account Category:

Petty Cash is an asset account. **Bank Deposit** is an asset account.

Step 2 Determine Debit/Credit

The normal balance of asset accounts is debit. **Petty Cash** is debited by $1,500. **Bank Deposit** is credited by $1,500.

Step 3 Record in T-accounts

Petty Cash	
Debit	Credit
1,500	

Bank Deposit	
Debit	Credit
	1,500

Step 4 Record in Journals

CASH PAYMENTS JOURNAL PAGE 1

	DATE		DOC. NO.	ACCOUNT NAME	POST. REF.	GENERAL		ACCOUNTS PAYABLE DEBIT	BANK DEPOSIT CREDIT	CASH ON HAND CREDIT	
						DEBIT	CREDIT				
1	Dec.	1	CS029	Petty Cash		1 500 00			1 500 00		1
2											2
3											3
4											4

TRANSACTION 2

On December 1, Han Liang borrowed $1,500 from accounting department for business trip. Han Liang is a staff in human resource department.

WHAT TO DO?

There is no record for this transaction since most small and medium companies in the United States do not allow borrowings for business trip. Employees should first pay the bills by themselves and then get reimbursement from the companies. Therefore, it is assumed that Xinle does not allow borrowings for business trip.

TRANSACTION 3

On December 1, Ling Lin went back from her business trip. She borrowed $1,000 from accounting department but only spent $800 during the trip. She is a staff in management department. Xinle collected the rest of the money. The source document is INVOICE NO. 324.

Hilton Inn **INVOICE NO. 324**

132 Clown Plaza
Shanghai, China 200000

DATE: Nov. 30, 2016
TERMS: Payable in 30 days

TO APT 11723
271 Zhongshan ST
Xiangshan, China 315700

ROOM #	NAME	CHECK-IN	CHECK-OUT	PRICE/NITE	TOTAL
201	Ling Lin	11/29/2016	11/30/2016	$ 800.00	$ 800.00

WHAT TO DO?

Just as mentioned in last transaction, most small and medium companies in the United States do not allow borrowings for business trip. It is assumed that Xinle does not allow borrowings for business trip. Therefore, this transaction is treated as this employee paid the bills herself first and then tried to get reimbursement from the company. Suppose that the company would reimburse the fees by cash.

Step 1 Analyze Transaction

Accounts Affected:

There are two accounts affected by this transaction. They are **M&A Travel Expense** and **Cash on Hand.**

Increase/Decrease:

M&A Travel Expense is increased by $800. **Cash on Hand** is decreased by $800.

Account Category:

M&A Travel Expense is an expense account. **Cash on Hand** is an asset account.

Step 2 Determine Debit/Credit

–The normal balance of expense accounts is debit. **M&A Travel Expense** is debited by $800.

–The normal balance of asset accounts is debit. **Cash on Hand** is credited by $800.

Step 3 Record in T-accounts

M&A Travel Expense

Debit	Credit
800	

Cash on Hand

Debit	Credit
	800

Step 4 Record in Journals

CASH PAYMENTS JOURNAL											PAGE 1
	DATE		DOC. NO.	ACCOUNT NAME	POST. REF.	GENERAL		ACCOUNTS PAYABLE DEBIT	BANK DEPOSIT CREDIT	CASH ON HAND CREDIT	
						DEBIT	CREDIT				
2	Dec.	1	INV324	M&A Travel Expense		800 00				800 00	2
3											3
4											4
5											5

TRANSACTION 4

On December 1, Xinle paid $30 for bank service fee. The source document is RECEIPT NO. 12.

China Construction Bank
155 Yuji ST
Xiangshan, China 315700

RECEIPT

No. 12

Dec. 1 2016

RECEIVED FROM Xinle Air-blower Co., Ltd. $ 30.00

Thirty and no/100 DOLLARS

FOR Checks Purchase 12/01/2016

RECEIVED BY *Yu Li*

WHAT TO DO?

Step 1 Analyze Transaction

Accounts Affected:

There are two accounts affected by this transaction. They are **Bank Fee Expense** and **Bank Deposit.**

Increase/Decrease:

Bank Fee Expense is increased by $30. **Bank Deposit** is decreased by $30.

Account Category:

Bank Fee Expense is an expense account. **Bank Deposit** is an asset account.

Step 2 Determine Debit/Credit

–The normal balance of expense accounts is debit. **Bank Fee Expense** is debited by $30.

–The normal balance of asset accounts is debit. **Bank Deposit** is credited by $30.

Step 3 Record in T-accounts

Bank Fee Expense	
Debit	Credit
30	

Bank Deposit	
Debit	Credit
	30

Step 4 Record in Journals

CASH PAYMENTS JOURNAL											PAGE 1
	DATE		DOC. NO.	ACCOUNT NAME	POST. REF.	GENERAL		ACCOUNTS PAYABLE DEBIT	BANK DEPOSIT CREDIT	CASH ON HAND CREDIT	
						DEBIT	CREDIT				
3	Dec.	1	REC12	Bank Fee Expense		30 00			30 00		3
4											4
5											5
6											6

TRANSACTION 5

On December 2, Xinle purchased a saw machine at the after-tax price of $234,000. The installment fee was $2,000. The source document is CHECK STUB NO. 030. The product price was $200,000, and the sales tax rate in the United States is 9% instead of 17%. Therefore, the after-tax price is no longer $234,000. Instead, it should have been $218,000. There is no tax on service. In other words, the installment fee is tax free. Xinle should have paid $220,000 to Ninghai Machinery Co., Ltd.

$ 220,000.00 **CHECK STUB NO. 030**

Date December 2 2016

To Ninghai Machinery Co., Ltd.

For Saw Machine Purchase

	Dollars	Cents
Balance brought forward	2,350,470	00
Add deposits		
Total	2,350,470	00
Less this check	220,000	00
Balance carried forward	2,130,470	00

WHAT TO DO?

Step 1 Analyze Transaction

Accounts Affected:

There are two accounts affected by this transaction. They are **Saw Machine** and **Bank Deposit.**

Increase/Decrease:

Saw Machine is increased by $220,000. **Bank Deposit** is decreased by $220,000.

Account Category:

Saw Machine is an asset account. **Bank Deposit** is an asset account.

Step 2 Determine Debit/Credit

The normal balance of asset accounts is debit. **Saw Machine** is debited by $220,000. **Bank Deposit** is credited by $220,000.

Step 3 Record in T-accounts

Saw Machine

Debit	Credit
220,000	

Bank Deposit

Debit	Credit
	220,000

Step 4 Record in Journals

CASH PAYMENTS JOURNAL PAGE 1

	DATE		DOC. NO.	ACCOUNT NAME	POST. REF.	GENERAL		ACCOUNTS PAYABLE DEBIT	BANK DEPOSIT CREDIT	CASH ON HAND CREDIT	
						DEBIT	CREDIT				
4	Dec.	2	CS030	Saw Machine		220 000 00			220 000 00		4
5											5
6											6
7											7

TRANSACTION 6

On December 2, Xinle collected $100,000 accounts receivable from Fenghua Air-blower Co., Ltd. The source document is REMITTANCE ADVICE NO. 291.

REMITTANCE ADVICE

NO. 291

Fenghua Air-blower
116 Yunhui ST
Fenghua
China 315500

Date: 12/02/2016

To: Xinle Air-blower
23 Tulan ST
Xiangshan
China 315700

Date	Invoice No.	Amount
11/21/2016	291	100,000.00
		100,000.00

WHAT TO DO?

Step 1 Analyze Transaction

Accounts Affected:

There are two accounts affected by this transaction. They are **Bank Deposit** and **Accounts Receivable–Fenghua Air-blower.**

Increase/Decrease:

Bank Deposit is increased by $100, 000. **Accounts Receivable–Fenghua Air–blower** is decreased by $100,000.

Account Category:

Bank Deposit is an asset account. **Accounts Receivable–Fenghua Air–blower** is an asset account.

Step 2 Determine Debit/Credit

The normal balance of asset accounts is debit. Bank Deposit is debited by $100, 000. **Accounts Receivable–Fenghua Air-blower** is credited by $100,000.

Step 3 Record in T-accounts

Bank Deposit	
Debit	Credit
100,000	

Accounts Receivable–Fenghua Air-blower	
Debit	Credit
	100,000

Step 4 Record in Journals

CASH RECEIPTS JOURNAL											PAGE 1
	DATE	DOC. NO.	ACCOUNT NAME	POST. REF.	GENERAL CREDIT	SALES CREDIT	SALES TAX PAYABLE CREDIT	ACCOUNTS RECEIVABLE CREDIT	BANK DEPOSIT DEBIT	CASH ON HAND DEBIT	
1	Dec. 2	RA291	AR-FHAB					100 000 00	100 000 00		1
2											2
3											3
4											4

TRANSACTION 7

On December 2, Xinle purchased 20-ton steel plates from Beijing Steel Co., Ltd. Unit price was $8,000/ton. Delivery fee was $4,000. The source document is CHECK STUB NO. 031. Since sales tax rate in the United States is 9%, sales tax should be $14,400. After-tax price was $174,400. There is no tax on service. In other words, delivery fee is tax free. Xinle should have paid $178,400 to Beijing Steel Co., Ltd.

$ 178,400.00 CHECK STUB NO. 031

Date December 2 2016

To Beijing Steel Co., Ltd.

For 20-ton Steel Plates and Delivery Fee

	Dollars	Cents
Balance brought forward	2,230,470	00
Add deposits		
Total	2,230,470	00
Less this check	178,400	00
Balance carried forward	2,052,070	00

WHAT TO DO?

Suppose that Xinle currently uses standard costing method. The standard cost of steel plates is $7,500/ton. Therefore, standard total cost of those steel plates is $150,000.

Step 1 Analyze Transaction

Accounts Affected:

There are four accounts affected by this transaction. They are **Steel Plates, Material Price Variance, Factory Overhead Incurred** and **Bank Deposit.**

Increase/Decrease:

Steel Plates is increased by $150,000. **Material Price Variance** is increased by $10,000.

Factory Overhead Incurred is increased by $18,400. **Bank Deposit** is decreased by $178,400.

Account Category:

Steel Plates is an asset account. **Material Price Variance** is an asset account. **Factory Overhead Incurred** is an asset account. **Bank Deposit** is an asset account.

Step 2 Determine Debit/Credit

The normal balance of asset accounts is debit. **Steel Plates** is debited by $150,000. **Material Price Variance** is debited by $10,000. **Factory Overhead Incurred** is debited by $18,400. **Bank Deposit** is credited by $178,400.

Step 3 Record in T-accounts

Steel Plates

Debit	Credit
150,000	

Material Price Variance

Debit	Credit
10,000	

Factory Overhead Incurred

Debit	Credit
18,400	

Bank Deposit

Debit	Credit
	178,400

Step 4 Record in Journals

CASH PAYMENTS JOURNAL PAGE 1

	DATE		DOC. NO.	ACCOUNT NAME	POST. REF.	GENERAL DEBIT	GENERAL CREDIT	ACCOUNTS PAYABLE DEBIT	BANK DEPOSIT CREDIT	CASH ON HAND CREDIT	
5	Dec.	2	CS031	Steel Plates		150 000 00			178 400 00		5
6				Material Pric. Var.		10 000 00					6
7				Fac. O/H Incurred		18 400 00					7
8											8

TRANSACTION 8

On December 3, Xinle purchased 10-ton iron castings from Beijing Steel Co., Ltd. Unit price was $5,000/ton. Delivery fee was $2,000. The source document is CHECK STUB NO. 032. Since sales tax rate in the United States is 9%, sales tax should be $4,500. After-tax price was $54,500. There is no tax on service. In other words, delivery fee is tax free. Xinle should have paid $56,500 to Beijing Steel Co., Ltd.

$ 56,500.00 **CHECK STUB NO. 032**

Date December 3 2016

To Beijing Steel Co., Ltd.

For 10-ton Iron Castings and Delivery Fee

	Dollars	Cents
Balance brought forward	2,052,070	00
Add deposits		
Total	2,052,070	00
Less this check	56,500	00
Balance carried forward	1,995,570	00

WHAT TO DO?

Suppose that Xinle currently uses standard costing method. The standard cost of iron castings is $4,500/ton. Therefore, standard total cost of those iron castings is $45,000.

Step 1 Analyze Transaction

Accounts Affected:

There are four accounts affected by this transaction. They are **Iron Castings, Material Price Variance, Factory Overhead Incurred** and **Bank Deposit.**

Increase/Decrease:

Iron Castings is increased by $45,000. **Material Price Variance** is increased by $5,000. **Factory Overhead Incurred** is increased by $6,500. **Bank Deposit** is decreased by $56,500.

Account Category:

Iron Castings is an asset account. **Material Price Variance** is an asset account. **Factory Overhead Incurred** is an asset account. **Bank Deposit** is an asset account.

Step 2 Determine Debit/Credit

The normal balance of asset accounts is debit. **Iron Castings** is debited by $45,000. **Material Price Variance** is debited by $5,000. **Factory Overhead Incurred** is debited by $6,500. **Bank Deposit** is credited by $56,500.

Step 3 Record in T-accounts

Iron Castings

Debit	Credit
45,000	

Material Price Variance

Debit	Credit
5,000	

Factory Overhead Incurred	
Debit	Credit
6,500	

Bank Deposit	
Debit	Credit
	56,500

Step 4 Record in Journals

CASH PAYMENTS JOURNAL PAGE 1

	DATE		DOC. NO.	ACCOUNT NAME	POST. REF.	GENERAL DEBIT	GENERAL CREDIT	ACCOUNTS PAYABLE DEBIT	BANK DEPOSIT CREDIT	CASH ON HAND CREDIT	
8	Dec.	3	CS032	Iron Castings		45 000 00			56 500 00		8
9				Material Pric. Var.		5 000 00					9
10				Fac. O/H Incurred		6 500 00					10
11											11

TRANSACTION 9

On December 3, Xinle reimbursed $1,200 for telecommunication fee by cash. The source document is RECEIPT NO. 229.

China Unicom RECEIPT

341 Minghai ST

Xiangshan, China 315700 No. 229

Dec. 3 2016

RECEIVED FROM Xinle Air-blower Co., Ltd. $ 1,200.00

One thousand and two hundred and no/100 DOLLARS

FOR Telecommunication Fee 12/03/2016

RECEIVED BY *Yu Li*

WHAT TO DO?

Step 1 Analyze Transaction

Accounts Affected:

There are two accounts affected by this transaction. They are **Telecommunication Expense** and **Cash on Hand.**

Increase/Decrease:

Telecommunication Expense is increased by $1,200. **Cash on Hand** is decreased by $1,200.

Account Category:

Telecommunication Expense is an expense account. **Cash on Hand** is an asset account.

Step 2 Determine Debit/Credit

–The normal balance of expense accounts is debit. **Telecommunication Expense** is debited by $1,200.

–The normal balance of asset accounts is debit. **Cash on Hand** is credited by $1,200.

Step 3 Record in T-accounts

Telecommunication Expense	
Debit	Credit
1,200	

Cash on Hand	
Debit	Credit
	1,200

Step 4 Record in Journals

CASH PAYMENTS JOURNAL PAGE 1

	DATE		DOC. NO.	ACCOUNT NAME	POST. REF.	GENERAL DEBIT	GENERAL CREDIT	ACCOUNTS PAYABLE DEBIT	BANK DEPOSIT CREDIT	CASH ON HAND CREDIT	
11	Dec.	3	REC229	Tele. Expense		1 2 0 0 00				1 2 0 0 00	11
12											12
13											13
14											14

TRANSACTION 10

On December 3, Xinle purchased 50 packing boxes from Zhenhai Supplies Co., Ltd. Unit price was $40 per box. There was no delivery fee. The source document is CHECK STUB NO. 033. Since sales tax rate in the United States is 9%, sales tax should be $180. After-tax price was $2,180. Xinle should have paid $2,180 to Zhenhai Supplies Co., Ltd.

$ 2,180.00 CHECK STUB NO. 033

Date December 3 2016

To Zhenhai Supplies Co., Ltd.

For 50 Packing Boxes

	Dollars	Cents
Balance brought forward	1,995,570	00
Add deposits		
Total	1,995,570	00
Less this check	2,180	00
Balance carried forward	1,993,390	00

WHAT TO DO?

Suppose that Xinle currently uses standard costing method. Packing boxes are indirect material, and therefore the concept of standard cost cannot apply to it.

Step 1 Analyze Transaction

Accounts Affected:

There are three accounts affected by this transaction. They are **Packing Boxes, Factory Overhead Incurred** and **Bank Deposit.**

Increase/Decrease:

Packing Boxes is increased by $2, 000. **Factory Overhead Incurred** is increased by $180. **Bank Deposit** is decreased by $2,180.

Account Category:

Packing Boxes is an asset account. **Factory Overhead Incurred** is an asset account. **Bank Deposit** is an asset account.

Step 2 Determine Debit/Credit

The normal balance of asset accounts is debit. **Packing Boxes** is debited by $2,000. **Factory Overhead Incurred** is debited by $180. **Bank Deposit** is credited by $2,180.

Step 3 Record in T-accounts

Packing Boxes

Debit	Credit
2,000	

Factory Overhead Incurred

Debit	Credit
180	

Bank Deposit

Debit	Credit
	2,180

Step 4 Record in Journals

CASH PAYMENTS JOURNAL PAGE 1

	DATE		DOC. NO.	ACCOUNT NAME	POST. REF.	GENERAL DEBIT	GENERAL CREDIT	ACCOUNTS PAYABLE DEBIT	BANK DEPOSIT CREDIT	CASH ON HAND CREDIT	
12	Dec.	3	CS033	Packing Boxes		2 0 0 0 00			2 1 8 0 00		12
13				Fac. O/H Incurred		1 8 0 00					13
14											14
15											15

TRANSACTION 11

On December 4, Xinle sold 1 000 small air-blowers to Fenghua Air-blower Co., Ltd. The unit price was $350. Since sales tax rate in the United States is 9%, sales tax should be $31,500. After-tax price was $381,500. The source document is SALES SLIP NO. 68.

Xinle Air-blower					
23 Tulan ST, Xiangshan, China 315700					
DATE: December 4, 2016			NO. 68		
SOLD TO	Fenghua Air-blower 116 Yunhui ST Fenghua, China 315500				
CLERK B.E.	CASH	CHARGE √	TERMS N/A		
QTY.	DESCRIPTION	UNIT PRICE	AMOUNT		
1 000	Small Air-blowers	$ 350.00	$ 350,000	00	
Thank You!		SUBTOTAL	$ 350,000	00	
		SALES TAX	31,500	00	
		TOTAL	$ 381,500	00	

The delivery fee was $3,000. Xinle paid it for Fenghua Air-blower Co., Ltd. The source document is CHECK STUB NO. 034.

$ 3,000.00 **CHECK STUB NO. 034**

Date December 4 2016

To Fenghua Air-blower Co., Ltd.

For Delivery Fee

	Dollars	Cents
Balance brought forward	1,993,390	00
Add deposits		
Total	1,993,390	00
Less this check	3,000	00
Balance carried forward	1,990,390	00

WHAT TO DO?

For this transaction, three entries should be made. The first one is to record the sales of 1 000 small air-blowers. The second one is to record the delivery fee paid by Xinle. The third one is to record the change in inventory system. The unit cost of small air-blower is $250, and therefore cost of goods sold should be $250,000.

Step 1 Analyze Transaction

Accounts Affected:

- For the first entry, there are three accounts affected by this transaction. They are **Accounts Receivable–Fenghua Air-blower, Sales Revenue–Small Air-blower** and **Sales Tax Payable.**
- For the second entry, there are two accounts affected by this transaction. They are **Other Receivable–Fenghua Air-blower** and **Bank Deposit.**
- For the third entry, there are two accounts affected by this transaction. They are **Cost of Goods Sold–Small Air-blower** and **Finished Goods–Small Air-blower.**

Increase/Decrease:

- **Accounts Receivable–Fenghua Air-blower** is increased by $381,500. **Sales Revenue–Small Air-blower** is increased by $350,000. **Sales Tax Payable** is increased by $31,500.
- **Other Receivables–Fenghua Air-blower** is increased by $3,000. **Bank Deposit** is decreased by $3,000.
- **Cost of Goods Sold–Small Air-blower** is increased by $250,000. **Finished Goods–Small Air-blower** is decreased by $250,000.

Account Category:

- **Accounts Receivable–Fenghua Air-blower** is an asset account. **Sales Revenue–Small Air-blower** is a revenue account. **Sales Tax Payable** is a liability account.
- **Other Receivables–Fenghua Air-blower** is an asset account. **Bank Deposit** is an asset account.
- **Cost of Goods Sold–Small Air-blower** is an expense account. **Finished Goods–Small Air-blower** is an asset account.

Step 2 Determine Debit/Credit

- The normal balance of asset accounts is debit. **Accounts Receivable–Fenghua Air-blower** is debited by $381,500.
- The normal balance of revenue accounts is credit. **Sales Revenue–Small Air-blower** is credited by $350,000.
- The normal balance of liability accounts is credit. **Sales Tax Payable** is credited by $31,500.

- The normal balance of asset accounts is debit. **Other Receivables–Fenghua Air-blower** is debited by $3,000.
- The normal balance of asset accounts is debit. **Bank Deposit** is credited by $3,000.

- The normal balance of expense accounts is debit. **Cost of Goods Sold–Small Air-blower** is debited by $250,000.

–The normal balance of asset accounts is debit. **Finished Goods–Small Air-blower** is credited by $250,000.

Step 3 Record in T-accounts

Accounts Receivable–Fenghua Air-blower

Debit	Credit
381,500	

Sales Revenue–Small Air-blower

Debit	Credit
	350,000

Sales Tax Payable

Debit	Credit
	31,500

Other Receivables–Fenghua Air-blower

Debit	Credit
3,000	

Bank Deposit

Debit	Credit
	3,000

Cost of Goods Sold–Small Air-blower

Debit	Credit
250,000	

Finished Goods–Small Air-blower

Debit	Credit
	250,000

Step 4 Record in Journals

SALES JOURNAL PAGE 1

	DATE		SALES SLIP NO.	CUSTOMER'S ACCOUNT DEBITED	POST. REF.	SALES CREDIT	SALES TAX PAYABLE CREDIT	ACCOUNTS RECEIVABLE DEBIT	
1	Dec.	4	68	Fenghua Air-blower–Small Air-blower		350 0 0 0 00	31 5 0 0 00	381 5 0 0 00	1
2									2
3									3
4									4

GENERAL JOURNAL							PAGE 1
	DATE		DESCRIPTION	POST. REF.	DEBIT	CREDIT	
1	Dec.	4	Other Receivables–Fenghua Air-blower		3 0 0 0 00		1
2			Bank Deposit			3 0 0 0 00	2
3			*CHECK STUB 034*				3
4	Dec.	4	Cost of Goods Sold–Small Air-blower		250 0 0 0 00		4
5			Finished Goods–Small Air-blower			250 0 0 0 00	5
6			*SALES SLIP 68*				6
7							7

TRANSACTION 12

On December 4, Xinle issued a cash check to withdraw $2,000 for petty cash. The source document is CHECK STUB NO. 035.

$ 2,000.00 CHECK STUB NO. 035

Date December 4 2016

To Xinle Air-blower Co., Ltd.

For Petty Cash

	Dollars	Cents
Balance brought forward	1,990,390	00
Add deposits		
Total	1,990,390	00
Less this check	2,000	00
Balance carried forward	1,988,390	00

WHAT TO DO?

Step 1 Analyze Transaction

Accounts Affected:

There are two accounts affected by this transaction. They are **Petty Cash** and **Bank Deposit.**

Increase/Decrease:

Petty Cash is increased by $2,000. **Bank Deposit** is decreased by $2,000.

Account Category:

Petty Cash is an asset account. **Bank Deposit** is an asset account.

Step 2 Determine Debit/Credit

The normal balance of asset accounts is debit. **Petty Cash** is debited by $2,000. **Bank Deposit** is credited by $2,000.

Step 3 Record in T-accounts

Petty Cash	
Debit	Credit
2,000	

Bank Deposit	
Debit	Credit
	2,000

Step 4 Record in Journals

CASH PAYMENTS JOURNAL PAGE 1

	DATE		DOC. NO.	ACCOUNT NAME	POST. REF.	GENERAL DEBIT	GENERAL CREDIT	ACCOUNTS PAYABLE DEBIT	BANK DEPOSIT CREDIT	CASH ON HAND CREDIT	
14	Dec.	4	CS035	Petty Cash		2 000 00			2 000 00		14
15											15
16											16
17											17

TRANSACTION 13

On December 4, Xinle paid value - added tax, corporate income tax, construction and maintenance tax, education surcharge, local education surcharge, and employee income tax. Value-added Tax was $658,000. Corporate Income Tax was $472,800. Construction and Maintenance Tax was $46,060. Education Surcharge was $19,740. Local Education Surcharge was $6,580. Employee Income Tax was $2,016. The source document is CHECK STUB NO. 036.

$ 1,205,196.00 CHECK STUB NO. 036

Date December 4 2016

To Ningbo Tax Bureau

For Value-added Tax, Corporate Income Tax, Construction and Maintenance Tax, Education Surcharge, Local Education Surcharge, and Employee Income Tax

	Dollars	Cents
Balance brought forward	1,988,390	00
Add deposits		
Total	1,988,390	00
Less this check	1,205,196	00
Balance carried forward	783,194	00

WHAT TO DO?

Since tax system in China is different from that in the United States, those taxes should be adjusted to satisfy tax system in the United States. Corporate Income Tax Payable is divided into two accounts, and each account accounts for a half of the balance of Corporate Income Tax Payable, which is $236, 400. Those two accounts are Federal Income Tax Payable and State Income Tax Payable. Besides, the rest amount of Tax Payable is equally added to those two accounts. Therefore, the balance of each account should be $601, 590. Employee Income Tax Payable is also divided into two accounts. Those two accounts are Employee Federal Income Tax Payable and Employee State Income Tax Payable. Employee Federal Income Tax Payable accounts for 1/3 of the balance of Employee Income Tax Payable, which is $672. Employee State Income Tax Payable accounts for 2/3 of the balance of Employee Income Tax Payable, which is $1,344. This can be described in following table:

Accounts	Amount	Adaption
Value-added Tax	$658,000	–Federal Income Tax: $601,590 –State Income Tax: $601,590
Corporate Income Tax	472,800	
Construction and Maintenance Tax	46,060	
Education Surcharge	19,740	
Local Education Surcharge	6,580	
Employee Income Tax	2,016	–Employee Federal Income Tax Payable: $672 –Employee State Income Tax Payable: $1,344

Step 1 Analyze Transaction

Accounts Affected:

There are five accounts affected by this transaction. They are **Federal Income Tax Payable, State Income Tax Payable, Employee Federal Income Tax Payable, Employee State Income Tax Payable** and **Bank Deposit.**

Increase/Decrease:

Federal Income Tax Payable is decreased by $601, 590. **State Income Tax Payable** is decreased by $601,590. **Employee Federal Income Tax Payable** is decreased by $672. **Employee State Income Tax Payable** is decreased by $1,344. **Bank Deposit** is decreased by $1,205,196.

Account Category:

Federal Income Tax Payable is a liability account. **State Income Tax Payable** is a liability account. **Employee Federal Income Tax Payable** is a liability account. **Employee State Income Tax Payable** is a liability account. **Bank Deposit** is an asset account.

Step 2 Determine Debit/Credit

–The normal balance of liability accounts is credit. **Federal Income Tax Payable** is debited by $601, 590. **State Income Tax Payable** is debited by $601, 590. **Employee Federal Income Tax Payable** is debited by $672. **Employee State Income Tax Payable** is debited by $1,344.

–The normal balance of asset accounts is debit. **Bank Deposit** is credited by $1,205,196.

Step 3 Record in T-accounts

Federal Income Tax Payable

Debit	Credit
601,590	

State Income Tax Payable

Debit	Credit
601,590	

Employee Federal Income Tax Payable

Debit	Credit
672	

Employee State Income Tax Payable

Debit	Credit
1,344	

Bank Deposit

Debit	Credit
	1,205,196

Step 4 Record in Journals

CASH PAYMENTS JOURNAL										PAGE 1	
	DATE		DOC. NO.	ACCOUNT NAME	POST. REF.	GENERAL DEBIT	GENERAL CREDIT	ACCOUNTS PAYABLE DEBIT	BANK DEPOSIT CREDIT	CASH ON HAND CREDIT	
15	Dec.	4	CS036	FITP		601 590 00			1205 196 00		15
16				SITP		601 590 00					16
17				Employee FITP		672 00					17
18				Employee SITP		1344 00					18
19											19

TRANSACTION 14

On December 4, Xinle paid $90, 000 for next - year insurance. The source document is CHECK STUB NO. 037.

CHECK STUB NO. 037

$ 90,000.00

Date December 4 2016

To China Life Insurance Co., Ltd.

For 2017 Insurance Fee

	Dollars	Cents
Balance brought forward	783,194	00
Add deposits		
Total	783,194	00
Less this check	90,000	00
Balance carried forward	693,194	00

WHAT TO DO?

Step 1 Analyze Transaction

Accounts Affected:

There are two accounts affected by this transaction. They are **Prepaid Insurance** and **Bank Deposit.**

Increase/Decrease:

Prepaid Insurance is increased by $90,000. **Bank Deposit** is decreased by $90,000.

Account Category:

Prepaid Insurance is an asset account. **Bank Deposit** is an asset account.

Step 2 Determine Debit/Credit

The normal balance of asset accounts is debit. **Prepaid Insurance** is debited by $90, 000. **Bank Deposit** is credited by $90,000.

Step 3 Record in T-accounts

Prepaid Insurance	
Debit	Credit
90,000	

Bank Deposit	
Debit	Credit
	90,000

Step 4 Record in Journals

CASH PAYMENTS JOURNAL											PAGE 1
	DATE		DOC. NO.	ACCOUNT NAME	POST. REF.	GENERAL		ACCOUNTS PAYABLE DEBIT	BANK DEPOSIT CREDIT	CASH ON HAND CREDIT	
						DEBIT	CREDIT				
19	Dec.	4	CS037	Prepaid Insurance		90 000 00			90 000 00		19
20											20
21											21
22											22

TRANSACTION 15

On December 4, Xinle borrowed $600,000 and put it in the bank. The source document is LOAN 38.

LOAN 38

$ 600,000.00

Six months ______ after date Xinle Air-blower Co., Ltd. promise to pay to

China Construction Bank Co., Ltd. ______ the sum of

Six hundred thousand dollars ______ with interest at the rate of

6.84% ______ per year.

Due date May 4, 2017

Ming Li

WHAT TO DO?

Step 1 Analyze Transaction

Accounts Affected:

There are two accounts affected by this transaction. They are **Bank Deposit** and **Short-term Borrowings–China Construction Bank.**

Increase/Decrease:

Bank Deposit is increased by $600,000. **Short-term Borrowings–China Construction Bank** is decreased by $600,000.

Account Category:

Bank Deposit is an asset account. **Short - term Borrowings–China Construction Bank** is an asset account.

Step 2 Determine Debit/Credit

The normal balance of asset accounts is debit. **Bank Deposit** is debited by $600,000. **Short-term Borrowings–China Construction Bank** is credited by $600,000.

Step 3 Record in T-accounts

Bank Deposit	
Debit	Credit
600,000	

Short-term Borrowings–China Construction Bank	
Debit	Credit
	600,000

Step 4 Record in Journals

	CASH RECEIPTS JOURNAL										PAGE 1
	DATE	DOC. NO.	ACCOUNT NAME	POST. REF.	GENERAL CREDIT	SALES CREDIT	SALES TAX PAYABLE CREDIT	ACCOUNTS RECEIVABLE CREDIT	BANK DEPOSIT DEBIT	CASH ON HAND DEBIT	
2	DEC. 4	L38	STB–CCB		600000 00				600000 00		2
3											3
4											4
5											5

TRANSACTION 16

On December 5, Xinle purchased 6-ton copper line from Hebei Steel Co., Ltd. Unit price was $18,000/ton. Delivery fee was $1,000. The source document is CHECK STUB NO. 038. Since sales tax rate in the United States is 9%, sales tax should be $9,720. After-tax price was $117,720. There is no tax on service. In other words, delivery fee is tax free. Xinle should have paid $118,720 to Hebei Steel Co., Ltd.

$ 118,720.00 **CHECK STUB NO. 038**

Date December 5 2016

To Hebei Steel Co., Ltd.

For 6-ton Copper Line and Delivery Fee

	Dollars	Cents
Balance brought forward	1,293,194	00
Add deposits		
Total	1,293,194	00
Less this check	118,720	00
Balance carried forward	1,174,474	00

WHAT TO DO?

Suppose that Xinle currently uses standard costing method. The standard cost of copper line is $17,500/ton. Therefore, standard total cost of those copper line is $105,000.

Step 1 Analyze Transaction

Accounts Affected:

There are four accounts affected by this transaction. They are **Copper Line, Material Price Variance, Factory Overhead Incurred** and **Bank Deposit.**

Increase/Decrease:

Copper Line is increased by $105, 000. **Material Price Variance** is increased by $3, 000.

Factory Overhead Incurred is increased by $6,500. **Bank Deposit** is decreased by $56,500.

Account Category:

Copper Line is an asset account. **Material Price Variance** is an asset account. **Factory Overhead Incurred** is an asset account. **Bank Deposit** is an asset account.

Step 2 Determine Debit/Credit

The normal balance of asset accounts is debit. **Copper Line** is debited by $105,000. **Material Price Variance** is debited by $3, 000. **Factory Overhead Incurred** is debited by $6, 500. **Bank Deposit** is credited by $56,500.

Step 3 Record in T-accounts

Copper Line

Debit	Credit
105,000	

Material Price Variance

Debit	Credit
3,000	

Factory Overhead Incurred

Debit	Credit
10,720	

Bank Deposit

Debit	Credit
	118,720

Step 4 Record in Journals

CASH PAYMENTS JOURNAL PAGE 1

	DATE		DOC. NO.	ACCOUNT NAME	POST. REF.	GENERAL DEBIT	GENERAL CREDIT	ACCOUNTS PAYABLE DEBIT	BANK DEPOSIT CREDIT	CASH ON HAND CREDIT	
20	Dec.	5	CS038	Copper Line		105 000 00			118 720 00		20
21				Material Pric. Var.		3 000 00					21
22				Fac. O/H Incurred		10 720 00					22
23											23

TRANSACTION 17

On December 5, Xinle purchased 6 barrels of refrigeration oil from Ningbo Jiashan Trade Co., Ltd. Unit price was $5,000/ton. The source document is CHECK STUB NO. 039. Since sales tax rate in the United States is 9%, sales tax should be $2,700. After-tax price was $32,700. Xinle should have paid $32,700 to Ningbo Jiashan Trade Co., Ltd.

$ 32,700	CHECK STUB NO. 039	
Date December 5		2016
To Ningbo Jiashan Trade Co., Ltd.		
For 6 Barrels of Refrigeration Oil		
	Dollars	Cents
Balance brought forward	1,174,474	00
Add deposits		
Total	1,174,474	00
Less this check	32,700	00
Balance carried forward	1,141,774	00

WHAT TO DO?

Suppose that Xinle currently uses standard costing method. The standard cost of barrels of refrigeration oil is $5,000/ton. Therefore, standard total cost of those barrels of refrigeration oil is $30,000.

Step 1 Analyze Transaction

Accounts Affected:

There are three accounts affected by this transaction. They are **Refrigeration Oil, Factory Overhead Incurred** and **Bank Deposit.**

Increase/Decrease:

Refrigeration Oil is increased by $30,000. **Factory Overhead Incurred** is increased by $2,700. **Bank Deposit** is decreased by $32,700.

Account Category:

Refrigeration Oil is an asset account. **Factory Overhead Incurred** is an asset account. **Bank Deposit** is an asset account.

Step 2 Determine Debit/Credit

The normal balance of asset accounts is debit. **Refrigeration Oil** is debited by $30, 000. **Factory Overhead Incurred** is debited by $2,700. **Bank Deposit** is credited by $32,700.

Step 3 Record in T-accounts

Refrigeration Oil

Debit	Credit
30,000	

Factory Overhead Incurred

Debit	Credit
2,700	

Bank Deposit	
Debit	Credit
	32,700

Step 4 Record in Journals

CASH PAYMENTS JOURNAL											PAGE 1
	DATE		DOC. NO.	ACCOUNT NAME	POST. REF.	GENERAL		ACCOUNTS PAYABLE DEBIT	BANK DEPOSIT CREDIT	CASH ON HAND CREDIT	
						DEBIT	CREDIT				
23	Dec.	5	CS039	Refrigeration Oil		30 000 00			32 700 00		23
24				Fac. O/H Incurred		2 700 00					24

TRANSACTION 18

On December 6, Xinle opened a special bank account in Shandong for purchase purpose and deposited $100,000 in that account.

WHAT TO DO?

There is no record for this transaction since most small and medium companies in the United States do not allow purchase like that. Most companies use current bank account to deal with their business. Therefore, it is assumed that Xinle does not allow a new bank account for purchase.

TRANSACTION 19

On December 7, Xinle purchased 10-ton steel plates from Shandong Steel Co., Ltd. Unit price was $8,000/ton. Delivery fee was $2,000. The source document is CHECK STUB NO. 040. Since sales tax rate in the United States is 9%, sales tax should be $7,200. After-tax price was $87,200. There is no tax on service. In other words, delivery fee is tax free. Xinle should have paid $89,200 to Shandong Steel Co., Ltd.

$ 89,200.00 **CHECK STUB NO. 040**
Date December 7 2016
To Shandong Steel Co., Ltd.
For 10-ton Steel Plates and Delivery Fee

	Dollars	Cents
Balance brought forward	1,141,774	00
Add deposits		
Total	1,141,774	00
Less this check	89,200	00
Balance carried forward	1,052,574	00

WHAT TO DO?

Suppose that Xinle currently uses standard costing method. The standard cost of steel plates is \$7,500/ton. Therefore, standard total cost of those steel plates is \$75,000.

Step 1 Analyze Transaction

Accounts Affected:

There are four accounts affected by this transaction. They are **Steel Plates, Material Price Variance, Factory Overhead Incurred** and **Bank Deposit.**

Increase/Decrease:

Steel Plates is increased by \$75,000. **Material Price Variance** is increased by \$5,000. **Factory Overhead Incurred** is increased by \$9,200. **Bank Deposit** is decreased by \$89,200.

Account Category:

Steel Plates is an asset account. **Material Price Variance** is an asset account. **Factory Overhead Incurred** is an asset account. **Bank Deposit** is an asset account.

Step 2 Determine Debit/Credit

The normal balance of asset accounts is debit. **Steel Plates** is debited by \$75,000. **Material Price Variance** is debited by \$5, 000. **Factory Overhead Incurred** is debited by \$9, 200. **Bank Deposit** is credited by \$89,200.

Step 3 Record in T-accounts

Steel Plates

Debit	Credit
75,000	

Material Price Variance

Debit	Credit
5,000	

Factory Overhead Incurred

Debit	Credit
9,200	

Bank Deposit

Debit	Credit
	89,200

Step 4 Record in Journals

CASH PAYMENTS JOURNAL PAGE 2

	DATE		DOC. NO.	ACCOUNT NAME	POST. REF.	GENERAL DEBIT	GENERAL CREDIT	ACCOUNTS PAYABLE DEBIT	BANK DEPOSIT CREDIT	CASH ON HAND CREDIT	
1	Dec.	7	CS040	Steel Plates		75 000 00			89 200 00		1
2				Material Pric. Var.		5 000 00					2
3				Fac. O/H Incurred		9 200 00					3
4											4

TRANSACTION 20

On December 7, Xinle collected the rest money from the special bank account opened in December 6, 2016, and put the rest money into its China Construction Bank account.

WHAT TO DO?

There is no record for this transaction since it is assumed that Xinle had not opened the special bank account in Shandong for purchase purpose. Therefore, Xinle does not need to close this bank account.

TRANSACTION 21

On December 7, Xinle sold 2 000 large air-blowers to Ningbo Air-blower Co., Ltd. The unit price was $400. Since sales tax rate in the United States is 9%, sales tax should be $72,000. After-tax price should be $872,000. Xinle had already collected the money. The source document is SALES SLIP NO. 69 and CHECK STUB NO. 041.

Xinle Air-blower

23 Tulan ST, Xiangshan, China 315700

DATE: December 7, 2016			NO. 69	
SOLD TO	Ningbo Air-blower 31 Liuyun ST Ningbo, China 315000			
CLERK B.E.	CASH	CHARGE √	TERMS N/A	
QTY.	DESCRIPTION	UNIT PRICE	AMOUNT	
2 000	Large Air-blowers	$ 400.00	$ 800,000	00
Thank You!		SUBTOTAL	$800,000	00
		SALES TAX	72,000	00
		TOTAL	$872,000	00

$ 872,000.00 CHECK STUB NO. 041

Date December 7 2016

To Ningbo Air-blower Co., Ltd.

For Sales of 2 000 Large Air-blowers

	Dollars	Cents
Balance brought forward	1,052,574	00
Add deposits	872,000	00
Total	1,924,574	00
Less this check		
Balance carried forward	1,924,574	00

WHAT TO DO?

For this transaction, two entries should be made. The first one is to record the sales of 2 000 large air-blowers. The second one is to record the change in inventory system. The unit cost of large air-blower is $260, and therefore cost of goods sold should be $520,000.

Step 1 Analyze Transaction

Accounts Affected:

- For the first entry, there are three accounts affected by this transaction. They are **Bank Deposit, Sales Revenue–Large Air-blower** and **Sales Tax Payable.**
- For the second entry, there are two accounts affected by this transaction. They are **Cost of Goods Sold–Large Air-blower** and **Finished Goods–Large Air-blower.**

Increase/Decrease:

- **Bank Deposit** is increased by $872,000. **Sales Revenue–Large Air-blower** is increased by $800,000. **Sales Tax Payable** is increased by $72,000.
- **Cost of Goods Sold–Large Air-blower** is increased by $520,000. **Finished Goods–Large Air-blower** is decreased by $520,000.

Account Category:

- **Bank Deposit** is an asset account. **Sales Revenue–Large Air-blower** is a revenue account. **Sales Tax Payable** is a liability account.
- **Cost of Goods Sold–Large Air-blower** is an expense account. **Finished Goods–Large Air-blower** is an asset account.

Step 2 Determine Debit/Credit

- The normal balance of asset accounts is debit. **Bank Deposit** is debited by $872,000.
- The normal balance of revenue accounts is credit. **Sales Revenue–Large Air-blower** is credited by $800,000.
- The normal balance of liability accounts is credit. **Sales Tax Payable** is credited by $72,000.
- The normal balance of expense accounts is debit. **Cost of Goods Sold–Large Air-blower** is debited by $520,000.
- The normal balance of asset accounts is debit. **Finished Goods–Large Air-blower** is credited by $520,000.

Step 3 Record in T-accounts

Bank Deposit

Debit	Credit
872,000	

Sales Revenue–Large Air-blower

Debit	Credit
	800,000

Sales Tax Payable

Debit	Credit
	72,000

Cost of Goods Sold–Large Air-blower

Debit	Credit
520,000	

Finished Goods–Large Air-blower

Debit	Credit
	520,000

Step 4 Record in Journals

CASH RECEIPTS JOURNAL PAGE 1

	DATE		DOC. NO.	ACCOUNT NAME	POST. REF.	GENERAL CREDIT	SALES CREDIT	SALES TAX PAYABLE CREDIT	ACCOUNTS RECEIVABLE CREDIT	BANK DEPOSIT DEBIT	CASH ON HAND DEBIT	
3	Dec.	7	NO.69/CS041	Large Air-blower			800 000 00	72 000 00		872 000 00		3
4												4
5												5
6												6

GENERAL JOURNAL PAGE 1

	DATE		DESCRIPTION	POST. REF.	DEBIT	CREDIT	
7	Dec.	7	Cost of Goods Sold–Large Air-blower		520 000 00		7
8			Finished Goods–Large Air-blower			520 000 00	8
9			*SALES SLIP 69*				9
10							10

TRANSACTION 22

On December 7, Xinle sold 1 000 small air-blowers to Xiangshan Air-blower Co., Ltd. The unit price was $350. Since sales tax rate in the United States is 9%, sales tax should be $31,500. After-tax price was $381,500. Xinle had already collected the money. The source document is SALES SLIP NO. 70 and CHECK STUB NO. 042.

Xinle Air-blower					
23 Tulan ST, Xiangshan, China 315700					
DATE: December 7, 2016				NO. 70	
SOLD TO	Xiangshan Air-blower 24 Lihai ST Xiangshan, China 315700				
CLERK B.E.	CASH	CHARGE √		TERMS N/A	
QTY.	DESCRIPTION	UNIT PRICE		AMOUNT	
1 000	Small Air-blowers	$ 350.00		$ 350,000	00
		SUBTOTAL		$350,000	00
Thank You!		SALES TAX		31,500	00
		TOTAL		$381,500	00

$ 381,500.00 **CHECK STUB NO. 042**

Date December 7 2016

To Xiangshan Air-blower Co., Ltd.

For Sales of 1 000 Small Air-blowers

	Dollars	Cents
Balance brought forward	1,924,574	00
Add deposits	381,500	00
Total	2,306,074	00
Less this check		
Balance carried forward	2,306,074	00

WHAT TO DO?

For this transaction, two entries should be made. The first one is to record the sales of 1 000 small air-blowers. The second one is to record the change in inventory system. The unit cost of small air-blower is $250, and therefore cost of goods sold should be $250,000.

Step 1 Analyze Transaction

Accounts Affected:

- For the first entry, there are three accounts affected by this transaction. They are **Bank Deposit, Sales Revenue–Small Air-blower** and **Sales Tax Payable.**
- For the second entry, there are two accounts affected by this transaction. They are **Cost of Goods Sold–Small Air-blower** and **Finished Goods–Small Air-blower.**

Increase/Decrease:

- **Bank Deposit** is increased by $381,500. **Sales Revenue–Small Air-blower** is increased by $350,000. **Sales Tax Payable** is increased by $31,500.
- **Cost of Goods Sold–Small Air-blower** is increased by $250,000. **Finished Goods–Small Air-blower** is decreased by $250,000.

Account Category:

- **Bank Deposit** is an asset account. **Sales Revenue–Small Air-blower** is a revenue account. **Sales Tax Payable** is a liability account.
- **Cost of Goods Sold–Small Air-blower** is an expense account. **Finished Goods–Small Air-blower** is an asset account.

Step 2 Determine Debit/Credit

- The normal balance of asset accounts is debit. **Bank Deposit** is debited by $381,500.
- The normal balance of revenue accounts is credit. **Sales Revenue–Small Air-blower** is credited by $350,000.
- The normal balance of liability accounts is credit. **Sales Tax Payable** is credited by $31,500.

- The normal balance of expense accounts is debit. **Cost of Goods Sold–Small Air-blower** is debited by $250,000.
- The normal balance of asset accounts is debit. **Finished Goods–Small Air-blower** is credited by $250,000.

Step 3 Record in T-accounts

Bank Deposit

Debit	Credit
381,500	

Sales Revenue–Small Air-blower

Debit	Credit
	350,000

Sales Tax Payable

Debit	Credit
	31,500

Cost of Goods Sold–Small Air-blower

Debit	Credit
250,000	

Finished Goods–Small Air-blower

Debit	Credit
	250,000

Step 4 Record in Journals

CASH RECEIPTS JOURNAL — PAGE 1

	DATE		DOC. NO.	ACCOUNT NAME	POST. REF.	GENERAL CREDIT	SALES CREDIT	SALES TAX PAYABLE CREDIT	ACCOUNTS RECEIVABLE CREDIT	BANK DEPOSIT DEBIT	CASH ON HAND DEBIT	
4	Dec.	7	NO.70/CS042	Small Air-blower			350 000 00	31 500 00		381 500 00		4
5												5
6												6
7												7

GENERAL JOURNAL — PAGE 1

	DATE		DESCRIPTION	POST. REF.	DEBIT	CREDIT	
10	Dec.	7	Cost of Goods Sold–Small Air-blower		250 000 00		10
11			Finished Goods–Small Air-blower			250 000 00	11
12			*SALES SLIP 70*				12
13							13

TRANSACTION 23

On December 7, Xinle purchased 10-ton iron castings from Beijing Steel Co., Ltd. Unit price was \$5,000/ton. Delivery fee was \$2,000. Xinle had not paid the money yet. The source document is INVOICE NO. 523. Since sales tax rate in the United States is 9%, sales tax should be \$4,500. After-tax price was \$54,500. There is no tax on service. In other words, delivery fee is tax free. Xinle should have paid \$56,500 to Beijing Steel Co., Ltd.

Beijing Steel Co., Ltd.
217 Sihai ST
Beijing, China 100000

INVOICE NO. 523

DATE: Dec. 7, 2016
ORDER NO.: 92837
SHIPPED BY: Truck
TERMS: Payable in 30 days

TO Xinle Air-blower
23 Tulan ST
Xiangshan, China 315700

TON	ITEM	UNIT PRICE	TOTAL
10	Iron Castings	\$ 5,000.00	\$ 50,000.00

WHAT TO DO?

Suppose that Xinle currently uses standard costing method. The standard cost of iron castings is $4,500/ton. Therefore, standard total cost of those iron castings is $45,000.

Step 1 Analyze Transaction

Accounts Affected:

There are four accounts affected by this transaction. They are **Iron Castings, Material Price Variance, Factory Overhead Incurred** and **Accounts Payable–Beijing Steel.**

Increase/Decrease:

Iron Castings is increased by $45, 000. **Material Price Variance** is increased by $5, 000. **Factory Overhead Incurred** is increased by $6,500. **Accounts Payable–Beijing Steel** is increased by $56,500.

Account Category:

Iron Castings is an asset account. **Material Price Variance** is an asset account. **Factory Overhead Incurred** is an asset account. **Accounts Payable–Beijing Steel** is a liability account.

Step 2 Determine Debit/Credit

The normal balance of asset accounts is debit. **Iron Castings** is debited by $45,000. **Material Price Variance** is debited by $5,000. **Factory Overhead Incurred** is debited by $6,500. **Accounts Payable–Beijing Steel** is credited by $56,500.

Step 3 Record in T-accounts

Iron Castings

Debit	Credit
45,000	

Material Price Variance

Debit	Credit
5,000	

Factory Overhead Incurred

Debit	Credit
6,500	

Accounts Payable–Beijing Steel

Debit	Credit
	56,500

Step 4 Record in Journals

PURCHASES JOURNAL										PAGE 1
	DATE	INVOICE NO.	CREDITOR'S ACCOUNT CREDITED	TYPE	POST. REF.	ACCOUNTS PAYABLE CREDIT	PURCHASES DEBIT	GENERAL ACCOUNT DEBITED	GENERAL POST. REF.	GENERAL DEBIT
1	Dec. 7	INV523	Beijing Steel	IC		56 500 00	45 000 00	Fac. O/H Incurred		6 500 00
2								Material Pric. Var.		5 000 00
3										
4										

TRANSACTION 24

On December 7, Xinle sold 1 000 large air-blowers to Xiangshan Air-blower Co., Ltd. The unit price was $400. Since sales tax rate in the United States is 9%, sales tax should be $36,000. After-tax price was $436,000. Xinle had already collected the money. The source document is SALES SLIP NO. 71 and CHECK STUB NO. 043.

Xinle Air-blower

23 Tulan ST, Xiangshan, China 315700

DATE: December 7, 2016			NO. 71
SOLD TO	Xiangshan Air-blower 24 Lihai ST Xiangshan, China 315700		
CLERK B.E.	CASH	CHARGE √	TERMS N/A
QTY.	DESCRIPTION	UNIT PRICE	AMOUNT
1 000	Large Air-blowers	$ 400.00	$ 400,000 00
		SUBTOTAL	$400,000 00
	Thank You!	SALES TAX	36,000 00
		TOTAL	$436,000 00

$ 436,000.00 **CHECK STUB NO. 043**

Date December 7 2016

To Xiangshan Air-blower Co., Ltd.

For Sales of 1 000 Large Air-blowers

	Dollars	Cents
Balance brought forward	2,306,074	00
Add deposits	436,000	00
Total	2,742,074	00
Less this check		
Balance carried forward	2,742,074	00

WHAT TO DO?

For this transaction, two entries should be made. The first one is to record the sales of 1 000 large air-blowers. The second one is to record the change in inventory system. The unit cost of large air-blower is $260, and therefore cost of goods sold should be $260,000.

Step 1 Analyze Transaction

Accounts Affected:

- For the first entry, there are three accounts affected by this transaction. They are **Bank Deposit, Sales Revenue–Large Air-blower** and **Sales Tax Payable.**
- For the second entry, there are two accounts affected by this transaction. They are **Cost of Goods Sold–Large Air-blower** and **Finished Goods–Large Air-blower.**

Increase/Decrease:

- **Bank Deposit** is increased by $436,000. **Sales Revenue–Large Air-blower** is increased by $400,000. **Sales Tax Payable** is increased by $36,000.
- **Cost of Goods Sold–Large Air-blower** is increased by $260,000. **Finished Goods–Large Air-blower** is decreased by $260,000.

Account Category:

- **Bank Deposit** is an asset account. **Sales Revenue–Large Air-blower** is a revenue account. **Sales Tax Payable** is a liability account.
- **Cost of Goods Sold–Large Air-blower** is an expense account. **Finished Goods–Large Air-blower** is an asset account.

Step 2 Determine Debit/Credit

- The normal balance of asset accounts is debit. **Bank Deposit** is debited by $436,000.
- The normal balance of revenue accounts is credit. **Sales Revenue–Large Air-blower** is credited by $400,000.
- The normal balance of liability accounts is credit. **Sales Tax Payable** is credited by $36,000.

- The normal balance of expense accounts is debit. **Cost of Goods Sold–Large Air-blower** is debited by $260,000.
- The normal balance of asset accounts is debit. **Finished Goods–Large Air-blower** is credited by $260,000.

Step 3 Record in T-accounts

Bank Deposit

Debit	Credit
436,000	

Sales Revenue–Large Air-blower

Debit	Credit
	400,000

Sales Tax Payable

Debit	Credit
	36,000

Cost of Goods Sold–Large Air-blower

Debit	Credit
260,000	

Finished Goods–Large Air-blower

Debit	Credit
	260,000

Step 4 Record in Journals

CASH RECEIPTS JOURNAL PAGE 1

	DATE		DOC. NO.	ACCOUNT NAME	POST. REF.	GENERAL CREDIT	SALES CREDIT	SALES TAX PAYABLE CREDIT	ACCOUNTS RECEIVABLE CREDIT	BANK DEPOSIT DEBIT	CASH ON HAND DEBIT	
5	Dec.	7	NO.71/CS043	Large Air-blower			400 000 00	36 000 00		436 000 00		5
6												6
7												7
8												8

GENERAL JOURNAL PAGE 1

	DATE		DESCRIPTION	POST. REF.	DEBIT	CREDIT	
13	Dec.	7	Cost of Goods Sold–Large Air-blower		260 000 00		13
14			Finished Goods–Large Air-blower			260 000 00	14
15			*SALES SLIP 71*				15
16							16

TRANSACTION 25

On December 8, Xinle reimbursed $3,000 for training fee by cash. This lump sum of training fee is used for staff in selling department. The source document is RECEIPT NO. 116.

Xiangshan Training Center RECEIPT

46 Haihe ST

No. 116

Xiangshan, China 315700

Dec. 8 2016

RECEIVED FROM Xinle Air-blower Co., Ltd. $ 3,000.00

Three thousand and no/100 DOLLARS

FOR Training 12/08/2016

RECEIVED BY *Yu Li*

WHAT TO DO?

Step 1 Analyze Transaction

Accounts Affected:

There are two accounts affected by this transaction. They are **Sales Training Expense** and **Cash on Hand.**

Increase/Decrease:

Sales Training Expense is increased by $3,000. **Cash on Hand** is decreased by $3,000.

Account Category:

Sales Training Expense is an expense account. **Cash on Hand** is an asset account.

Step 2 Determine Debit/Credit

–The normal balance of expense accounts is debit. **Sales Training Expense** is debited by $3,000.

–The normal balance of asset accounts is debit. **Cash on Hand** is credited by $3,000.

Step 3 Record in T-accounts

Sales Training Expense

Debit	Credit
3,000	

Cash on Hand

Debit	Credit
	3,000

Step 4 Record in Journals

CASH PAYMENTS JOURNAL											PAGE 2
	DATE		DOC. NO.	ACCOUNT NAME	POST. REF.	GENERAL DEBIT	GENERAL CREDIT	ACCOUNTS PAYABLE DEBIT	BANK DEPOSIT CREDIT	CASH ON HAND CREDIT	
4	Dec.	8	REC116	Sales Training Expense		3 000 00				3 000 00	4
5											5
6											6
7											7

TRANSACTION 26

On December 8, Xinle paid $1,000 for invitation fee by bank deposit. The source document is INVOICE NO. 316 and CHECK STUB NO. 044.

Xiangshan Local Food Co., Ltd. INVOICE NO. 316

37 Heming ST

Beijing, China 100000 DATE: Dec. 8, 2016

TERMS: Payable in 30 days

TO Xinle Air-blower
23 Tulan ST
Xiangshan, China 315700

Room #	ITEM	UNIT PRICE	TOTAL
205	Meal	$ 1,000.00	$ 1,000.00

$ 1,000.00 CHECK STUB NO. 044

Date December 8 2016

To Xinle Air-blower Co., Ltd.

For Invitation Fee

	Dollars	Cents
Balance brought forward	2,742,074	00
Add deposits		
Total	2,742,074	00
Less this check	1,000	00
Balance carried forward	2,741,074	00

WHAT TO DO?

Step 1 Analyze Transaction

Accounts Affected:

There are two accounts affected by this transaction. They are **Invitation Fee Expense** and **Bank Deposit.**

Increase/Decrease:

Invitation Fee Expense is increased by $1,000. **Bank Deposit** is decreased by $1,000.

Account Category:

Invitation Fee Expense is an expense account. **Bank Deposit** is an asset account.

Step 2 Determine Debit/Credit

–The normal balance of expense accounts is debit. **Invitation Fee Expense** is debited by $1,000.

–The normal balance of asset accounts is debit. **Bank Deposit** is credited by $1,000.

Step 3 Record in T-accounts

Invitation Fee Expense	
Debit	Credit
1,000	

Bank Deposit	
Debit	Credit
	1,000

Step 4 Record in Journals

CASH PAYMENTS JOURNAL PAGE 2

	DATE		DOC. NO.	ACCOUNT NAME	POST. REF.	GENERAL DEBIT	GENERAL CREDIT	ACCOUNTS PAYABLE DEBIT	BANK DEPOSIT CREDIT	CASH ON HAND CREDIT	
5	Dec.	8	INV316	Invitation Fee Expense		1 0 0 0 00			1 0 0 0 00		5
6											6
7											7
8											8

TRANSACTION 27

On December 8, Xinle reimbursed $2, 000 for office supplies fee by cash. Those office supplies will be used in financial department. The source document is INVOICE NO. 823.

Xiangshan Office Supplies Co., Ltd.
634 Liuxiang ST
Xiangshan, China 315700

INVOICE NO. 823

DATE: Dec. 8, 2016
TERMS: Payable in 30 days

TO
Xinle Air-blower
23 Tulan ST
Xiangshan, China 315700

QTY.	ITEM	UNIT PRICE	TOTAL
250	Accounting Books	$8.00	$ 2,000.00

WHAT TO DO?

Step 1 Analyze Transaction

Accounts Affected:

There are two accounts affected by this transaction. They are **M&A Office Supplies** and **Cash on Hand.**

Increase/Decrease:

M&A Office Supplies is increased by $2,000. **Cash on Hand** is decreased by $2,000.

Account Category:

M&A Office Supplies is an asset account. **Cash on Hand** is an asset account.

Step 2 Determine Debit/Credit

–The normal balance of asset accounts is debit. **M&A Office Supplies** is debited by $2,000.

–The normal balance of asset accounts is debit. **Cash on Hand** is credited by $2,000.

Step 3 Record in T-accounts

M&A Office Supplies	
Debit	Credit
2,000	

Cash on Hand	
Debit	Credit
	2,000

Step 4 Record in Journals

CASH PAYMENTS JOURNAL											PAGE 2
	DATE		DOC. NO.	ACCOUNT NAME	POST. REF.	GENERAL		ACCOUNTS PAYABLE DEBIT	BANK DEPOSIT CREDIT	CASH ON HAND CREDIT	
						DEBIT	CREDIT				
6	Dec.	8	INV823	M&A Office Supplies		2000 00				2000 00	6
7											7
8											8
9											9

TRANSACTION 28

On December 8, Xinle issued a cash check to withdraw $2,000 for petty cash. The source document is CHECK STUB NO. 045.

CHECK STUB NO. 045

$ 2,000.00

Date December 8 2016

To Xinle Air-blower Co., Ltd.

For Petty Cash

	Dollars	Cents
Balance brought forward	2,741,074	00
Add deposits		
Total	2,741,074	00
Less this check	2,000	00
Balance carried forward	2,739,074	00

WHAT TO DO?

Step 1 Analyze Transaction

Accounts Affected:

There are two accounts affected by this transaction. They are **Petty Cash** and **Bank Deposit.**

Increase/Decrease:

Petty Cash is increased by $2,000. **Bank Deposit** is decreased by $2,000.

Account Category:

Petty Cash is an asset account. **Bank Deposit** is an asset account.

Step 2 Determine Debit/Credit

The normal balance of asset accounts is debit. **Petty Cash** is debited by $2,000. **Bank Deposit** is credited by $2,000.

Step 3 Record in T-accounts

Petty Cash	
Debit	Credit
2,000	

Bank Deposit	
Debit	Credit
	2,000

Step 4 Record in Journals

CASH PAYMENTS JOURNAL											PAGE 2
	DATE		DOC. NO.	ACCOUNT NAME	POST. REF.	GENERAL DEBIT	GENERAL CREDIT	ACCOUNTS PAYABLE DEBIT	BANK DEPOSIT CREDIT	CASH ON HAND CREDIT	
7	Dec.	8	CS045	Petty Cash		2 000 00			2 000 00		7
8											8
9											9
10											10

TRANSACTION 29

On December 8, Xinle purchased 50 packing boxes from Zhenhai Supplies Co., Ltd. Unit price was $40 per box. There was no delivery fee. The source document is CHECK STUB NO. 046. Since sales tax rate in the United States is 9%, sales tax should be $180. After-tax price was $2,180. Xinle should have paid $2,180 to Zhenhai Supplies Co., Ltd.

$ 2,180.00 CHECK STUB NO. 046

Date December 8 2016

To Zhenhai Supplies Co., Ltd.

For 50 Packing Boxes

	Dollars	Cents
Balance brought forward	2,739,074	00
Add deposits		
Total	2,739,074	00
Less this check	2,180	00
Balance carried forward	2,736,894	00

WHAT TO DO?

Suppose that Xinle currently uses standard costing method. Packing boxes are indirect material, and therefore the concept of standard cost cannot apply to it.

Step 1 Analyze Transaction

Accounts Affected:

There are three accounts affected by this transaction. They are **Packing Boxes, Factory Overhead Incurred** and **Bank Deposit.**

Increase/Decrease:

Packing Boxes is increased by $2, 000. **Factory Overhead Incurred** is increased by $180. **Bank Deposit** is decreased by $2,180.

Account Category:

Packing Boxes is an asset account. **Factory Overhead Incurred** is an asset account. **Bank Deposit** is an asset account.

Step 2 Determine Debit/Credit

The normal balance of asset accounts is debit. **Packing Boxes** is debited by $2,000. **Factory Overhead Incurred** is debited by $180. **Bank Deposit** is credited by $2,180.

Step 3 Record in T-accounts

Packing Boxes

Debit	Credit
2,000	

Factory Overhead Incurred

Debit	Credit
180	

Bank Deposit

Debit	Credit
	2,180

Step 4 Record in Journals

CASH PAYMENTS JOURNAL PAGE 2

	DATE		DOC. NO.	ACCOUNT NAME	POST. REF.	GENERAL DEBIT	GENERAL CREDIT	ACCOUNTS PAYABLE DEBIT	BANK DEPOSIT CREDIT	CASH ON HAND CREDIT	
8	Dec.	8	CS046	Packing Boxes		2 0 0 0 00			2 1 8 0 00		8
9				Fac. O/H Incurred		1 8 0 00					9
10											10
11											11

TRANSACTION 30

On December 8, Xinle borrowed $500,000 and put it in the bank. The source document is LOAN 192.

LOAN 192

$ 500,000.00

Six months after date Xinle Air-blower Co., Ltd. promise to pay to

Bank of China Co., Ltd. the sum of

Five hundred thousand dollars with interest at the rate of

6.84% per year.

Due date May 8, 2017

Ming Li

WHAT TO DO?

Step 1 Analyze Transaction

Accounts Affected:

There are two accounts affected by this transaction. They are **Bank Deposit** and **Short-term Borrowings–Bank of China.**

Increase/Decrease:

Bank Deposit is increased by $500,000. **Short-term Borrowings–Bank of China** is decreased by $500,000.

Account Category:

Bank Deposit is an asset account. **Short-term Borrowings–Bank of China** is an asset account.

Step 2 Determine Debit/Credit

The normal balance of asset accounts is debit. **Bank Deposit** is debited by $500,000. **Short-term Borrowings–Bank of China** is credited by $500,000.

Step 3 Record in T-accounts

Bank Deposit	
Debit	Credit
500,000	

Short-term Borrowings-Bank of China	
Debit	Credit
	500,000

Step 4 Record in Journals

CASH RECEIPTS JOURNAL										PAGE 1	
	DATE	DOC. NO.	ACCOUNT NAME	POST. REF.	GENERAL CREDIT	SALES CREDIT	SALES TAX PAYABLE CREDIT	ACCOUNTS RECEIVABLE CREDIT	BANK DEPOSIT DEBIT	CASH ON HAND DEBIT	
6	DEC. 8	L192	STB-BOC		500 000 00				500 000 00		6
7											7
8											8
9											9

TRANSACTION 31

On December 9, Xinle issued a check to pay broadband fees for next year, which was $120,000. The source document is CHECK STUB NO. 047.

$ 120,000.00 **CHECK STUB NO. 047**

Date December 9 2016

To Xiangshan Broadband Co., Ltd.

For 2017 Broadband Fees

	Dollars	Cents
Balance brought forward	3,236,894	00
Add deposits		
Total	3,236,894	00
Less this check	120,000	00
Balance carried forward	3,116,894	00

WHAT TO DO?

Step 1 Analyze Transaction

Accounts Affected:

There are two accounts affected by this transaction. They are **Prepaid Broadband** and **Bank Deposit.**

Increase/Decrease:

Prepaid Broadband is increased by $120,000. **Bank Deposit** is decreased by $120,000.

Account Category:

Prepaid Broadband is an asset account. **Bank Deposit** is an asset account.

Step 2 Determine Debit/Credit

The normal balance of asset accounts is debit. **Prepaid Broadband** is debited by $120,000. **Bank Deposit** is credited by $120,000.

Step 3 Record in T-accounts

Prepaid Broadband	
Debit	Credit
120,000	

Bank Deposit	
Debit	Credit
	120,000

Step 4 Record in Journals

CASH PAYMENTS JOURNAL PAGE 2

	DATE		DOC. NO.	ACCOUNT NAME	POST. REF.	GENERAL DEBIT	GENERAL CREDIT	ACCOUNTS PAYABLE DEBIT	BANK DEPOSIT CREDIT	CASH ON HAND CREDIT	
10	Dec.	9	CS047	Prepaid Broadband		120 000 00			120 000 00		10
11											11
12											12
13											13

TRANSACTION 32

On December 9, Xinle sold 1 000 small air-blowers to Ningbo Air-blower Co., Ltd. The unit price was $350. Since sales tax rate in the United States is 9%, sales tax should be $31,500. After-tax price was $381,500. The source document is SALES SLIP NO. 72.

Xinle Air-blower

23 Tulan ST, Xiangshan, China 315700

DATE: December 9, 2016			NO. 72
SOLD TO	Ningbo Air-blower 31 Liuyun ST Ningbo, China 315000		
CLERK B.E.	CASH	CHARGE √	TERMS N/A
QTY.	DESCRIPTION	UNIT PRICE	AMOUNT
1 000	Small Air-blowers	$ 350.00	$ 350,000 00
		SUBTOTAL	$ 350,000 00
		SALES TAX	31,500 00
Thank You!		TOTAL	$ 381,500 00

The delivery fee was $3, 000. Xinle paid it for Ningbo Air-blower Co., Ltd. The source document is CHECK STUB NO. 048.

$ 3,000.00	CHECK STUB NO. 048	
Date December 9	2016	
To Ningbo Air-blower Co., Ltd.		
For Delivery Fee		
	Dollars	Cents
Balance brought forward	3,116,894	00
Add deposits		
Total	3,116,894	00
Less this check	3,000	00
Balance carried forward	3,113,894	00

WHAT TO DO?

For this transaction, three entries should be made. The first one is to record the sales of 1 000 small air-blowers. The second one is to record the delivery fee paid by Xinle. The third one is to record the change in inventory system. The unit cost of small air-blower is $250, and therefore cost of goods sold should be $250,000.

Step 1 Analyze Transaction

Accounts Affected:

- For the first entry, there are three accounts affected by this transaction. They are **Accounts Receivable–Ningbo Air-blower, Sales Revenue–Small Air-blower** and **Sales Tax Payable.**
- For the second entry, there are two accounts affected by this transaction. They are **Other Receivables–Ningbo Air-blower** and **Bank Deposit.**
- For the third entry, there are two accounts affected by this transaction. They are **Cost of Goods Sold–Small Air-blower** and **Finished Goods–Small Air-blower.**

Increase/Decrease:

- **Accounts Receivable–Ningbo Air-blower** is increased by $381,500. **Sales Revenue–Small Air-blower** is increased by $350,000. **Sales Tax Payable** is increased by $31,500.
- **Other Receivables–Ningbo Air-blower** is increased by $3,000. **Bank Deposit** is decreased by $3,000.
- **Cost of Goods Sold–Small Air-blower** is increased by $250,000. **Finished Goods–Small Air-blower** is decreased by $250,000.

Account Category:

- **Accounts Receivable–Ningbo Air-blower** is an asset account. **Sales Revenue–Small Air-blower** is a revenue account. **Sales Tax Payable** is a liability account.
- **Other Receivables–Ningbo Air-blower** is an asset account. **Bank Deposit** is an asset account.
- **Cost of Goods Sold–Small Air-blower** is an expense account. **Finished Goods–Small Air-blower**

is an asset account.

Step 2 Determine Debit/Credit

- The normal balance of asset accounts is debit. **Accounts Receivable–Ningbo Air-blower** is debited by $381,500.
- The normal balance of revenue accounts is credit. **Sales Revenue–Small Air-blower** is credited by $350,000.
- The normal balance of liability accounts is credit. **Sales Tax Payable** is credited by $31,500.

- The normal balance of asset accounts is debit. **Other Receivables–Ningbo Air-blower** is debited by $3,000.
- The normal balance of asset accounts is debit. **Bank Deposit** is credited by $3,000.

- The normal balance of expense accounts is debit. **Cost of Goods Sold–Small Air-blower** is debited by $250,000.
- The normal balance of asset accounts is debit. **Finished Goods–Small Air-blower** is credited by $250,000.

Step 3 Record in T-accounts

Accounts Receivable–Ningbo Air-blower

Debit	Credit
381,500	

Sales Revenue–Small Air-blower

Debit	Credit
	350,000

Sales Tax Payable

Debit	Credit
	31,500

Other Receivables–Ningbo Air-blower

Debit	Credit
3,000	

Bank Deposit

Debit	Credit
	3,000

Cost of Goods Sold–Small Air-blower

Debit	Credit
250,000	

Finished Goods–Small Air-blower

Debit	Credit
	250,000

Step 4 Record in Journals

SALES JOURNAL									PAGE 1
	DATE		SALES SLIP NO.	CUSTOMER'S ACCOUNT DEBITED	POST. REF.	SALES CREDIT	SALES TAX PAYABLE CREDIT	ACCOUNTS RECEIVABLE DEBIT	
2	Dec.	9	72	Ningbo Air-blower–Small Air-blower		350000 00	31500 00	381500 00	2
3									3
4									4
5									5

GENERAL JOURNAL							PAGE 1
	DATE		DESCRIPTION	POST. REF.	DEBIT	CREDIT	
16	Dec.	9	Other Receivables–Ningbo Air-blower		3000 00		16
17			Bank Deposit			3000 00	17
18			*Check Stub 048*				18
19	Dec.	9	Cost of Goods Sold–Small Air-blower		250000 00		19
20			Finished Goods–Small Air-blower			250000 00	20
21			*SALES SLIP 72*				21
22							22

TRANSACTION 33

On December 10, Xinle purchased 4 barrels of refrigeration oil from Ningbo Jiashan Trade Co., Ltd. Unit price was $5,000/ton. The source document is CHECK STUB NO. 049. Since sales tax rate in the United States is 9%, sales tax should be $1,800. After-tax price was $21,800. Xinle should have paid $21,800 to Ningbo Jiashan Trade Co., Ltd.

CHECK STUB NO. 049

$ 21,800

Date December 10 2016

To Ningbo Jiashan Trade Co., Ltd.

For 4 Barrels of Refrigeration Oil

	Dollars	Cents
Balance brought forward	3,113,894	00
Add deposits		
Total	3,113,894	00
Less this check	21,800	00
Balance carried forward	3,092,094	00

WHAT TO DO?

Suppose that Xinle currently uses standard costing method. The standard cost of barrels of refrigeration oil is \$5,000/ton. Therefore, standard total cost of those barrels of refrigeration oil is \$20,000.

Step 1 Analyze Transaction

Accounts Affected:

There are three accounts affected by this transaction. They are **Refrigeration Oil, Factory Overhead Incurred** and **Bank Deposit.**

Increase/Decrease:

Refrigeration Oil is increased by \$20,000. **Factory Overhead Incurred** is increased by \$1,800. **Bank Deposit** is decreased by \$21,800.

Account Category:

Refrigeration Oil is an asset account. **Factory Overhead Incurred** is an asset account. **Bank Deposit** is an asset account.

Step 2 Determine Debit/Credit

The normal balance of asset accounts is debit. **Refrigeration Oil** is debited by \$20, 000. **Factory Overhead Incurred** is debited by \$1,800. **Bank Deposit** is credited by \$21,800.

Step 3 Record in T-accounts

Refrigeration Oil

Debit	Credit
20,000	

Factory Overhead Incurred

Debit	Credit
1,800	

Bank Deposit

Debit	Credit
	21,800

Step 4 Record in Journals

CASH PAYMENTS JOURNAL PAGE 2

	DATE		DOC. NO.	ACCOUNT NAME	POST. REF.	GENERAL DEBIT	GENERAL CREDIT	ACCOUNTS PAYABLE DEBIT	BANK DEPOSIT CREDIT	CASH ON HAND CREDIT	
11	Dec.	10	CS049	Refrigeration Oil		20 000 00			21 800 00		11
12				Fac. O/H Incurred		1 800 00					12
13											13
14											14

TRANSACTION 34

On December 11, Xinle sold 1 000 large air-blowers to Xiangshan Air-blower Co., Ltd. The unit price was $400. Since sales tax rate in the United States is 9%, sales tax should be $36,000. After-tax price was $436,000. Xinle had already collected the money. The source document is SALES SLIP NO. 73 and CHECK STUB NO. 050.

Xinle Air-blower					
23 Tulan ST, Xiangshan, China 315700					
DATE: December 11, 2016				NO. 73	
SOLD TO	Xiangshan Air-blower 24 Lihai ST Xiangshan, China 315700				
CLERK B.E.	CASH	CHARGE √		TERMS N/A	
QTY.	DESCRIPTION		UNIT PRICE	AMOUNT	
1 000	Large Air-blowers		$ 400.00	$ 400,000	00
Thank You!			SUBTOTAL	$400,000	00
			SALES TAX	36,000	00
			TOTAL	$436,000	00

CHECK STUB NO. 050

$ 436,000.00

Date December 11 2016

To Xiangshan Air-blower Co., Ltd.

For Sales of 1 000 Large Air-blowers

	Dollars	Cents
Balance brought forward	3,092,094	00
Add deposits	436,000	00
Total	3,528,094	00
Less this check		
Balance carried forward	3,528,094	00

WHAT TO DO?

For this transaction, two entries should be made. The first one is to record the sales of 1 000 large air-blowers. The second one is to record the change in inventory system. The unit cost of large air-blower is $260, and therefore cost of goods sold should be $260,000.

Step 1 Analyze Transaction

Accounts Affected:

- For the first entry, there are three accounts affected by this transaction. They are **Bank Deposit, Sales Revenue–Large Air-blower** and **Sales Tax Payable.**
- For the second entry, there are two accounts affected by this transaction. They are **Cost of Goods Sold–Large Air-blower** and **Finished Goods–Large Air-blower.**

Increase/Decrease:

- **Bank Deposit** is increased by $436,000. **Sales Revenue–Large Air-blower** is increased by $400,000. **Sales Tax Payable** is increased by $36,000.
- **Cost of Goods Sold–Large Air-blower** is increased by $260,000. **Finished Goods–Large Air-blower** is decreased by $260,000.

Account Category:

- **Bank Deposit is** an asset account. **Sales Revenue–Large Air–blower** is a revenue account. **Sales Tax Payable** is a liability account.
- **Cost of Goods Sold–Large Air-blower** is an expense account. **Finished Goods–Large Air–blower** is an asset account.

Step 2 Determine Debit/Credit

- The normal balance of asset accounts is debit. **Bank Deposit** is debited by $436,000.
- The normal balance of revenue accounts is credit. **Sales Revenue–Large Air-blower** is credited by $400,000.
- The normal balance of liability accounts is credit. **Sales Tax Payable** is credited by $36,000.

- The normal balance of expense accounts is debit. **Cost of Goods Sold–Large Air-blower** is debited by $260,000.
- The normal balance of asset accounts is debit. **Finished Goods–Large Air-blower** is credited by $260,000.

Step 3 Record in T-accounts

Bank Deposit

Debit	Credit
436,000	

Sales Revenue–Large Air-blower

Debit	Credit
	400,000

Sales Tax Payable

Debit	Credit
	36,000

Cost of Goods Sold–Large Air-blower

Debit	Credit
260,000	

Finished Goods–Large Air-blower

Debit	Credit
	260,000

Step 4 Record in Journals

CASH RECEIPTS JOURNAL PAGE 1

	DATE		DOC. NO.	ACCOUNT NAME	POST. REF.	GENERAL CREDIT	SALES CREDIT	SALES TAX PAYABLE CREDIT	ACCOUNTS RECEIVABLE CREDIT	BANK DEPOSIT DEBIT	CASH ON HAND DEBIT	
7	Dec.	11	NO.73/CS050	Large Air-blower			400 000 00	36 000 00		436 000 00		7
8												8
9												9
10												10

GENERAL JOURNAL PAGE 1

	DATE		DESCRIPTION	POST. REF.	DEBIT	CREDIT	
22	Dec.	11	Cost of Goods Sold–Large Air-blower		260 000 00		22
23			Finished Goods–Large Air-blower			260 000 00	23
24			*SALES SLIP 73*				24
25							25

TRANSACTION 35 & 36

On December 11, Xinle disposed a lathe. The original cost of the lathe was $150, 000. Accumulated depreciation was $135, 000. The source document is MEMORANDUM 32. On December 11, Xinle sold the lathe mentioned in last transaction, and got $10,000 and put the money into bank. The source document is MEMORANDUM 33. Those two transactions are treated as one in the United States.

Xinle Air-blower Co., Ltd. MEMORANDUM 32

23 Tulan ST

Xiangshan, China 315700

TO: Machine Management Department

FROM: Peter Pan

DATE: December 11, 2016

SUBJECT: Disposal of Lathe

The lathe #23 should be disposed since it cannot be used.

Xinle Air-blower Co., Ltd. MEMORANDUM 33

23 Tulan ST

Xiangshan, China 315700

TO: Accounting Department

FROM: Machine Management Department

DATE: December 11, 2016

SUBJECT: Disposable Value of Lathe

The lathe #23 has been sold at $10,000.

WHAT TO DO?

Since there are only 35 rows on one page of general journal book, Row 32 to Row 35 on page 1 should be crossed off. One transaction cannot be recorded on different pages.

Step 1 Analyze Transaction

Accounts Affected:

There are four accounts affected by transactions. They are **Bank Deposit, Loss on Disposal of Lathe, Accumulated Depreciation–Lathe** and **Lathe.**

Increase/Decrease:

Bank Deposit is increased by $10,000. **Loss on Disposal of Lathe** is increased by $5,000.

Accumulated Depreciation–Lathe is decreased by $135,000. **Lathe** is decreased by $150,000.

<u>*Account Category:*</u>

Bank Deposit is an asset account. **Loss on Disposal of Lathe** is a loss account. **Accumulated Depreciation–Lathe** is a contra-asset account. **Lathe** is an asset account.

Step 2 Determine Debit/Credit

–The normal balance of asset accounts is debit. **Bank Deposit** is debited by $10,000.

–The normal balance of loss accounts is debit. **Loss on Disposal of Lathe** is debited by $5,000.

–The normal balance of contra-asset accounts is credit. **Accumulated Depreciation–Lathe** is debited by $135,000.

–The normal balance of asset accounts is debit. **Lathe** is credited by $150,000.

Step 3 Record in T-accounts

Bank Deposit

Debit	Credit
10,000	

Loss on Disposal of Lathe

Debit	Credit
5,000	

Accumulated Depreciation–Lathe

Debit	Credit
135,000	

Lathe

Debit	Credit
	150,000

Step 4 Record in Journals

GENERAL JOURNAL PAGE 1

	DATE		DESCRIPTION	POST. REF.	DEBIT	CREDIT	
25	Dec.	11	Bank Deposit		10 000 00		25
26			Loss on Disposal of Lathe		5 000 00		26
27			Accumulated Depreciation–Lathe		135 000 00		27
28			Lathe			150 000 00	28
29			*Memorandum 32 & 33*				29
30							30

TRANSACTION 37

On December 11, Xinle reimbursed $1,500 for factory office supplies fee by check. The source document is INVOICE NO. 114 and CHECK STUB NO. 051.

Xiangshan Bookstore Co., Ltd.

INVOICE NO. 114

73 Sanming ST

Xiangshan, China 315700

DATE: Dec. 11, 2016

TERMS: Payable in 30 days

TO Xinle Air-blower
23 Tulan ST
Xiangshan, China 315700

QTY.	ITEM	UNIT PRICE	TOTAL
3	Pens	$500.00	$ 1,500.00

CHECK STUB NO. 051

$ 1,500.00

Date December 11 2016

To Xiangshan Bookstore Co., Ltd.

For Purchase of 3 Pens

	Dollars	Cents
Balance brought forward	3,538,094	00
Add deposits		
Total	3,538,094	00
Less this check	1,500	00
Balance carried forward	3,536,594	00

WHAT TO DO?

Step 1 Analyze Transaction

Accounts Affected:

There are two accounts affected by this transaction. They are **Factory Office Supplies** and **Bank Deposit.**

Increase/Decrease:

Factory Office Supplies is increased by $1,500. **Bank Deposit** is decreased by $1,500.

Account Category:

Factory Office Supplies is an asset account. **Bank Deposit** is an asset account.

Step 2 Determine Debit/Credit

–The normal balance of asset accounts is debit. **Factory Office Supplies** is debited by $1,500.

–The normal balance of asset accounts is debit. **Bank Deposit** is credited by $1,500.

Step 3 Record in T-accounts

Factory Office Supplies	
Debit	Credit
1,500	

Bank Deposit	
Debit	Credit
	1,500

Step 4 Record in Journals

CASH PAYMENTS JOURNAL												PAGE 2
	DATE		DOC. NO.	ACCOUNT NAME	POST. REF.	GENERAL		ACCOUNTS PAYABLE DEBIT	BANK DEPOSIT CREDIT	CASH ON HAND CREDIT	
						DEBIT	CREDIT				
13	Dec.	11	INV114	Factory Office Supplies		1 500 00			1 500 00		13
14											14
15											15
16											16

TRANSACTION 38

On December 11, Xinle issued a check to pay newspaper and magazine fees for next year, which was $9,600. The source document is CHECK STUB NO. 052.

$ 9,600.00 **CHECK STUB NO. 052**

Date December 11 2016

To Xiangshan Newspaper Co., Ltd.

For 2017 Newspaper and Magazine Fees

	Dollars	Cents
Balance brought forward	3,536,594	00
Add deposits		
Total	3,536,594	00
Less this check	9,600	00
Balance carried forward	3,526,994	00

WHAT TO DO?

Step 1 Analyze Transaction

Accounts Affected:

There are two accounts affected by this transaction. They are **Prepaid Subscription** and **Bank Deposit.**

Increase/Decrease:

Prepaid Subscription is increased by $9,600. **Bank Deposit** is decreased by $9,600.

Account Category:

Prepaid Subscription is an asset account. **Bank Deposit** is an asset account.

Step 2 Determine Debit/Credit

The normal balance of asset accounts is debit. **Prepaid Subscription** is debited by $9,600. **Bank Deposit** is credited by $9,600.

Step 3 Record in T-accounts

Prepaid Subscription

Debit	Credit
9,600	

Bank Deposit

Debit	Credit
	9,600

Step 4 Record in Journals

CASH PAYMENTS JOURNAL PAGE 2

	DATE		DOC. NO.	ACCOUNT NAME	POST. REF.	GENERAL DEBIT	GENERAL CREDIT	ACCOUNTS PAYABLE DEBIT	BANK DEPOSIT CREDIT	CASH ON HAND CREDIT	
14	Dec.	11	CS052	Prepaid Subscription		9 600 00			9 600 00		14
15											15
16											16
17											17

TRANSACTION 39

On December 11, Xinle purchased 10-ton iron castings from Beijing Steel Co., Ltd. Unit price was $5,000/ton. Delivery fee was $2,000. The source document is CHECK STUB NO. 053. Since sales tax rate in the United States is 9%, sales tax should be $4,500. After-tax price was $54,500. There is no tax on service. In other words, delivery fee is tax free. Xinle should have paid $56,500 to

Beijing Steel Co., Ltd.

$ 56,500.00	CHECK STUB NO. 053
Date December 11	2016
To Beijing Steel Co., Ltd.	
For 10-ton Iron Castings and Delivery Fee	

	Dollars	Cents
Balance brought forward	3,526,994	00
Add deposits		
Total	3,526,994	00
Less this check	56,500	00
Balance carried forward	3,470,494	00

WHAT TO DO?

Suppose that Xinle currently uses standard costing method. The standard cost of iron castings is $4,500/ton. Therefore, standard total cost of those iron castings is $45,000.

Step 1 Analyze Transaction

Accounts Affected:

There are four accounts affected by this transaction. They are **Iron Castings, Material Price Variance, Factory Overhead Incurred** and **Bank Deposit.**

Increase/Decrease:

Iron Castings is increased by $45, 000. **Material Price Variance** is increased by $5, 000. **Factory Overhead Incurred** is increased by $6,500. **Bank Deposit** is decreased by $56,500.

Account Category:

Iron Castings is an asset account. **Material Price Variance** is an asset account. **Factory Overhead Incurred** is an asset account. **Bank Deposit** is an asset account.

Step 2 Determine Debit/Credit

The normal balance of asset accounts is debit. **Iron Castings** is debited by $45,000. **Material Price Variance** is debited by $5, 000. **Factory Overhead Incurred** is debited by $6, 500. **Bank Deposit** is credited by $56,500.

Step 3 Record in T-accounts

Iron Castings

Debit	Credit
45,000	

Material Price Variance

Debit	Credit
5,000	

Factory Overhead Incurred	
Debit	Credit
6,500	

Bank Deposit	
Debit	Credit
	56,500

Step 4 Record in Journals

CASH PAYMENTS JOURNAL PAGE 2

	DATE		DOC. NO.	ACCOUNT NAME	POST. REF.	GENERAL		ACCOUNTS PAYABLE DEBIT	BANK DEPOSIT CREDIT	CASH ON HAND CREDIT	
						DEBIT	CREDIT				
15	Dec.	11	CS053	Iron Castings		45 000 00			56 500 00		15
16				Material Pric. Var.		5 000 00					16
17				Fac. O/H Incurred		6 500 00					17
18											18

TRANSACTION 40

On December 12, Xinle sold 2 000 small air-blowers to Xiangshan Air-blower Co., Ltd. The unit price was $350. Since sales tax rate in the United States is 9%, sales tax should be $63,000. After-tax price was $763,000. Xinle had already collected the money. The source document is SALES SLIP NO. 74 and CHECK STUB NO. 054.

Xinle Air-blower

23 Tulan ST, Xiangshan, China 315700

DATE: December 12, 2016			NO. 74	
SOLD TO	Xiangshan Air-blower 24 Lihai ST Xiangshan, China 315700			
CLERK B.E.	CASH	CHARGE √	TERMS N/A	
QTY.	DESCRIPTION	UNIT PRICE	AMOUNT	
2 000	Small Air-blowers	$ 350.00	$ 700,000	00
		SUBTOTAL	$700,000	00
	Thank You!	SALES TAX	63,000	00
		TOTAL	$763,000	00

$ 763,000.00 **CHECK STUB NO. 054**

Date December 12 2016

To Xiangshan Air-blower Co., Ltd.

For Sales of 2 000 Small Air-blowers

	Dollars	Cents
Balance brought forward	3,470,494	00
Add deposits	763,000	00
Total	4,233,494	00
Less this check		
Balance carried forward	4,233,494	00

WHAT TO DO?

For this transaction itself, two entries should be made. The first one is to record the sales of 2 000 small air-blowers. The second one is to record the change in inventory system. The unit cost of small air-blower is $250, and therefore cost of goods sold should be $500,000.

Step 1 Analyze Transaction

Accounts Affected:

- For the first entry, there are three accounts affected by this transaction. They are **Bank Deposit, Sales Revenue–Small Air-blower** and **Sales Tax Payable.**
- For the second entry, there are two accounts affected by this transaction. They are **Cost of Goods Sold–Small Air-blower** and **Finished Goods–Small Air-blower.**

Increase/Decrease:

- **Bank Deposit** is increased by $763,000. **Sales Revenue–Small Air-blower** is increased by $700,000. **Sales Tax Payable** is increased by $63,000.
- **Cost of Goods Sold–Small Air-blower** is increased by $500,000. **Finished Goods–Small Air-blower** is decreased by $500,000.

Account Category:

- **Bank Deposit** is an asset account. **Sales Revenue–Small Air-blower** is a revenue account. **Sales Tax Payable** is a liability account.
- **Cost of Goods Sold–Small Air-blower** is an expense account. **Finished Goods–Small Air-blower** is an asset account.

Step 2 Determine Debit/Credit

– The normal balance of asset accounts is debit. **Bank Deposit** is debited by $763,000.

– The normal balance of revenue accounts is credit. **Sales Revenue–Small Air-blower** is credited by $700,000.

– The normal balance of liability accounts is credit. **Sales Tax Payable** is credited by $63,000.

– The normal balance of expense accounts is debit. **Cost of Goods Sold–Small Air-blower** is debited by $500,000.

– The normal balance of asset accounts is debit. **Finished Goods–Small Air-blower** is credited by $500,000.

Step 3 Record in T-accounts

Bank Deposit

Debit	Credit
763,000	

Sales Revenue–Small Air-blower

Debit	Credit
	700,000

Sales Tax Payable

Debit	Credit
	63,000

Cost of Goods Sold–Small Air-blower

Debit	Credit
500,000	

Finished Goods–Small Air-blower

Debit	Credit
	500,000

Step 4 Record in Journals

CASH RECEIPTS JOURNAL PAGE 1

	DATE		DOC. NO.	ACCOUNT NAME	POST. REF.	GENERAL CREDIT	SALES CREDIT	SALES TAX PAYABLE CREDIT	ACCOUNTS RECEIVABLE CREDIT	BANK DEPOSIT DEBIT	CASH ON HAND DEBIT	
8	Dec.	12	NO.74/CS054	Small Air-blower			700 000 00	63 000 00		763 000 00		8
9												9
10												10
11												11

	GENERAL JOURNAL					PAGE 1
	DATE		DESCRIPTION	POST. REF.	DEBIT	CREDIT	
30	Dec.	12	Cost of Goods Sold–Small Air-blower		500 0 0 0 00		30
31			Finished Goods–Small Air-blower			500 0 0 0 00	31
32			*SALES SLIP 74*				32
33							33

TRANSACTION 41

On December 12, Xinle paid $10, 000 for advertising fee by bank deposit. The source document is INVOICE NO. 521 and CHECK STUB NO. 055.

Xiangshan Advertising Co., Ltd. INVOICE NO. 521

164 Lanxin ST
Xiangshan, China 315700

DATE: Dec. 12, 2016
TERMS: Payable in 30 days

TO
Xinle Air-blower
23 Tulan ST
Xiangshan, China 315700

ORDER #	ITEM	UNIT PRICE	TOTAL
1273	Advertisement	$ 10,000.00	$ 10,000.00

$ 10,000.00 CHECK STUB NO. 055

Date December 12 2016

To Xiangshan Advertising Co., Ltd.

For Advertisement

	Dollars	Cents
Balance brought forward	4,233,494	00
Add deposits		
Total	4,233,494	00
Less this check	10,000	00
Balance carried forward	4,223,494	00

WHAT TO DO?

Step 1 Analyze Transaction

Accounts Affected:

There are two accounts affected by this transaction. They are **Advertising Expense** and **Bank Deposit.**

Increase/Decrease:

Advertising Expense is increased by $10,000. **Bank Deposit** is decreased by $10,000.

Account Category:

Advertising Expense is an expense account. **Bank Deposit** is an asset account.

Step 2 Determine Debit/Credit

–The normal balance of expense accounts is debit. **Advertising Expense** is debited by $10,000.

–The normal balance of asset accounts is debit. **Bank Deposit** is credited by $10,000.

Step 3 Record in T-accounts

Advertising Expense	
Debit	Credit
10,000	

Bank Deposit	
Debit	Credit
	10,000

Step 4 Record in Journals

CASH PAYMENTS JOURNAL											PAGE 2
	DATE		DOC. NO.	ACCOUNT NAME	POST. REF.	GENERAL		ACCOUNTS PAYABLE DEBIT	BANK DEPOSIT CREDIT	CASH ON HAND CREDIT	
						DEBIT	CREDIT				
18	Dec.	12	INV521	Advertising Expense		10 000 00			10 000 00		18
19											19
20											20
21											21

TRANSACTION 42

On December 12, Xinle reimbursed $1,000 for office supplies fee by check. Those office supplies will be used in selling department. The source document is INVOICE NO. 923 and CHECK STUB NO. 056.

Xiangshan Bookstore Co., Ltd.
73 Sanming ST
Xiangshan, China 315700

INVOICE NO. 923

DATE: Dec. 12, 2016
TERMS: Payable in 30 days

TO
Xinle Air-blower
23 Tulan ST
Xiangshan, China 315700

QTY.	ITEM	UNIT PRICE	TOTAL
2	Pens	$500.00	$ 1,000.00

$ 1,000.00 CHECK STUB NO. 056

Date December 12 2016

To Xiangshan Bookstore Co., Ltd.

For Purchase of 2 Pens

	Dollars	Cents
Balance brought forward	4,223,494	00
Add deposits		
Total	4,223,494	00
Less this check	1,000	00
Balance carried forward	4,222,494	00

WHAT TO DO?

Step 1 Analyze Transaction

Accounts Affected:

There are two accounts affected by this transaction. They are **Sales Office Supplies** and **Bank Deposit.**

Increase/Decrease:

Sales Office Supplies is increased by $1,000. **Bank Deposit** is decreased by $1,000.

Account Category:

Sales Office Supplies is an asset account. **Bank Deposit** is an asset account.

Step 2 Determine Debit/Credit

–The normal balance of asset accounts is debit. **Sales Office Supplies** is debited by $1,000.

–The normal balance of asset accounts is debit. **Bank Deposit** is credited by $1,000.

Step 3 Record in T-accounts

Sales Office Supplies	
Debit	Credit
1,000	

Bank Deposit	
Debit	Credit
	1,000

Step 4 Record in Journals

CASH PAYMENTS JOURNAL											PAGE 2
	DATE		DOC. NO.	ACCOUNT NAME	POST. REF.	GENERAL DEBIT	GENERAL CREDIT	ACCOUNTS PAYABLE DEBIT	BANK DEPOSIT CREDIT	CASH ON HAND CREDIT	
19	Dec.	12	INV923	Sales Office Supplies		1 000 00			1 000 00		19
20											20
21											21
22											22

TRANSACTION 43

On December 12, Xinle purchased a lathe at the after-tax price of $210,600. The source document is CHECK STUB NO. 057. The product price was $180,000, and the sales tax rate in the United States is 9% instead of 17%. Therefore, the after-tax price is no longer $210,600. Instead, it should have been $196,200. In other words, Xinle should have paid $196,200 to Ninghai Machinery Co., Ltd.

$ 196,200.00 **CHECK STUB NO. 057**

Date December 12 2016

To Ninghai Machinery Co., Ltd.

For Lathe Purchase

	Dollars	Cents
Balance brought forward	4,222,494	00
Add deposits		
Total	4,222,494	00
Less this check	196,200	00
Balance carried forward	4,026,294	00

WHAT TO DO?

Step 1 Analyze Transaction

Accounts Affected:

There are two accounts affected by this transaction. They are **Lathe** and **Bank Deposit.**

Increase/Decrease:

Lathe is increased by $196,200. **Bank Deposit** is decreased by $196,200.

Account Category:

Lathe is an asset account. **Bank Deposit** is an asset account.

Step 2 Determine Debit/Credit

The normal balance of asset accounts is debit. **Lathe** is debited by $196,200. **Bank Deposit** is credited by $196,200.

Step 3 Record in T-accounts

Lathe	
Debit	Credit
196,200	

Bank Deposit	
Debit	Credit
	196,200

Step 4 Record in Journals

CASH PAYMENTS JOURNAL — PAGE 2

	DATE		DOC. NO.	ACCOUNT NAME	POST. REF.	GENERAL DEBIT	GENERAL CREDIT	ACCOUNTS PAYABLE DEBIT	BANK DEPOSIT CREDIT	CASH ON HAND CREDIT	
20	Dec.	12	CS057	Lathe		196 2 0 0 00			196 2 0 0 00		20
21											21
22											22
23											23

TRANSACTION 44

On December 13, Xinle paid $3,000 for installment fee. The source document is CHECK STUB NO. 058. There is no tax on service. In other words, the installment fee is tax free. Xinle should have paid $3,000 to Ninghai Machinery Co., Ltd.

$ 3,000.00 **CHECK STUB NO. 058**

Date December 13 2016

To Ninghai Machinery Co., Ltd.

For Installment Fee for Lathe

	Dollars	Cents
Balance brought forward	4,026,294	00
Add deposits		
Total	4,026,294	00
Less this check	3,000	00
Balance carried forward	4,023,294	00

WHAT TO DO?

Step 1 Analyze Transaction

Accounts Affected:

There are two accounts affected by this transaction. They are **Lathe** and **Bank Deposit.**

Increase/Decrease:

Lathe is increased by $3,000. **Bank Deposit** is decreased by $3,000.

Account Category:

Lathe is an asset account. **Bank Deposit** is an asset account.

Step 2 Determine Debit/Credit

The normal balance of asset accounts is debit. **Lathe** is debited by $3,000. **Bank Deposit** is credited by $3,000.

Step 3 Record in T-accounts

Lathe		Bank Deposit	
Debit	Credit	Debit	Credit
3,000			3,000

Step 4 Record in Journals

	CASH PAYMENTS JOURNAL									PAGE 2	
	DATE		DOC. NO.	ACCOUNT NAME	POST. REF.	GENERAL		ACCOUNTS PAYABLE DEBIT	BANK DEPOSIT CREDIT	CASH ON HAND CREDIT	
						DEBIT	CREDIT				
21	Dec.	13	CS058	Lathe		3 000 00			3 000 00		21
22											22
23											23

TRANSACTION 45

On December 13, Xinle purchased 6-ton copper line from Hebei Steel Co., Ltd. Unit price was $18,000/ton. Delivery fee was $1,000. The source document is CHECK STUB NO. 059. Since sales tax rate in the United States is 9%, sales tax should be $9,720. After-tax price was $117,720. There is no tax on service. In other words, delivery fee is tax free. Xinle should have paid $118,720 to Hebei Steel Co., Ltd.

$ 118,720.00 **CHECK STUB NO. 059**

Date December 13 2016

To Hebei Steel Co., Ltd.

For 6-ton Copper Line and Delivery Fee

	Dollars	Cents
Balance brought forward	4,023,294	00
Add deposits		
Total	4,023,294	00
Less this check	118,720	00
Balance carried forward	3,904,574	00

WHAT TO DO?

Suppose that Xinle currently uses standard costing method. The standard cost of copper line is $17,500/ton. Therefore, standard total cost of those copper line is $105,000.

Step 1 Analyze Transaction

Accounts Affected:

There are four accounts affected by this transaction. They are **Copper Line, Material Price Variance, Factory Overhead Incurred** and **Bank Deposit.**

Increase/Decrease:

Copper Line is increased by $105, 000. **Material Price Variance** is increased by $3, 000. **Factory Overhead Incurred** is increased by $6,500. **Bank Deposit** is decreased by $56,500.

Account Category:

Copper Line is an asset account. **Material Price Variance** is an asset account. **Factory Overhead Incurred** is an asset account. **Bank Deposit** is an asset account.

Step 2 Determine Debit/Credit

The normal balance of asset accounts is debit. **Copper Line** is debited by $105,000. **Material Price Variance** is debited by $3, 000. **Factory Overhead Incurred** is debited by $6, 500. **Bank Deposit** is credited by $56,500.

Step 3 Record in T-accounts

Copper Line

Debit	Credit
105,000	

Material Price Variance

Debit	Credit
3,000	

Factory Overhead Incurred

Debit	Credit
10,720	

Bank Deposit

Debit	Credit
	118,720

Step 4 Record in Journals

CASH PAYMENTS JOURNAL PAGE 3

	DATE		DOC. NO.	ACCOUNT NAME	POST. REF.	GENERAL DEBIT	GENERAL CREDIT	ACCOUNTS PAYABLE DEBIT	BANK DEPOSIT CREDIT	CASH ON HAND CREDIT	
1	Dec.	13	CS059	Copper Line		105 000 00			118 720 00		1
2				Material Pric. Var.		3 000 00					2
3				Fac. O/H Incurred		10 720 00					3
4											4

TRANSACTION 46

On December 14, Xinle issued a check for employee payroll. The money distributed to employees was $535,184. Salaries Payable was $680,000. Housing fund fee was $68,000. Medical insurance fee was $13, 600. Unemployment insurance fee was $6, 800. Pension fee was $54, 400. Employee Income Tax was $2,016. One example of the source document is CHECK STUB NO. 060. There were 105 checks issued to employees in Xinle.

$ 3,000.00 **CHECK STUB NO. 060**

Date December 14 2016

To Han Liang

For Payroll of November 2016

	Dollars	Cents
Balance brought forward	3,904,574	00
Add deposits		
Total	3,904,574	00
Less this check	3,000	00
Balance carried forward	3,901,574	00

WHAT TO DO?

Step 1 Analyze Transaction

Accounts Affected:

There are two accounts affected by this transaction. They are **Salaries Payable** and **Bank Deposit.**

Increase/Decrease:

Salaries Payable is decreased by $535,184. **Bank Deposit** is decreased by $535,184.

Account Category:

Salaries Payable is a liability account. **Bank Deposit** is an asset account.

Step 2 Determine Debit/Credit

–The normal balance of liability accounts is credit. **Salaries Payable** is debited by $535,184.

–The normal balance of asset accounts is debit. **Bank Deposit** is credited by $535,184.

Step 3 Record in T-accounts

Salaries Payable	
Debit	Credit
535,184	

Bank Deposit	
Debit	Credit
	535,184

Step 4 Record in Journals

CASH PAYMENTS JOURNAL PAGE 3

	DATE		DOC. NO.	ACCOUNT NAME	POST. REF.	GENERAL DEBIT	GENERAL CREDIT	ACCOUNTS PAYABLE DEBIT	BANK DEPOSIT CREDIT	CASH ON HAND CREDIT	
4	Dec.	14	CS060 -CS164	Salaries Payable		535 184 00			535 184 00		4
5											5
6											6
7											7

TRANSACTION 47

On December 15, Xinle issued a check to pay housing fund fee.

WHAT TO DO?

Since employee payroll tax system in China is different from that in the United States, those employee payroll taxes should be adjusted to satisfy tax system in the United States. Medical Insurance Fee Payable is changed to Medicare Tax Payable. Unemployment Insurance Fee Payable is divided into two accounts. They are Federal Unemployment Tax Payable and State Unemployment Tax Payable. Federal Unemployment Tax Payable accounts for 12.9032% of Unemployment Insurance Fee Payable, which should be $877. State Unemployment Tax Payable accounts for 87.0968% of Unemployment Insurance Fee Payable, which should be $5, 923. Employee Income Tax Payable is also divided into two accounts. Those two accounts are Employee Federal Income Tax Payable and Employee State Income Tax Payable. Employee Federal Income Tax Payable accounts for 1/3 of the balance of Employee Income Tax Payable, which is $672. Employee State Income Tax Payable accounts for 2/3 of the balance of Employee Income Tax Payable, which is $1,344. However, this fee had already been paid on December 4, 2016. Besides, the rest amount of Payroll Tax Payable is collected to Social Security Tax Payable, which should be $122,400. This can be described in following table (the highlighted row had already been paid):

Employee Payroll		
Accounts	Amount	Adaption
Housing Fund Fee	$68,000	Social Security Tax Payable: $122,400
Pension Fee	54,400	
Medical Insurance Fee	13,600	Medicare Tax Payable: $13,600
Unemployment Insurance Fee	6,800	-Federal Unemployment Tax Payable: $877 -State Unemployment Tax Payable: $5,923
Employee Income Tax	2,016	-Employee Federal Income Tax Payable: $672 -Employee State Income Tax Payable: $1,344

Above description is for employee payroll section. In the United States, employers still need to pay for employee payroll tax. In other words, the initial balance of Xinle should also be adjusted. Adjustment rules for employer payroll are similar to that for employee payroll. There are only two differences. First, Employee Income Tax is also collected to Social Security Tax Payable since double employee tax system is not applicable in the United States. Second, Maternity Insurance Fee and Employee Income Tax are also collected to Social Security Tax Payable. This adaption is illustrated in following table:

Employer Payroll		
Accounts	Amount	Adaption
Housing Fund Fee	$68,000	Social Security Tax Payable: $213,496
Pension Fee	136,000	
Employment Injury Insurance Fee	2,040	
Maternity Insurance Fee	5,440	
Employee Income Tax	2,016	
Medical Insurance Fee	47,600	Medicare Tax Payable: $47,600
Unemployment Insurance Fee	13,600	-Federal Unemployment Tax Payable: $1,755 -State Unemployment Tax Payable: $11,845

There is still one problem for this adjustment. In the United States, the amount of Employee Social Security Tax should be equal to Employer Social Security Tax. The amount of Employee Medicare Tax should be equal to Employer Medicare Tax. Based on the analysis, Housing Fund Fee cannot be paid separately to the government in the United States. Therefore, there is no record for this transaction.

TRANSACTION 48

On December 15, Xinle issued a check to pay the five kinds of insurance undertaken by both employers and employees. The source document is CHECK STUB NO. 163. Based on previous analysis, total amount of the fee should be $417,496. Employee income tax had already been paid on December 4, 2016 and therefore should not be paid twice.

$ 417,496.00 **CHECK STUB NO. 163**

Date December 15 2016

To California Tax Bureau

For Payroll Tax of November 2016

	Dollars	Cents
Balance brought forward	3,369,390	00
Add deposits		
Total	3,369,390	00
Less this check	417,496	00
Balance carried forward	2,951,894	00

WHAT TO DO?

Based on previous analysis, the accumulative balance of payroll tax accounts can be illustrated in following table:

Account	Employee	Employer	Total
Social Security Tax Payable	$122,400	$213,496	$335,896
Medicare Tax Payable	13,600	47,600	61,200
Federal Unemployment Tax Payable	877	1,755	2,632
State Unemployment Tax Payable	5,923	11,845	17,768
Employee Federal Income Tax Payable	672		672
Employee State Income Tax Payable	1,344		1,344

Step 1 Analyze Transaction

Accounts Affected:

There are five accounts affected by this transaction. They are **Social Security Tax Payable, Medicare Tax Payable, Federal Unemployment Tax Payable, State Unemployment Tax Payable** and **Bank Deposit.**

Increase/Decrease:

Social Security Tax Payable is decreased by $335,896. **Medicare Tax Payable** is decreased by $61,200. **Federal Unemployment Tax Payable** is decreased by $2,632. **State Unemployment Tax Payable** is decreased by $17,768. **Bank Deposit** is decreased by $417,496.

Account Category:

Social Security Tax Payable is a liability account. **Medicare Tax Payable** is a liability account. **Federal Unemployment Tax Payable** is a liability account. **State Unemployment Tax Payable** is a liability account. **Bank Deposit** is an asset account.

Step 2 Determine Debit/Credit

–The normal balance of liability accounts is credit. **Social Security Tax Payable** is debited by $335, 896. **Medicare Tax Payable** is debited by $61, 200. **Federal Unemployment Tax Payable** is debited by $2,632. **State Unemployment Tax Payable** is debited by $17,768.

–The normal balance of asset accounts is debit. **Bank Deposit** is credited by $417,496.

Step 3 Record in T-accounts

Social Security Tax Payable

Debit	Credit
335,896	

Medicare Tax Payable

Debit	Credit
61,200	

Federal Unemployment Tax Payable

Debit	Credit
2,632	

State Unemployment Tax Payable

Debit	Credit
17,768	

Bank Deposit

Debit	Credit
	417,496

Step 4 Record in Journals

CASH PAYMENTS JOURNAL PAGE 3

	DATE		DOC. NO.	ACCOUNT NAME	POST. REF.	GENERAL DEBIT	GENERAL CREDIT	ACCOUNTS PAYABLE DEBIT	BANK DEPOSIT CREDIT	CASH ON HAND CREDIT	
5	Dec.	15	CS163	Social Sec. Tax Pay.		335 896 00			417 496 00		5
6				Med. Tax Pay.		61 200 00					6
7				FUTP		2 632 00					7
8				SUTP		17 768 00					8
9											9

TRANSACTION 49

On December 15, Xinle purchased 10-ton iron castings from Beijing Steel Co., Ltd. Unit price was $5,000/ton. Delivery fee was $2,000. The source document is CHECK STUB NO. 164. Since sales tax rate in the United States is 9%, sales tax should be $4,500. After-tax price was $54, 500. There is no tax on service. In other words, delivery fee is tax free. Xinle should have paid $56, 500 to Beijing Steel Co., Ltd.

$ 56,500.00 CHECK STUB NO. 164

Date December 15 2016

To Beijing Steel Co., Ltd.

For 10-ton Iron Castings and Delivery Fee

	Dollars	Cents
Balance brought forward	2,951,894	00
Add deposits		
Total	2,951,894	00
Less this check	56,500	00
Balance carried forward	2,895,394	00

WHAT TO DO?

Suppose that Xinle currently uses standard costing method. The standard cost of iron castings is $4,500/ton. Therefore, standard total cost of those iron castings is $45,000.

Step 1 Analyze Transaction

Accounts Affected:

There are four accounts affected by this transaction. They are **Iron Castings, Material Price Variance, Factory Overhead Incurred** and **Bank Deposit.**

Increase/Decrease:

Iron Castings is increased by $45, 000. **Material Price Variance** is increased by $5, 000. **Factory Overhead Incurred** is increased by $6,500. **Bank Deposit** is decreased by $56,500.

Account Category:

Iron Castings is an asset account. **Material Price Variance** is an asset account. **Factory Overhead Incurred** is an asset account. **Bank Deposit** is an asset account.

Step 2 Determine Debit/Credit

The normal balance of asset accounts is debit. **Iron Castings** is debited by $45,000. **Material Price Variance** is debited by $5, 000. **Factory Overhead Incurred** is debited by $6, 500. **Bank Deposit** is credited by $56,500.

Step 3 Record in T-accounts

Iron Castings

Debit	Credit
45,000	

Material Price Variance

Debit	Credit
5,000	

Factory Overhead Incurred

Debit	Credit
6,500	

Bank Deposit

Debit	Credit
	56,500

Step 4 Record in Journals

CASH PAYMENTS JOURNAL											PAGE 3
	DATE		DOC. NO.	ACCOUNT NAME	POST. REF.	GENERAL		ACCOUNTS PAYABLE DEBIT	BANK DEPOSIT CREDIT	CASH ON HAND CREDIT	
						DEBIT	CREDIT				
9	Dec.	15	CS164	Iron Castings		45 000 00			56 500 00		9
10				Material Pric. Var.		5 000 00					10
11				Fac. O/H Incurred		6 500 00					11
12											12

TRANSACTION 50

On December 15, Xinle sold 2 000 large air-blowers to Fenghua Air-blower Co., Ltd. The unit price was $400. Since sales tax rate in the United States is 9%, sales tax should be $72,000. After-tax price was $872,000. Xinle had already collected the money. The source document is SALES SLIP NO. 75 and CHECK STUB NO. 165.

Xinle Air-blower					
23 Tulan ST, Xiangshan, China 315700					
DATE: December 15, 2016				NO. 75	
SOLD TO	Fenghua Air-blower 116 Yunhui ST Fenghua, China 315500				
CLERK B.E.	CASH	CHARGE √		TERMS N/A	
QTY.	DESCRIPTION		UNIT PRICE	AMOUNT	
2,000	Large Air-blowers		$ 400.00	$ 800,000	00
			SUBTOTAL	$800,000	00
Thank You!			SALES TAX	72,000	00
			TOTAL	$872,000	00

$ 872,000.00	CHECK STUB NO. 165
Date December 15	2016
To Fenghua Air-blower Co., Ltd.	
For Sales of 2 000 Large Air-blowers	

	Dollars	Cents
Balance brought forward	2,895,394	00
Add deposits	872,000	00
Total	3,767,394	00
Less this check		
Balance carried forward	3,767,394	00

WHAT TO DO?

For this transaction, two entries should be made. The first one is to record the sales of 2 000 large air-blowers. The second one is to record the change in inventory system. The unit cost of large air-blower is $260, and therefore cost of goods sold should be $520,000.

Step 1 Analyze Transaction

Accounts Affected:

- For the first entry, there are three accounts affected by this transaction. **They are Bank Deposit, Sales Revenue–Large Air-blower** and **Sales Tax Payable.**
- For the second entry, there are two accounts affected by this transaction. They are **Cost of Goods Sold–Large Air-blower** and **Finished Goods–Large Air-blower.**

Increase/Decrease:

- **Bank Deposit** is increased by $872,000. **Sales Revenue–Large Air-blower** is increased by $800,000. **Sales Tax Payable** is increased by $72,000.
- **Cost of Goods Sold–Large Air-blower** is increased by $520,000. **Finished Goods–Large Air-blower** is decreased by $520,000.

Account Category:

- **Bank Deposit** is an asset account. **Sales Revenue–Large Air-blower** is a revenue account. **Sales Tax Payable** is a liability account.
- **Cost of Goods Sold–Large Air-blower** is an expense account. **Finished Goods–Large Air-blower** is an asset account.

Step 2 Determine Debit/Credit

- The normal balance of asset accounts is debit. **Bank Deposit** is debited by $872,000.
- The normal balance of revenue accounts is credit. **Sales Revenue–Large Air-blower** is credited by $800,000.

–The normal balance of liability accounts is credit. **Sales Tax Payable** is credited by $72,000.

–The normal balance of expense accounts is debit. **Cost of Goods Sold–Large Air-blower** is debited by $520,000.

–The normal balance of asset accounts is debit. **Finished Goods–Large Air-blower** is credited by $520,000.

Step 3 Record in T-accounts

Bank Deposit

Debit	Credit
872,000	

Sales Revenue–Large Air-blower

Debit	Credit
	800,000

Sales Tax Payable

Debit	Credit
	72,000

Cost of Goods Sold–Large Air-blower

Debit	Credit
520,000	

Finished Goods–Large Air-blower

Debit	Credit
	520,000

Step 4 Record in Journals

CASH PAYMENTS JOURNAL PAGE 1

	DATE		DOC. NO.	ACCOUNT NAME	POST. REF.	GENERAL CREDIT	SALES CREDIT	SALES TAX PAYABLE CREDIT	ACCOUNTS RECEIVABLE CREDIT	BANK DEPOSIT DEBIT	CASH ON HAND DEBIT	
9	Dec.	15	NO.75/CS165	Large Air-blower			800000 00	72 000 00		872000 00		9
10												10
11												11
12												12

GENERAL JOURNAL							PAGE 1
	DATE		DESCRIPTION	POST. REF.	DEBIT	CREDIT	
33	Dec.	15	Cost of Goods Sold–Large Air-blower		520 0 0 0 00		33
34			Finished Goods–Large Air-blower			520 0 0 0 00	34
35			*SALES SLIP 75*				35
36							36

TRANSACTION 51

On December 16, Xinle purchased 20-ton steel plates from Beijing Steel Co., Ltd. Unit price was $8,000/ton. Delivery fee was $4,000. The source document is CHECK STUB NO. 166. Since sales tax rate in the United States is 9%, sales tax should be S14,400. After-tax price was $174,400. There is no tax on service. In other words, delivery fee is tax free. Xinle should have paid $178,400 to Beijing Steel Co., Ltd. Xinle had already paid $4,000 delivery fee.

$ 4,000.00 **CHECK STUB NO. 166**

Date December 16, 2016

To Beijing Steel Co., Ltd.

For Delivery Fee of 20-ton Steel Plates

	Dollars	Cents
Balance brought forward	3,767,394	00
Add deposits		
Total	3,767,394	00
Less this check	4,000	00
Balance carried forward	3,763,394	00

WHAT TO DO?

Suppose that Xinle currently uses standard costing method. The standard cost of steel plates is $7,500/ton. Therefore, standard total cost of those steel plates is $150,000.

Step 1 Analyze Transaction

Accouns Affected:

There are five accounts affected by this transaction. They are **Steel Plates, Material Price Variance, Factory Overhead Incurred, Bank Deposit** and **Accounts Payable–Beijing Steel.**

Increase/Decrease:

Steel Plates is increased by $150, 000. **Material Price Variance** is increased by $10, 000. **Factory Overhead Incurred** is increased by $18, 400. **Bank Deposit** is decreased by $4, 000. **Accounts Payable–Beijing Steel** is increased by $174,400.

Account Category:

Steel Plates is an asset account. **Material Price Variance** is an asset account. **Factory Overhead Incurred** is an expense account. **Bank Deposit** is an asset account. **Accounts Payable–Beijing Steel** is a liability account.

Step 2 Determine Debit/Credit

The normal balance of asset accounts is debit. **Steel Plates** is debited by $150,000. **Material Price Variance** is debited by $10,000. Bank Deposit is credited by $4,000.

The normal balance of expense accounts is debit. **Factory Overhead Incurred** is debited by $18,400.

The normal balance of liability accounts is credit. **Accounts Payable–Beijing Steel** is credited by $174,400.

Step 3 Record in T-accounts

Steel Plates

Debit	Credit
150,000	

Material Price Variance

Debit	Credit
10,000	

Factory Overhead Incurred

Debit	Credit
18,400	

Bank Deposit

Debit	Credit
	4,000

Accounts Payable–Beijing Steel

Debit	Credit
	174,400

Step 4 Record in Journals

	GENERAL JOURNAL									PAGE 3	
	DATE		DOC. NO.	ACCOUNT NAME	POST. REF.	GENERAL DEBIT	GENERAL CREDIT	ACCOUNTS PAYABLE DEBIT	BANK DEPOSIT CREDIT	CASH ON HAND CREDIT	
12	Dec.	16	CS166	Fac. O/H Incurred		4 000 00			4 000 00		12
13											13
14											14
15											15

	PURCHASES JOURNAL										PAGE 1	
	DATE		INVOICE NO.	CREDITOR'S ACCOUNT CREDITED	TYPE	POST. REF.	ACCOUNTS PAYABLE CREDIT	PURCHASES DEBIT	GENERAL ACCOUNT DEBITED	GENERAL POST. REF.	GENERAL DEBIT	
3	Dec.	16	CS166	Beijing Steel	SP		174 400 00	150 000 00	Material Pric. Var.		10 000 00	3
4									Fac. O/H Incurred		14 400 00	4
5												5
6												6

TRANSACTION 52

On December 16, Xinle reimbursed $1,000 for office supplies fee by cash. Those office supplies will be used in human resource department. The source document is INVOICE NO. 235.

Xiangshan Bookstore Co., Ltd. INVOICE NO. 235

73 Sanming ST

Xiangshan, China 315700

DATE: Dec. 16, 2016

TERMS: Payable in 30 days

TO Xinle Air-blower
23 Tulan ST
Xiangshan, China 315700

QTY.	ITEM	UNIT PRICE	TOTAL
2	Pen	$ 500.00	$ 1,000.00

WHAT TO DO?

Step 1 Analyze Transaction

Accounts Affected:

There are two accounts affected by this transaction. They are **M&A Office Supplies** and **Cash on Hand.**

Increase/Decrease:

M&A Office Supplies is increased by $1,000. **Cash on Hand** is decreased by $1,000.

Account Category:

M&A Office Supplies is an asset account. **Cash on Hand** is an asset account.

Step 2 Determine Debit/Credit

−The normal balance of asset accounts is debit. **M&A Office Supplies** is debited by $1,000.

−The normal balance of asset accounts is debit. **Cash on Hand** is credited by $1,000.

Step 3 Record in T-accounts

M&A Office Supplies		Cash on Hand	
Debit	Credit	Debit	Credit
1,000			1,000

Step 4 Record in Journals

CASH PAYMENTS JOURNAL PAGE 3

	DATE		DOC. NO.	ACCOUNT NAME	POST. REF.	GENERAL DEBIT	GENERAL CREDIT	ACCOUNTS PAYABLE DEBIT	BANK DEPOSIT CREDIT	CASH ON HAND CREDIT	
13	Dec.	16	INV235	M&A Office Supplies		1 000 00				1 000 00	13
14											14
15											15
16											16

TRANSACTION 53

On December 16, Yu Li went back from her business trip. She borrowed $4, 000 from accounting department but spent $4,500 during the trip. She is a staff in selling department. Xinle reimbursed the rest of the money. The source document is INVOICE NO. 145.

Marriott Inn INVOICE NO. 145

132 Clown Plaza

Shanghai, China 200000

DATE: Dec. 16, 2016

TERMS: Payable in 30 days

TO APT 44364
23 Liuxu ST
Xiangshan, China 315700

ROOM #	NAME	CHECK-IN	CHECK-OUT	PRICE/NITE	TOTAL
523	Yu Li	12/14/2016	12/16/2016	$ 2,250.00	$ 4,500.00

WHAT TO DO?

Just as mentioned in last transaction, most small and medium companies in the United States do not allow borrowings for business trip. It is assumed that Xinle does not allow borrowings for business trip. Therefore, this transaction is treated as this employee paid the bills herself first and then tried to get reimbursement from the company. Suppose that the company reimburse the fees by cash.

Step 1 Analyze Transaction

Accounts Affected:

There are two accounts affected by this transaction. They are **Sales Travel Expense** and **Cash on Hand.**

Increase/Decrease:

Sales Travel Expense is increased by $4,500. **Cash on Hand** is decreased by $4,500.

Account Category:

Sales Travel Expense is an expense account. **Cash on Hand** is an asset account.

Step 2 Determine Debit/Credit

–The normal balance of expense accounts is debit. **Sales Travel Expense** is debited by $4,500.

–The normal balance of asset accounts is debit. **Cash on Hand** is credited by $4,500.

Step 3 Record in T-accounts

Sales Travel Expense		Cash on Hand	
Debit	Credit	Debit	Credit
4,500			4,500

Step 4 Record in Journals

CASH PAYMENTS JOURNAL											PAGE 3
	DATE		DOC. NO.	ACCOUNT NAME	POST. REF.	GENERAL		ACCOUNTS PAYABLE	BANK DEPOSIT	CASH ON HAND	
						DEBIT	CREDIT	DEBIT	CREDIT	CREDIT	
14	Dec.	16	INV145	Sales Travel Expense		4 500 00				4 500 00	14
15											15
16											16
17											17

TRANSACTION 54

On December 17, Xinle purchased 300 work jackets at the unit price of $35,300 work shoes at the unit price of $30, and 1,000 heat-resistant gloves at the unit price of $5 from Zhenhai Supplies Co., Ltd. There was no delivery fee. The source document is CHECK STUB NO. 167. Since sales tax rate in the United States is 9%, sales tax should be $2,205. After-tax price was $26, 705. Xinle should have paid $26,705 to Zhenhai Supplies Co., Ltd.

$ 26,705.00 **CHECK STUB NO. 167**

Date December 17, 2016

To Zhenhai Supplies Co., Ltd.

For 300 Work Jackets, 300 Work Shoes and 1,000 Heat-resistant Gloves

	Dollars	Cents
Balance brought forward	3,763,394	00
Add deposits		
Total	3,763,394	00
Less this check	26,705	00
Balance carried forward	3,736,689	00

WHAT TO DO?

Suppose that Xinle currently uses standard costing method. Work jackets, work shoes and heat-resistant gloves are not treated as direct or indirect materials. Instead, they are treated as Factory Overhead when they are used.

Step 1 Analyze Transaction

Accounts Affected:

There are five accounts affected by this transaction. They are Work Jackets, **Work Shoes, Heat-resistant Gloves, Factory Overhead Incurred** and **Bank Deposit.**

Increase/Decrease:

Work Jackets is increased by $10,500. **Work Shoes** is increased by $9,000. **Heat-resistant Gloves** is increased by $5,000. **Factory Overhead Incurred** is increased by $2,205. **Bank Deposit** is decreased by $26,705.

Account Category:

Work Jackets is an asset account. **Work Shoes** is an asset account. **Heat-resistant Gloves** is an asset account. **Factory Overhead Incurred** is an expense account. **Bank Deposit** is an asset account.

Step 2 Determine Debit/Credit

The normal balance of asset accounts is debit. **Work Jackets** is debited by $10,500. **Work Shoes** is debited by $9,000. **Heat-resistant Gloves** is debited by $5,000. **Bank Deposit** is credited by $26,705.

The normal balance of expense accounts is debit. **Factory Overhead Incurred** is debited by $2,205.

Step 3 Record in T-accounts

Work Jackets

Debit	Credit
10,500	

Work Shoes

Debit	Credit
9,000	

Heat-resistant Gloves

Debit	Credit
5,000	

Factory Overhead Incurred

Debit	Credit
2,205	

Bank Deposit	
Debit	Credit
	26,705

Step 4 Record in Journals

CASH PAYMENTS JOURNAL PAGE 3

	DATE		DOC. NO.	ACCOUNT NAME	POST. REF.	GENERAL DEBIT	GENERAL CREDIT	ACCOUNTS PAYABLE DEBIT	BANK DEPOSIT CREDIT	CASH ON HAND CREDIT	
15	Dec.	17	CS167	Work Jackets		10 500 00			26 705 00		15
16				Work Shoes		9 000 00					16
17				Heat-resistant Gloves		5 000 00					17
18				Fac. O/H Incurred		2 205 00					18
19											19

TRANSACTION 55

On December 17, Xinle sold 2,000 large air-blowers to Ningbo Air-blower Co., Ltd. The unit price was $400. Since sales tax rate in the United States is 9%, sales tax should be $72,000. After-tax price should be $872,000. Xinle had already collected the money. The source document is SALES SLIP NO. 76 and CHECK STUB NO. 168.

Xinle Air-blower

23 Tulan ST, Xiangshan, China 315700

DATE: December 17, 2016			NO. 76
SOLD TO	Ningbo Air-blower 31 Liuyun ST Ningbo, China 315000		
CLERK B.E.	CASH	CHARGE √	TERMS N/A
QTY.	DESCRIPTION	UNIT PRICE	AMOUNT
2, 000	Large Air-blowers	$ 400.00	$ 800,000 00
		SUBTOTAL	$ 800,000 00
	Thank You!	SALES TAX	$ 72,000 00
		TOTAL	$ 872,000 00

The delivery fee was $2,000. Xinle paid it for Ningbo Air-blower Co., Ltd. The source document is CHECK STUB NO. 168.

$ 2,000.00 **CHECK STUB NO. 168**

Date December 17, 2016

To Ningbo Air-blower Co., Ltd.

For Delivery Fee

	Dollars	Cents
Balance brought forward	3,736,689	00
Add deposits		
Total	3,736,689	00
Less this check	2,000	00
Balance carried forward	3,734,689	00

WHAT TO DO?

For this transaction, two entries should be made. The first one is to record the sales of 2,000 large air-blowers. The second one is to record the change in inventory system. The unit cost of large air-blower is $260, and therefore cost of goods sold should be $520,000.

Step 1 Analyze Transaction

Accounts Affected:

- For the first entry, there are three accounts affected by this transaction. They are **Accounts Receivable–Ningbo Air-blower, Sales Revenue–Large Air-blower** and **Sales Tax Payable.**
- For the second entry, there are two accounts affected by this transaction. They are **Other Receivable–Ningbo Air-blower** and **Bank Deposit.**
- For the third entry, there are two accounts affected by transactions. They are **Cost of Goods Sold–Large Air-blower** and **Finished Goods–Large Air-blower.**

Increase/Decrease:

- **Accounts Receivable–Ningbo Air-blower** is increased by $872,000. **Sales Revenue–Large Air-blower** is increased by $800,000. **Sales Tax Payable** is increased by $72,000.
- **Other Receivables–Ningbo Air-blower** is increased by $2,000. **Bank Deposit** is decreased by $2,000.
- **Cost of Goods Sold–Large Air-blower** is increased by $520,000. **Finished Goods–Large Air-blower** is decreased by $520,000.

Account Category:

- **Accounts Receivable–Ningbo Air-blower** is an asset account. **Sales Revenue–Large Air-blower** is a revenue account. **Sales Tax Payable** is a liability account.
- **Other Receivable–Ningbo Air-blower** is an asset account. **Bank Deposit** is an asset account.

–**Cost of Goods Sold–Large Air-blower** is an expense account. **Finished Goods–Large Air-blower** is an asset account.

Step 2 Determine Debit/Credit

–The normal balance of asset accounts is debit. **Accounts Receivable–Ningbo Air-blower** is debited by $872,000.

–The normal balance of revenue accounts is credit. **Sales Revenue–Large Air-blower** is credited by $800,000.

–The normal balance of liability accounts is credit. **Sales Tax Payable** is credited by $72,000.

–The normal balance of asset accounts is debit. **Other Receivables–Ningbo Air-blower** is debited by $2,000.

–The normal balance of asset accounts is debit. **Bank Deposit** is credited by $2,000.

–The normal balance of expense accounts is debit. **Cost of Goods Sold–Large Air-blower** is debited by $520,000.

–The normal balance of asset accounts is debit. **Finished Goods–Large Air-blower** is credited by $520,000.

Step 3 Record in T-accounts

Accounts Receivable–Ningbo Air-blower

Debit	Credit
872,000	

Sales Revenue–Large Air-blower

Debit	Credit
	800,000

Sales Tax Payable

Debit	Credit
	72,000

Other Receivables–Ningbo Air-blower

Debit	Credit
2,000	

Bank Deposit

Debit	Credit
	2,000

Cost of Goods Sold–Large Air-blower

Debit	Credit
520,000	

Finished Goods–Large Air-blower

Debit	Credit
	520,000

Step 4 Record in Journals

SALES JOURNAL PAGE 1

	DATE		SALES SLIP NO.	CUSTOMER'S ACCOUNT DEBITED	POST. REF.	SALES CREDIT	SALES TAX PAYABLE CREDIT	ACCOUNTS RECEIVABLE DEBIT	
3	Dec.	17	76	Ningbo Air-blower–Large Air-blower		800 000 00	72 000 00	872 000 00	3
4									4
5									5
6									6

GENERAL JOURNAL PAGE 1

	DATE		DESCRIPTION	POST. REF.	DEBIT	CREDIT	
36	Dec.	17	Other Receivables–Ningbo Air-blower		2 000 00		36
37			Bank Deposit			2 000 00	37
38			*CHECK STUB 168*				38
39	Dec.	17	Cost of Goods Sold–Large Air-blower		520 000 00		39
40			Finished Goods–Large Air-blower			520 000 00	40
41			*SALES SLIP 76*				41
42							42

TRANSACTION 56

On December 17, Xinle sold 1,000 small air-blowers to Xiangshan Air-blower Co., Ltd. The unit price was \$350. Since sales tax rate in the United States is 9%, sales tax should be \$31,500. After-tax price should be \$381,500. Xinle had already collected the money. The source document is SALES SLIP NO. 77 and CHECK STUB NO. 169.

Xinle Air-blower			
23 Tulan ST, Xiangshan, China 315700			
DATE: December 17, 2016			NO. 77
SOLD TO	Xiangshan Air-blower 24 Lihai ST Xiangshan, China 315700		
CLERK B.E.	CASH	CHARGE √	TERMS N/A
QTY.	DESCRIPTION	UNIT PRICE	AMOUNT
1, 000	Small Air-blowers	$ 350.00	$ 350,000 00
		SUBTOTAL	$ 350,000 00
	Thank You!	SALES TAX	$ 31,500 00
		TOTAL	$ 381,500 00

$ 381,500.00 **CHECK STUB NO. 169**

Date December 17, 2016

To Xiangshan Air-blower Co., Ltd.

For Sales of 1, 000 Small Air-blowers

	Dollars	Cents
Balance brought forward	3,734,689	00
Add deposits	381,500	00
Total	4,116,189	00
Less this check		
Balance carried forward	4,116,189	00

WHAT TO DO?

For this transaction, two entries should be made. The first one is to record the sales of 1,000 small air-blowers. The second one is to record the delivery fee paid by Xinle. The third one is to record the change in inventory system. The unit cost of small air-blower is $250, and therefore cost of goods sold should be $250,000.

Step 1 Analyze Transaction

Accounts Affected:

- For the first entry, there are three accounts affected by this transaction. They are **Bank Deposit, Sales Revenue–Small Air-blower** and **Sales Tax Payable.**
- For the second entry, there are two accounts affected by transactions. They are **Cost of**

Goods Sold–Small Air-blower and **Finished Goods–Small Air-blower.**

Increase/Decrease:

- **Bank Deposit** is increased by $381,500. **Sales Revenue–Small Air-blower** is increased by $350,000. **Sales Tax Payable** is increased by $31,500.
- **Cost of Goods Sold–Small Air-blower** is increased by $250,000. **Finished Goods–Small Air-blower** is decreased by $250,000.

Account Category:

- **Bank Deposit** is an asset account. **Sales Revenue–Small Air-blower** is a revenue account. **Sales Tax Payable** is a liability account.
- **Cost of Goods Sold–Small Air-blower** is an expense account. **Finished Goods–Small Air-blower** is an asset account.

Step 2 Determine Debit/Credit

- The normal balance of asset accounts is debit. **Bank Deposit** is debited by $381,500.
- The normal balance of revenue accounts is credit. **Sales Revenue–Small Air-blower** is credited by $350,000.
- The normal balance of liability accounts is credit. **Sales Tax Payable** is credited by $31,500.

- The normal balance of expense accounts is debit. **Cost of Goods Sold–Small Air-blower** is debited by $250,000.
- The normal balance of asset accounts is debit. **Finished Goods–Small Air-blower** is credited by $250,000.

Step 3 Record in T-accounts

Bank Deposit

Debit	Credit
381,500	

Sales Revenue–Small Air-blower

Debit	Credit
	350,000

Sales Tax Payable

Debit	Credit
	31,500

Cost of Goods Sold–Small Air-blower	
Debit	Credit
250,000	

Finished Goods–Small Air-blower	
Debit	Credit
	250,000

Step 4 Record in Journals

CASH RECEIPTS JOURNAL PAGE 1

	DATE		DOC. NO.	ACCOUNT NAME	POST. REF.	GENERAL CREDIT	SALES CREDIT	SALES TAX PAYABLE CREDIT	ACCOUNTS RECEIVABLE CREDIT	BANK DEPOSIT DEBIT	CASH ON HAND DEBIT	
10	Dec.	17	NO.77/CS169	Small Air-blower			350 000 00	31 500 00		381 500 00		10
11												11
12												12
13												13

GENERAL JOURNAL PAGE 1

	DATE		DESCRIPTION	POST. REF.	DEBIT	CREDIT	
42	Dec.	17	Cost of Goods Sold–Small Air-blower		250 000 00		42
43			Finished Goods–Small Air-blower			250 000 00	43
44			SALES SLIP 77				44
45							45

TRANSACTION 57

On December 17, Xinle sold 1,000 large air-blowers to Fenghua Air-blower Co., Ltd. The unit price was $400. Since sales tax rate in the United States is 9%, sales tax should be $36,000. After-tax price should be $436,000. Xinle had already collected the money. The source document is SALES SLIP NO. 78 and CHECK STUB NO. 170.

Xinle Air-blower					
23 Tulan ST, Xiangshan, China 315700					
DATE: December 17, 2016				NO. 78	
SOLD TO	Fenghua Air-blower 116 Yunhui ST Fenghua, China 315500				
CLERK B.E.	CASH	CHARGE √		TERMS N/A	
QTY.	DESCRIPTION		UNIT PRICE	AMOUNT	
1,000	Large Air-blowers		$ 400.00	$ 400,000	00
			SUBTOTAL	$ 400,000	00
Thank You!			SALES TAX	$ 36,000	00
			TOTAL	$ 436,000	00

$ 436,000.00 **CHECK STUB NO. 170**

Date December 17, 2016

To Fenghua Air-blower Co., Ltd.

For Sales of 1,000 Large Air-blowers

	Dollars	Cents
Balance brought forward	4,116,189	00
Add deposits	436,000	00
Total	4,552,189	00
Less this check		
Balance carried forward	4,552,189	00

WHAT TO DO?

For this transaction, two entries should be made. The first one is to record the sales of 1,000 small air-blowers. The second one is to record the change in inventory system. The unit cost of small air-blower is $260, and therefore cost of goods sold should be $260,000.

Step 1 Analyze Transaction

Accounts Affected:

– For the first entry, there are three accounts affected by this transaction. They are **Bank**

Deposit, Sales Revenue–Large Air-blower and **Sales Tax Payable.**

– For the second entry, there are two accounts affected by transactions. They are **Cost of Goods Sold–Large Air-blower** and **Finished Goods–Large Air-blower.**

Increase/Decrease:

– **Bank Deposit** is increased by $436,000. **Sales Revenue–Large Air-blower** is increased by $400,000. **Sales Tax Payable** is increased by $36,000.

– **Cost of Goods Sold–Large Air-blower** is increased by $260,000. **Finished Goods–Large Air-blower** is decreased by $260,000.

Account Category:

– **Bank Deposit** is an asset account. **Sales Revenue–Large Air-blower** is a revenue account. **Sales Tax Payable** is a liability account.

– **Cost of Goods Sold–Large Air-blower** is an expense account. **Finished Goods–Large Air-blower** is an asset account.

Step 2 Determine Debit/Credit

– The normal balance of asset accounts is debit. **Bank Deposit** is debited by $436,000.

– The normal balance of revenue accounts is credit. **Sales Revenue–Large Air-blower** is credited by $400,000.

– The normal balance of liability accounts is credit. **Sales Tax Payable** is credited by $36,000.

– The normal balance of expense accounts is debit. **Cost of Goods Sold–Large Air-blower** is debited by $260,000.

– The normal balance of asset accounts is debit. **Finished Goods–Large Air-blower** is credited by $260,000.

Step 3 Record in T-accounts

Bank Deposit

Debit	Credit
436,000	

Sales Tax Payable

Debit	Credit
	400,000

Sales Revenue–Large Air-blower

Debit	Credit
	36,000

Cost of Goods Sold–Large Air-blower	
Debit	Credit
260,000	

Finished Goods–Large Air-blower	
Debit	Credit
	260,000

Step 4 Record in Journals

CASH RECEIPTS JOURNAL PAGE 1

	DATE		DOC. NO.	ACCOUNT NAME	POST. REF.	GENERAL CREDIT	SALES CREDIT	SALES TAX PAYABLE CREDIT	ACCOUNTS RECEIVABLE CREDIT	BANK DEPOSIT DEBIT	CASH ON HAND DEBIT	
11	Dec.	17	NO.78/CS170	Large Air-blower			400000 00	36 000 00		436000 00		11
12												12
13												13
14												14

GENERAL JOURNAL PAGE 1

	DATE		DESCRIPTION	POST. REF.	DEBIT	CREDIT	
45	Dec.	17	Cost of Goods Sold–Large Air-blower		260 0 0 0 00		45
46			Finished Goods–Large Air-blower			260 0 0 0 00	46
47			SALES SLIP 78				47
48							48

TRANSACTION 58

On December 17, Xinle purchased 50 packing boxes from Zhenhai Supplies Co., Ltd. Unit price was $40 per box. There was no delivery fee. The source document is CHECK STUB NO. 171. Since sales tax rate in the United States is 9%, sales tax should be $180. After-tax price was $2,180. Xinle should have paid $2,180 to Zhenhai Supplies Co., Ltd.

$ 2,180.00 **CHECK STUB NO. 171**

Date December 17, 2016

To Zhenhai Supplies Co., Ltd.

For 50 Packing Boxes

	Dollars	Cents
Balance brought forward	4,552,189	00
Add deposits		
Total	4,552,189	00
Less this check	2,180	00
Balance carried forward	4,550,009	00

WHAT TO DO?

Suppose that Xinle currently uses standard costing method. Packing boxes are indirect material, and therefore the concept of standard cost cannot apply to it.

Step 1 Analyze Transaction

Accounts Affected:

There are three accounts affected by this transaction. They are **Packing Boxes, Factory Overhead Incurred** and **Bank Deposit.**

Increase/Decrease:

Packing Boxes is increased by $2, 000. **Factory Overhead Incurred** is increased by $180. **Bank Deposit** is decreased by $2,180.

Account Category:

Packing Boxes is an asset account. **Factory Overhead Incurred** is an expense account. **Bank Deposit** is an asset account.

Step 2 Determine Debit/Credit

The normal balance of asset accounts is debit. **Packing Boxes** is debited by $2, 000. **Bank Deposit** is credited by $2,180.

The normal balance of expense accounts is debit. **Factory Overhead Incurred** is debited by $180.

Step 3 Record in T-accounts

Packing Boxes		Factory Overhead Incurred	
Debit	Credit	Debit	Credit
2,000		180	

Bank Deposit	
Debit	Credit
	2,180

Step 4 Record in Journals

CASH PAYMENTS JOURNAL											PAGE 3
	DATE		DOC. NO.	ACCOUNT NAME	POST. REF.	GENERAL		ACCOUNTS PAYABLE DEBIT	BANK DEPOSIT CREDIT	CASH ON HAND CREDIT	
						DEBIT	CREDIT				
19	Dec.	17	CS171	Packing Boxes		2 000 00			2 180 00		19
20				Fac. O/H Incurred		180 00					20
21											21
22											22

TRANSACTION 59

On December 17, Xinle paid $5, 000 for advertising fee by bank deposit. The source document is INVOICE NO. 349 and CHECK STUB NO. 172.

Xiangshan Advertising Co., Ltd. INVOICE NO. 349

164 Lanxin ST

Xiangshan, China 315700

DATE: Dec. 17, 2016

TERMS: Payable in 30 days

TO
Xinle Air-blower
23 Tulan ST
Xiangshan, China 315700

Order #	ITEM	UNIT PRICE	TOTAL
1632	Advertisement	$ 5,000.00	$ 5,000.00

$ 5,000.00 CHECK STUB NO. 172

Date December 17, 2016

To Xiangshan Advertising Co., Ltd.

For Advertisements

	Dollars	Cents
Balance brought forward	4,550,009	00
Add deposits		
Total	4,550,009	00
Less this check	5,000	00
Balance carried forward	4,545,009	00

WHAT TO DO?

Step 1 Analyze Transaction

Accounts Affected:

There are two accounts affected by this transaction. They are **Advertising Expense** and **Bank Deposit.**

Increase/Decrease:

Advertising Expense is increased by $5,000. **Bank Deposit** is decreased by $5,000.

Account Category:

Advertising Expense is an expense account. **Bank Deposit** is an asset account.

Step 2 Determine Debit/Credit

–The normal balance of expense accounts is debit. **Advertising Expense** is debited by $5,000.

–The normal balance of asset accounts is debit. **Bank Deposit** is credited by $5,000.

Step 3 Record in T-accounts

Advertising Expense		Bank Deposit	
Debit	Credit	Debit	Credit
5,000			5,000

Step 4 Record in Journals

CASH PAYMENTS JOURNAL											PAGE 3
	DATE		DOC. NO.	ACCOUNT NAME	POST. REF.	GENERAL		ACCOUNTS PAYABLE	BANK DEPOSIT	CASH ON HAND	
						DEBIT	CREDIT	DEBIT	CREDIT	CREDIT	
21	Dec.	17	INV349	Advertising Expense		5 000 00			5 000 00		21
22											22
23											23

TRANSACTION 60

On December 17, Xinle submitted property tax form, land use tax form and vehicle and vessel usage tax form. The annual property tax rate is 1.2%. The net property is $3,606,000. The source document is MEMORANDUM 36.

Xinle Air-blower Co., Ltd. **MEMORANDUM 36**
23 Tulan ST
Xiangshan, China 315700

TO:	California Tax Bureau
FROM:	Amy Strong
DATE:	December 17, 2016
SUBJECT:	Application for Property

The Property Tax Form has been mailed to you.

WHAT TO DO?

Land use tax does not exist in the United States. This is because land can be owned by individuals. Vehicle and vessel usage tax does not exist in the United States, either. Therefore, only property tax should be recorded. The annual property tax rate in the United States is around 3%. Property tax rate can be different in different states. Therefore, half-year property tax should be $54,090.

Step 1 Analyze Transaction

Accounts Affected:

There are two accounts affected by transactions. They are **Property Tax Expense** and **Property**

Tax Payable.

Increase/Decrease:

Property Tax Expense is increased by $54,090. **Property Tax Payable** is increased by $54,090.

Account Category:

Property Tax Expense is an expense account. **Property Tax Payable** is a liability account.

Step 2 Determine Debit/Credit

– The normal balance of expense accounts is debit. **Property Tax Expense** is debited by $54,090.

– The normal balance of liability accounts is credit. **Property Tax Payable** is credited by $54,090.

Step 3 Record in T-accounts

Property Tax Expense

Debit	Credit
54,090	

Property Tax Payable

Debit	Credit
	54,090

Step 4 Record in Journals

GENERAL JOURNAL PAGE 1

	DATE		DESCRIPTION	POST. REF.	DEBIT	CREDIT	
48	Dec.	18	Property Tax Expense		54 090 00		48
49			Property Tax Payable			54 090 00	49
50			*MEMORANDUM 36*				50
51							51

TRANSACTION 61

On December 17, Xinle paid $240 for television fee by bank deposit. The source document is INVOICE NO. 112 and CHECK STUB NO. 173.

Xiangshan Television Co., Ltd. INVOICE NO. 112

52 Sijin ST

Xiangshan, China 315700

DATE: Dec. 17, 2016

TERMS: Payable in 30 days

TO
Xinle Air-blower
23 Tulan ST
Xiangshan, China 315700

Order #	ITEM	UNIT PRICE	TOTAL
27332	Television	$ 240.00	$ 240.00

$ 240.00 CHECK STUB NO. 173

Date December 17, 2016

To Xiangshan Television Co., Ltd.

For Television Fee

	Dollars	Cents
Balance brought forward	4,545,009	00
Add deposits		
Total	4,545,009	00
Less this check	240	00
Balance carried forward	4,544,769	00

WHAT TO DO?

Step 1 Analyze Transaction

Accounts Affected:

There are two accounts affected by this transaction. They are **Television Expense** and **Bank**

Deposit.

Increase/Decrease:

Television Expense is increased by $240. **Bank Deposit** is decreased by $240.

Account Category:

Television Expense is an expense account. **Bank Deposit** is an asset account.

Step 2 Determine Debit/Credit

–The normal balance of expense accounts is debit. **Television Expense** is debited by $240.

–The normal balance of asset accounts is debit. **Bank Deposit** is credited by $240.

Step 3 Record in T-accounts

Television Expense	
Debit	Credit
240	

Bank Deposit	
Debit	Credit
	240

Step 4 Record in Journals

CASH PAYMENTS JOURNAL PAGE 3

	DATE		DOC. NO.	ACCOUNT NAME	POST. REF.	GENERAL DEBIT	GENERAL CREDIT	ACCOUNTS PAYABLE DEBIT	BANK DEPOSIT CREDIT	CASH ON HAND CREDIT	
22	Dec.	17	INV112	Television Expense		240 00			240 00		22
23											23

TRANSACTION 62

On December 17, Xinle paid $99,684 for electricity fee by bank deposit. Xinle used 120,000 kWh. The unit price was $0.71. The sales tax was 17% in China. The source document is INVOICE NO. 32 and CHECK STUB NO. 174. In the United States, sales tax is 9%. Therefore, after-tax price should be $92,868.

Xiangshan Electricity Co., Ltd. INVOICE NO. 32

722 Luoming ST

Xiangshan, China 315700

DATE: Dec. 17, 2016

TERMS: Payable in 30 days

TO Xinle Air-blower
23 Tulan ST
Xiangshan, China 315700

QTY.	ITEM	UNIT PRICE	TOTAL
120,000	Electricity	$ 0.71	$ 85,200.00

$ 92,868.00 CHECK STUB NO. 174

Date December 17, 2016

To Xiangshan Electricity Co., Ltd.

For Electricity Fee

	Dollars	Cents
Balance brought forward	4,544,769	00
Add deposits		
Total	4,544,769	00
Less this check	92,868	00
Balance carried forward	4,451,901	00

WHAT TO DO?

Step 1 Analyze Transaction

Accounts Affected:

There are two accounts affected by this transaction. They are **Factory Overhead Incurred** and

Bank Deposit.

Increase/Decrease:
Factory Overhead Incurred is increased by $92,868. **Bank Deposit** is decreased by $92,868.

Account Category:
Factory Overhead Incurred is an expense account. **Bank Deposit** is an asset account.

Step 2 Determine Debit/Credit

–The normal balance of expense accounts is debit. **Factory Overhead Incurred** is debited by $92,868.

–The normal balance of asset accounts is debit. **Bank Deposit** is credited by $92,868.

Step 3 Record in T-accounts

Factory Overhead Incurred	
Debit	Credit
92,868	

Bank Deposit	
Debit	Credit
	92,868

Step 4 Record in Journals

CASH PAYMENTS JOURNAL PAGE 3

	DATE		DOC. NO.	ACCOUNT NAME	POST. REF.	GENERAL DEBIT	GENERAL CREDIT	ACCOUNTS PAYABLE DEBIT	BANK DEPOSIT CREDIT	CASH ON HAND CREDIT	
23	Dec.	17	INV32	Fac. O/H Incurred		92 8 6 8 00			92 8 6 8 00		23

TRANSACTION 63

On December 17, Xinle paid $7,380.78 for water fee by bank deposit. Xinle used 2,950-ton water. The unit price was $2.11. The sales tax was 6% in China. Additional water tax is 10%. The source document is INVOICE NO. 329 and CHECK STUB NO. 175. In the United States, water sales tax is 8%. Therefore, after-tax price should be $6,722.46.

Xiangshan Electricity Co., Ltd. INVOICE NO. 329

823 Xiangjun ST

Xiangshan, China 315700

DATE: Dec. 17, 2016

TERMS: Payable in 30 days

TO Xinle Air-blower
23 Tulan ST
Xiangshan, China 315700

QTY.	ITEM	UNIT PRICE	TOTAL
2,950	Water	$ 2.11	$ 6,224.50

$ 7,380.78 CHECK STUB NO. 175

Date December 17, 2016

To Xiangshan Electricity Co., Ltd.

For Water Fee

	Dollars	Cents
Balance brought forward	4,451,901	00
Add deposits		
Total	4,451,901	00
Less this check	6,722.46	00
Balance carried forward	4,445,178.54	00

WHAT TO DO?

Step 1 Analyze Transaction

Accounts Affected:

There are two accounts affected by this transaction. They are **Factory Overhead Incurred** and **Bank Deposit.**

Increase/Decrease:

Factory Overhead Incurred is increased by $6,722.46. **Bank Deposit** is decreased by

$6,722.46.

Account Category:

Factory Overhead Incurred is an expense account. **Bank Deposit** is an asset account.

Step 2 Determine Debit/Credit

–The normal balance of expense accounts is debit. **Factory Overhead Incurred** is debited by $6,722.46.

–The normal balance of asset accounts is debit. **Bank Deposit** is credited by $6,722.46.

Step 3 Record in T-accounts

Factory Overhead Incurred	
Debit	Credit
6,722.46	

Bank Deposit	
Debit	Credit
	6,722.46

Step 4 Record in Journals

CASH PAYMENTS JOURNAL PAGE 4

	DATE		DOC. NO.	ACCOUNT NAME	POST. REF.	GENERAL DEBIT	GENERAL CREDIT	ACCOUNTS PAYABLE DEBIT	BANK DEPOSIT CREDIT	CASH ON HAND CREDIT	
1	Dec.	17	INV329	Fac. O/H Incurred		6 7 2 2 46			6 7 2 2 46		1
2											2
3											3
4											4

TRANSACTION 64

On December 17, Xinle paid $1,000,000 back to China Construction Bank with $17,499 interest fee. Within those interest fees, $5, 833 was accrued for current month. The source document is CHECK STUB NO. 176.

$ 1,017,499.00 CHECK STUB NO. 176

Date December 17, 2016

To China Construction Bank Co., Ltd.

For Payment for Bank Loan

	Dollars	Cents
Balance brought forward	4,445,178.54	00
Add deposits		
Total	4,445,178.54	00
Less this check	1,017,499	00
Balance carried forward	3,427,679.54	00

WHAT TO DO?

Step 1 Analyze Transaction

Accounts Affected:

There are four accounts affected by this transaction. They are **Short-term Borrowings–China Construction Bank, Interest Payable, Interest Expense** and **Bank Deposit.**

Increase/Decrease:

Short - term Borrowings–China Construction Bank is decreased by $1, 000, 000. **Interest Payable** is decreased by $11, 666. **Interest Expense** is increased by $5, 833. **Bank Deposit** is decreased by $1,017,499.

Account Category:

Short-term Borrowings–China Construction Bank is a liability account. **Interest Payable** is a liability account. **Interest Expense** is an expense account. **Bank Deposit** is an asset account.

Step 2 Determine Debit/Credit

– The normal balance of liability accounts is credit. **Short - term Borrowings–China Construction Bank** is debited by $1,000,000. **Interest Payable** is debited by $11,666.

–The normal balance of expense accounts is debit. **Interest Expense** is debited by $5,833.

–The normal balance of asset accounts is debit. **Bank Deposit** is credited by $1,017,499.

Step 3 Record in T-accounts

Short-term Borrowings–China Construction Bank

Debit	Credit
1,000,000	

Interest Payable

Debit	Credit
11,666	

Interest Expense

Debit	Credit
5,833	

Bank Deposit

Debit	Credit
	1,017,499

Step 4 Record in Journals

CASH PAYMENTS JOURNAL PAGE 4

	DATE		DOC. NO.	ACCOUNT NAME	POST. REF.	GENERAL DEBIT	GENERAL CREDIT	ACCOUNTS PAYABLE DEBIT	BANK DEPOSIT CREDIT	CASH ON HAND CREDIT	
2	Dec.	17	CS176	ST Bo.–CCB		1000 000 00			1017 499 00		2
3				Interest Pay.		11 666 00					3
4				Interest Exp.		5 833 00					4
5											5

TRANSACTION 65

On December 18, Xinle collected $97,875 note receivable from Xiangshan Air-blower Co., Ltd. The face value is $100,000. Discount rate is 8.5%. The beginning date of this note is October 21, 2016, while the due date is March 21, 2017. The source document is CHECK STUB NO. 177.

$ 97,875.00 CHECK STUB NO. 177

Date December 18, 2016

To Xiangshan Air-blower Co., Ltd.

For Note Receivable

	Dollars	Cents
Balance brought forward	3,427,679.54	00
Add deposits	97,875	00
Total	3,525,554.54	00
Less this check		
Balance carried forward	3,525,554.54	00

WHAT TO DO?

Step 1 Analyze Transaction

Accounts Affected:

There are three accounts affected by this transaction. They are **Bank Deposit, Discounts on Notes Receivable–Xiangshan Air-blower** and **Notes Receivable–Xiangshan Air-blower.**

Increase/Decrease:

Bank Deposit is increased by $97,875. **Discounts on Notes Receivable–Xiangshan Air-blower** is decreased by $2,125. **Notes Receivable–Xiangshan Air-blower** is decreased by $100,000.

Account Category:

Bank Deposit is an asset account. **Discounts on Notes Receivable–Xiangshan Air-blower** is a contra–asset account. **Notes Receivable–Xiangshan Air-blower** is an asset account.

Step 2 Determine Debit/Credit

– The normal balance of asset accounts is debit. **Bank Deposit** is debited by $97,875. **Notes Receivable–Xiangshan Air-blower** is credited by $100,000.

– The normal balance of contra-asset accounts is credit. **Discounts on Notes Receivable–Xiangshan Air-blower** is debited by $2,125.

Step 3 Record in T-accounts

Bank Deposit

Debit	Credit
97,875	

Discounts on Notes Receivable–Xiangshan Air-blower

Debit	Credit
2,125	

Notes Receivable–Xiangshan Air-blower

Debit	Credit
	100,000

Step 4 Record in Journals

GENERAL JOURNAL						PAGE 1
	DATE	DESCRIPTION	POST. REF.	DEBIT	CREDIT	
51	Dec. 18	Bank Deposit		97 875 00		51
52		Discounts on N/R-Xiangshan AB		2 125 00		52
53		N/R-Xiangshan AB			100 000 00	53
54		*CHECK STUB 177*				54
55						55

TRANSACTION 66

On December 18, Xinle reimbursed $3, 000 for training fee by cash. This lump sum of training fees is used for staff in accounting department. The source document is RECEIPT NO. 723.

Xiangshan Training Center RECEIPT

46 Haihe ST

Xiangshan, China 315700

No. 723

Dec. 18 2016

RECEIVED FROM RECEIVED FROM Xinle Air-blower Co., Ltd. $ 3,000.00

Three thousand and no/100 DOLLARS

FOR Training 12/18/2016

RECEIVED BY *Yu Li*

WHAT TO DO?

Step 1 Analyze Transaction

Accounts Affected:

There are two accounts affected by this transaction. They are **M&A Training Expense** and **Cash on Hand.**

Increase/Decrease:

M&A Training Expense is increased by $3,000. **Cash on Hand** is decreased by $3,000.

Account Category:

M&A Training Expense is an expense account. **Cash on Hand** is an asset account.

Step 2 Determine Debit/Credit

–The normal balance of expense accounts is debit. **M&A Training Expense** is debited by $3,000.

–The normal balance of asset accounts is debit. **Cash on Hand** is credited by $3,000.

Step 3 Record in T-accounts

M&A Training Expense

Debit	Credit
3,000	

Cash on Hand

Debit	Credit
	3,000

Step 4 Record in Journals

CASH PAYMENTS JOURNAL PAGE 4

	DATE		DOC. NO.	ACCOUNT NAME	POST. REF.	GENERAL DEBIT	GENERAL CREDIT	ACCOUNTS PAYABLE DEBIT	BANK DEPOSIT CREDIT	CASH ON HAND CREDIT	
5	Dec.	18	REC723	M&A Training Expense		3 000 00				3 000 00	5
6											6
7											7
8											8

TRANSACTION 67

On December 18, Xinle received $3,000 cash for fine. The source document is RECEIPT NO.56.

Xinle Air-blower Co., Ltd. RECEIPT

24 Lihai ST

Xiangshan, China 315700 No. 56

Dec. 18 2016

RECEIVED FROM Liu Ming $ 3,000.00

Three thousand and no/100 DOLLARS

FOR Fine 12/18/2016

RECEIVED BY Yu Li

WHAT TO DO?

Step 1 Analyze Transaction

Accounts Affected:

There are two accounts affected by this transaction. They are **Cash on Hand** and **Other Revenue.**

Increase/Decrease:

Cash on Hand is increased by $3,000. **Other Revenue** is increased by $3,000.

Account Category:

Cash on Hand is an asset account. **Other Revenue** is a revenue account.

Step 2 Determine Debit/Credit

–The normal balance of asset accounts is debit. **Cash on Hand** is debited by $3,000.

–The normal balance of revenue accounts is credit. **Other Revenue** is credited by $3,000.

Step 3 Record in T-accounts

Cash on Hand

Debit	Credit
3,000	

Other Revenue

Debit	Credit
	3,000

Step 4 Record in Journals

CASH RECEIPTS JOURNAL PAGE 1

	DATE		DOC. NO.	ACCOUNT NAME	POST. REF.	GENERAL CREDIT	SALES CREDIT	SALES TAX PAYABLE CREDIT	ACCOUNTS RECEIVABLE CREDIT	BANK DEPOSIT DEBIT	CASH ON HAND DEBIT	
12	Dec.	18	REC56	Other Rev.		3 000 00					3 000 00	12
13												13
14												14
15												15

TRANSACTION 68

On December 19, Xinle paid $10,000 for factory repair and maintenance fee to Ninghai Machinery Co., Ltd. The source document is CHECK STUB NO. 178.

$ 10,000.00 CHECK STUB NO. 178

Date December 19, 2016

To Ninghai Machinery Co., Ltd.

For Repair and Mintenance Fee

	Dollars	Cents
Balance brought forward	3,525,554.54	00
Add deposits		
Total	3,525,554.54	00
Less this check	10,000	00
Balance carried forward	3,515,554.54	00

WHAT TO DO?

Step 1 Analyze Transaction

Accounts Affected:

There are two accounts affected by this transaction. They are **Factory Overhead Incurred** and **Bank Deposit.**

Increase/Decrease:

Factory Overhead Incurred is increased by $10,000. **Bank Deposit** is decreased by $10,000.

Account Category:

Factory Overhead Incurred is an expense account. **Bank Deposit** is an asset account.

Step 2 Determine Debit/Credit

–The normal balance of expense accounts is debit. **Factory Overhead Incurred** is debited by $10,000.

–The normal balance of asset accounts is debit. **Bank Deposit** is credited by $10,000.

Step 3 Record in T-accounts

Factory Overhead Incurred	
Debit	Credit
10,000	

Bank Deposit	
Debit	Credit
	10,000

Step 4 Record in Journals

CASH PAYMENTS JOURNAL PAGE 4

	DATE		DOC. NO.	ACCOUNT NAME	POST. REF.	GENERAL DEBIT	GENERAL CREDIT	ACCOUNTS PAYABLE DEBIT	BANK DEPOSIT CREDIT	CASH ON HAND CREDIT	
6	Dec.	19	CS178	Fac. O/H Incurred		10 000 00			10 000 00		6
7											7
8											8
9											9

TRANSACTION 69

On December 19, Xinle purchased 50 packing boxes from Zhenhai Supplies Co., Ltd. Unit price was $40 per box. There was no delivery fee. The source document is CHECK STUB NO. 179. Since sales tax rate in the United States is 9%, sales tax should be $180. After-tax price was $2,180. Xinle should have paid $2,180 to Zhenhai Supplies Co., Ltd.

$ 2,180.00 **CHECK STUB NO. 179**

Date December 19, 2016

To Zhenhai Supplies Co., Ltd.

For 50 Packing Boxes

	Dollars	Cents
Balance brought forward	3,515,554.54	00
Add deposits		
Total	3,515,554.54	00
Less this check	2,180	00
Balance carried forward	3,513,374.54	00

WHAT TO DO?

Suppose that Xinle currently uses standard costing method. Packing boxes are indirect material, and therefore the concept of standard cost cannot apply to it.

Step 1 Analyze Transaction

Accounts Affected:

There are three accounts affected by this transaction. They are **Packing Boxes, Factory Overhead Incurred** and **Bank Deposit.**

Increase/Decrease:

Packing Boxes is increased by \$2,000. **Factory Overhead Incurred** is increased by \$180. **Bank Deposit** is decreased by \$2,180.

Account Category:

Packing Boxes is an asset account. **Factory Overhead Incurred** is an expense account. **Bank Deposit** is an asset account.

Step 2 Determine Debit/Credit

The normal balance of asset accounts is debit. **Packing Boxes** is debited by \$2,000. **Bank Deposit** is credited by \$2,180.

The normal balance of expense accounts is debit. **Factory Overhead Incurred** is debited by \$180.

Step 3 Record in T-accounts

Packing Boxes

Debit	Credit
2,000	

Factory Overhead Incurred

Debit	Credit
180	

Bank Deposit

Debit	Credit
	2,180

Step 4 Record in Journals

CASH PAYMENTS JOURNAL PAGE 4

	DATE		DOC. NO.	ACCOUNT NAME	POST. REF.	GENERAL DEBIT	GENERAL CREDIT	ACCOUNTS PAYABLE DEBIT	BANK DEPOSIT CREDIT	CASH ON HAND CREDIT	
7	Dec.	19	CS179	Packing Boxes		2 000 00			2 180 00		7
8				Fac. O/H Incurred		180 00					8
9											9
10											10

TRANSACTION 70

On December 19, Xinle purchased 10-ton iron castings from Beijing Steel Co., Ltd. Unit price was $5,000/ton. Delivery fee was $2,000. Xinle had not paid the product yet but had already paid the delivery fee. The source document is INVOICE NO. 723 and CHECK STUB NO. 180. Since sales tax rate in the United States is 9%, sales tax should be $4,500. After-tax price was $54, 500. There is no tax on service. In other words, delivery fee is tax free. Xinle should have paid $56, 500 to Beijing Steel Co., Ltd. and had already paid $2,000.

Beijing Steel Co., Ltd.

217 Sihai ST

Beijing, China 100000

INVOICE NO. 723

DATE: Dec. 19, 2016

ORDER NO.: 82374

SHIPPED BY: Truck

TERMS: Payable in 30 days

TO Xinle Air-blower
23 Tulan ST
Xiangshan, China 315700

QTY.	ITEM	UNIT PRICE	TOTAL
10	Iron Castings	$ 5,000.00	$ 50,000.00

$ 2,000.00 **CHECK STUB NO. 180**

Date December 19, 2016

To Beijing Steel Co., Ltd.

For Delivery Fee of 10-ton Iron Castings

	Dollars	Cents
Balance brought forward	3,513,374.54	00
Add deposits		
Total	3,513,374.54	00
Less this check	2,000	00
Balance carried forward	3,511,374.54	00

WHAT TO DO?

Suppose that Xinle currently uses standard costing method. The standard cost of iron castings is $4,500/ton. Therefore, standard total cost of those iron castings is $45,000.

Step 1 Analyze Transaction

Accounts Affected:

There are five accounts affected by this transaction. They are **Iron Castings, Material Price Variance, Factory Overhead Incurred, Accounts Payable–Beijing Steel** and **Bank Deposit.**

Increase/Decrease:

Iron Castings is increased by $45,000. **Material Price Variance** is increased by $5,000. **Factory Overhead Incurred** is increased by $6,500. **Accounts Payable–Beijing Steel** is increased by $54,500. **Bank Deposit** is decreased by $2,000.

Account Category:

Iron Castings is an asset account. **Material Price Variance** is an asset account. **Factory Overhead Incurred** is an expense account. **Accounts Payable–Beijing Steel** is a liability account. **Bank Deposit** is an asset account.

Step 2 Determine Debit/Credit

The normal balance of asset accounts is debit. **Iron Castings** is debited by $45,000. **Material Price Variance** is debited by $5,000. **Bank Deposit** is credited by $2,000.

The normal balance of expense accounts is debit. **Factory Overhead Incurred** is debited by $6,500.

The normal balance of liability accounts is credit. **Accounts Payable–Beijing Steel** is credited by $54,500.

Step 3 Record in T-accounts

Iron Castings

Debit	Credit
45,000	

Material Price Variance

Debit	Credit
5,000	

Factory Overhead Incurred

Debit	Credit
6,500	

Accounts Payable–Beijing Steel

Debit	Credit
	54,500

Bank Deposit

Debit	Credit
	2,000

Step 4 Record in Journals

CASH PAYMENTS JOURNAL PAGE 4

	DATE		DOC. NO.	ACCOUNT NAME	POST. REF.	GENERAL DEBIT	GENERAL CREDIT	ACCOUNTS PAYABLE DEBIT	BANK DEPOSIT CREDIT	CASH ON HAND CREDIT	
9	Dec.	19	CS180	Fac. O/H Incurred		2 000 00			2 000 00		9
10											10
11											11
12											12

PURCHASES JOURNAL PAGE 1

	DATE		INVOICE NO.	CREDITOR'S ACCOUNT CREDITED	TYPE	POST. REF.	ACCOUNTS PAYABLE CREDIT	PURCHASES DEBIT	GENERAL ACCOUNT DEBITED	GENERAL POST. REF.	GENERAL DEBIT	
5	Dec.	19	INV723	Beijing Steel	IC		54 500 00	45 000 00	Fac. O/H Incurred		4 500 00	5
6									Material Pric. Var.		5 000 00	6
7												7
8												8

TRANSACTION 71

On December 19, Xinle sold 3,000 small air-blowers to Fenghua Air-blower Co., Ltd. The unit price was $350. Since sales tax rate in the United States is 9%, sales tax should be $ 94,500. After - tax price should be $1, 144, 500. Xinle had already collected the money. The source document is SALES SLIP NO. 79 and CHECK STUB NO. 181.

Xinle Air-blower

23 Tulan ST, Xiangshan, China 315700

DATE: December 19, 2016			NO. 79	
SOLD TO	Fenghua Air-blower 116 Yunhui ST Fenghua, China 315500			
CLERK B.E.	CASH	CHARGE √	TERMS N/A	
QTY.	DESCRIPTION	UNIT PRICE	AMOUNT	
3,000	Small Air-blowers	$ 350.00	$ 1,050,000	00
		SUBTOTAL	$1,050,000	00
	Thank You!	SALES TAX	$ 94,500	00
		TOTAL	$1,144,500	00

$ 1,144,500.00

CHECK STUB NO. 181

Date December 19, 2016

To Fenghua Air-blower Co., Ltd.

For Sales of 3,000 Small Air-blowers

	Dollars	Cents
Balance brought forward	3,511,374.54	00
Add deposits	1,144,500	00
Total	4,655,874.54	00
Less this check		
Balance carried forward	4,655,874.54	00

WHAT TO DO?

For this transaction, two entries should be made. The first one is to record the sales of 3,000 small air-blowers. The second one is to record the delivery fee paid by Xinle. The third one is to record the change in inventory system. The unit cost of small air-blower is $250, and therefore cost of goods sold should be $750,000.

Step 1 Analyze Transaction

Accounts Affected:

- For the first entry, there are three accounts affected by this transaction. They are **Bank Deposit, Sales Revenue–Small Air-blower** and **Sales Tax Payable.**
- For the second entry, there are two accounts affected by transactions. They are **Cost of Goods Sold–Small Air-blower** and **Finished Goods–Small Air-blower.**

Increase/Decrease:

- **Bank Deposit** is increased by $1,144,500. **Sales Revenue–Small Air-blower** is increased by $1,050,000. **Sales Tax Payable** is increased by $94,500.
- **Cost of Goods Sold–Small Air-blower** is increased by $750,000. **Finished Goods–Small Air-blower** is decreased by $750,000.

Account Category:

- **Bank Deposit** is an asset account. **Sales Revenue–Small Air-blower** is a revenue account. **Sales Tax Payable** is a liability account.
- **Cost of Goods Sold–Small Air-blower** is an expense account. **Finished Goods–Small Air-blower** is an asset account.

Step 2 Determine Debit/Credit

- The normal balance of asset accounts is debit. **Bank Deposit** is debited by $1,144,500.
- The normal balance of revenue accounts is credit. **Sales Revenue–Small Air-blower** is credited by $1,050,000.
- The normal balance of liability accounts is credit. **Sales Tax Payable** is credited by $94,500.

- The normal balance of expense accounts is debit. **Cost of Goods Sold–Small Air-blower** is debited by $750,000.
- The normal balance of asset accounts is debit. **Finished Goods–Small Air-blower** is credited by $750,000.

Step 3 Record in T-accounts

Bank Deposit

Debit	Credit
1,144,500	

Sales Revenue–Small Air-blower

Debit	Credit
	1,050,000

Sales Tax Payable

Debit	Credit
	94,500

Cost of Goods Sold–Small Air-blower

Debit	Credit
750,000	

Finished Goods–Small Air-blower

Debit	Credit
	750,000

Step 4 Record in Journals

CASH RECEIPTS JOURNAL PAGE 1

	DATE		DOC. NO.	ACCOUNT NAME	POST. REF.	GENERAL CREDIT	SALES CREDIT	SALES TAX PAYABLE CREDIT	ACCOUNTS RECEIVABLE CREDIT	BANK DEPOSIT DEBIT	CASH ON HAND DEBIT	
13	Dec.	19	NO.79/CS181	Small Air-blower			1050000 00	94500 00		1144500 00		13
14												14
15												15
16												16

GENERAL JOURNAL PAGE 1

	DATE		DESCRIPTION	POST. REF.	DEBIT	CREDIT	
55	Dec.	19	Cost of Goods Sold–Small Air-blower		750000 00		55
56			Finished Goods–Small Air-blower			750000 00	56
57			SALES SLIP 79				57
58							58

TRANSACTION 72

On December 21, Xinle received a grinder invested by Hefeng Co., Ltd. The fair value of the grinder is $50,000. The source document is MEMORANDUM 38.

Xinle Air-blower Co., Ltd. MEMORANDUM 38

23 Tulan ST

Xiangshan, China 315700

TO: Accounting Department

FROM: John Thompson

DATE: December 21, 2016

SUBJECT: Receive a Grinder

I have received a grinder from Hefeng Co., Ltd.

WHAT TO DO?

Step 1 Analyze Transaction

Accounts Affected:

There are two accounts affected by this transaction. They are **Grinder and Capital–Hefeng.**

Increase/Decrease:

Grinder is increased by $50,000. **Capital–Hefeng** is increased by $50,000.

Account Category:

Grinder is an asset account. **Capital–Hefeng** is an equity account.

Step 2 Determine Debit/Credit

–The normal balance of asset accounts is debit. **Grinder** is debited by $50,000.

–The normal balance of equity accounts is credit. **Capital–Hefeng** is credited by $50,000.

Step 3 Record in T-accounts

Grinder	
Debit	Credit
50,000	

Capital−Hefeng	
Debit	Credit
	50,000

Step 4 Record in Journals

GENERAL JOURNAL						PAGE 2
	DATE		DESCRIPTION	POST. REF.	DEBIT	CREDIT	
1	Dec.	21	Grinder		50 000 00		1
2			Capital−Hefeng			50 000 00	2
3			MEMORANDUM 38				3
4							4

TRANSACTION 73

On December 21, Xinle paid $1,500 for invitation fee by bank deposit. The source document is INVOICE NO. 554 and CHECK STUB NO. 182.

Xiangshan Local Food Co., Ltd. INVOICE NO. 554

37 Heming ST

Xiangshan, China 315700 DATE: Dec. 21, 2016

TERMS: Payable in 30 days

TO Xinle Air-blower
23 Tulan ST
Xiangshan, China 315700

Room #	ITEM	UNIT PRICE	TOTAL
723	Meal	$ 1,500.00	$ 1,500.00

$ 1,500.00 **CHECK STUB NO. 182**

Date December 21, 2016

To Xiangshan Local Food Co., Ltd.

For Invitation Fee

	Dollars	Cents
Balance brought forward	4,655,874.54	00
Add deposits		
Total	4,655,874.54	00
Less this check	1,500	00
Balance carried forward	4,654,374.54	00

WHAT TO DO?

Step 1 Analyze Transaction

Accounts Affected:

There are two accounts affected by this transaction. They are **Invitation Fee Expense** and **Bank Deposit.**

Increase/Decrease:

Invitation Fee Expense is increased by $1,500. **Bank Deposit** is decreased by $1,500.

Account Category:

Invitation Fee Expense is an expense account. **Bank Deposit** is an asset account.

Step 2 Determine Debit/Credit

–The normal balance of expense accounts is debit. **Invitation Fee Expense** is debited by $1,500.

–The normal balance of asset accounts is debit. **Bank Deposit** is credited by $1,500.

Step 3 Record in T-accounts

Invitation Fee Expense

Debit	Credit
1,500	

Bank Deposit

Debit	Credit
	1,500

Step 4 Record in Journals

CASH PAYMENTS JOURNAL											PAGE 4
	DATE		DOC. NO.	ACCOUNT NAME	POST. REF.	GENERAL		ACCOUNTS PAYABLE	BANK DEPOSIT	CASH ON HAND	
						DEBIT	CREDIT	DEBIT	CREDIT	CREDIT	
10	Dec.	21	INV554	Invitation Fee Expense		1 500 00			1 500 00		10
11											11
12											12
13											13

TRANSACTION 74

On December 21, Xinle purchased 4 barrels of refrigeration oil from Ningbo Jiashan Trade Co., Ltd. Unit price was $5,000/ton. The source document is CHECK STUB NO. 183. Since sales tax rate in the United States is 9%, sales tax should be $1,800. After-tax price was $21,800. Xinle should have paid $21,800 to Ningbo Jiashan Trade Co., Ltd.

$ 21,800 **CHECK STUB NO. 183**

Date December 21, 2016

To Ningbo Jiashan Trade Co., Ltd.

For 4 Barrels of Refrigeration Oil

	Dollars	Cents
Balance brought forward	4,654,374.54	00
Add deposits		
Total	4,654,374.54	00
Less this check	21,800	00
Balance carried forward	4,632,574.54	00

WHAT TO DO?

Suppose that Xinle currently uses standard costing method. The standard cost of refrigeration oil is $5 000/ton. Therefore, standard total cost of those refrigeration oil is $20 000.

Step 1 Analyze Transaction

Accounts Affected:

There are three accounts affected by this transaction. They are **Refrigeration Oil, Factory**

Overhead Incurred and **Bank Deposit.**

Increase/Decrease:

Refrigeration Oil is increased by $20,000. **Factory Overhead Incurred** is increased by $1,800. **Bank Deposit** is decreased by $21,800.

Account Category:

Refrigeration Oil is an asset account. **Factory Overhead** Incurred is an expense account. **Bank Deposit** is an asset account.

Step 2 Determine Debit/Credit

The normal balance of asset accounts is debit. **Refrigeration Oil** is debited by $20,000. **Bank Deposit** is credited by $21,800.

The normal balance of expense accounts is debit. **Factory Overhead Incurred** is debited by $1,800.

Step 3 Record in T-accounts

Refrigeration Oil

Debit	Credit
20,000	

Factory Overhead Incurred

Debit	Credit
1,800	

Bank Deposit

Debit	Credit
	21,800

Step 4 Record in Journals

CASH PAYMENTS JOURNAL PAGE 4

	DATE		DOC. NO.	ACCOUNT NAME	POST. REF.	GENERAL DEBIT	GENERAL CREDIT	ACCOUNTS PAYABLE DEBIT	BANK DEPOSIT CREDIT	CASH ON HAND CREDIT	
11	Dec.	21	CS183	Refrigeration Oil		20 000 00			21 800 00		11
12				Fac. O/H Incurred		1 800 00					12
13											13
14											14

TRANSACTION 75

On December 22, Xinle sold 2,000 small air-blowers to Fenghua Air-blower Co., Ltd. The unit price was $350. Since sales tax rate in the United States is 9%, sales tax should be $63,000. After-tax price should be $763,000. Xinle had not collected the money yet. The source document is SALES SLIP NO. 80.

Xinle Air-blower

23 Tulan ST, Xiangshan, China 315700

DATE: December 22, 2016			NO. 80	
SOLD TO	Fenghua Air-blower 116 Yunhui ST Fenghua, China 315500			
CLERK B.E.	CASH	CHARGE √	TERMS N/A	
QTY.	DESCRIPTION	UNIT PRICE	AMOUNT	
2,000	Small Air-blowers	$ 350.00	$ 700,000	00
		SUBTOTAL	$ 700,000	00
Thank You!		SALES TAX	$ 63,000	00
		TOTAL	$ 763,000	00

WHAT TO DO?

For this transaction, three entries should be made. The first one is to record the sales of 2,000 small air-blowers. The second one is to record the delivery fee paid by Xinle. The third one is to record the change in inventory system. The unit cost of small air-blower is $250, and therefore cost of goods sold should be $500,000.

Step 1 Analyze Transaction

<u>*Accounts Affected:*</u>

- For the first entry, there are three accounts affected by this transaction. They are **Accounts Receivable–Fenghua Air-blower, Sales Revenue–Small Air-blower** and **Sales Tax Payable.**
- For the second entry, there are two accounts affected by transactions. They are **Cost of Goods Sold–Small Air-blower** and **Finished Goods–Small Air-blower.**

<u>*Increase/Decrease:*</u>

- **Accounts Receivable–Fenghua Air-blower** is increased by $763,000. **Sales Revenue–Small Air-blower** is increased by $700,000. **Sales Tax Payable** is increased by $63,000.

–**Cost of Goods Sold–Small Air-blower** is increased by $500,000. **Finished Goods–Small Air-blower** is decreased by $500,000.

Account Category:

–**Accounts Receivable–Fenghua Air-blower** is an asset account. **Sales Revenue–Small Air-blower** is a revenue account. **Sales Tax Payable** is a liability account.

–**Cost of Goods Sold–Small Air-blower** is an expense account. **Finished Goods–Small Air-blower** is an asset account.

Step 2 Determine Debit/Credit

–The normal balance of asset accounts is debit. **Accounts Receivable–Fenghua Air-blower** is debited by $763,000.

–The normal balance of revenue accounts is credit. **Sales Revenue–Small Air-blower** is credited by $700,000.

–The normal balance of liability accounts is credit. **Sales Tax Payable** is credited by $63,000.

–The normal balance of expense accounts is debit. **Cost of Goods Sold–Small Air-blower** is debited by $500,000.

–The normal balance of asset accounts is debit. **Finished Goods–Small Air-blower** is credited by $500,000.

Step 3 Record in T-accounts

Accounts Receivable–Fenghua Air-blower

Debit	Credit
763,000	

Sales Revenue–Small Air-blower

Debit	Credit
	700,000

Sales Tax Payable

Debit	Credit
	63,000

Cost of Goods Sold–Small Air-blower

Debit	Credit
500,000	

Finished Goods–Small Air-blower

Debit	Credit
	500,000

Step 4 Record in Journals

GENERAL JOURNAL							PAGE 2
	DATE		DESCRIPTION	POST. REF.	DEBIT	CREDIT	
4	Dec.	22	Cost of Goods Sold–Small Air-blower		500 0 0 0 00		4
5			Finished Goods–Small Air-blower			500 0 0 0 00	5
6			SALES SLIP 80				6
7							7

SALES JOURNAL									PAGE 1
	DATE		SALES SLIP NO.	CUSTOMER'S ACCOUNT DEBITED	POST. REF.	SALES CREDIT	SALES TAX PAYABLE CREDIT	ACCOUNTS RECEIVABLE DEBIT	
4	Dec.	22	80	Fenghua Air-blower–Small Air-blower		700 0 0 0 00	63 0 0 0 00	763 0 0 0 00	4
5									5
6									6
7									7

TRANSACTION 76

On December 22, Xinle purchased 4-ton copper line from Hebei Steel Co., Ltd. Unit price was $18,000/ton. Delivery fee was $800. The source document is CHECK STUB NO. 184. Since sales tax rate in the United States is 9%, sales tax should be $6,480. After-tax price was $78,480. There is no tax on service. In other words, delivery fee is tax free. Xinle should have paid $79,280 to Hebei Steel Co., Ltd.

CHECK STUB NO. 184

$ 79,280.00

Date December 22, 2016

To Hebei Steel Co., Ltd.

For 4 ton Copper Line and Delivery Fee

	Dollars	Cents
Balance brought forward	4,632,574.54	00
Add deposits		
Total	4,632,574.54	00
Less this check	79,280	00
Balance carried forward	4,553,294.54	00

WHAT TO DO?

Suppose that Xinle currently uses standard costing method. The standard cost of copper line is $17,500/ton. Therefore, standard total cost of those copper line is $70,000.

Step 1 Analyze Transaction

Accounts Affected:

There are four accounts affected by this transaction. They are **Copper Line, Material Price Variance, Factory Overhead Incurred** and **Bank Deposit.**

Increase/Decrease:

Copper Line is increased by $70, 000. **Material Price Variance** is increased by $2, 000. **Factory Overhead Incurred** is increased by $7,280. **Bank Deposit** is decreased by $79,280.

Account Category:

Copper Line is an asset account. **Material Price Variance** is an asset account. **Factory Overhead Incurred** an expense account. **Bank Deposit** is an asset account.

Step 2 Determine Debit/Credit

The normal balance of asset accounts is debit. **Copper Line** is debited by $70,000. **Material Price Variance** is debited by $2,000. **Bank Deposit** is credited by $79,280.

The normal balance of expense accounts is debit. **Factory Overhead Incurred** is debited by $7,280.

Step 3 Record in T-accounts

Copper Line

Debit	Credit
70,000	

Material Price Variance

Debit	Credit
2,000	

Factory Overhead Incurred

Debit	Credit
7,280	

Bank Deposit

Debit	Credit
	79,280

Step 4 Record in Journals

CASH PAYMENTS JOURNAL PAGE 4

	DATE		DOC. NO.	ACCOUNT NAME	POST. REF.	GENERAL DEBIT	GENERAL CREDIT	ACCOUNTS PAYABLE DEBIT	BANK DEPOSIT CREDIT	CASH ON HAND CREDIT	
13	Dec.	22	CS184	Copper Line		70 000 00			79 280 00		13
14				Material Pric. Var.		2 000 00					14
15				Fac. O/H Incurred		7 280 00					15
16											16

TRANSACTION 77

On December 23, Xinle purchased 10-ton steel plates from Shandong Steel Co., Ltd. Unit price was $8,000/ton. Delivery fee was $2,000. The source document is BILL 117. Since sales tax rate in the United States is 9%, sales tax should be $7,200. After-tax price was $87,200. There is no tax on service. In other words, delivery fee is tax free. Xinle should have paid $89,200 to Shandong Steel Co., Ltd.

BILL 117

$ 89,200.00

one year after date Xinle Air-blower Co., Ltd. promise to pay to

Shandong Steel Co., Ltd. the sum of

Eighty nine thousand and two hundred dollars on

December 23, 2016 per year

Due date December 23, 2017

Ming Li

WHAT TO DO?

Suppose that Xinle currently uses standard costing method. The standard cost of steel plates is $7,500/ton. Therefore, standard total cost of those steel plates is $75,000.

Step 1 Analyze Transaction

Accounts Affected:

There are four accounts affected by this transaction. They are **Steel Plates, Material Price Variance, Factory Overhead Incurred** and **Commercial Acceptance Bill Payable.**

Increase/Decrease:

Steel Plates is increased by $75,000. **Material Price Variance** is increased by $5,000. **Factory Overhead Incurred** is increased by $9,200. **Commercial Acceptance Bill Payable** is decreased by $89,200.

Account Category:

Steel Plates is an asset account. **Material Price Variance** is an asset account. **Factory Overhead Incurred** is an expense account. **Commercial Acceptance Bill Payable** is a liability account.

Step 2 Determine Debit/Credit

- The normal balance of asset accounts is debit. **Steel Plates** is debited by $75,000. **Material Price Variance** is debited by $5,000.
- The normal balance of expense accounts is debit. **Factory Overhead Incurred** is debited by $9,200.
- The normal balance of liability accounts is credit. **Commercial Acceptance Bill Payable** is credited by $89,200.

Step 3 Record in T-accounts

Steel Plates

Debit	Credit
75,000	

Material Price Variance

Debit	Credit
5,000	

Factory Overhead Incurred

Debit	Credit
9,200	

Commercial Acceptance Bill Payable

Debit	Credit
	89,200

Step 4 Record in Journals

GENERAL JOURNAL PAGE 2

	DATE		DESCRIPTION	POST. REF.	DEBIT	CREDIT	
7	Dec.	23	Steel Plates		75 000 00		7
8			Material Price Variance		5 000 00		8
9			Factory Overhead Incurred		9 200 00		9
10			Commercial Acceptance Bill Pay.			89 200 00	10
11			*BILL 117*				11
12							12

TRANSACTION 78

On December 23, Xinle purchased 10-ton iron castings from Beijing Steel Co., Ltd. Unit price was $5,000/ton. Delivery fee was $2,000. The source document is CHECK STUB NO. 185. Since sales tax rate in the United States is 9%, sales tax should be $4,500. After-tax price was $54,500. There is no tax on service. In other words, delivery fee is tax free. Xinle should have paid $56,500 to Beijing Steel Co., Ltd.

$ 56,500.00 CHECK STUB NO. 185

Date December 23, 2016

To Beijing Steel Co., Ltd.

For 10-ton Iron Castings and Delivery Fee

	Dollars	Cents
Balance brought forward	4,553,294.54	00
Add deposits		
Total	4,553,294.54	00
Less this check	56,500	00
Balance carried forward	4,496,794.54	00

WHAT TO DO?

Suppose that Xinle currently uses standard costing method. The standard cost of iron castings is $4,500/ton. Therefore, standard total cost of those iron castings is $45,000.

Step 1 Analyze Transaction

Accounts Affected:

There are four accounts affected by this transaction. They are **Iron Castings, Material Price Variance, Factory Overhead Incurred** and **Bank Deposit.**

Increase/Decrease:

Iron Castings is increased by $45, 000. **Material Price Variance** is increased by $5, 000. **Factory Overhead Incurred** is increased by $6,500. **Bank Deposit** is decreased by $56,500.

Account Category:

Iron Castings is an asset account. **Material Price Variance** is an asset account. **Factory Overhead Incurred** an expense account. **Bank Deposit** is an asset account.

Step 2 Determine Debit/Credit

The normal balance of asset accounts is debit. **Iron Castings** is debited by $45,000. **Material Price Variance** is debited by $5,000. **Bank Deposit** is credited by $56,500.

The normal balance of expense accounts is debit. **Factory Overhead** Incurred is debited by $6,500.

Step 3 Record in T-accounts

Iron Castings	
Debit	Credit
45,000	

Material Price Variance	
Debit	Credit
5,000	

Factory Overhead Incurred	
Debit	Credit
6,500	

Bank Deposit	
Debit	Credit
	56,500

Step 4 Record in Journals

CASH PAYMENTS JOURNAL PAGE 4

	DATE		DOC. NO.	ACCOUNT NAME	POST. REF.	GENERAL DEBIT	GENERAL CREDIT	ACCOUNTS PAYABLE DEBIT	BANK DEPOSIT CREDIT	CASH ON HAND CREDIT	
16	Dec.	23	CS185	Iron Castings		45 000 00			56 500 00		16
17				Material Pric. Var.		5 000 00					17
18				Fac. O/H Incurred		6 500 00					18
19											19

TRANSACTION 79

On December 23, Xinle issued a check to pay $30,000 for air-blower trademark to Xiangshan Trademark Bureau. The source document is CHECK STUB NO. 186.

$ 30,000.00 **CHECK STUB NO. 186**

Date December 23, 2016

To Xiangshan Trademark Bureau

For Trademark Purchase

	Dollars	Cents
Balance brought forward	4,496,794.54	00
Add deposits		
Total	4,496,794.54	00
Less this check	30,000	00
Balance carried forward	4,466,794.54	00

WHAT TO DO?

Step 1 Analyze Transaction

Accounts Affected:

There are two accounts affected by this transaction. They are **Trademark** and **Bank Deposit.**

Increase/Decrease:

Trademark is increased by $30,000. **Bank Deposit** is decreased by $30,000.

Account Category:

Trademark is an asset account. **Bank Deposit** is an asset account.

Step 2 Determine Debit/Credit

The normal balance of asset accounts is debit. **Trademark** is debited by $30, 000. **Bank Deposit** is credited by $30,000.

Step 3 Record in T-accounts

Trademark

Debit	Credit
30,000	

Bank Deposit

Debit	Credit
	30,000

Step 4 Record in Journals

CASH PAYMENTS JOURNAL PAGE 4

	DATE		DOC. NO.	ACCOUNT NAME	POST. REF.	GENERAL		ACCOUNTS PAYABLE	BANK DEPOSIT	CASH ON HAND	
						DEBIT	CREDIT	DEBIT	CREDIT	CREDIT	
19	Dec.	23	CS186	Trademark		30 000 00			30 000 00		19
20											20
21											21
22											22

TRANSACTION 80

On December 23, Xinle put $1 500 cash into bank. The source document is RECEIPT NO. 926.

China Construction Bank RECEIPT

155 Yuji ST

Xiangshan, China 315700

No.926

Dec. 23 2016

RECEIVED FROM Xinle Air-blower Co., Ltd. $ 1,500.00

One thousand and five hundred and no/100- DOLLARS

FOR Deposit Money 12/23/2016

RECEIVED BY *Yu Li*

WHAT TO DO?

Step 1 Analyze Transaction

Accounts Affected:

There are two accounts affected by this transaction. They are **Bank Deposit** and **Cash on Hand.**

Increase/Decrease:

Bank Deposit is increased by $1,500. **Cash on Hand** is decreased by $1,500.

Account Category:

Bank Deposit is an asset account. **Cash on Hand** is an asset account.

Step 2 Determine Debit/Credit

The normal balance of asset accounts is debit. **Bank Deposit** is debited by $1,500. **Cash on**

Hand is credited by $1,500.

Step 3 Record in T-accounts

Bank Deposit	
Debit	Credit
1,500	

Cash on Hand	
Debit	Credit
	1,500

Step 4 Record in Journals

GENERAL JOURNAL							PAGE 2
	DATE		DESCRIPTION	POST. REF.	DEBIT	CREDIT	
12	Dec.	23	Bank Deposit		1 500 00		12
13			Cash on Hand			1 500 00	13
14			*RECEIPT 926*				14
15							15

TRANSACTION 81

On December 24, Xinle sold 1,000 large air-blowers to Ningbo Air-blower Co., Ltd. The unit price was $400. Since sales tax rate in the United States is 9%, sales tax should be $36,000. After-tax price should be $436,000. Xinle had already collected the money. However, the products had not been delivered yet. The source document is SALES SLIP NO. 81 and CHECK STUB NO. 187.

Xinle Air-blower				
23 Tulan ST, Xiangshan, China 315700				
DATE: December 24, 2016			NO. 81	
SOLD TO	Ningbo Air-blower 31 Liuyun ST Ningbo, China 315000			
CLERK B.E.	CASH	CHARGE √	TERMS N/A	
QTY.	DESCRIPTION	UNIT PRICE	AMOUNT	
1,000	Large Air-blowers	$ 400.00	$ 400,000	00
Thank You!		SUBTOTAL	$ 400,000	00
		SALES TAX	$ 36,000	00
		TOTAL	$ 436,000	00

$ 436,000.00 CHECK STUB NO. 187

Date December 24, 2016

To Ningbo Air-blower Co., Ltd.

For Sales of 1,000 Large Air-blowers

	Dollars	Cents
Balance brought forward	4,468,294.54	00
Add deposits	436,000	00
Total	4,904,294.54	00
Less this check		
Balance carried forward	4,904,294.54	00

WHAT TO DO?

Step 1 Analyze Transaction

Accounts Affected:

There are three accounts affected by this transaction. They are **Bank Deposit, Unearned Revenue-Ningbo Air-blower** and **Sales Tax Payable.**

Increase/Decrease:

Bank Deposit is increased by $436,000. **Unearned Revenue–Ningbo Air-blower** is increased by $400,000. **Sales Tax Payable** is increased by $36,000.

Account Category:

Bank Deposit is an asset account. **Unearned Revenue–Ningbo Air - blower** is a Liability account. **Sales Tax Payable** is a liability account.

Step 2 Determine Debit/Credit

–The normal balance of asset accounts is debit. **Bank Deposit** is debited by $436,000.

–The normal balance of Liability accounts is credit. **Unearned Revenue–Ningbo Air-blower** is credited by $400,000.

–The normal balance of liability accounts is credit. **Sales Tax Payable** is credited by $36,000.

Step 3 Record in T-accounts

Bank Deposit	
Debit	Credit
436,000	

Unearned Revenue–Ningbo Air-blower	
Debit	Credit
	400,000

Sales Tax Payable	
Debit	Credit
	36,000

Step 4 Record in Journals

CASH RECEIPTS JOURNAL PAGE 1

	DATE		DOC. NO.	ACCOUNT NAME	POST. REF.	GENERAL CREDIT	SALES CREDIT	SALES TAX PAYABLE CREDIT	ACCOUNTS RECEIVABLE CREDIT	BANK DEPOSIT DEBIT	CASH ON HAND DEBIT	
14	Dec.	24	NO.81/CS187	Unearned Rev.–NBAB		400 0 0 0 00		36 000 00		436000 00		14
15												15
16												16
17												17

TRANSACTION 82

On December 26, Xinle sold 1,000 small air-blowers to Xiangshan Air-blower Co., Ltd. The unit price was \$350. Since sales tax rate in the United States is 9%, sales tax should be \$31,500. After-tax price should be \$381,500. Xiangshan Air-blower had prepaid the money. The source document is SALES SLIP NO. 82 and CHECK STUB NO. 188.

Xinle Air-blower

23 Tulan ST, Xiangshan, China 315700

DATE: December 26, 2016				NO. 82	
SOLD TO	Xiangshan Air-blower 24 Lihai ST Xiangshan, China 315700				
CLERK B.E.	CASH	CHARGE √		TERMS N/A	
QTY.	DESCRIPTION		UNIT PRICE	AMOUNT	
1,000	Small Air-blowers		$ 350.00	$ 350,000	00
Thank You!			SUBTOTAL	$ 350,000	00
			SALES TAX	$ 31,500	00
			TOTAL	$ 381,500	00

$ 381,500.00 CHECK STUB NO. 188

Date December 26, 2016

To Xinle Air-blower Co., Ltd.

For Prepayment of 1,000 Small Air-blowers

	Dollars	Cents
Balance brought forward	4,904,294.54	00
Add deposits	381,500	00
Total	5,285,794.54	00
Less this check		
Balance carried forward	5,285,794.54	00

WHAT TO DO?

Step 1 Analyze Transaction

Accounts Affected:

There are three accounts affected by this transaction. They are **Bank Deposit, Unearned**

Revenue–Xiangshan Air-blower and **Sales Tax Payable.**

Increase/Decrease:

Bank Deposit is increased by $381, 500. **Unearned Revenue–Xiangshan Air-blower** is increased by $350,000. **Sales Tax Payable** is increased by $31,500.

Account Category:

Bank Deposit is an asset account. **Unearned Revenue–Xiangshan Air-blower** is a liability account. **Sales Tax Payable** is a liability account.

Step 2 Determine Debit/Credit

–The normal balance of asset accounts is debit. **Bank Deposit** is debited by $381,500.

–The normal balance of liablity accounts is credit. **Unearned Revenue–Xiangshan Air-blower** is credited by $350,000.

–The normal balance of liability accounts is credit. **Sales Tax Payable** is credited by $31,500.

Step 3 Record in T-accounts

Bank Deposit

Debit	Credit
381,500	

Unearned Revenue–Xiangshan Air-blower

Debit	Credit
	350,000

Sales Tax Payable

Debit	Credit
	31,500

Step 4 Record in Journals

	CASH RECEIPTS JOURNAL											PAGE 1
	DATE		DOC. NO.	ACCOUNT NAME	POST. REF.	GENERAL CREDIT	SALES CREDIT	SALES TAX PAYABLE CREDIT	ACCOUNTS RECEIVABLE CREDIT	BANK DEPOSIT DEBIT	CASH ON HAND DEBIT	
15	Dec.	26	NO.82/CS188	Unearned Rev.-XSAB		350 000 00		31 500 00		381 500 00		15
16												16
17												17
18												18

TRANSACTION 83

On December 27, Xinle purchased 10-ton iron castings from Beijing Steel Co., Ltd. Unit price was $5,000/ton. Delivery fee was $2,000. Xinle had not paid the product yet but had already paid the delivery fee. The source document is INVOICE NO. 872 and CHECK STUB NO. 189. Since sales tax rate in the United States is 9%, sales tax should be $4,500. After-tax price was $54,500. There is no tax on service. In other words, delivery fee is tax free. Xinle should have paid $56,500 to Beijing Steel Co., Ltd. and had already paid $2,000.

Beijing Steel Co., Ltd. INVOICE NO. 872

217 Sihai ST

Beijing, China 100000

DATE: Dec. 27, 2016

ORDER NO.: 92834

SHIPPED BY: Truck

TERMS: Payable in 30 days

TO Xinle Air-blower
23 Tulan ST
Xiangshan, China 315700

TON	ITEM	UNIT PRICE	TOTAL
10	Iron Castings	$ 5,000.00	$ 50,000.00

$ 2,000.00 **CHECK STUB NO. 189**

Date December 27, 2016

To Beijing Steel Co., Ltd.

For Delivery Fee of 10-ton Iron Castings

	Dollars	Cents
Balance brought forward	5,285,794.54	00
Add deposits		
Total	5,285,794.54	00
Less this check	2,000	00
Balance carried forward	5,283,794.54	00

WHAT TO DO?

Suppose that Xinle currently uses standard costing method. The standard cost of iron castings is $4,500/ton. Therefore, standard total cost of those iron castings is $45,000.

Step 1 Analyze Transaction

Accounts Affected:

There are five accounts affected by this transaction. They are **Iron Castings, Material Price Variance, Factory Overhead Incurred, Accounts Payable–Beijing Steel** and **Bank Deposit.**

Increase/Decrease:

Iron Castings is increased by $45, 000. **Material Price Variance** is increased by $5, 000. **Factory Overhead Incurred** is increased by $6,500. **Accounts Payable–Beijing Steel** is increased by $54,500. **Bank Deposit** is decreased by $2,000.

Account Category:

Iron Castings is an asset account. **Material Price Variance** is an asset account. **Factory Overhead Incurred** is an expense account. **Accounts Payable–Beijing Steel** is a liability account. **Bank Deposit** is an asset account.

Step 2 Determine Debit/Credit

The normal balance of asset accounts is debit. **Iron Castings** is debited by $45,000. **Material Price Variance** is debited by $5,000. **Bank Deposit** is credited by $2,000.

The normal balance of expense accounts is debit. **Factory Overhead Incurred** is debited by $6,500.

The normal balance of liability accounts is credit. **Accounts Payable–Beijing Steel** is credited by $56,500.

Step 3 Record in T-accounts

Iron Castings	
Debit	Credit
45,000	

Material Price Variance	
Debit	Credit
5,000	

Factory Overhead Incurred	
Debit	Credit
6,500	

Accounts Payable–Beijing Steel	
Debit	Credit
	54,500

Bank Deposit	
Debit	Credit
	2,000

Step 4 Record in Journals

CASH PAYMENTS JOURNAL — PAGE 4

	DATE		DOC. NO.	ACCOUNT NAME	POST. REF.	GENERAL DEBIT	GENERAL CREDIT	ACCOUNTS PAYABLE DEBIT	BANK DEPOSIT CREDIT	CASH ON HAND CREDIT	
20	Dec.	27	CS189	Fac. O/H Incurred		2 000 00			2 000 00		20
21											21
22											22
23											23

PURCHASES JOURNAL — PAGE 1

	DATE		INVOICE NO.	CREDITOR'S ACCOUNT CREDITED	TYPE	POST. REF.	ACCOUNTS PAYABLE CREDIT	PURCHASES DEBIT	GENERAL ACCOUNT DEBITED	GENERAL POST. REF.	GENERAL DEBIT	
7	Dec.	27	INV872	Beijing Steel	IC		54 5 0 0 00	45 0 0 0 00	Fac. O/H Incurred		450000	7
8									Material Pric. Var.		500000	8
9												9
10												10

TRANSACTION 84

On December 27, Xinle counted cash on hand and discovered that $50 was lost. The source document is MEMORANDUM 39.

Xinle Air-blower Co., Ltd. MEMORANDUM 39

23 Tulan ST

Xiangshan, China 315700

TO: Accounting Department

FROM: Amy Hilton

DATE: December 27, 2016

SUBJECT: Lost Cash

I found $50 cash was lost.

WHAT TO DO?

Step 1 Analyze Transaction

Accounts Affected:

There are two accounts affected by this transaction. They are **Cash Lost Expense** and **Cash on Hand.**

Increase/Decrease:

Cash Lost Expense is increased by $50. **Cash on Hand** is decreased by $50.

Account Category:

Cash Lost Expense is an expense account. **Cash on Hand** is an asset account.

Step 2 Determine Debit/Credit

–The normal balance of expense accounts is debit. **Cash Lost Expense** is debited by $50.

–The normal balance of asset accounts is debit. **Cash on Hand** is credited by $50.

Step 3 Record in T-accounts

Cash Lost Expense	
Debit	Credit
50	

Cash on Hand	
Debit	Credit
	50

Step 4 Record in Journals

GENERAL JOURNAL							PAGE 2
	DATE		DESCRIPTION	POST. REF.	DEBIT	CREDIT	
15	Dec.	27	Cash Lost Expense		50 00		15
16			Cash on Hand			50 00	16
17			*MEMORANDUM 39*				17
18							18

TRANSACTION 85

On December 27, Yang Zhang paid $50 for the lost cash in last transaction. The source document is MEMORANDUM 40.

Xinle Air-blower Co., Ltd. MEMORANDUM 40

23 Tulan ST

Xiangshan, China 315700

TO: Accounting Department

FROM: Amy Hilton

DATE: December 27, 2016

SUBJECT: Reimbursement of Lost Cash

Yang Zhang paid $50 for the lost cash.

WHAT TO DO?

Step 1 Analyze Transaction

Accounts Affected:

There are two accounts affected by this transaction. They are **Cash on Hand** and **Cash Lost Expense.**

Increase/Decrease:

Cash on Hand is increased by $50. **Cash Lost Expense** is decreased by $50.

Account Category:

Cash on Hand is an asset account. **Cash Lost Expense** is an expense account.

Step 2 Determine Debit/Credit

–The normal balance of asset accounts is debit. **Cash on Hand** is debited by $50.

–The normal balance of expense accounts is debit. **Cash Lost Expense** is credited by $50.

Step 3 Record in T-accounts

Cash on Hand	
Debit	Credit
50	

Cash Lost Expense	
Debit	Credit
	50

Step 4 Record in Journals

GENERAL JOURNAL						PAGE 2	
	DATE		DESCRIPTION	POST. REF.	DEBIT	CREDIT	
18	Dec.	27	Cash on Hand		50 00		18
19			Cash Lost Expense			50 00	19
20			*MEMORANDUM 40*				20
21							21

TRANSACTION 86

On December 27, Xinle paid $8,000 for telephone fee by bank deposit. The source document is INVOICE NO. 45 and CHECK STUB NO. 190.

Xiangshan Advertising Co., Ltd. INVOICE NO. 45

11 Wulun ST

Xiangshan, China 315700

DATE: Dec. 27, 2016

TERMS: Payable in 30 days

TO
Xinle Air-blower
23 Tulan ST
Xiangshan, China 315700

ORDER #	ITEM	UNIT PRICE	TOTAL
819273	Advertisement	$ 8,000.00	$ 8,000.00

$ 8,000.00 CHECK STUB NO. 190

Date December 27, 2016

To Xiangshan Advertising Co., Ltd.

For Telephone Fee

	Dollars	Cents
Balance brought forward	5,283,794.54	00
Add deposits		
Total	5,283,794.54	00
Less this check	8,000	00
Balance carried forward	5,275,794.54	00

WHAT TO DO?

Step 1 Analyze Transaction

Accounts Affected:

There are two accounts affected by this transaction. They are **Telephone Expense** and **Bank Deposit.**

Increase/Decrease:

Telephone Expense is increased by $8,000. **Bank Deposit** is decreased by $8,000.

Account Category:

Telephone Expense is an expense account. **Bank Deposit** is an asset account.

Step 2 Determine Debit/Credit

–The normal balance of expense accounts is debit. **Telephone Expense** is debited by $8,000.

–The normal balance of asset accounts is debit. **Bank Deposit** is credited by $8,000.

Step 3 Record in T-accounts

Telephone Expense	
Debit	Credit
8,000	

Bank Deposit	
Debit	Credit
	8,000

Step 4 Record in Journals

CASH PAYMENTS JOURNAL PAGE 4

	DATE		DOC. NO.	ACCOUNT NAME	POST. REF.	GENERAL DEBIT	GENERAL CREDIT	ACCOUNTS PAYABLE DEBIT	BANK DEPOSIT CREDIT	CASH ON HAND CREDIT	
21	Dec.	27	INV45	Telephone Expense		8 000 00			8 000 00		21
22											22
23											23

TRANSACTION 87

On December 28, Xinle sold 2,000 large air-blowers to Xiangsha Air-blower Co., Ltd. The unit price was $400. Since sales tax rate in the United States is 9%, sales tax should be $72,000. After-tax price should be $872,000. Xinle had already collected the money. The source document is SALES SLIP NO. 83 and CHECK STUB NO. 191.

Xinle Air-blower				
23 Tulan ST, Xiangshan, China 315700				
DATE: December 28, 2016			NO. 83	
SOLD TO	Xiangshan Air-blower 24 Lihai ST Xiangshan, China 315700			
CLERK B.E.	CASH	CHARGE √	TERMS N/A	
QTY.	DESCRIPTION	UNIT PRICE	AMOUNT	
2,000	Large Air-blowers	$ 400.00	$ 800,000	00
		SUBTOTAL	$ 800,000	00
	Thank You!	SALES TAX	$ 72,000	00
		TOTAL	$ 872,000	00

$ 872,000.00 CHECK STUB NO. 191

Date December 28, 2016

To Xiangshan Air-blower Co., Ltd.

For Sales of 2,000 Large Air-blowers

	Dollars	Cents
Balance brought forward	5,275,794.54	00
Add deposits	872,000	00
Total	6,147,794.54	00
Less this check		
Balance carried forward	6,147,794.54	00

WHAT TO DO?

For this transaction, two entries should be made. The first one is to record the sales of 2,000 large air-blowers. The second one is to record the change in inventory system. The unit cost of small air-blower is $260, and therefore cost of goods sold should be $520,000.

Step 1 Analyze Transaction

Accounts Affected:

– For the first entry, there are three accounts affected by this transaction. They are **Bank Deposit, Sales Revenue–Large Air-blower** and **Sales Tax Payable.**

– For the second entry, there are two accounts affected by transactions. They are **Cost of Goods Sold–Large Air-blower** and **Finished Goods–Large Air-blower.**

Increase/Decrease:

– **Bank Deposit** is increased by $872,000. **Sales Revenue–Large Air-blower** is increased by $800,000. **Sales Tax Payable** is increased by $72,000.

– **Cost of Goods Sold-Large Air-blower** is increased by $520,000. **Finished Goods–Large Air-blower** is decreased by $520,000.

Account Category:

– **Bank Deposit** is an asset account. **Sales Revenue-Large Air–blower** is a revenue account. **Sales Tax Payable** is a liability account.

– **Cost of Goods Sold–Large Air-blower** is an expense account. **Finished Goods–Large Air-blower** is an asset account.

Step 2 Determine Debit/Credit

–The normal balance of asset accounts is debit. **Bank Deposit** is debited by $872,000.

–The normal balance of revenue accounts is credit. **Sales Revenue–Large Air-blower** is credited by $800,000.

–The normal balance of liability accounts is credit. **Sales Tax Payable** is credited by $72,000.

–The normal balance of expense accounts is debit. **Cost of Goods Sold–Large Air-blower** is debited by $520,000.

–The normal balance of asset accounts is debit. **Finished Goods–Large Air-blower** is credited by $520,000.

Step 3 Record in T-accounts

Bank Deposit

Debit	Credit
872,000	

Sales Revenue–Large Air-blower

Debit	Credit
	800,000

Sales Tax Payable

Debit	Credit
	72,000

Cost of Goods Sold–Large Air-blower	
Debit	Credit
520,000	

Finished Goods–Large Air-blower	
Debit	Credit
	520,000

Step 4 Record in Journals

CASH RECEIPTS JOURNAL PAGE 1

	DATE		DOC. NO.	ACCOUNT NAME	POST. REF.	GENERAL CREDIT	SALES CREDIT	SALES TAX PAYABLE CREDIT	ACCOUNTS RECEIVABLE CREDIT	BANK DEPOSIT DEBIT	CASH ON HAND DEBIT	
16	Dec.	28	NO.83/CS191	Large Air-blower			800 000 00	72 000 00		872 000 00		16
17												17
18												18
19												19

GENERAL JOURNAL PAGE 2

	DATE		DESCRIPTION	POST. REF.	DEBIT	CREDIT	
21	Dec.	28	Cost of Goods Sold–Large Air-blower		520 000 00		21
22			Finished Goods–Large Air-blower			520 000 00	22
23			*SALES SLIP 83*				23
24							24

TRANSACTION 88

On December 28, Xinle paid property tax form, land use tax form and vehicle and vessel usage tax form. The source document is CHECK STUB NO. 192. Just as mentioned before, urban land use tax does not exist in the United States. This is because land can be owned by individuals. Vehicle and vessel tax does not exist in the United States, either. Therefore, only property tax should be recorded. The annual property tax rate in the United States is around 3%. Property tax rate can be different in different states. Therefore, half-year property tax should be $54,090. Xinle had already submitted the tax for to California Tax Bureau.

$ 54,090.00		CHECK STUB NO. 192
Date December 28, 2016		
To California Tax Bureau		
For Payment of Property Tax		
	Dollars	Cents
Balance brought forward	6,147,794.54	00
Add deposits		
Total	6,147,794.54	00
Less this check	54,090	00
Balance carried forward	6,093,704.54	00

WHAT TO DO?

Step 1 Analyze Transaction

Accounts Affected:

There are two accounts affected by transactions. They are **Property Tax Payable** and **Bank Deposit.**

Increase/Decrease:

Property Tax Payable is increased by $54,090. **Bank Deposit** is decreased by $54,090.

Account Category:

Property Tax Payable is a liability account. **Bank Deposit** is an asset account.

Step 2 Determine Debit/Credit

-The normal balance of liability accounts is credit. **Property Tax Payable** is debited by $54,090.

-The normal balance of asset accounts is debit. **Bank Deposit** is credited by $54,090.

Step 3 Record in T-accounts

Property Tax Payable		Bank Deposit	
Debit	Credit	Debit	Credit
54,090			54,090

Step 4 Record in Journals

CASH PAYMENTS JOURNAL										PAGE 4
	DATE	DOC. NO.	ACCOUNT NAME	POST. REF.	GENERAL		ACCOUNTS PAYABLE	BANK DEPOSIT	CASH ON HAND	
					DEBIT	CREDIT	DEBIT	CREDIT	CREDIT	
22	Dec. 28	CS192	Property Tax Pay		54 0 9 0 00			54 0 9 0 00		22
23										23

TRANSACTION SUMMARY

Period journal entries have been completed at this point. Regular transactions have already been collected in General Journal and four special journals. General Journal is illustrated in following table.

GENERAL JOURNAL						PAGE 1
	DATE	DESCRIPTION	POST. REF.	DEBIT	CREDIT	
1	Dec. 4	Other Receivables–Fenghua Air-blower		3 0 0 0 00		1
2		Bank Deposit			3 0 0 0 00	2
3		*CHECK STUB 34*				3
4	Dec. 4	Cost of Goods Sold–Small Air-blower		250 0 0 0 00		4
5		Finished Goods–Small Air-blower			250 0 0 0 00	5
6		*SALES SLIP 68*				6
7	Dec. 7	Cost of Goods Sold–Large Air-blower		520 0 0 0 00		7
8		Finished Goods–Large Air-blower			520 0 0 0 00	8
9		*SALES SLIP 69*				9
10	Dec. 7	Cost of Goods Sold–Small Air-blower		250 0 0 0 00		10
11		Finished Goods–Small Air-blower			250 0 0 0 00	11
12		*SALES SLIP 70*				12
13	Dec. 7	Cost of Goods Sold–Large Air-blower		260 0 0 0 00		13
14		Finished Goods–Large Air-blower			260 0 0 0 00	14
15		*SALES SLIP 71*				15
16	Dec. 9	Other Receivables–Ningbo Air-blower		3 0 0 0 00		16

continued

	DATE		DESCRIPTION	POST. REF.	DEBIT		CREDIT		
17			Bank Deposit				3000	00	17
18			*CHECK STUB 48*						18
19	Dec.	9	Cost of Goods Sold-Small Air-blower		250000	00			19
20			Finished Goods-Small Air-blower				250000	00	20
21			*SALES SLIP 72*						21
22	Dec.	11	Cost of Goods Sold-Large Air-blower		260000	00			22
23			Finished Goods-Large Air-blower				260000	00	23
24			*SALES SLIP 73*						24
25	Dec.	11	Bank Deposit		10000	00			25
26			Loss on Disposal of Lathe		5000	00			26
27			Accumulated Depreciation-Lathe		135000	00			27
28			Lathe				150000	00	28
29			*MEMORANDUM 32 & 33*						29
30	Dec.	12	Cost of Goods Sold-Small Air-blower		500000	00			30
31			Finished Goods-Small Air-blower				500000	00	31
32			*SALES SLIP 74*						32
33	Dec.	15	Cost of Goods Sold-Large Air-blower		520000	00			33
34			Finished Goods-Large Air-blower				520000	00	34
35			*SALES SLIP 75*						35
36	Dec.	17	Other Receivables-Ningbo Air-blower		2000	00			36
37			Bank Deposit				2000	00	37
38			*CHECK STUB 168*						38
39	Dec.	17	Cost of Goods Sold-Large Air-blower		520000	00			39
40			Finished Goods-Large Air-blower				520000	00	40
41			*SALES SLIP 76*						41
42	Dec.	17	Cost of Goods Sold-Small Air-blower		250000	00			42
43			Finished Goods-Small Air-blower				250000	00	43

continued

	DATE		DESCRIPTION	POST. REF.	DEBIT	CREDIT	
44			*SALES SLIP 77*				44
45	Dec.	17	Cost of Goods Sold-Large Air-blower		260 000 00		45
46			Finished Goods-Large Air-blower			260 000 00	46
47			*SALES SLIP 78*				47
48	Dec.	17	Property Tax Expense		54 090 00		48
49			Property Tax Payable			54 090 00	49
50			*MEMORANDUM 36*				50
51	Dec.	18	Bank Deposit		97 875 00		51
52			Discounts on N/R-Xiangshan AB		2 125 00		52
53			N/R-Xiangshan AB			100 000 00	53
54			*CHECK STUB 177*				54
55	Dec.	19	Cost of Goods Sold-Small Air-blower		750 000 00		55
56			Finished Goods-Small Air-blower			750 000 00	56
57			*SALES SLIP 79*				57
58							
59							
60							

GENERAL JOURNAL PAGE 2

	DATE		DESCRIPTION	POST. REF.	DEBIT	CREDIT	
1	Dec.	21	Grinder		50 000 00		1
2			Capital-Hefeng			50 000 00	2
3			*MEMORANDUM 38*				3
4	Dec.	22	Cost of Goods Sold-Small Air-blower		500 000 00		4
5			Finished Goods-Small Air-blower			500 000 00	5
6			*SALES SLIP 80*				6
7	Dec.	23	Steel Plates		75 000 00		7

continued

	DATE		DESCRIPTION	POST. REF.	DEBIT	CREDIT	
8			Material Price Variance		5 000 00		8
9			Factory Overhead Incurred		9 200 00		9
10			Commercial Acceptance Bill Pay.			89 200 00	10
11			*BILL 117*				11
12	Dec.	23	Bank Deposit		1 500 00		12
13			Cash on Hand			1 500 00	13
14			*RECEIPT 926*				14
15	Dec.	27	Cash Lost Expense		50 00		15
16			Cash on Hand			50 00	16
17			*MEMORANDUM 39*				17
18	Dec.	27	Cash on Hand		50 00		18
19			Cash Lost Expense			50 00	19
20			*MEMORANDUM 40*				20
21	Dec.	28	Cost of Goods Sold-Large Air-blower		520 000 00		21
22			Finished Goods-Large Air-blower			520 000 00	22
23			*SALES SLIP 83*				23

Cash Receipts Journal, Cash Payments Journal, Sales Journal and Purchases Journal are illustrated in following tables.

CASH RECEIPTS JOURNAL PAGE 1

	DATE		DOC. NO.	ACCOUNT NAME	POST. REF.	GENERAL CREDIT	SALES CREDIT	SALES TAX PAYABLE CREDIT	ACCOUNTS RECEIVABLE CREDIT	BANK DEPOSIT DEBIT	CASH ON HAND DEBIT	
1	Dec.	2	RA291	AR-FHAB					100 000 00	100 000 00		1
2	Dec.	4	L38	STB-CCB		600 000 00				600 000 00		2
3	Dec.	7	NO.69/CS041	Large Air-blower			800 000 00	72 000 00		872 000 00		3
4	Dec.	7	NO.70/CS042	Small Air-blower			350 000 00	31 500 00		381 500 00		4

continued

	DATE		DOC. NO.	ACCOUNT NAME	POST. REF.	GENERAL CREDIT	SALES CREDIT	SALES TAX PAYABLE CREDIT	ACCOUNTS RECEIVABLE CREDIT	BANK DEPOSIT DEBIT	CASH ON HAND DEBIT	
5	Dec.	7	NO.71/CS043	Large Air-blower			400 000 00	36 000 00		436 000 00		5
6	Dec.	8	L192	STB-BOC		500 000 00				500 000 00		6
7	Dec.	11	NO.73/CS050	Large Air-blower			400 000 00	36 000 00		436 000 00		7
8	Dec.	12	NO.74/CS054	Small Air-blower			700 000 00	63 000 00		763 000 00		8
9	Dec.	15	NO.75/CS165	Large Air-blower			800 000 00	72 000 00		872 000 00		9
10	Dec.	17	NO.77/CS169	Small Air-blower			350 000 00	31 500 00		381 500 00		10
11	Dec.	17	NO.78/CS170	Large Air-blower			400 000 00	36 000 00		436 000 00		11
12	Dec.	18	REC56	Other Rev.		3 000 00					3 000 00	12
13	Dec.	19	NO.79/CS181	Small Air-blower			1050 000 00	94 500 00		1144 500 00		13
14	Dec.	24	NO.81/CS187	Unearned Rev.-NBAB		400 000 00		36 000 00		436 000 00		14
15	Dec.	26	NO.82/CS188	Unearned Rev.-XSAB		350 000 00		31 500 00		381 500 00		15
16	Dec.	28	NO.83/CS191	Large Air-blower			800 000 00	72 000 00		872 000 00		16

CASH PAYMENTS JOURNAL PAGE 1

	DATE		DOC. NO.	ACCOUNT NAME	POST. REF.	GENERAL		ACCOUNTS PAYABLE DEBIT	BANK DEPOSIT CREDIT	CASH ON HAND CREDIT	
						DEBIT	CREDIT				
1	Dec.	1	CS029	Petty Cash		1 500 00			1 500 00		1
2	Dec.	1	INV324	M&A Travel Expense		800 00				800 00	2
3	Dec.	1	REC12	Bank Fee Expense		30 00			30 00		3

continued

	DATE		DOC. NO.	ACCOUNT NAME	POST. REF.	GENERAL		ACCOUNTS PAYABLE DEBIT	BANK DEPOSIT CREDIT	CASH ON HAND CREDIT	
						DEBIT	CREDIT				
4	Dec.	2	CS030	Saw Machine		220000 00			220000 00		4
5	Dec.	2	CS031	Steel Plates		150000 00			178400 00		5
6				Material Pric. Var.		10000 00					6
7				Fac. O/H Incurred		18400 00					7
8	Dec.	3	CS032	Iron Castings		45000 00			56500 00		8
9				Material Pric. Var.		5000 00					9
10				Fac. O/H Incurred		6500 00					10
11	Dec.	3	REC229	Tele. Expense		1200 00				1200 00	11
12	Dec.	3	CS033	Packing Boxes		2000 00			2180 00		12
13				Fac. O/H Incurred		180 00					13
14	Dec.	4	CS035	Petty Cash		2000 00			2000 00		14
15	Dec.	4	CS036	FITP		601590 00			1205196 00		15
16				SITP		601590 00					16
17				Employee FITP		672 00					17
18				Employee SITP		1344 00					18
19	Dec.	4	CS037	Prepaid Insurance		90000 00			90000 00		19
20	Dec.	5	CS038	Copper Line		105000 00			118720 00		20
21				Material Pric. Var.		3000 00					21
22				Fac. O/H Incurred		10720 00					22
23	Dec.	5	CS039	Refrigeration Oil		30000 00			32700 00		23
24				Fac. O/H Incurred		2700 00					24

CASH PAYMENTS JOURNAL											PAGE 2
	DATE		DOC. NO.	ACCOUNT NAME	POST. REF.	GENERAL		ACCOUNTS PAYABLE	BANK DEPOSIT	CASH ON HAND	
						DEBIT	CREDIT	DEBIT	CREDIT	CREDIT	
1	Dec.	7	CS040	Steel Plates		75000 00			89200 00		1
2				Material Pric. Var.		5000 00					2
3				Fac. O/H Incurred		9200 00					3
4	Dec.	8	REC116	Sales Training Expense		3000 00				3000 00	4
5	Dec.	8	INV316	Invitation Fee Expense		1000 00			1000 00		5
6	Dec.	8	INV823	M&A Office Supplies		2000 00				2000 00	6
7	Dec.	8	CS045	Petty Cash		2000 00			2000 00		7
8	Dec.	8	CS046	Packing Boxes		2000 00			2180 00		8
9				Fac. O/H Incurred		180 00					9
10	Dec.	9	CS047	Prepaid Broadband		120000 00			120000 00		10
11	Dec.	10	CS049	Refrigeration Oil		20000 00			21800 00		11
12				Fac. O/H Incurred		1800 00					12
13	Dec.	11	INV114	Factory Office Supplies		1500 00			1500 00		13
14	Dec.	11	CS052	Prepaid Subscription		9600 00			9600 00		14
15	Dec.	11	CS053	Iron Castings		45000 00			56500 00		15
16				Material Pric. Var.		5000 00					16
17				Fac. O/H Incurred		6500 00					17
18	Dec.	12	INV521	Advertising Expense		10000 00			10000 00		18
19	Dec.	12	INV923	Sales Office Supplies		1000 00			1000 00		19
20	Dec.	12	CS057	Lathe		196200 00			196200 00		20
21	Dec.	13	CS058	Lathe		3000 00			3000 00		21
22											22
23											23

CASH PAYMENTS JOURNAL PAGE 3

	DATE		DOC. NO.	ACCOUNT NAME	POST. REF.	GENERAL DEBIT	GENERAL CREDIT	ACCOUNTS PAYABLE DEBIT	BANK DEPOSIT CREDIT	CASH ON HAND CREDIT	
1	Dec.	13	CS059	Copper Line		105 000 00			118 720 00		1
2				Material Pric. Var.		3 000 00					2
3				Fac. O/H Incurred		10 720 00					3
4	Dec.	14	CS060 –CS162	Salaries Payable		535 184 00			535 184 00		4
5	Dec.	15	CS163	Social Sec. Tax Pay.		335 896 00			417 496 00		5
6				Med. Tax Pay.		61 200 00					6
7				FUTP		2 632 00					7
8				SUTP		17 768 00					8
9	Dec.	15	CS164	Iron Castings		45 000 00			56 500 00		9
10				Material Pric. Var.		5 000 00					10
11				Fac. O/H Incurred		6 500 00					11
12	Dec.	16	CS166	Fac. O/H Incurred		4 000 00			4 000 00		12
13	Dec.	16	INV235	M&A Office Supplies		1 000 00				1 000 00	13
14	Dec.	16	INV145	Sales Travel Expense		4 500 00				4 500 00	14
15	Dec.	17	CS167	Work Jackets		10 500 00			26 705 00		15
16				Work Shoes		9 000 00					16
17				Heat-resistant Gloves		5 000 00					17
18				Fac. O/H Incurred		2 205 00					18
19	Dec.	17	CS171	Packing Boxes		2 000 00			2 180 00		19
20				Fac. O/H Incurred		180 00					20
21	Dec.	17	INV349	Advertising Expense		5 000 00			5 000 00		21
22	Dec.	17	INV112	Television Expense		240 00			240 00		22
23	Dec.	17	INV32	Fac. O/H Incurred		92 868 00			92 868 00		23

CASH PAYMENTS JOURNAL										PAGE 4
	DATE	DOC. NO.	ACCOUNT NAME	POST. REF.	GENERAL		ACCOUNTS PAYABLE	BANK DEPOSIT	CASH ON HAND	
					DEBIT	CREDIT	DEBIT	CREDIT	CREDIT	
1	Dec. 17	INV329	Fac. O/H Incurred		6722 46			6722 46		1
2	Dec. 17	CS176	ST Bo.-CCB		1 000000 00			1 017499 00		2
3			Interest Pay.		11666 00					3
4			Interest Exp.		5833 00					4
5	Dec. 18	REC723	A&M Training Expense		3000 00				3000 00	5
6	Dec. 19	CS178	Fac. O/H Incurred		10000 00			10000 00		6
7	Dec. 19	CS179	Packing Boxes		2000 00			2180 00		7
8			Fac. O/H Incurred		180 00					8
9	Dec. 19	CS180	Fac. O/H Incurred		2000 00			2000 00		9
10	Dec. 21	INV554	Invitation Fee Expense		1500 00			1500 00		10
11	Dec. 21	CS183	Refrigeration Oil		20000 00			21800 00		11
12			Fac. O/H Incurred		1800 00					12
13	Dec. 22	CS184	Copper Line		70000 00			79280 00		13
14			Material Pric. Var.		2000 00					14
15			Fac. O/H Incurred		7280 00					15
16	Dec. 23	CS185	Iron Castings		45000 00			56500 00		16
17			Material Pric. Var.		5000 00					17
18			Fac. O/H Incurred		6500 00					18
19	Dec. 23	CS186	Trademark		30000 00			30000 00		19
20	Dec. 27	CS189	Fac. O/H Incurred		2000 00			2000 00		20
21	Dec. 27	INV45	Telephone Expense		8000 00			8000 00		21
22	Dec. 28	CS192	Property Tax Pay.		54090 00			54090 00		22
23										23

SALES JOURNAL								PAGE 1
	DATE		SALES SLIP NO.	CUSTOMER'S ACCOUNT DEBITED	POST. REF.	SALES CREDIT	SALES TAX PAYABLE CREDIT	ACCOUNTS RECEIVABLE DEBIT	
1	Dec.	4	68	Fenghua Air-blower–Small Air-blower		350000 00	31500 00	381500 00	1
2	Dec.	9	72	Ningbo Air-blower–Small Air-blower		350000 00	31500 00	381500 00	2
3	Dec.	17	76	Ningbo Air-blower–Large Air-blower		800000 00	72000 00	872000 00	3
4	Dec.	22	80	Fenghua Air-blower–Small Air-blower		700000 00	63000 00	763000 00	4

PURCHASES JOURNAL											PAGE 1
	DATE		INVOICE NO.	CREDITOR'S ACCOUNT CREDITED	TYPE	POST. REF.	ACCOUNTS PAYABLE CREDIT	PURCHASES DEBIT	GENERAL			
									ACCOUNT DEBITED	POST. REF.	DEBIT	
1	Dec.	7	INV523	Beijing Steel	IC		56500 00	45000 00	Fac. O/H Incurred		6500 00	1
2									Material Pric. Var.		5000 00	2
3	Dec.	16	CS166	Beijing Steel	SP		174400 00	150000 00	Material Pric. Var.		10000 00	3
4									Fac. O/H Incurred		14400 00	4
5	Dec.	19	INV723	Beijing Steel	IC		54500 00	45000 00	Fac. O/H Incurred		4500 00	5
6									Material Pric. Var.		5000 00	6
7	Dec.	27	INV872	Beijing Steel	IC		54500 00	45000 00	Fac. O/H Incurred		4500 00	7
8									Material Pric. Var.		5000 00	8

T-accounts book is one of the most important places to collect all transactions. The sets of T-accounts at the moment are illustrated as following table. There are four sets of T-accounts. They are asset T-accounts, liability T-accounts, equity T-accounts and income/expense T-accounts. The first three sets are balance sheet T-accounts. The last one is income statement T-accounts. B means beginning balance and U means unadjusted ending balance. * means the account is a control account. ** means the account is a second-level subsidiary account. *** and **** indicate that the account is a third-level and fourth-level subsidiary account.

Cash on Hand*

	Debit	Credit
B	51,000	
		800
		1,200
		3,000
		2,000
		1,000
		4,500
		3,000
	3,000	
		1,500
		50
	50	
U	37,000	

Bank Deposit*

	Debit	Credit
B	2,352,000	
		1,500
		30
		220,000
	100,000	
		178,400
		56,500
		2,180
		3,000
		2,000
		1,205,196
		90,000
	600,000	
		118,720
		32,700
		89,200
	872,000	
	381,500	
	436,000	
		1,000
		2,000
		2,180
	500,000	
		120,000
		3,000
		21,800
	436,000	
	10,000	
		1,500
		9,600
		56,500
	763,000	
		10,000
		1,000
		196,200
		3,000
		118,720
		535,184
		417,496
		56,500
	872,000	
		4,000
		26,705
		2,000
	381,500	
	436,000	
		2,180
		5,000
		240
		92,868
		6,722.46
		1,017,499
	97,875	
		10,000
		2,180
		2,000
	1,144,500	
		1,500
		21,800
		79,280
		56,500
		30,000
	1,500	
	436,000	
	381,500	
		2,000
		8,000
	872,000	
		54,090
U	6,093,704.54	

Bank Draft*

	Debit	Credit
B	60,408	
U	60,408	

Notes Receivable*

	Debit	Credit	
B	302,125		
		100,000	
U	202,125		

Notes Receivable–Fenghua Air-blower**

	Debit	Credit
B	202,125	
U	202,125	

Notes Receivable–Xiangshan Air-blower**

	Debit	Credit
B	100,000	
		100,000
U	0	

Discounts on Notes Receivable*

Debit	Credit	
	2,125	B
2,125		
	0	U

Debit	Credit

Debit	Credit

Accounts Receivable*

	Debit	Credit
B	700,000	
	1,044,500	
	1,253,500	
U	2,998,000	

Accounts Receivable–Fenghua Air-blower**

	Debit	Credit
B	200,000	
		100,000
	381,500	
	763,000	
U	1,244,500	

Accounts Receivable–Ningbo Air-blower**

	Debit	Credit
	381,500	
	872,000	
U	1,253,500	

Accounts Receivable–Xiangshan Air-blower**

	Debit	Credit
B	500,000	
U	500,000	

Debit	Credit

Debit	Credit

Allowance for Doubtful Debts*

Debit	Credit	
	6,000	B
	6,000	U

Debit	Credit

Debit	Credit

Prepaid Expense*

	Debit	Credit
B	12,500	
	120,000	
	9,600	
	90,000	
U	232,100	

Prepaid Broadband**

	Debit	Credit
B	1,200	
	120,000	
U	121,200	

Prepaid Subscription**

	Debit	Credit
B	1,500	
	9,600	
U	11,100	

Prepaid Insurance**

	Debit	Credit
B	9,800	
	90,000	
U	99,800	

Debit	Credit

Debit	Credit

Other Receivables*

	Debit	Credit
	5,500	
	3,000	
	5,000	
U	13,500	

Petty Cash**

	Debit	Credit
	1,500	
	2,000	
	2,000	
U	5,500	

Other Receivables–Fenghua Air-blower**

	Debit	Credit
	3,000	
U	3,000	

Other Receivables–Ningbo Air-blower**

	Debit	Credit
	3,000	
	2,000	
U	5,000	

Debit	Credit

Debit	Credit

Inventory*

	Debit	Credit
B	5,612,121	
	1,123,000	
	-5,610,000	
U	1,125,121	

Raw Material**

	Debit	Credit
B	516,200	
	1,045,000	
	78,000	
U	1,639,200	

Direct Material***

	Debit	Credit
B	510,000	
	450,000	
	280,000	
	315,000	
U	1,555,000	

Indirect Material***

	Debit	Credit
B	6,200	
	70,000	
	8,000	
U	84,200	

Steel Plates****

	Debit	Credit
B	230,000	
	150,000	
	75,000	
	150,000	
	75,000	
U	680,000	

Copper Line****

	Debit	Credit
B	180,000	
	105,000	
	105,000	
	70,000	
U	460,000	

Iron Castings****

	Debit	Credit
B	100,000	
	45,000	
	45,000	
	45,000	
	45,000	
	45,000	
	45,000	
	45,000	
U	415,000	

Refrigeration Oil****

	Debit	Credit
B	5,000	
	30,000	
	20,000	
	20,000	
U	75,000	

Packing Boxes****

	Debit	Credit
B	1,200	
	2,000	
	2,000	
	2,000	
	2,000	
U	9,200	

Material Price Variance*

	Debit	Credit
B	18,000	
	10,000	
	5,000	
	3,000	
	5,000	
	5,000	
	5,000	
	3,000	
	5,000	
	10,000	
	5,000	
	2,000	
	5,000	
	5,000	
	5,000	
U	91,000	

Debit	Credit

Debit	Credit

Work-in-process**

	Debit	Credit
B	315,921	
U	315,921	

Work-in-process–Small Air-blower***

	Debit	Credit
B	219,800	
U	219,800	

Work-in-process–Large Air-blower***

	Debit	Credit
B	96,121	
U	96,121	

Work-in-process–Small Air-blower–Stamping Workshop****

	Debit	Credit
B	75,760	
U	75,760	

Work-in-process–Small Air-blower–Machining Workshop****

	Debit	Credit
B	60,860	
U	60,860	

Work-in-process–Small Air-blower–Assembling Workshop****

	Debit	Credit
B	83,180	
U	83,180	

Work-in-process–Large Air-blower–Stamping Workshop****

	Debit	Credit
B	24,630	
U	24,630	

Work-in-process–Large Air-blower–Machining Workshop****

	Debit	Credit
B	32,210	
U	32,210	

Work-in-process–Large Air-blower–Assembling Workshop****

	Debit	Credit
B	39,281	
U	39,281	

Factory Overhead*

	Debit	Credit
	18,400	
	6,500	
	180	
	10,720	
	2,700	
	9,200	
	6,500	
	180	
	1,800	
	6,500	
	10,720	
	6,500	
	18,400	
	2,205	
	180	
	92,868	
	6,722.46	
	10,000	
	180	
	6,500	
	1,800	
	7,280	
	9,200	
	6,500	
	6,500	
U	248,235.46	

Debit	Credit

Debit	Credit

Finished Goods**

	Debit	Credit
B	4,780,000	
		2,750,000
		2,860,000
U	-830,000	

Finished Goods–Small Air-blower***

	Debit	Credit
B	2,000,000	
		250,000
		250,000
		250,000
		500,000
		250,000
		750,000
		500,000
U	-750,000	

Finished Goods–Large Air-blower***

	Debit	Credit
B	2,780,000	
		520,000
		260,000
		260,000
		520,000
		520,000
		260,000
		520,000
U	-80,000	

Supplies*

	Debit	Credit
B	4,000	
	3,000	
	1,000	
	26,000	
U	34,000	

M&A Office Supplies**

	Debit	Credit
	2,000	
	1,000	
U	3,000	

Sales Office Supplies**

	Debit	Credit
	1,000	
U	1,000	

Factory Supplies**

	Debit	Credit
B	4,000	
	10,500	
	9,000	
	5,000	
	1,500	
U	30,000	

Work Jackets***

	Debit	Credit
B	2,400	
	10,500	
U	12,900	

Work Shoes***

	Debit	Credit
B	1,150	
	9,000	
U	10,150	

Heat-resistant Gloves***

	Debit	Credit
B	450	
	5,000	
U	5,450	

Factory Office Supplies***

	Debit	Credit
	1,500	
U	1,500	

Debit	Credit

Plant, Property & Equipment*

	Debit	Credit
B	12,000,000	
		150,000
	220,000	
	199,200	
	50,000	
U	12,319,200	

Lathe (Old)**

	Debit	Credit
B	150,000	
		150,000
U	0	

Saw machine**

	Debit	Credit
	220,000	
U	220,000	

Lathe (New)**

	Debit	Credit	
	196,200		
	3,000		
U	199,200		

Grinder**

	Debit	Credit	
	50,000		
U	50,000		

Debit	Credit

Accumulated Depreciation*

	Debit	Credit	
		2,500,000	B
	135,000		
		2,365,000	U

Accumulated Depreciation–Lathe**

	Debit	Credit	
		135,000	B
	135,000		
		0	U

Debit	Credit

Land*

	Debit	Credit	
B	2,600,000		
U	2,600,000		

Debit	Credit

Debit	Credit

Intangible Assets*

	Debit	Credit	
B	500,000		
	30,000		
U	530,000		

Patent**

	Debit	Credit	
B	500,000		
U	500,000		

Trademark**

	Debit	Credit	
	30000		
U	30,000		

Accumulated Amortization*

	Debit	Credit	
		200,000	B
		200,000	U

Accumulated Amortization–Patent**

	Debit	Credit	
B		200,000	B
		200,000	U

Debit	Credit

Short-term Borrowings*

	Debit	Credit	
		2,428,000	B
	400,000		
		500,000	
		2,528,000	U

Short-term Borrowings–China Construction Bank**

	Debit	Credit	
		1,000,000	B
		600,000	
	1,000,000		
		600,000	U

Short-term Borrowings–Bank of China**

	Debit	Credit	
		1,428,000	B
		500,000	
		1,928,000	U

Notes Payable*

	Debit	Credit	
		110,000	B
		110,000	U

Notes Payable–Beijing Steel**

	Debit	Credit	
		68,000	B
		68,000	U

Notes Payable–Hebei Steel**

	Debit	Credit	
		42,000	B
		42,000	U

Accounts Payable*

Debit	Credit	
	102,000	B
	339,900	
	441,900	U

Accounts Payable–Beijing Steel**

Debit	Credit	
	60,000	B
	56,500	
	174,400	
	54,500	
	54,500	
	399,900	U

Accounts Payable–Hebei Steel**

Debit	Credit	
	42,000	B
	42,000	U

Unearned Revenue*

Debit	Credit	
	441,570	B
	400,000	
	350,000	
	1,191,570	U

Unearned Revenue–Ningbo Air-blower**

Debit	Credit	
	290,047	B
	400,000	
	690,047	U

Unearned Revenue–Xiangshan Air-blower**

Debit	Credit	
	151,523	B
	350,000	
	501,523	U

Payroll Liabilities*

Debit	Credit	
	954,696	B
535,184		
335,896		
61,200		
2,632		
17,768		
672		
1,344		
	0	U

Salaries Payable**

Debit	Credit	
	535,184	B
535,184		
	0	U

Social Security Tax Payable**

Debit	Credit	
	335,896	B
335,896		
	0	U

Medicare Tax Payable**

Debit	Credit	
	61,200	B
61,200		
	0	U

Federal Unemployment Tax Payable**

Debit	Credit	
	2,632	B
2,632		
	0	U

State Unemployment Tax Payable**

Debit	Credit	
	17,768	B
17,768		
	0	U

Employee Federal Income Tax Payable**

Debit	Credit	
	672	B
672		
	0	U

Employee State Income Tax Payable**

Debit	Credit	
	1,344	B
1,344		
	0	U

Debit	Credit

Taxes Payable*

Debit	Credit	
	1,203,180	B
	810,000	
1,203,180		
	810,000	U

Sales Tax Payable**

Debit	Credit	
	31,500	
	72,000	
	31,500	
	36,000	
	31,500	
	36,000	
	63,000	
	72,000	
	72,000	
	31,500	
	36,000	
	94,500	
	63,000	
	36,000	
	31,500	
	72,000	
	810,000	U

Property Tax Payable**

Debit	Credit	
	54,090	
54,090		
	0	U

Income Taxes Payable**

Debit	Credit	
	1,203,180	B
601,590		
601,590		
	0	U

Federal Income Tax Payable***

Debit	Credit	
	601,590	B
601,590		
	0	U

State Income Tax Payable***

Debit	Credit	
	601,590	B
601,590		
	0	U

Interests Payable*

Debit	Credit	
	14,583	B
11,666		
	2,917	U

Commercial Acceptance Bill Payable*

Debit	Credit	
	89,200	
	89,200	U

Debit	Credit

Capital, Hefeng*

Debit	Credit	
	12,800,000	B
	50,000	
	12,850,000	U

Capital Reserve*

Debit	Credit	
	550,000	B
	550,000	U

Retained Earnings*

Debit	Credit	
	2,900,000	B
	2,900,000	U

Sales Revenue*

Debit	Credit	
	3,850,000	
	4,400,000	
	8,250,000	U

Sales Revenue-Small Air-blower**

Debit	Credit	
	350,000	
	350,000	
	350,000	
	700,000	
	350,000	
	1,050,000	
	700,000	
	3,850,000	U

Sales Revenue-Large Air-blower**

Debit	Credit	
	800,000	
	400,000	
	400,000	
	800,000	
	800,000	
	400,000	
	800,000	
	4,400,000	U

Other Revenue*

Debit	Credit	
	3,000	
	3,000	U

Debit	Credit

Debit	Credit

Cost of Goods Sold*

	Debit	Credit
	2,750,000	
	2,860,000	
U	5,610,000	

Cost of Goods Sold-Small Air-blower**

	Debit	Credit
	250,000	
	250,000	
	250,000	
	500,000	
	250,000	
	750,000	
	500,000	
U	2,750,000	

Cost of Goods Sold-Large Air-blower**

	Debit	Credit
	520,000	
	260,000	
	260,000	
	520,000	
	520,000	
	260,000	
	520,000	
U	2,860,000	

Selling Expense*

	Debit	Credit
	4,500	
	3,000	
	15,000	
	8,000	
U	30,500	

Administrative & Managerial Expense*

	Debit	Credit
	800	
	3,000	
	30	
	1,200	
	2,500	
	240	
	5,833	
U	13,603	

Other Expense*

	Debit	Credit
U	0	

M&A Travel Expense**

	Debit	Credit
	800	
U	800	

Sales Travel Expense**

	Debit	Credit
	4,500	
U	4,500	

Debit	Credit

Sales Training Expense**

	Debit	Credit
	3,000	
U	3,000	

M&A Training Expense**

	Debit	Credit
	3,000	
U	3,000	

Debit	Credit

Bank Fee Expense**

	Debit	Credit
	30	
U	30	

Telecommunication Expense**

	Debit	Credit
	1,200	
U	1,200	

Invitation Fee Expense**

	Debit	Credit
	1,000	
	1,500	
U	2,500	

Advertising Expense**

	Debit	Credit
	10,000	
	5,000	
U	15,000	

Television Expense**

	Debit	Credit
	240	
U	240	

Interest Expense**

	Debit	Credit
	5,833	
U	5,833	

Cash Lost Expense**

	Debit	Credit
	50	
		50
U	0	

Telephone Expense**

	Debit	Credit
	8,000	
U	8,000	

Debit	Credit

Taxes Expense*

	Debit	Credit
	54,090	
U	54,090	

Property Tax Expense**

	Debit	Credit
	54,090	
U	54,090	

Debit	Credit

Loss on Disposal of PP&E*

	Debit	Credit
	5,000	
U	5,000	

Loss on Disposal of Lathe**

	Debit	Credit
	5,000	
U	5,000	

Debit	Credit

CHAPTER 3 POST TO THE LEDGER

The second step of accounting cycle is to post transactions recorded in journal books to the ledger. Since account number and account name are necessary for posting, accounts list is illustrated in following table.

Control Account #	Sub-account Level 1 #	Sub-account Level 2 #	Sub-account Level 3 #	Account Name
101				Cash on Hand
102				Bank Deposit
103				Bank Draft
104				Notes Receivable
	1041			Notes Receivable–Fenghua Air-blower
	1042			Notes Receivable–Xiangshan Air-blower
105				Discounts on Notes Receivable
106				Accounts Receivable
	1061			Accounts Receivable–Fenghua Air-blower
	1062			Accounts Receivable–Ningbo Air-blower
	1063			Accounts Receivable–Xiangshan Air-blower
107				Allowance for Doubtful Debts
108				Prepaid Expense
	1081			Prepaid Broadband
	1082			Prepaid Subscription
	1083			Prepaid Insurance
109				Other Receivables
	1091			Petty Cash
	1092			Other Receivables–Fenghua Air-blower
	1093			Other Receivables–Ningbo Air-blower
110				Inventory
	1101			Raw Material
		11011		Direct Material

continued

Control Account #	Sub-account Level 1 #	Sub-account Level 2 #	Sub-account Level 3 #	Account Name
			110111	Steel Plates
			110112	Copper Line
			110113	Iron Castings
		11012		Indirect Material
			110121	Refrigeration Oil
			110122	Packing Boxes
	1102			Work-in-process
		11021		Work-in-process–Small Air-blower
		11022		Work-in-process–Large Air-blower
	1103			Finished Goods
		11031		Finished Goods–Small Air-blower
		11032		Finished Goods–Large Air-blower
111				Material Price Variance
112				Material Quantity Variance
113				Factory Overhead
114				Supplies
	1141			M&A Office Supplies
	1142			Sales Office Supplies
	1143			Factory Supplies
		11431		Work Jackets
		11432		Work Shoes
		11433		Heat-resistant Gloves
		11434		Factory Office Supplies
115				Plant, Property & Equipment
	1151			Lathe (Old)
	1152			Saw Machine
	1153			Lathe (New)
	⋮			⋮

continued

Control Account #	Sub-account Level 1 #	Sub-account Level 2 #	Sub-account Level 3 #	Account Name
	1159			Grinder
116				Accumulated Depreciation
	1161			Accumulated Depreciation-Lathe
	⋮			⋮
117				Land
118				Intangible Assets
	1181			Patent
	1182			Trademark
119				Accumulated Amortization
	1191			Accumulated Amortization-Patent
	1192			Accumulated Amortization-Trademark
120				Direct Labor
121				Labor Efficiency Variance
122				Labor Rate Variance
201				Short-term Borrowings
	2011			Short-term Borrowings-China Construction Bank
	2012			Short-term Borrowings-Bank of China
202				Notes Payable
	2021			Notes Payable-Beijing Steel
	2022			Notes Payable-Hebei Steel
203				Accounts Payable
	2031			Accounts Payable-Beijing Steel
	2032			Accounts Payable-Hebei Steel
204				Unearned Revenue
	2041			Unearned Revenue-Ningbo Air-blower
	2042			Unearned Revenue-Xiangshan Air-blower
205				Payroll Liabilities
	2051			Salaries Payable

continued

Control Account #	Sub-account Level 1 #	Sub-account Level 2 #	Sub-account Level 3 #	Account Name
	2052			Social Security Tax Payable
	2053			Medicare Tax Payable
	2054			Federal Unemployment Tax Payable
	2055			State Unemployment Tax Payable
	2056			Employee Federal Income Tax Payable
	2057			Employee State Income Tax Payable
206				Taxes Payable
	2061			Sales Tax Payable
	2062			Property Tax Payable
	2063			Income Taxes Payable
		20631		Federal Income Tax Payable
		20632		State Income Tax Payable
207				Interests Payable
208				Commercial Acceptance Bill Payable
301				Capital, Hefeng
302				Capital Reserve
303				Retained Earnings
401				Sales Revenue
	4011			Sales Revenue–Small Air-blower
	4012			Sales Revenue–Large Air-blower
402				Other Revenue
403				Investment Earnings
501				Cost of Goods Sold
	5011			Cost of Goods Sold–Small Air-blower
	5012			Cost of Goods Sold–Large Air-blower
502				Selling Expense
	5021			Sales Travel Expense
	5022			Sales Training Expense
	5023			Advertising Expense

continued

Control Account #	Sub-account Level 1 #	Sub-account Level 2 #	Sub-account Level 3 #	Account Name
	5024			Telephone Expense
	5025			Sales Salaries Expense
503				Administrative & Managerial Expense
	5031			M&A Travel Expense
	5032			M&A Training Expense
	5033			Bank Fee Expense
	5034			Telecommunication Expense
	5035			Invitation Fee Expense
	5036			Television Expense
	5037			Interest Expense
	5038			Cash Lost Expense
	5039			M&A Broadband Expense
	50310			M&A Depreciation Expense
	50311			Amortization Expense
		503111		Amortization Expense-Patent
		503112		Amortization Expense-Trademark
	50312			Subscription Expense
	50313			Insurance Expense
	50314			M&A Salaries Expense
	50315			Payroll Tax Expense
	50316			Bad Debt Expense
504				Other Expense
505				Taxes Expense
	5051			Income Taxes Expense
	5052			Property Tax Expense
506				Loss on Disposal of PP&E
	5061			Loss on Disposal of Lathe
601				Income Summary

In the following part of this section, general ledger and subsidiary ledgers will be recorded for all transactions of Xinle Air-blower Co., Ltd. These will be illustrated in following transaction. Totals of Special journals are posted directly to the ledger.

ACCOUNT *Cash on Hand* ACCOUNT NO. 101

	DATE		DESCRIPTION	POST. REF.	DEBIT	CREDIT	BALANCE		
							DEBIT	CREDIT	
1	Dec.	1	Balance	√			51 000 00		1
2	Dec.	23	Deposit money	G2		1 500 00	49 500 00		2
3	Dec.	27	Cash lost	G2		50 00	49 450 00		3
4	Dec.	27	Reimbursement of cash lost	G2	50 00		49 500 00		4
5	Dec.	28	Cash Receipts Journal	CRJ1	3 000 00		52 500 00		5
6	Dec.	28	Cash Payments Journal	CPJ4		15 500 00	37 000 00		6
7									7
8									8
9									9
10									10

ACCOUNT *Bank Deposit* ACCOUNT NO. 102

	DATE		DESCRIPTION	POST. REF.	DEBIT	CREDIT	BALANCE		
							DEBIT	CREDIT	
1	Dec.	1	Balance	√			2 352 000 00		1
2	Dec.	4	Delivery fee	G1		3 000 00	2 349 000 00		2
3	Dec.	9	Delivery fee	G1		3 000 00	2 346 000 00		3
4	Dec.	11	Disposal of Lathe	G1	10 000 00		2 356 000 00		4
5	Dec.	17	Delivery fee	G1		2 000 00	2 354 000 00		5
6	Dec.	18	Collection of the note	G1	97 875 00		2 451 875 00		6
7	Dec.	23	Deposit money	G2	1 500 00		2 453 375 00		7
8	Dec.	31	Cash Receipts Journal	CRJ1	8 612 000 00		11 065 375 00		8
9	Dec.	31	Cash Payments Journal	CPJ4		4 971 670 46	6 093 704 54		9
10									10

ACCOUNT *Bank Draft* ACCOUNT NO. 103

	DATE		DESCRIPTION	POST. REF.	DEBIT	CREDIT	BALANCE DEBIT	BALANCE CREDIT	
1	Dec.	1	Balance	√			60 408 00		1
2									2
3									3
4									4
5									5
6									6
7									7
8									8
9									9
10									10

ACCOUNT *Notes Receivable* ACCOUNT NO. 104

	DATE		DESCRIPTION	POST. REF.	DEBIT	CREDIT	BALANCE DEBIT	BALANCE CREDIT	
1	Dec.	1	Balance	√			302 125 00		1
2	Dec.	28	Xiangshan Air-blower	1042		100 000 00	202 125 00		2
3									3
4									4
5									5
6									6
7									7
8									8
9									9
10									10

ACCOUNT *Notes Receivable–Fenghua Air-blower* ACCOUNT NO. 1041

	DATE		DESCRIPTION	POST. REF.	DEBIT	CREDIT	BALANCE DEBIT	BALANCE CREDIT	
1	Dec.	1	Balance	√			202 125 00		1
2									2
3									3
4									4
5									5
6									6
7									7
8									8
9									9
10									10

ACCOUNT *Notes Receivable–Xiangshan Air-blower* ACCOUNT NO. 1042

	DATE		DESCRIPTION	POST. REF.	DEBIT	CREDIT	BALANCE DEBIT	BALANCE CREDIT	
1	Dec.	1	Balance	√			100 000 00		1
2	Dec.	18	Collection of the note	G1		100 000 00	~~0 000 00~~		2
3									3
4									4
5									5
6									6
7									7
8									8
9									9
10									10

ACCOUNT *Discounts on Notes Receivable* ACCOUNT NO. 105

	DATE		DESCRIPTION	POST. REF.	DEBIT	CREDIT	BALANCE DEBIT	BALANCE CREDIT	
1	Dec.	1	Balance	√				2 125 00	1
2	Dec.	18	Collection of the note	G1	2 125 00			~~0 000 00~~	2
3									3
4									4
5									5
6									6
7									7
8									8
9									9
10									10

ACCOUNT *Accounts Receivable* ACCOUNT NO. 106

	DATE		DESCRIPTION	POST. REF.	DEBIT	CREDIT	BALANCE DEBIT	BALANCE CREDIT	
1	Dec.	1	Balance	√			700 000 00		1
2	Dec.	28	Fenghua Air-blower	1061	1 044 500 00		1 744 500 00		2
3	Dec.	28	Ningbo Air-blower	1062	1 253 500 00		2 998 000 00		3
4									4
5									5
6									6
7									7
8									8
9									9
10									10

ACCOUNT *Accounts Receivable–Fenghua Air-blower* ACCOUNT NO. 1061

	DATE		DESCRIPTION	POST. REF.	DEBIT	CREDIT	BALANCE		
							DEBIT	CREDIT	
1	Dec.	1	Balance	√			200 000 00		1
2	Dec.	28	Collect accounts receivable	CRJ1		100 000 00	100 000 00		2
3	Dec.	28	Sales Journal	SJ1	1 144 500 00		1 244 500 00		3
4									4
5									5
6									6
7									7
8									8
9									9
10									10

ACCOUNT *Accounts Receivable–Ningbo Air-blower* ACCOUNT NO. 1062

	DATE		DESCRIPTION	POST. REF.	DEBIT	CREDIT	BALANCE		
							DEBIT	CREDIT	
1	Dec.	28	Sales Journal	SJ1	1 253 500 00		1 253 500 00		1
2									2
3									3
4									4
5									5
6									6
7									7
8									8
9									9
10									10

ACCOUNT *Accounts Receivable–Xiangshan Air-blower* ACCOUNT NO. 1063

	DATE		DESCRIPTION	POST. REF.	DEBIT	CREDIT	BALANCE		
							DEBIT	CREDIT	
1	Dec.	1	Balance	√			500 000 00		1
2									2
3									3
4									4
5									5
6									6
7									7
8									8
9									9
10									10

ACCOUNT *Allowance for Doubtful Debts* ACCOUNT NO. 107

	DATE		DESCRIPTION	POST. REF.	DEBIT	CREDIT	BALANCE		
							DEBIT	CREDIT	
1	Dec.	1	Balance	√				6 000 00	1
2									2
3									3
4									4
5									5
6									6
7									7
8									8
9									9
10									10

ACCOUNT *Prepaid Expense* ACCOUNT NO. 108

	DATE		DESCRIPTION	POST. REF.	DEBIT	CREDIT	BALANCE		
							DEBIT	CREDIT	
1	Dec.	1	Balance	√			12 500 00		1
2	Dec.	28	Prepaid Broadband	1081	120 000 00		132 500 00		2
3	Dec.	28	Prepaid Subscription	1082	9 600 00		142 100 00		3
4	Dec.	28	Prepaid Insurance	1083	90 000 00		232 100 00		4
5									5
6									6
7									7
8									8
9									9
10									10

ACCOUNT *Prepaid Broadband* ACCOUNT NO. 1081

	DATE		DESCRIPTION	POST. REF.	DEBIT	CREDIT	BALANCE		
							DEBIT	CREDIT	
1	Dec.	1	Balance	√			1 200 00		1
2	Dec.	28	Pay broadband fee	CPJ2	120 000 00		121 200 00		2
3									3
4									4
5									5
6									6
7									7
8									8
9									9
10									10

ACCOUNT *Prepaid Subscription* ACCOUNT NO. 1082

	DATE		DESCRIPTION	POST. REF.	DEBIT	CREDIT	BALANCE		
							DEBIT	CREDIT	
1	Dec.	1	Balance	√			1 500 00		1
2	Dec.	28	Pay subscription fee	CPJ2	9 600 00		11 100 00		2
3									3
4									4
5									5
6									6
7									7
8									8
9									9
10									10

ACCOUNT *Prepaid Insurance* ACCOUNT NO. 1083

	DATE		DESCRIPTION	POST. REF.	DEBIT	CREDIT	BALANCE		
							DEBIT	CREDIT	
1	Dec.	1	Balance	√			9 800 00		1
2	Dec.	31	Pay insurance fee	CPJ1	90 000 00		99 800 00		2
3									3
4									4
5									5
6									6
7									7
8									8
9									9
10									10

ACCOUNT *Other Receivables* ACCOUNT NO. 109

	DATE		DESCRIPTION	POST. REF.	DEBIT	CREDIT	BALANCE		
							DEBIT	CREDIT	
1	Dec.	28	Petty Cash	1091	5 500 00				1
2	Dec.	28	Fenghua Air-blower	1092	3 000 00				2
3	Dec.	28	Ningbo Air-blower	1093	5 000 00		13 500 00		3
4									4
5									5
6									6
7									7
8									8
9									9
10									10

ACCOUNT *Petty Cash* ACCOUNT NO. 1091

	DATE		DESCRIPTION	POST. REF.	DEBIT	CREDIT	BALANCE		
							DEBIT	CREDIT	
1	Dec.	28	Bank transfer	CPJ1	1 500 00		1 500 00		1
2	Dec.	28	Bank transfer	CPJ1	2 000 00		3 500 00		2
3	Dec.	28	Bank transfer	CPJ2	2 000 00		5 500 00		3
4									4
5									5
6									6
7									7
8									8
9									9
10									10

ACCOUNT *Other Receivables–Fenghua Air-blower* ACCOUNT NO. 1092

	DATE		DESCRIPTION	POST. REF.	DEBIT	CREDIT	BALANCE		
							DEBIT	CREDIT	
1	Dec.	4	Delivery fee	G1	3 000 00		3 000 00		1
2									2
3									3
4									4
5									5
6									6
7									7
8									8
9									9
10									10

ACCOUNT *Other Receivables–Ningbo Air-blower* ACCOUNT NO. 1093

	DATE		DESCRIPTION	POST. REF.	DEBIT	CREDIT	BALANCE		
							DEBIT	CREDIT	
1	Dec.	9	Delivery fee	G1	3 000 00		3 000 00		1
2	Dec.	17	Delivery fee	G1	2 000 00		5 000 00		2
3									3
4									4
5									5
6									6
7									7
8									8
9									9
10									10

ACCOUNT *Inventory* ACCOUNT NO. 110

	DATE		DESCRIPTION	POST. REF.	DEBIT	CREDIT	BALANCE		
							DEBIT	CREDIT	
1	Dec.	1	Balance	√			5 612 121 00		1
2	Dec.	28	Raw Material	1101	1 123 000 00		6 735 121 00		2
3	Dec.	28	Finished Goods	1103		5 610 000 00	1 125 121 00		3
4									4
5									5
6									6
7									7
8									8
9									9
10									10

ACCOUNT *Raw Material* ACCOUNT NO. 1101

	DATE		DESCRIPTION	POST. REF.	DEBIT	CREDIT	BALANCE		
							DEBIT	CREDIT	
1	Dec.	1	Balance	√			516 200 00		1
2	Dec.	28	Direct Material	11011	1 045 000 00		1 561 200 00		2
3	Dec.	28	Indirect Material	11012	78 000 00		1 639 200 00		3
4									4
5									5
6									6
7									7
8									8
9									9
10									10

ACCOUNT *Direct Material* ACCOUNT NO. 11011

	DATE		DESCRIPTION	POST. REF.	DEBIT	CREDIT	BALANCE		
							DEBIT	CREDIT	
1	Dec.	1	Balance	√			510 000 00		1
2	Dec.	28	Steel Plates	110111	450 000 00		960 000 00		2
3	Dec.	28	Copper Line	110112	280 000 00		1 240 000 00		3
4	Dec.	28	Iron Castings	110113	315 000 00		1 555 000 00		4
5									5
6									6
7									7
8									8
9									9
10									10

ACCOUNT *Steel Plates* ACCOUNT NO. 110111

	DATE		DESCRIPTION	POST. REF.	DEBIT	CREDIT	BALANCE		
							DEBIT	CREDIT	
1	Dec.	1	Balance	√			230 000 00		1
2	Dec.	23	Purchase steel plates	G2	75 000 00		305 000 00		2
3	Dec.	28	Purchase steel plates	CPJ1	150 000 00		455 000 00		3
4	Dec.	28	Purchase steel plates	CPJ2	75 000 00		530 000 00		4
5	Dec.	28	Purchases Journal	PJ1	150 000 00		680 000 00		5
6									6
7									7
8									8
9									9
10									10

ACCOUNT *Copper Line* ACCOUNT NO. 110112

	DATE		DESCRIPTION	POST. REF.	DEBIT	CREDIT	BALANCE		
							DEBIT	CREDIT	
1	Dec.	1	Balance	√			180 000 00		1
2	Dec.	28	Purchase copper line	CPJ1	105 000 00		285 000 00		2
3	Dec.	28	Purchase copper line	CPJ3	105 000 00		390 000 00		3
4	Dec.	28	Purchase copper line	CPJ4	70 000 00		460 000 00		4
5									5
6									6
7									7
8									8
9									9
10									10

ACCOUNT *Iron Castings* ACCOUNT NO. 110113

	DATE		DESCRIPTION	POST. REF.	DEBIT	CREDIT	BALANCE		
							DEBIT	CREDIT	
1	Dec.	1	Balance	√			100 000 00		1
2	Dec.	28	Purchase iron castings	CPJ1	45 000 00		145 000 00		2
3	Dec.	28	Purchase iron castings	CPJ2	45 000 00		190 000 00		3
4	Dec.	28	Purchase iron castings	CPJ3	45 000 00		235 000 00		4
5	Dec.	28	Purchase iron castings	CPJ4	45 000 00		280 000 00		5
6	Dec.	28	Purchases Journal	PJ1	135 000 00		415 000 00		6
7									7
8									8
9									9
10									10

ACCOUNT *Indirect Material* ACCOUNT NO. 11012

	DATE		DESCRIPTION	POST. REF.	DEBIT	CREDIT	BALANCE		
							DEBIT	CREDIT	
1	Dec.	1	Balance	√			6 200 00		1
2	Dec.	28	Refrigeration oil	110121	70 000 00		76 200 00		2
3	Dec.	28	Packing boxes	110122	8 000 00		84 200 00		3
4									4
5									5
6									6
7									7
8									8
9									9
10									10

ACCOUNT *Refrigeration Oil* ACCOUNT NO. 110121

	DATE		DESCRIPTION	POST. REF.	DEBIT	CREDIT	BALANCE		
							DEBIT	CREDIT	
1	Dec.	1	Balance	√			5 000 00		1
2	Dec.	28	Purchase refrigeration oil	CPJ1	30 000 00		35 000 00		2
3	Dec.	28	Purchase refrigeration oil	CPJ2	20 000 00		55 000 00		3
4	Dec.	28	Purchase refrigeration oil	CPJ4	20 000 00		75 000 00		4
5									5
6									6
7									7
8									8
9									9
10									10

ACCOUNT *Packing Boxes* ACCOUNT NO. 110122

	DATE		DESCRIPTION	POST. REF.	DEBIT	CREDIT	BALANCE		
							DEBIT	CREDIT	
1	Dec.	1	Balance	√			1 200 00		1
2	Dec.	28	Purchase packing boxes	CPJ1	2 000 00		3 200 00		2
3	Dec.	28	Purchase packing boxes	CPJ2	2 000 00		5 200 00		3
4	Dec.	28	Purchase packing boxes	CPJ3	2 000 00		7 200 00		4
5	Dec.	28	Purchase packing boxes	CPJ4	2 000 00		9 200 00		5
6									6
7									7
8									8
9									9
10									10

ACCOUNT *Work-in-process* ACCOUNT NO. 1102

	DATE		DESCRIPTION	POST. REF.	DEBIT	CREDIT	BALANCE		
							DEBIT	CREDIT	
1	Dec.	1	Balance	√			315 9 2 1 00		1
2									2
3									3
4									4
5									5
6									6
7									7
8									8
9									9
10									10

ACCOUNT *Work-in-process—Small Air-blower* ACCOUNT NO. 11021

	DATE		DESCRIPTION	POST. REF.	DEBIT	CREDIT	BALANCE		
							DEBIT	CREDIT	
1	Dec.	1	Balance	√			219 8 0 0 00		1
2									2
3									3
4									4
5									5
6									6
7									7
8									8
9									9
10									10

ACCOUNT *Work-in-process—Large Air-blower* ACCOUNT NO. 11022

	DATE		DESCRIPTION	POST. REF.	DEBIT	CREDIT	BALANCE		
							DEBIT	CREDIT	
1	Dec.	1	Balance	√			96 1 2 1 00		1
2									2
3									3
4									4
5									5
6									6
7									7
8									8
9									9
10									10

ACCOUNT *Finished Goods* ACCOUNT NO. 1103

	DATE		DESCRIPTION	POST. REF.	DEBIT	CREDIT	BALANCE		
							DEBIT	CREDIT	
1	Dec.	1	Balance	√			4 780 000 00		1
2	Dec.	28	Small Air-blower	11031		2 750 000 00	2 030 000 00		2
3	Dec.	28	Large Air-blower	11032		2 860 000 00	−830 000 00		3
4									4
5									5
6									6
7									7
8									8
9									9
10									10

ACCOUNT *Finished Goods−Small Air-blower* ACCOUNT NO. 11031

	DATE		DESCRIPTION	POST. REF.	DEBIT	CREDIT	BALANCE		
							DEBIT	CREDIT	
1	Dec.	1	Balance	√			2 000 000 00		1
2	Dec.	4	Sold products	G1		250 000 00	1 750 000 00		2
3	Dec.	7	Sold products	G1		250 000 00	1 500 000 00		3
4	Dec.	9	Sold products	G1		250 000 00	1 250 000 00		4
5	Dec.	12	Sold products	G1		500 000 00	750 000 00		5
6	Dec.	17	Sold products	G1		250 000 00	500 000 00		6
7	Dec.	19	Sold products	G1		750 000 00	−250 000 00		7
8	Dec.	22	Sold products	G2		500 000 00	−750 000 00		8
9									9
10									10

ACCOUNT *Finished Goods−Large Air-blower* ACCOUNT NO. 11032

	DATE		DESCRIPTION	POST. REF.	DEBIT	CREDIT	BALANCE		
							DEBIT	CREDIT	
1	Dec.	1	Balance	√			2 780 000 00		1
2	Dec.	7	Sold products	G1		520 000 00	2 260 000 00		2
3	Dec.	7	Sold products	G1		260 000 00	2 000 000 00		3
4	Dec.	11	Sold products	G1		260 000 00	1 740 000 00		4
5	Dec.	15	Sold products	G1		520 000 00	1 220 000 00		5
6	Dec.	17	Sold products	G1		520 000 00	700 000 00		6
7	Dec.	17	Sold products	G1		260 000 00	440 000 00		7
8	Dec.	28	Sold products	G2		520 000 00	−80 000 00		8
9									9
10									10

ACCOUNT *Material Price Variance* ACCOUNT NO. 111

	DATE		DESCRIPTION	POST. REF.	DEBIT	CREDIT	BALANCE DEBIT	BALANCE CREDIT	
1	Dec.	1	Balance	√			18 000 00		1
2	Dec.	23	Purchase steel plates	G2	5 000 00		23 000 00		2
3	Dec.	28	Purchase steel plates	CPJ1	10 000 00		33 000 00		3
4	Dec.	28	Purchase iron castings	CPJ1	5 000 00		38 000 00		4
5	Dec.	28	Purchase copper line	CPJ1	3 000 00		41 000 00		5
6	Dec.	28	Purchase steel plates	CPJ2	5 000 00		46 000 00		6
7	Dec.	28	Purchase iron castings	CPJ2	5 000 00		51 000 00		7
8	Dec.	28	Purchase copper line	CPJ3	3 000 00		54 000 00		8
9	Dec.	28	Purchase iron castings	CPJ3	5 000 00		59 000 00		9
10	Dec.	28	Purchase copper line	CPJ4	2 000 00		61 000 00		10
11	Dec.	28	Purchase iron castings	CPJ4	5 000 00		66 000 00		11
12	Dec.	28	Sales Journal	CJ1	25 000 00		91 000 00		12

ACCOUNT *Factory Overhead* ACCOUNT NO. 113

	DATE		DESCRIPTION	POST. REF.	DEBIT	CREDIT	BALANCE DEBIT	BALANCE CREDIT	
1	Dec.	23	Purchase steel plates	G2	9 200 00		9 200 00		1
2	Dec.	28	Purchase steel plates	CPJ1	18 400 00		27 600 00		2
3	Dec.	28	Purchase iron castings	CPJ1	6 500 00		34 100 00		3
4	Dec.	28	Purchase packing boxes	CPJ1	180 00		34 280 00		4
5	Dec.	28	Purchase copper line	CPJ1	10 720 00		45 000 00		5
6	Dec.	28	Purchase refrigeration oil	CPJ1	2 700 00		47 700 00		6
7	Dec.	28	Purchase steel plates	CPJ2	9 200 00		56 900 00		7
8	Dec.	28	Purchase packing boxes	CPJ1	180 00		57 080 00		8
9	Dec.	28	Purchase refrigeration oil	CPJ2	1 800 00		58 880 00		9
10	Dec.	28	Purchase iron castings	CPJ2	6 500 00		65 380 00		10

continued

	DATE		DESCRIPTION	POST. REF.	DEBIT	CREDIT	BALANCE		
							DEBIT	CREDIT	
11	Dec.	28	Purchase copper line	CPJ3	10 720 00		76 100 00		11
12	Dec.	28	Purchase iron castings	CPJ3	6 500 00		82 600 00		12
13	Dec.	28	Delivery fee	CPJ3	4 000 00		86 600 00		13
14	Dec.	28	Purchase factory supplies	CPJ3	2 205 00		88 805 00		14
15	Dec.	28	Purchase packing boxes	CPJ3	180 00		88 985 00		15
16	Dec.	28	Pay electricity fee	CPJ3	92 868 00		181 853 00		16
17	Dec.	28	Pay water fee	CPJ4	6 722 46		188 575 46		17
18	Dec.	28	Pay repair and maintenance fee	CPJ4	10 000 00		198 575 46		18
19	Dec.	28	Purchase packing boxes	CPJ4	180 00		198 755 46		19
20	Dec.	28	Delivery fee	CPJ4	2 000 00		200 755 46		20
21	Dec.	28	Purchase refrigeration oil	CPJ4	1 800 00		202 555 46		21
22	Dec.	28	Purchase copper line	CPJ4	7 280 00		209 835 46		22
23	Dec.	28	Purchase iron castings	CPJ4	6 500 00		216 335 46		23
24	Dec.	28	Delivery fee	CPJ4	2 000 00		218 335 46		24
25	Dec.	28	Sales Journal	CJ1	29 900 00		248 235 46		25

ACCOUNT *Supplies* ACCOUNT NO. 114

	DATE		DESCRIPTION	POST. REF.	DEBIT	CREDIT	BALANCE		
							DEBIT	CREDIT	
1	Dec.	1	Balance	√			4 000 00		1
2	Dec.	28	M&A Office Supplies	1141	3 000 00		7 000 00		2
3	Dec.	28	Sales Office Supplies	1142	1 000 00		8 000 00		3
4	Dec.	28	Factory Supplies	1143	26 000 00		34 000 00		4
5									5
6									6
7									7
8									8
9									9
10									10

ACCOUNT *M&A Office Supplies* ACCOUNT NO. 1141

	DATE		DESCRIPTION	POST. REF.	DEBIT	CREDIT	BALANCE DEBIT	BALANCE CREDIT	
1	Dec.	28	Pay office supplies fee	CPJ2	2 000 00		2 000 00		1
2	Dec.	28	Pay office supplies fee	CPJ3	1 000 00		3 000 00		2
3									3
4									4
5									5
6									6
7									7
8									8
9									9
10									10

ACCOUNT *Sales Office Supplies* ACCOUNT NO. 1142

	DATE		DESCRIPTION	POST. REF.	DEBIT	CREDIT	BALANCE DEBIT	BALANCE CREDIT	
1	Dec.	28	Pay office supplies fee	CPJ2	1 000 00		1 000 00		1
2									2
3									3
4									4
5									5
6									6
7									7
8									8
9									9
10									10

ACCOUNT *Factory Supplies* ACCOUNT NO. 1143

	DATE		DESCRIPTION	POST. REF.	DEBIT	CREDIT	BALANCE DEBIT	BALANCE CREDIT	
1	Dec.	1	Balance	√			4 000 00		1
2	Dec.	28	Work Jackets	11431	10 500 00		14 500 00		2
3	Dec.	28	Work Shoes	11432	9 000 00		23 500 00		3
4	Dec.	28	Heat-resistant Gloves	11433	5 000 00		28 500 00		4
5	Dec.	28	Factory Office Supplies	11434	1 500 00		30 000 00		5
6									6
7									7
8									8
9									9
10									10

ACCOUNT *Work Jackets* ACCOUNT NO. 11431

	DATE		DESCRIPTION	POST. REF.	DEBIT	CREDIT	BALANCE DEBIT	BALANCE CREDIT	
1	Dec.	1	Balance	√			2 400 00		1
2	Dec.	28	Pay work jackets	CPJ3	10 500 00		12 900 00		2
3									3
4									4
5									5
6									6
7									7
8									8
9									9
10									10

ACCOUNT *Work Shoes* ACCOUNT NO. 11432

	DATE		DESCRIPTION	POST. REF.	DEBIT	CREDIT	BALANCE DEBIT	BALANCE CREDIT	
1	Dec.	1	Balance	√			1 150 00		1
2	Dec.	28	Pay work shoes	CPJ3	9 000 00		10 150 00		2
3									3
4									4
5									5
6									6
7									7
8									8
9									9
10									10

ACCOUNT *Heat-resistant Gloves* ACCOUNT NO. 11433

	DATE		DESCRIPTION	POST. REF.	DEBIT	CREDIT	BALANCE DEBIT	BALANCE CREDIT	
1	Dec.	1	Balance	√			450 00		1
2	Dec.	28	Pay heat-resistant gloves	CPJ3	5 000 00		5 450 00		2
3									3
4									4
5									5
6									6
7									7
8									8
9									9
10									10

ACCOUNT *Factory Office Supplies* ACCOUNT NO. 11434

DATE		DESCRIPTION	POST. REF.	DEBIT	CREDIT	BALANCE	
						DEBIT	CREDIT
Dec.	28	Purchase factory office supplies	CPJ2	1 500 00		1 500 00	

ACCOUNT *Plant, Property & Equipment* ACCOUNT NO. 115

DATE		DESCRIPTION	POST. REF.	DEBIT	CREDIT	BALANCE	
						DEBIT	CREDIT
Dec.	1	Balance	√			12 000 000 00	
Dec.	28	Lathe(Old)	1151		150 000 00	11 850 000 00	
Dec.	28	Saw Machine	1152	220 000 00		12 070 000 00	
Dec.	28	Lathe(New)	1153	199 200 00		12 269 200 00	
Dec.	28	Grinder	1159	50 000 00		12 319 200 00	

ACCOUNT *Lathe (Old)* ACCOUNT NO. 1151

DATE		DESCRIPTION	POST. REF.	DEBIT	CREDIT	BALANCE	
						DEBIT	CREDIT
Dec.	1	Balance	√			150 000 00	
Dec.	11	Disposal of Lathe	G1		150 000 00	0 000 00	

ACCOUNT *Saw Machine* ACCOUNT NO. 1152

	DATE		DESCRIPTION	POST. REF.	DEBIT	CREDIT	BALANCE		
							DEBIT	CREDIT	
1	Dec.	31	Purchase of saw machine	CPJ1	220 000 00		220 000 00		1
2									2
3									3
4									4
5									5
6									6
7									7
8									8
9									9
10									10

ACCOUNT *Lathe (New)* ACCOUNT NO. 1153

	DATE		DESCRIPTION	POST. REF.	DEBIT	CREDIT	BALANCE		
							DEBIT	CREDIT	
1	Dec.	28	Pay the lathe	CPJ2	196 200 00		196 200 00		1
2	Dec.	28	Pay the lathe	CPJ2	3 000 00		199 200 00		2
3									3
4									4
5									5
6									6
7									7
8									8
9									9
10									10

ACCOUNT *Grinder* ACCOUNT NO. 1159

	DATE		DESCRIPTION	POST. REF.	DEBIT	CREDIT	BALANCE		
							DEBIT	CREDIT	
1	Dec.	21	Donation of Grinder	G2	50 000 00		50 000 00		1
2									2
3									3
4									4
5									5
6									6
7									7
8									8
9									9
10									10

ACCOUNT *Accumulated Depreciation* ACCOUNT NO. 116

	DATE		DESCRIPTION	POST. REF.	DEBIT	CREDIT	BALANCE DEBIT	BALANCE CREDIT	
1	Dec.	1	Balance	√				2 500 000 00	1
2	Dec.	28	Lathe	1161	135 000 00			2 365 000 00	2
3									3
4									4
5									5
6									6
7									7
8									8
9									9
10									10

ACCOUNT *Accumulated Depreciation–Lathe* ACCOUNT NO. 1161

	DATE		DESCRIPTION	POST. REF.	DEBIT	CREDIT	BALANCE DEBIT	BALANCE CREDIT	
1	Dec.	1	Balance	√				135 000 00	1
2	Dec.	11	Disposal of Lathe	G1	135 000 00			θ θθθ θθ	2
3									3
4									4
5									5
6									6
7									7
8									8
9									9
10									10

ACCOUNT *Land* ACCOUNT NO. 117

	DATE		DESCRIPTION	POST. REF.	DEBIT	CREDIT	BALANCE DEBIT	BALANCE CREDIT	
1	Dec.	1	Balance	√			2 600 000 00		1
2									2
3									3
4									4
5									5
6									6
7									7
8									8
9									9
10									10

ACCOUNT *Intangible Assets* ACCOUNT NO. 118

	DATE		DESCRIPTION	POST. REF.	DEBIT	CREDIT	BALANCE DEBIT	BALANCE CREDIT	
1	Dec.	1	Balance	√			500 000 00		1
2	Dec.	28	Trademark	1182	30 000 00		530 000 00		2
3									3
4									4
5									5
6									6
7									7
8									8
9									9
10									10

ACCOUNT *Patent* ACCOUNT NO. 1181

	DATE		DESCRIPTION	POST. REF.	DEBIT	CREDIT	BALANCE DEBIT	BALANCE CREDIT	
1	Dec.	1	Balance	√			500 000 00		1
2									2
3									3
4									4
5									5
6									6
7									7
8									8
9									9
10									10

ACCOUNT *Trademark* ACCOUNT NO. 1182

	DATE		DESCRIPTION	POST. REF.	DEBIT	CREDIT	BALANCE DEBIT	BALANCE CREDIT	
1	Dec.	28	Purchase patent	CPJ4	30 000 00		30 000 00		1
2									2
3									3
4									4
5									5
6									6
7									7
8									8
9									9
10									10

ACCOUNT *Accumulated Amortization* ACCOUNT NO. 119

	DATE		DESCRIPTION	POST. REF.	DEBIT	CREDIT	BALANCE		
							DEBIT	CREDIT	
1	Dec.	1	Balance	√				200 000 00	1
2									2
3									3
4									4
5									5
6									6
7									7
8									8
9									9
10									10

ACCOUNT *Accumulated Amortization-Patent* ACCOUNT NO. 1191

	DATE		DESCRIPTION	POST. REF.	DEBIT	CREDIT	BALANCE		
							DEBIT	CREDIT	
1	Dec.	1	Balance	√				200 000 00	1
2									2
3									3
4									4
5									5
6									6
7									7
8									8
9									9
10									10

ACCOUNT *Short-term Borrowings* ACCOUNT NO. 201

	DATE		DESCRIPTION	POST. REF.	DEBIT	CREDIT	BALANCE		
							DEBIT	CREDIT	
1	Dec.	1	Balance	√				2 428 000 00	1
2	Dec.	28	China Construction Bank	2011	400 000 00			2 828 000 00	2
3	Dec.	28	Bank of China	2012		500 000 00		2 528 000 00	3
4									4
5									5
6									6
7									7
8									8
9									9
10									10

ACCOUNT *Short-term Borrowings—China Construction Bank* ACCOUNT NO. 2011

	DATE		DESCRIPTION	POST. REF.	DEBIT	CREDIT	BALANCE DEBIT	BALANCE CREDIT	
1	Dec.	1	Balance	√				1 000 000 00	1
2	Dec.	28	Bank loan	CRJ1		600 000 00		1 600 000 00	2
3	Dec.	28	Pay debt	CPJ3	1 000 000 00			600 000 00	3
4									4
5									5
6									6
7									7
8									8
9									9
10									10

ACCOUNT *Short-term Borrowings—Bank of China* ACCOUNT NO. 2012

	DATE		DESCRIPTION	POST. REF.	DEBIT	CREDIT	BALANCE DEBIT	BALANCE CREDIT	
1	Dec.	1	Balance	√				1 428 000 00	1
2	Dec.	31	Bank loan	CRJ1		500 000 00		1 928 000 00	2
3									3
4									4
5									5
6									6
7									7
8									8
9									9
10									10

ACCOUNT *Notes Payable* ACCOUNT NO. 202

	DATE		DESCRIPTION	POST. REF.	DEBIT	CREDIT	BALANCE DEBIT	BALANCE CREDIT	
1	Dec.	1	Balance	√				110 000 00	1
2									2
3									3
4									4
5									5
6									6
7									7
8									8
9									9
10									10

ACCOUNT *Notes Payable—Beijing Steel* ACCOUNT NO. 2021

	DATE		DESCRIPTION	POST. REF.	DEBIT	CREDIT	BALANCE DEBIT	BALANCE CREDIT	
1	Dec.	1	Balance	√				68 000 00	1
2									2
3									3
4									4
5									5
6									6
7									7
8									8
9									9
10									10

ACCOUNT *Notes Payable—Hebei Steel* ACCOUNT NO. 2022

	DATE		DESCRIPTION	POST. REF.	DEBIT	CREDIT	BALANCE DEBIT	BALANCE CREDIT	
1	Dec.	1	Balance	√				42 000 00	1
2									2
3									3
4									4
5									5
6									6
7									7
8									8
9									9
10									10

ACCOUNT *Accounts Payable* ACCOUNT NO. 203

	DATE		DESCRIPTION	POST. REF.	DEBIT	CREDIT	BALANCE DEBIT	BALANCE CREDIT	
1	Dec.	1	Balance	√				102 000 00	1
2	Dec.	28	Beijing Steel	2031		339 900 00		441 900 00	2
3									3
4									4
5									5
6									6
7									7
8									8
9									9
10									10

ACCOUNT *Accounts Payable-Beijing Steel* ACCOUNT NO. 2031

	DATE		DESCRIPTION	POST. REF.	DEBIT	CREDIT	BALANCE DEBIT	BALANCE CREDIT	
1	Dec.	1	Balance	√				60 000 00	1
2	Dec.	28	Purchases Journal	PJ1		339 900 00		399 900 00	2
3									3
4									4
5									5
6									6
7									7
8									8
9									9
10									10

ACCOUNT *Accounts Payable-Hebei Steel* ACCOUNT NO. 2032

	DATE		DESCRIPTION	POST. REF.	DEBIT	CREDIT	BALANCE DEBIT	BALANCE CREDIT	
1	Dec.	1	Balance	√				42 000 00	1
2									2
3									3
4									4
5									5
6									6
7									7
8									8
9									9
10									10

ACCOUNT *Unearned Revenue* ACCOUNT NO. 204

	DATE		DESCRIPTION	POST. REF.	DEBIT	CREDIT	BALANCE DEBIT	BALANCE CREDIT	
1	Dec.	1	Balance	√				441 570 00	1
2	Dec.	28	Ningbo Air-blower	CRJ 1		400 000 00		841 570 00	2
3	Dec.	28	Xiangshan Air-blower	CRJ 1		350 000 00		1 191 570 00	3
4									4
5									5
6									6
7									7
8									8
9									9
10									10

ACCOUNT *Unearned Revenue–Ningbo Air-blower* ACCOUNT NO. 2041

	DATE		DESCRIPTION	POST. REF.	DEBIT	CREDIT	BALANCE DEBIT	BALANCE CREDIT	
1	Dec.	1	Balance	√				290 047 00	1
2	Dec.	28	Prepaid sales	CRJ1		400 000 00		690 047 00	2
3									3
4									4
5									5
6									6
7									7
8									8
9									9
10									10

ACCOUNT *Unearned Revenue–Xiangshan Air-blower* ACCOUNT NO. 2042

	DATE		DESCRIPTION	POST. REF.	DEBIT	CREDIT	BALANCE DEBIT	BALANCE CREDIT	
1	Dec.	1	Balance	√				151 523 00	1
2	Dec.	28	Prepaid sales	CRJ1		350 000 00		501 523 00	2
3									3
4									4
5									5
6									6
7									7
8									8
9									9
10									10

ACCOUNT *Payroll Liabilities* ACCOUNT NO. 205

	DATE		DESCRIPTION	POST. REF.	DEBIT	CREDIT	BALANCE DEBIT	BALANCE CREDIT	
1	Dec.	1	Balance	√				954 696 00	1
2	Dec.	28	Salaries Payable	2051	535 184 00			419 512 00	2
3	Dec.	28	Social Security Tax Payable	2052	335 896 00			83 616 00	3
4	Dec.	28	Medicare Tax Payable	2053	61 200 00			22 416 00	4
5	Dec.	28	Federal Unemployment Tax Payable	2054	2 632 00			19 784 00	5
6	Dec.	28	State Unemployment Tax Payable	2055	17 768 00			2 016 00	6
7	Dec.	28	Employee FITP	2056	672 00			1 344 00	7
8	Dec.	28	Employee SITP	2057	1 344 00			0 000 00	8
9									9
10									10

ACCOUNT *Salaries Payable* ACCOUNT NO. 2051

	DATE		DESCRIPTION	POST. REF.	DEBIT	CREDIT	BALANCE		
							DEBIT	CREDIT	
1	Dec.	1	Balance	√				535 1 8 4 00	1
2	Dec.	28	Pay salaries	CPJ3	535 1 8 4 00			0 0 0 0 00	2
3									3
4									4
5									5
6									6
7									7
8									8
9									9
10									10

ACCOUNT *Social Security Tax Payable* ACCOUNT NO. 2052

	DATE		DESCRIPTION	POST. REF.	DEBIT	CREDIT	BALANCE		
							DEBIT	CREDIT	
1	Dec.	1	Balance	√				335 8 9 6 00	1
2	Dec.	28	Pay social security tax	CPJ3	335 8 9 6 00			0 0 0 0 00	2
3									3
4									4
5									5
6									6
7									7
8									8
9									9
10									10

ACCOUNT *Medicare Tax Payable* ACCOUNT NO. 2053

	DATE		DESCRIPTION	POST. REF.	DEBIT	CREDIT	BALANCE		
							DEBIT	CREDIT	
1	Dec.	1	Balance	√				61 2 0 0 00	1
2	Dec.	28	Pay Medicare tax	CPJ3	61 2 0 0 00			0 0 0 0 00	2
3									3
4									4
5									5
6									6
7									7
8									8
9									9
10									10

ACCOUNT *Federal Unemployment Tax Payable* ACCOUNT NO. 2054

	DATE		DESCRIPTION	POST. REF.	DEBIT	CREDIT	BALANCE DEBIT	BALANCE CREDIT	
1	Dec.	1	Balance	√				2 632 00	1
2	Dec.	28	Pay federal unemployment tax	CPJ3	2 632 00			0 000 00	2
3									3
4									4
5									5
6									6
7									7
8									8
9									9
10									10

ACCOUNT *State Unemployment Tax Payable* ACCOUNT NO. 2055

	DATE		DESCRIPTION	POST. REF.	DEBIT	CREDIT	BALANCE DEBIT	BALANCE CREDIT	
1	Dec.	1	Balance	√				17 768 00	1
2	Dec.	28	Pay state unemployment tax	CPJ3	17 768 00			0 000 00	2
3									3
4									4
5									5
6									6
7									7
8									8
9									9
10									10

ACCOUNT *Employee Federal Income Tax Payable* ACCOUNT NO. 2056

	DATE		DESCRIPTION	POST. REF.	DEBIT	CREDIT	BALANCE DEBIT	BALANCE CREDIT	
1	Dec.	1	Balance	√				672 00	1
2	Dec.	31	Pay employee federal income tax	CPJ1	672 00			0 000 00	2
3									3
4									4
5									5
6									6
7									7
8									8
9									9
10									10

ACCOUNT *Employee State Income Tax Payable* ACCOUNT NO. 2057

	DATE		DESCRIPTION	POST. REF.	DEBIT	CREDIT	BALANCE		
							DEBIT	CREDIT	
1	Dec.	1	Balance	√				1 344 00	1
2	Dec.	28	Pay employee state income tax	CPJ1	1 344 00			0 000 00	2
3									3
4									4
5									5
6									6
7									7
8									8
9									9
10									10

ACCOUNT *Taxes Payable* ACCOUNT NO. 206

	DATE		DESCRIPTION	POST. REF.	DEBIT	CREDIT	BALANCE		
							DEBIT	CREDIT	
1	Dec.	1	Balance	√				1 203 180 00	1
2	Dec.	28	Sales Tax Payable	2061		810 000 00		2 013 180 00	2
3	Dec.	28	Income Taxes Payable	2063	1 203 180 00			810 000 00	3
4									4
5									5
6									6
7									7
8									8
9									9
10									10

ACCOUNT *Sales Tax Payable* ACCOUNT NO. 2061

	DATE		DESCRIPTION	POST. REF.	DEBIT	CREDIT	BALANCE		
							DEBIT	CREDIT	
1	Dec.	28	Collect sales tax	CRJ1		612 000 00		612 000 00	1
2	Dec.	28	Sales Journal	SJ1		198 000 00		810 000 00	2
3									3
4									4
5									5
6									6
7									7
8									8
9									9
10									10

ACCOUNT *Property Tax Payable* ACCOUNT NO. 2062

	DATE		DESCRIPTION	POST. REF.	DEBIT	CREDIT	BALANCE DEBIT	BALANCE CREDIT	
1	Dec.	17	Property Tax Submission	G1		54 090 00			1
2	Dec.	28	Pay property tax	CPJ4	54 090 00			0 000 00	2
3									3
4									4
5									5
6									6
7									7
8									8
9									9
10									10

ACCOUNT *Income Taxes Payable* ACCOUNT NO. 2063

	DATE		DESCRIPTION	POST. REF.	DEBIT	CREDIT	BALANCE DEBIT	BALANCE CREDIT	
1	Dec.	1	Balance	√				1 203 180 00	1
2	Dec.	28	Federal Income Tax Payable	20631	601 590 00			601 590 00	2
3	Dec.	28	State Income Tax Payable	20632	601 590 00			0 000 00	3
4									4
5									5
6									6
7									7
8									8
9									9
10									10

ACCOUNT *Federal Income Tax Payable* ACCOUNT NO. 20631

	DATE		DESCRIPTION	POST. REF.	DEBIT	CREDIT	BALANCE DEBIT	BALANCE CREDIT	
1	Dec.	1	Balance	√				601 590 00	1
2	Dec.	28	Payment of federal income tax	CPJ1	601 590 00			0 000 00	2
3									3
4									4
5									5
6									6
7									7
8									8
9									9
10									10

ACCOUNT *State Income Tax Payable* ACCOUNT NO. 20632

	DATE		DESCRIPTION	POST. REF.	DEBIT	CREDIT	BALANCE		
							DEBIT	CREDIT	
1	Dec.	1	Balance	√				601 590 00	1
2	Dec.	28	Payment of state income tax	CPJ1	601 590 00			0 000 00	2
3									3
4									4
5									5
6									6
7									7
8									8
9									9
10									10

ACCOUNT *Interests Payable* ACCOUNT NO. 207

	DATE		DESCRIPTION	POST. REF.	DEBIT	CREDIT	BALANCE		
							DEBIT	CREDIT	
1	Dec.	1	Balance	√				14 583 00	1
2	Dec.	28	Pay debt	CPJ4	11 666 00			2 917 00	2
3									3
4									4
5									5
6									6
7									7
8									8
9									9
10									10

ACCOUNT *Commercial Acceptance Bill Payable* ACCOUNT NO. 208

	DATE		DESCRIPTION	POST. REF.	DEBIT	CREDIT	BALANCE		
							DEBIT	CREDIT	
1	Dec.	23	Purchase steel plates	G2		89 200 00		89 200 00	1
2									2
3									3
4									4
5									5
6									6
7									7
8									8
9									9
10									10

ACCOUNT *Capital, Hefeng* ACCOUNT NO. 301

	DATE		DESCRIPTION	POST. REF.	DEBIT	CREDIT	BALANCE		
							DEBIT	CREDIT	
1	Dec.	1	Balance	√				12 800 000 00	1
2	Dec.	21	Donation of grinder	G2		50 000 00		12 850 000 00	2
3									3
4									4
5									5
6									6
7									7
8									8
9									9
10									10

ACCOUNT *Capital Reserve* ACCOUNT NO. 302

	DATE		DESCRIPTION	POST. REF.	DEBIT	CREDIT	BALANCE		
							DEBIT	CREDIT	
1	Dec.	1	Balance	√				550 000 00	1
2									2
3									3
4									4
5									5
6									6
7									7
8									8
9									9
10									10

ACCOUNT *Retained Earnings* ACCOUNT NO. 303

	DATE		DESCRIPTION	POST. REF.	DEBIT	CREDIT	BALANCE		
							DEBIT	CREDIT	
1	Dec.	1	Balance	√				2 900 000 00	1
2									2
3									3
4									4
5									5
6									6
7									7
8									8
9									9
10									10

ACCOUNT *Sales Revenue* ACCOUNT NO. 401

	DATE		DESCRIPTION	POST. REF.	DEBIT	CREDIT	BALANCE DEBIT	BALANCE CREDIT	
1	Dec.	28	Small Air-blower	4011		3 850 000 00		3 850 000 00	1
2	Dec.	28	Large Air-blower	4012		4 400 000 00		8 250 000 00	2
3									3
4									4
5									5
6									6
7									7
8									8
9									9
10									10

ACCOUNT *Sales Revenue-Small Air-blower* ACCOUNT NO. 4011

	DATE		DESCRIPTION	POST. REF.	DEBIT	CREDIT	BALANCE DEBIT	BALANCE CREDIT	
1	Dec.	28	Sold products	CRJ1		2 450 000 00		2 450 000 00	1
2	Dec.	28	Sales Journal	SJ1		1 400 000 00		3 850 000 00	2
3									3
4									4
5									5
6									6
7									7
8									8
9									9
10									10

ACCOUNT *Sales Revenue-Large Air-blower* ACCOUNT NO. 4012

	DATE		DESCRIPTION	POST. REF.	DEBIT	CREDIT	BALANCE DEBIT	BALANCE CREDIT	
1	Dec.	31	Sold products	CRJ1		3 600 000 00		3 600 000 00	1
2	Dec.	28	Sales Journal	SJ1		800 000 00		4 400 000 00	2
3									3
4									4
5									5
6									6
7									7
8									8
9									9
10									10

ACCOUNT *Other Revenue* ACCOUNT NO. 402

	DATE		DESCRIPTION	POST. REF.	DEBIT	CREDIT	BALANCE DEBIT	BALANCE CREDIT	
1	Dec.	31	Fine	CRJ1		3 000 00		3 000 00	1
2									2
3									3
4									4
5									5
6									6
7									7
8									8
9									9
10									10

ACCOUNT *Cost of Goods Sold* ACCOUNT NO. 501

	DATE		DESCRIPTION	POST. REF.	DEBIT	CREDIT	BALANCE DEBIT	BALANCE CREDIT	
1	Dec.	1	Balance	√					1
2	Dec.	28	Small Air-blower	5011	2 750 000 00		2 750 000 00		2
3	Dec.	28	Large Air-blower	5012	2 860 000 00		5 610 000 00		3
4									4
5									5
6									6
7									7
8									8
9									9
10									10

ACCOUNT *Cost of Goods Sold-Small Air-blower* ACCOUNT NO. 5011

	DATE		DESCRIPTION	POST. REF.	DEBIT	CREDIT	BALANCE DEBIT	BALANCE CREDIT	
1	Dec.	4	Sold products	G1	250 000 00		250 000 00		1
2	Dec.	7	Sold products	G1	250 000 00		500 000 00		2
3	Dec.	9	Sold products	G1	250 000 00		750 000 00		3
4	Dec.	12	Sold products	G1	500 000 00		1 250 000 00		4
5	Dec.	17	Sold products	G1	250 000 00		1 500 000 00		5
6	Dec.	19	Sold products	G1	750 000 00		2 250 000 00		6
7	Dec.	22	Sold products	G2	500 000 00		2 750 000 00		7
8									8
9									9
10									10

ACCOUNT *Cost of Goods Sold-Large Air-blower* ACCOUNT NO. 5012

	DATE		DESCRIPTION	POST. REF.	DEBIT	CREDIT	BALANCE		
							DEBIT	CREDIT	
1	Dec.	7	Sold products	G1	520 000 00		520 000 00		1
2	Dec.	7	Sold products	G1	260 000 00		780 000 00		2
3	Dec.	11	Sold products	G1	260 000 00		1 040 000 00		3
4	Dec.	15	Sold products	G1	520 000 00		1 560 000 00		4
5	Dec.	17	Sold products	G1	520 000 00		2 080 000 00		5
6	Dec.	17	Sold products	G1	260 000 00		2 340 000 00		6
7	Dec.	28	Sold products	G2	520 000 00		2 860 000 00		7
8									8
9									9
10									10

ACCOUNT *Selling Expense* ACCOUNT NO. 502

	DATE		DESCRIPTION	POST. REF.	DEBIT	CREDIT	BALANCE		
							DEBIT	CREDIT	
1	Dec.	28	Sales Travel Expense	5021	4 500 00		4 500 00		1
2	Dec.	28	Sales Training Expense	5022	3 000 00		7 500 00		2
3	Dec.	28	Advertising Expense	5023	15 000 00		22 500 00		3
4	Dec.	28	Telephone Expense	5024	8 000 00		30 500 00		4
5									5
6									6
7									7
8									8
9									9
10									10

ACCOUNT *Sales Travel Expense* ACCOUNT NO. 5021

	DATE		DESCRIPTION	POST. REF.	DEBIT	CREDIT	BALANCE		
							DEBIT	CREDIT	
1	Dec.	28	Pay travel fee	CPJ3	4 500 00		4 500 00		1
2									2
3									3
4									4
5									5
6									6
7									7
8									8
9									9
10									10

ACCOUNT *Sales Training Expense* ACCOUNT NO. 5022

	DATE		DESCRIPTION	POST. REF.	DEBIT	CREDIT	BALANCE DEBIT	BALANCE CREDIT	
1	Dec.	28	Pay training fee	CPJ2	3 000 00		3 000 00		1
2									2
3									3
4									4
5									5
6									6
7									7
8									8
9									9
10									10

ACCOUNT *Advertising Expense* ACCOUNT NO. 5023

	DATE		DESCRIPTION	POST. REF.	DEBIT	CREDIT	BALANCE DEBIT	BALANCE CREDIT	
1	Dec.	28	Pay advertising fee	CPJ2	10 000 00		10 000 00		1
2	Dec.	28	Pay advertising fee	CPJ3	5 000 00		15 000 00		2
3									3
4									4
5									5
6									6
7									7
8									8
9									9
10									10

ACCOUNT *Telephone Expense* ACCOUNT NO. 5024

	DATE		DESCRIPTION	POST. REF.	DEBIT	CREDIT	BALANCE DEBIT	BALANCE CREDIT	
1	Dec.	28	Pay telephone fee	CPJ4	8 000 00		8 000 00		1
2									2
3									3
4									4
5									5
6									6
7									7
8									8
9									9
10									10

ACCOUNT *Administrative & Managerial Expense* ACCOUNT NO. 503

	DATE		DESCRIPTION	POST. REF.	DEBIT	CREDIT	BALANCE DEBIT	BALANCE CREDIT	
1	Dec.	28	M&A Travel Expense	5031	800 00		800 00		1
2	Dec.	28	M&A Training Expense	5032	3 000 00		3 800 00		2
3	Dec.	28	Bank Fee Expense	5033	30 00		3 830 00		3
4	Dec.	28	Telecommunication Expense	5034	1 200 00		5 030 00		4
5	Dec.	28	Invitation Fee Expense	5035	2 500 00		7 530 00		5
6	Dec.	28	Television Expense	5036	240 00		7 770 00		6
7	Dec.	28	Interest Expense	5037	5 833 00		13 603 00		7
8									8
9									9
10									10

ACCOUNT *M&A Travel Expense* ACCOUNT NO. 5031

	DATE		DESCRIPTION	POST. REF.	DEBIT	CREDIT	BALANCE DEBIT	BALANCE CREDIT	
1	Dec.	1	Reimbursement of travel fee	CPJ1	800 00		800 00		1
2									2
3									3
4									4
5									5
6									6
7									7
8									8
9									9
10									10

ACCOUNT *M&A Training Expense* ACCOUNT NO. 5032

	DATE		DESCRIPTION	POST. REF.	DEBIT	CREDIT	BALANCE DEBIT	BALANCE CREDIT	
1	Dec.	28	Pay training expense	CPJ4	3 000 00		3 000 00		1
2									2
3									3
4									4
5									5
6									6
7									7
8									8
9									9
10									10

ACCOUNT *Bank Fee Expense* ACCOUNT NO. 5033

	DATE		DESCRIPTION	POST. REF.	DEBIT	CREDIT	BALANCE DEBIT	BALANCE CREDIT	
1	Dec.	1	Payment of bank fee	CPJ1	30 00		30 00		1
2									2
3									3
4									4
5									5
6									6
7									7
8									8
9									9
10									10

ACCOUNT *Telecommunication Expense* ACCOUNT NO. 5034

	DATE		DESCRIPTION	POST. REF.	DEBIT	CREDIT	BALANCE DEBIT	BALANCE CREDIT	
1	Dec.	31	Payment of telecommunication fee	CPJ1	1 200 00		1 200 00		1
2									2
3									3
4									4
5									5
6									6
7									7
8									8
9									9
10									10

ACCOUNT *Invitation Fee Expense* ACCOUNT NO. 5035

	DATE		DESCRIPTION	POST. REF.	DEBIT	CREDIT	BALANCE DEBIT	BALANCE CREDIT	
1	Dec.	28	Pay invitation fee	CPJ2	1 000 00		1 000 00		1
2	Dec.	28	Pay invitation fee	CPJ4	1 500 00		2 500 00		2
3									3
4									4
5									5
6									6
7									7
8									8
9									9
10									10

ACCOUNT *Television Expense* ACCOUNT NO. 5036

DATE		DESCRIPTION	POST. REF.	DEBIT	CREDIT	BALANCE	
						DEBIT	CREDIT
Dec.	28	Pay television fee	CPJ3	240 00		240 00	

ACCOUNT *Interest Expense* ACCOUNT NO. 5037

DATE		DESCRIPTION	POST. REF.	DEBIT	CREDIT	BALANCE	
						DEBIT	CREDIT
Dec.	28	Pay debt	CPJ4	5 833 00		5 833 00	

ACCOUNT *Cash Lost Expense* ACCOUNT NO. 5038

DATE		DESCRIPTION	POST. REF.	DEBIT	CREDIT	BALANCE	
						DEBIT	CREDIT
Dec.	27	Cash lost	G2	50 00		50 00	
Dec.	27	Reimbursement of cash lost	G2		50 00	0 000 00	

ACCOUNT *Taxes Expense* ACCOUNT NO. 505

	DATE		DESCRIPTION	POST. REF.	DEBIT	CREDIT	BALANCE DEBIT	BALANCE CREDIT	
1	Dec.	28	Property Tax Expense	5052	54 090 00		54 090 00		1
2									2
3									3
4									4
5									5
6									6
7									7
8									8
9									9
10									10

ACCOUNT *Property Tax Expense* ACCOUNT NO. 5052

	DATE		DESCRIPTION	POST. REF.	DEBIT	CREDIT	BALANCE DEBIT	BALANCE CREDIT	
1	Dec.	17	Property Document Submission	G1	54 090 00		54 090 00		1
2									2
3									3
4									4
5									5
6									6
7									7
8									8
9									9
10									10

ACCOUNT *Loss on Disposal of PP&E* ACCOUNT NO. 506

	DATE		DESCRIPTION	POST. REF.	DEBIT	CREDIT	BALANCE DEBIT	BALANCE CREDIT	
1	Dec.	11	Lathe	5061	5 000 00		5 000 00		1
2									2
3									3
4									4
5									5
6									6
7									7
8									8
9									9
10									10

ACCOUNT *Loss on Disposal of Lathe*									ACCOUNT NO. 5061
	DATE		DESCRIPTION	POST. REF.	DEBIT	CREDIT	BALANCE		
							DEBIT	CREDIT	
1	Dec.	11	Disposal of Lathe	G1	5 000 00		5 000 00		1
2									2
3									3
4									4
5									5
6									6
7									7
8									8
9									9
10									10

All transactions in General Journal and four special journals have been posted to the ledger. Updated General Journal is illustrated in following table.

GENERAL JOURNAL							PAGE 1
	DATE		DESCRIPTION	POST. REF.	DEBIT	CREDIT	
1	Dec.	4	Other Receivables-Fenghua Air-blower	1092	3 000 00		1
2			Bank Deposit	102		3 000 00	2
3			Check Stub 34	√			3
4	Dec.	4	Cost of Goods Sold-Small Air-blower	5011	250 000 00		4
5			Finished Goods-Small Air-blower	11031		250 000 00	5
6			SALES SLIP 68	√			6
7	Dec.	7	Cost of Goods Sold-Large Air-blower	5012	520 000 00		7
8			Finished Goods-Large Air-blower	11032		520 000 00	8
9			SALES SLIP 69	√			9
10	Dec.	7	Cost of Goods Sold-Small Air-blower	5011	250 000 00		10
11			Finished Goods-Small Air-blower	11031		250 000 00	11
12			SALES SLIP 70	√			12
13	Dec.	7	Cost of Goods Sold-Large Air-blower	5012	260 000 00		13
14			Finished Goods-Large Air-blower	11032		260 000 00	14
15			SALES SLIP 71	√			15
16	Dec.	9	Other Receivables-Ningbo Air-blower	1093	3 000 00		16
17			Bank Deposit	102		3 000 00	17
18			Check Stub 48	√			18
19	Dec.	9	Cost of Goods Sold-Small Air-blower	5011	250 000 00		19
20			Finished Goods-Small Air-blower	11031		250 000 00	20
21			SALES SLIP 72	√			21
22	Dec.	11	Cost of Goods Sold-Large Air-blower	5012	260 000 00		22

continued

DATE		DESCRIPTION	POST. REF.	DEBIT	CREDIT
		Finished Goods–Large Air-blower	11032		260 000 00
		SALES SLIP 73	√		
Dec.	11	Bank Deposit	102	10 000 00	
		Loss on Disposal of Lathe	5061	5 000 00	
		Accumulated Depreciation–Lathe	1161	135 000 00	
		Lathe(Old)	1151		150 000 00
		Memorandum 32 & 33	√		
Dec.	12	Cost of Goods Sold–Small Air-blower	5011	500 000 00	
		Finished Goods–Small Air-blower	11031		500 000 00
		SALES SLIP 74	√		
Dec.	15	Cost of Goods Sold–Large Air-blower	5012	520 000 00	
		Finished Goods–Large Air-blower	11032		520 000 00
		SALES SLIP 75	√		
Dec.	17	Other Receivables–Ningbo Air-blower	1093	2 000 00	
		Bank Deposit	102		2 000 00
		Check Stub 168	√		
Dec.	17	Cost of Goods Sold–Large Air-blower	5012	520 000 00	
		Finished Goods–Large Air-blower	11032		520 000 00
		SALES SLIP 76	√		
Dec.	17	Cost of Goods Sold–Small Air-blower	5011	250 000 00	
		Finished Goods–Small Air-blower	11031		250 000 00
		SALES SLIP 77	√		
Dec.	17	Cost of Goods Sold–Large Air-blower	5012	260 000 00	
		Finished Goods–Large Air-blower	11032		260 000 00
		SALES SLIP 78	√		
Dec.	17	Property Tax Expense	5052	54 090 00	
		Property Tax Payable	2062		54 090 00
		Memorandum 36	√		
Dec.	18	Bank Deposit	102	97 875 00	
		Discounts on Notes Receivable–Xiangshan Air-blower	105	2 125 00	
		Notes Receivable–Xiangshan Air-blower	1042		100 000 00
		Check Stub 177	√		
Dec.	19	Cost of Goods Sold–Small Air-blower	5011	750 000 00	
		Finished Goods–Small Air-blower	11031		750 000 00
		SALES SLIP 79	√		

GENERAL JOURNAL PAGE 2

DATE		DESCRIPTION	POST. REF.	DEBIT	CREDIT
Dec.	21	Grinder	1159	50 000 00	
		Capital, Hefeng	301		50 000 00
		Memorandum 38	√		
Dec.	22	Cost of Goods Sold-Small Air-blower	5011	500 000 00	
		Finished Goods-Small Air-blower	11031		500 000 00
		SALES SLIP 80	√		
Dec.	23	Steel Plates	110111	75 000 00	
		Material Price Variance	111	5 000 00	
		Factory Overhead Incurred	113	9 200 00	
		Commercial Acceptance Bill Pay.	208		89 200 00
		Bill 117	√		
Dec.	23	Bank Deposit	102	1 500 00	
		Cash on Hand	101		1 500 00
		Receipt 926	√		
Dec.	27	Cash Lost Expense	5038	50 00	
		Cash on Hand	101		50 00
		Memorandum 39	√		
Dec.	27	Cash on Hand	101	50 00	
		Cash Lost Expense	5038		50 00
		Memorandum 40	√		
Dec.	28	Cost of Goods Sold-Large Air-blower	5012	520 000 00	
		Finished Goods-Large Air-blower	11032		520 000 00
		SALES SLIP 83	√		

Updated Cash Receipts Journal, Cash Payments Journal, Sales Journal and Purchases Journal are illustrated in following tables.

CASH RECEIPTS JOURNAL													PAGE 1
	DATE		DOC. NO.	ACCOUNT NAME	POST. REF.	GENERAL CREDIT	SALES CREDIT	SALES TAX PAYABLE CREDIT	ACCOUNTS RECEIVABLE CREDIT	BANK DEPOSIT DEBIT	CASH ON HAND DEBIT		
1	Dec.	2	RA291	AR–FHAB	1061				100 000 00	100 000 00		1	
2	Dec.	4	L38	STB–CCB	2011	600 000 00				600 000 00		2	
3	Dec.	7	NO.69/CS041	Large Air-blower	√		800 000 00	72 000 00		872 000 00		3	
4	Dec.	7	NO.70/CS042	Small Air-blower	√		350 000 00	31 500 00		381 500 00		4	
5	Dec.	7	NO.71/CS043	Large Air-blower	√		400 000 00	36 000 00		436 000 00		5	
6	Dec.	8	L192	STB–BOC	2012	500 000 00				500 000 00		6	
7	Dec.	11	NO.73/CS050	Large Air-blower	√		400 000 00	36 000 00		436 000 00		7	
8	Dec.	12	NO.74/CS054	Small Air-blower	√		700 000 00	63 000 00		763 000 00		8	
9	Dec.	15	NO.75/CS165	Large Air-blower	√		800 000 00	72 000 00		872 000 00		9	
10	Dec.	17	NO.77/CS169	Small Air-blower	√		350 000 00	31 500 00		381 500 00		10	
11	Dec.	17	NO.78/CS170	Large Air-blower	√		400 000 00	36 000 00		436 000 00		11	
12	Dec.	18	REC56	Other Rev.	402	3 000 00					3 000 00	12	
13	Dec.	19	NO.79/CS181	Small Air-blower	√		1 050 000 00	94 500 00		1 144 500 00		13	
14	Dec.	24	NO.81/CS187	Unearned Rev.–NBAB	CRJ1	400 000 00		36 000 00		436 000 00		14	
15	Dec.	26	NO.82/CS188	Unearned Rev.–XSAB	CRJ1	350 000 00		31 500 00		381 500 00		15	
16	Dec.	28	NO.83/CS191	Large Air-blower	√		800 000 00	72 000 00		872 000 00		16	
17	Dec.	28		Totals	√		6 050 000 00	612 000 00	100 000 00	8 612 000 00	3 000 00	17	

CASH PAYMENTS JOURNAL PAGE 1

	DATE		DOC. NO.	ACCOUNT NAME	POST. REF.	GENERAL DEBIT	GENERAL CREDIT	ACCOUNTS PAYABLE DEBIT	BANK DEPOSIT CREDIT	CASH ON HAND CREDIT	
1	Dec.	1	CS029	Petty Cash	1091	1 500 00			1 500 00		1
2	Dec.	1	INV324	M&A Travel Expense	5031	800 00				800 00	2
3	Dec.	1	REC12	Bank Fee Expense	5033	30 00			30 00		3
4	Dec.	2	CS030	Saw Machine	1152	220 000 00			220 000 00		4
5	Dec.	2	CS031	Steel Plates	110111	150 000 00			178 400 00		5
6				Material Pric. Var.	111	10 000 00					6
7				Fac. O/H Incurred	113	18 400 00					7
8	Dec.	3	CS032	Iron Castings	110113	45 000 00			56 500 00		8
9				Material Pric. Var.	111	5 000 00					9
10				Fac. O/H Incurred	113	6 500 00					10
11	Dec.	3	REC229	Tele. Expense	5034	1 200 00				1 200 00	11
12	Dec.	3	CS033	Packing Boxes	110122	2 000 00			2 180 00		12
13				Fac.O/H Incurred	113	180 00					13
14	Dec.	4	CS035	Petty Cash	1091	2 000 00			2 000 00		14
15	Dec.	4	CS036	FITP	20631	601 590 00			1 205 196 00		15
16				SITP	20632	601 590 00					16
17				Employee FITP	2056	672 00					17
18				Employee SITP	2057	1 344 00					18
19	Dec.	4	CS037	Prepaid Insurance	1083	90 000 00			90 000 00		19
20	Dec.	5	CS038	Copper Line	110112	105 000 00			118 720 00		20
21				Material Pric. Var.	111	3 000 00					21
22				Fac. O/H Incurred	113	10 720 00					22
23	Dec.	5	CS039	Refrigeration Oil	110121	30 000 00			32 700 00		23
24				Fac. O/H Incurred	113	2 700 00					24

CASH PAYMENTS JOURNAL PAGE 2

	DATE		DOC. NO.	ACCOUNT NAME	POST. REF.	GENERAL DEBIT	GENERAL CREDIT	ACCOUNTS PAYABLE DEBIT	BANK DEPOSIT CREDIT	CASH ON HAND CREDIT	
1	Dec.	7	CS040	Steel Plates	110111	75000 00			89200 00		1
2				Material Pric. Var.	111	5000 00					2
3				Fac. O/H Incurred	113	9200 00					3
4	Dec.	8	REC116	Sales Training Expense	5022	3000 00				3000 00	4
5	Dec.	8	INV316	Invitation Fee Expense	5035	1000 00			1000 00		5
6	Dec.	8	INV823	M&A Office Supplies	1141	2000 00				2000 00	6
7	Dec.	8	CS045	Petty Cash	1091	2000 00			2000 00		7
8	Dec.	8	CS046	Packing Boxes	110122	2000 00			2180 00		8
9				Fac. O/H Incurred	113	180 00					9
10	Dec.	9	CS047	Prepaid Broadband	1081	120000 00			120000 00		10
11	Dec.	10	CS049	Refrigeration Oil	110121	20000 00			21800 00		11
12				Fac. O/H Incurred	113	1800 00					12
13	Dec.	11	INV114	Factory Office Supplies	11434	1500 00			1500 00		13
14	Dec.	11	CS052	Prepaid Subscription	1082	9600 00			9600 00		14
15	Dec.	11	CS053	Iron Castings	110113	45000 00			56500 00		15
16				Material Pric. Var.	111	5000 00					16
17				Fac. O/H Incurred	113	6500 00					17
18	Dec.	12	INV521	Advertising Expense	5023	10000 00			10000 00		18
19	Dec.	12	INV923	Sales Office Supplies	1142	1000 00			1000 00		19
20	Dec.	12	CS057	Lathe	1153	196200 00			196200 00		20
21	Dec.	13	CS058	Lathe	1153	3000 00			3000 00		21
22											22
23											23

CASH PAYMENTS JOURNAL PAGE 3

	DATE		DOC. NO.	ACCOUNT NAME	POST. REF.	GENERAL DEBIT	GENERAL CREDIT	ACCOUNTS PAYABLE DEBIT	BANK DEPOSIT CREDIT	CASH ON HAND CREDIT	
1	Dec.	13	CS059	Copper Line	110112	105 000 00			118 720 00		1
2				Material Pric. Var.	111	3 000 00					2
3				Fac. O/H Incurred	113	10 720 00					3
4	Dec.	14	CS060–CS162	Salaries Payable	2051	535 184 00			535 184 00		4
5	Dec.	15	CS163	Social Sec. Tax Pay.	2052	335 896 00			417 496 00		5
6				Med. Tax Pay.	2053	61 200 00					6
7				FUTP	2054	2 632 00					7
8				SUTP	2055	17 768 00					8
9	Dec.	15	CS164	Iron Castings	110113	45 000 00			56 500 00		9
10				Material Pric. Var.	111	5 000 00					10
11				Fac. O/H Incurred	113	6 500 00					11
12	Dec.	16	CS166	Fac. O/H Incurred	113	4 000 00			4 000 00		12
13	Dec.	16	INV235	M&A Office Supplies	1141	1 000 00				1 000 00	13
14	Dec.	16	INV145	Sales Travel Expense	5021	4 500 00				4 500 00	14
15	Dec.	17	CS167	Work Jackets	11431	10 500 00			26 705 00		15
16				Work Shoes	11432	9 000 00					16
17				Heat-resistant Gloves	11433	5 000 00					17
18				Fac. O/H Incurred	113	2 205 00					18
19	Dec.	17	CS171	Packing Boxes	110122	2 000 00			2 180 00		19
20				Fac. O/H Incurred	113	180 00					20
21	Dec.	17	INV349	Advertising Expense	5023	5 000 00			5 000 00		21
22	Dec.	17	INV112	Television Expense	5036	240 00			240 00		22
23	Dec.	17	INV32	Fac. O/H Incurred	113	92 868 00			92 868 00		23

CASH PAYMENTS JOURNAL											PAGE 4
	DATE		DOC. NO.	ACCOUNT NAME	POST. REF.	GENERAL		ACCOUNTS PAYABLE DEBIT	BANK DEPOSIT CREDIT	CASH ON HAND CREDIT	
						DEBIT	CREDIT				
1	Dec.	17	INV329	Fac. O/H Incurred	113	6 722 46			6 722 46		1
2	Dec.	17	CS176	ST Bo.-CCB	2011	1 000 000 00			1 017 499 00		2
3				Interest Pay.	207	11 666 00					3
4				Interest Exp.	5037	5 833 00					4
5	Dec.	18	REC723	A&M Training Expense	5032	3 000 00				3 000 00	5
6	Dec.	19	CS178	Fac. O/H Incurred	113	10 000 00			10 000 00		6
7	Dec.	19	CS179	Packing Boxes	110122	2 000 00			2 180 00		7
8				Fac. O/H Incurred	113	180 00					8
9	Dec.	19	CS180	Fac. O/H Incurred	113	2 000 00			2 000 00		9
10	Dec.	21	INV554	Invitation Fee Expense	5035	1 500 00			1 500 00		10
11	Dec.	21	CS183	Refrigeration Oil	110121	20 000 00			21 800 00		11
12				Fac. O/H Incurred	113	1 800 00					12
13	Dec.	22	CS184	Copper Line	110112	70 000 00			79 280 00		13
14				Material Pric. Var.	111	2 000 00					14
15				Fac. O/H Incurred	113	7 280 00					15
16	Dec.	23	CS185	Iron Castings	110113	45 000 00			56 500 00		16
17				Material Pric. Var.	111	5 000 00					17
18				Fac. O/H Incurred	113	6 500 00					18
19	Dec.	23	CS186	Trademark	1181	30 000 00			30 000 00		19
20	Dec.	27	CS189	Fac. O/H Incurred	113	2 000 00			2 000 00		20
21	Dec.	27	INV45	Telephone Expense	5024	8 000 00			8 000 00		21
22	Dec.	28	CS192	Property Tax Pay.	2062	54 090 00			54 090 00		22
23	Dec.	28		Totals					4 971 670 46		23

SALES JOURNAL										PAGE 1
	DATE		SALES SLIP NO.	CUSTOMER'S ACCOUNT DEBITED	POST. REF.	SALES CREDIT	SALES TAX PAYABLE CREDIT	ACCOUNTS RECEIVABLE DEBIT		
1	Dec.	4	68	Fenghua Air-blower–Small Air-blower	√	350 0 0 0 00	31 5 0 0 00	381 5 0 0 00	1	
2	Dec.	9	72	Ningbo Air-blower–Small Air-blower	√	350 0 0 0 00	31 5 0 0 00	381 5 0 0 00	2	
3	Dec.	17	76	Ningbo Air-blower–Large Air-blower	√	800 0 0 0 00	72 0 0 0 00	872 0 0 0 00	3	
4	Dec.	22	80	Fenghua Air-blower–Small Air-blower	√	700 0 0 0 00	63 0 0 0 00	763 0 0 0 00	4	
5	Dec.	28		Totals	√	2 200 0 0 0 00	198 0 0 0 00	2 398 0 0 0 00	5	

PURCHASES JOURNAL													PAGE 1
	DATE		INVOICE NO.	CREDITOR'S ACCOUNT CREDITED	TYPE	POST. REF.	ACCOUNTS PAYABLE CREDIT	PURCHASES DEBIT	GENERAL				
									ACCOUNT DEBITED	POST. REF.	DEBIT		
1	Dec.	7	INV523	Beijing Steel	IC	113	56 5 0 0 00	45 0 0 0 00	Fac. O/H Incurred		6 5 0 0 00	1	
2						111			Material Pric. Var.		5 0 0 0 00	2	
3	Dec.	16	CS166	Beijing Steel	SP	111	174 4 0 0 00	150 0 0 0 00	Material Pric. Var.		10 0 0 0 00	3	
4						113			Fac. O/H Incurred		14 4 0 0 00	4	
5	Dec.	19	INV723	Beijing Steel	IC	113	54 5 0 0 00	45 0 0 0 00	Fac. O/H Incurred		4 5 0 0 00	5	
6						111			Material Pric. Var.		5 0 0 0 00	6	
7	Dec.	27	INV872	Beijing Steel	IC	113	54 5 0 0 00	45 0 0 0 00	Fac. O/H Incurred		4 5 0 0 00	7	
8	Dec.	28		Totals		111	339 9 0 0 00	285 0 0 0 00	Material Pric. Var.		5 0 0 0 00	8	

GENERAL JOURNAL							PAGE 1
	DATE		DESCRIPTION	POST. REF.	DEBIT	CREDIT	
1	Dec.	4	Other Receivables-Fenghua Air-blower	1092	3 0 0 0 00		1
2			Bank Deposit	102		3 0 0 0 00	2
3			Check Stub 34	√			3
4	Dec.	4	Cost of Goods Sold-Small Air-blower	5011	250 0 0 0 00		4
5			Finished Goods-Small Air-blower	11031		250 0 0 0 00	5
6			SALES SLIP 68	√			6
7	Dec.	7	Cost of Goods Sold-Large Air-blower	5012	520 0 0 0 00		7
8			Finished Goods-Large Air-blower	11032		520 0 0 0 00	8
9			SALES SLIP 69	√			9
10	Dec.	7	Cost of Goods Sold-Small Air-blower	5011	250 0 0 0 00		10
11			Finished Goods-Small Air-blower	11031		250 0 0 0 00	11
12			SALES SLIP 70	√			12
13	Dec.	7	Cost of Goods Sold-Large Air-blower	5012	260 0 0 0 00		13
14			Finished Goods-Large Air-blower	11032		260 0 0 0 00	14
15			SALES SLIP 71	√			15
16	Dec.	9	Other Receivables-Ningbo Air-blower	1093	3 0 0 0 00		16
17			Bank Deposit	102		3 0 0 0 00	17
18			Check Stub 48	√			18
19	Dec.	9	Cost of Goods Sold-Small Air-blower	5011	250 0 0 0 00		19
20			Finished Goods-Small Air-blower	11031		250 0 0 0 00	20
21			SALES SLIP 72	√			21
22	Dec.	11	Cost of Goods Sold-Large Air-blower	5012	260 0 0 0 00		22
23			Finished Goods-Large Air-blower	11032		260 0 0 0 00	23
24			SALES SLIP 73	√			24
25	Dec.	11	Bank Deposit	102	10 0 0 0 00		25
26			Loss on Disposal of Lathe	5061	5 0 0 0 00		26
27			Accumulated Depreciation-Lathe	1161	135 0 0 0 00		27
28			Lathe(Old)	1151		150 0 0 0 00	28
29			Memorandum 32 & 33	√			29
30	Dec.	12	Cost of Goods Sold-Small Air-blower	5011	500 0 0 0 00		30

continued

	DATE		DESCRIPTION	POST. REF.	DEBIT	CREDIT	
32			SALES SLIP 74	√			32
33	Dec.	15	Cost of Goods Sold-Large Air-blower	5012	520000 00		33
34			Finished Goods-Large Air-blower	11032		520000 00	34
35			SALES SLIP 75	√			35
36	Dec.	17	Other Receivables-Ningbo Air-blower	1093	2000 00		36
37			Bank Deposit	102		2000 00	37
38			Check Stub 168	√			38
39	Dec.	17	Cost of Goods Sold-Large Air-blower	5012	520000 00		39
40			Finished Goods-Large Air-blower	11032		520000 00	40
41			SALES SLIP 76	√			41
42	Dec.	17	Cost of Goods Sold-Small Air-blower	5011	250000 00		42
43			Finished Goods-Small Air-blower	11031		250000 00	43
44			SALES SLIP 77	√			44
45	Dec.	17	Cost of Goods Sold-Large Air-blower	5012	260000 00		45
46			Finished Goods-Large Air-blower	11032		260000 00	46
47			SALES SLIP 78	√			47
48	Dec.	17	Property Tax Expense	5052	54090 00		48
49			Property Tax Payable	2062		54090 00	49
50			Memorandum 36	√			50
51	Dec.	18	Bank Deposit	102	97875 00		51
52			Discounts on Notes Receivable-Xiangshan Air-blower	105	2125 00		52
53			Notes Receivable-Xiangshan Air-blower	1042		100000 00	53
54			Check Stub 177	√			54
55	Dec.	19	Cost of Goods Sold-Small Air-blower	5011	750000 00		55
56			Finished Goods-Small Air-blower	11031		750000 00	56
57			SALES SLIP 79	√			57
58							
59							
60							

GENERAL JOURNAL							PAGE 2
	DATE		DESCRIPTION	POST. REF.	DEBIT	CREDIT	
1	Dec.	21	Grinder	1159	50000 00		1
2			Capital, Hefeng	301		50000 00	2
3			Memorandum 38	√			3
4	Dec.	22	Cost of Goods Sold–Small Air-blower	5011	500000 00		4
5			Finished Goods–Small Air-blower	11031		500000 00	5
6			SALES SLIP 80	√			6
7	Dec.	23	Steel Plates	110111	75000 00		7
8			Material Price Variance	111	5000 00		8
9			Factory Overhead Incurred	113	9200 00		9
10			Commercial Acceptance Bill Payable	208		89200 00	10
11			Bill 117	√			11
12	Dec.	23	Bank Deposit	102	1500 00		12
13			Cash on Hand	101		1500 00	13
14			Receipt 926	√			14
15	Dec.	27	Cash Lost Expense	5038	50 00		15
16			Cash on Hand	101		50 00	16
17			Memorandum 39	√			17
18	Dec.	27	Cash on Hand	101	50 00		18
19			Cash Lost Expense	5038		50 00	19
20			Memorandum 40	√			20
21	Dec.	28	Cost of Goods Sold–Large Air-blower	5012	520000 00		21
22			Finished Goods–Large Air-blower	11032		520000 00	22
23			SALES SLIP 83	√			23
24	Dec.	28	Work-in-process–Small Air-blower		259875 00		24
25			Material Quantity Variance		2625 000		25
26			Steel Plates			262500 00	26
27			Memorandum 41				27
28			Work-in-process–Large Air-blower		226125 00		28
29			Material Quantity Variance		1875 00		29
30			Steel Plates			228000 00	30

continued

	DATE		DESCRIPTION	POST. REF.	DEBIT	CREDIT	
31			Memorandum 41				31
32			Factory Overhead Incurred		15 0 0 0 00		32
33			Steel Plates			15 0 0 0 00	33
34			Memorandum 41				34
35	Dec.	28	Work-in-process–Small Air-blower		111 3 7 5 00		35
36			Material Quantity Variance		1 1 2 5 00		36
37			Iron Castings			112 5 0 0 00	37
38			Memorandum 41				38
39			Work-in-process–Large Air-blower		111 3 7 5 00		39
40			Material Quantity Variance		2 2 5 00		40
41			Iron Castings			111 6 0 0 00	41
42			Memorandum 41				42
43			Factory Overhead Incurred		22 5 0 0 00		43
44			Iron Castings			22 5 0 0 00	44
45			Memorandum 41				45
46	Dec.	28	Work-in-process–Small Air-blower		173 2 5 0 00		46
47			Material Quantity Variance		1 7 5 0 00		47
48			Copper Line			175 0 0 0 00	48
49			Memorandum 41				49
50			Work-in-process–Large Air-blower		149 6 2 5 00		50
51			Material Quantity Variance		4 3 7 5 00		51
52			Copper Line			154 0 0 0 00	52
53			Memorandum 41				53
54	Dec.	28	Factory Overhead Incurred		30 0 0 0 00		54
55			Refrigeration Oil			30 0 0 0 00	55
56			Memorandum 41				56
57			Factory Overhead Incurred		37 5 0 0 00		57
58			Refrigeration Oil			37 5 0 0 00	58
59			Memorandum 41				59
60							60

GENERAL JOURNAL							PAGE 3
DATE		DESCRIPTION	POST. REF.	DEBIT		CREDIT	
Dec.	28	Factory Overhead Incurred		4000	00		
		Packing Boxes				4000	00
		Memorandum 41					
		Factory Overhead Incurred		3200	00		
		Packing Boxes				3200	00
		Memorandum 41					
Dec.	28	Factory Overhead Incurred		1018	42		
		Work Jackets				1018	42
		Memorandum 41					
		Factory Overhead Incurred		1760	12		
		Work Shoes				1760	12
		Memorandum 41					
		Factory Overhead Incurred		1486	36		
		Heat-resistant Gloves				1486	36
		Memorandum 41					
Dec.	29	Amortization Expense-Patent		2000	00		
		Accum. Amortization-Patent				2000	00
		Memorandum 42					
		Amortization Expense-Trademark		250	00		
		Accum. Amortization-Trademark				250	00
		Memorandum 42					
Dec.	29	Subscription Expense		9600	00		
		Prepaid Subscription				9600	00
		Memorandum 43					
		Insurance Expense		90000	00		
		Prepaid Insurance				90000	00
		Memorandum 43					
Dec.	29	Factory Overhead Incurred		7114	56		
		M&A Broadband Expense		2885	44		
		Prepaid Broadband				10000	00

continued

	DATE		DESCRIPTION	POST. REF.	DEBIT	CREDIT	
31			Memorandum 44				31
32	Dec.	29	Factory Overhead Incurred		87 302 56		32
33			M&A Depreciation Expense		15 984 70		33
34			Plant, Property & Equipment			103 287 26	34
35			Memorandum 45				35
36	Dec.	30	Cost of Goods Sold-Small Air-blower		44 607 84		36
37			Cost of Goods Sold-Large Air-blower		46 392 16		37
38			Material Price Variance			91 000 00	38
39			Memorandum 46				39
40			Cost of Goods Sold-Small Air-blower		5 870 10		40
41			Cost of Goods Sold-Large Air-blower		6 104 90		41
42			Material Quantity Variance			11 975 00	42
43			Memorandum 46				43
44	Dec.	30	Direct Labor		493 050 00		44
45			Labor Efficiency Variance		5 700 00		45
46			Labor Rate Variance		1 002 00		46
47			Factory Overhead Incurred		72 252 00		47
48			Sales Salaries Expense		10 000 00		48
49			M&A Salaries Expense		140 015 00		49
50			Social Security Tax Payable			129 963 42	50
51			Medicare Tax Payable			14 440 38	51
52			FUTP			931 64	52
53			SUTP			6 288 55	53
54			Employee FITP			904 67	54
55			Employee SITP			1 809 33	55
56			Salaries Payable			567 681 01	56
57			Memorandum 47				57
58							58
59							59
60							60

	GENERAL JOURNAL							PAGE 4
	DATE		DESCRIPTION	POST. REF.	DEBIT		CREDIT		
1	Dec.	30	Payroll Tax Expense		177 616	67			1
2			Social Security Tax Payable				129 963	42	2
3			Medicare Tax Payable				14 440	38	3
4			FUTP				4 332	11	4
5			SUTP				28 880	76	5
6			Memorandum 47						6
7	Dec.	30	Work-in-process–Small Air-blower		266 475	00			7
8			Work-in-process–Large Air-blower		226 575	00			8
9			Direct Labor				493 050	00	9
10			Memorandum 47						10
11	Dec.	30	Cost of Goods Sold–Small Air-blower		491	18			11
12			Cost of Goods Sold–Large Air-blower		510	82			12
13			Labor Rate Variance				1 002	00	13
14			Memorandum 47						14
15			Cost of Goods Sold–Small Air-blower		2 794	12			15
16			Cost of Goods Sold–Large Air-blower		2 905	88			16
17			Labor Efficiency Variance				5 700	00	17
18			Memorandum 47						18
19	Dec.	31	Bad Debt Expense		23 980	00			19
20			Allowance for Doubtful Debts				23 980	00	20
21			Memorandum 48						21
22	Dec.	31	Interest Expense		5 184	00			22
23			Interest Payable				5 184	00	23
24			Memorandum 49						24
25	Dec.	31	Work-in-process–Small Air-blower		288 420	00			25
26			Work-in-process–Large Air-blower		242 880	00			26
27			Factory Overhead Applied				531 300	00	27
28			Memorandum 50						28
29	Dec.	31	Cost of Goods Sold–Small Air-blower		34	06			29
30			Cost of Goods Sold–Large Air-blower		35	42			30
31			Factory Overhead				69	48	31
32			Memorandum 51						32
33	Dec.	31	Finished Goods–Small Air-blower		1 161 416	42			33
34			WIP–Small Air-blower				1 161 416	42	34
35			Memorandum 52						35
36	Dec.	31	Finished Goods–Large Air-blower		961 716	37			36
37			WIP–Large Air-blower				961 716	37	37
38			Memorandum 52						38

CHAPTER 4 PREPARE UNADJUSTED TRIAL BALANCE

The third step of accounting cycle is to prepare unadjusted trial balance. The purpose of worksheet unadjusted trial balance is to make sure that all debits equals to all credits before adjusting entries are made. Just as mentioned before, this helps reduce the time that accountants spend in searching for errors and therefore improves the efficiency. This is illustrated in following table.

	Debit	Credit
Cash on Hand	37,000.00	
Bank Deposit	6,093,704.54	
Bank Draft	60,408.00	
Notes Receivable	202,125.00	
Discounts on Notes Receivable		0.00
Accounts Receivable	2,998,000.00	
Allowance for Doubtful Debts		6,000.00
Prepaid Expense	232,100.00	
Other Receivables	13,500.00	
Inventory	1,125,121.00	
Material Price Variance	91,000.00	
Factory Overhead	248,235.46	
Supplies	34,000.00	
Plant, Property & Equipment	12,319,200.00	
Accumulated Depreciation		2,365,000.00
Land	2,600,000.00	
Intangible Assets, Net	530,000.00	
Accumulated Amortization		200,000.00
Short-term Borrowings		2,528,000.00
Notes Payable		110,000.00

continued

	Debit	Credit
Accounts Payable		441,900.00
Unearned Revenue		1,191,570.00
Payroll Liabilities		0.00
Taxes Payable		810,000.00
Interests Payable		2,917.00
Commercial Acceptance Bill Payable		89,200.00
Capital, Hefeng		12,850,000.00
Capital Reserve		550,000.00
Retained Earnings		2,900,000.00
Sales Revenue		8,250,000.00
Other Revenue		3,000.00
Cost of Goods Sold	5,610,000.00	
Selling Expense	30,500.00	
Administrative & Managerial Expense	13,603.00	
Other Expense	0.00	
Taxes Expense	54,090.00	
Loss on Disposal of PP&E	5,000.00	
Total	32,297,587.00	32,297,587.00

CHAPTER 5 PREPARE ADJUSTING ENTRIES AND POST TO THE LEDGER

The fourth step of accounting cycle is to make adjusting journal entries and record those transactions in T-accounts. At this moment, there are no longer two types of journals. Only one journal book should be used, which is General Journal Book. The recording and posting methods are similar to the ones for period transactions. Those entries should also be posted to the ledger. When journal entries are posted to the ledger, post reference should be recorded.

In the following part of this section, adjusting entries will be made for of Xinle Air-blower Co., Ltd. in December. Those adjusting entries will also be recorded in T-accounts book. These will be illustrated in following transaction.

TRANSACTION 89

On December 28, Xinle checked the materials and transfer them to the warehouse, and recorded material variance.

WHAT TO DO?

There is no record for this transaction since most small and medium companies in the United States record material variance when they purchase those materials. Therefore, it is assumed that Xinle does not allow after-purchase recording for material variance.

TRANSACTION 90

On December 28, raw materials had been allocated by accounting department. The source document is MEMORANDUM 41.

Xinle Air-blower Co., Ltd.
23 Tulan ST
Xiangshan, China 315700

MEMORANDUM 41

TO: Accounting Department
FROM: Sean Movasia
DATE: December 28, 2016
SUBJECT: Allocation of Raw Materials

I have made adjusting entries to allocate raw materials.

WHAT TO DO?

For this transaction, three entries should be recorded for the allocation of steel plates. Under the standard costing system, a standard usage rate of each type of materials is pre-set. However, only direct materials have variance account. Variance measurement of indirect materials is not necessary. There are three direct materials. They are steel plates, iron castings and copper line. Refrigeration oil is indirect materials. Each type of materials will be allocated one by one. Steel plates come to the first.

Allocation of Steel Plates

The standard usage rate of steel plates is 3.15kg/small air-blower and 3.35kg/large air-blower. The output of small air-blowers in December was 11,000 units. The output of large air-blowers in December was 9,000 units. The standard unit cost of steel plate is \$7,500/ton. Therefore, the standard deduction of steel plates for small air-blowers should be \$259,875 (3.15×11,000/1,000×7,500). The standard deduction of steel plates for large air-blowers should be \$226,125 (3.35×9,000/1,000×7,500). The actual usage of steel plates for small air-blowers was 35 tons and for large air-blowers was 30.4 tons. Deduction in steel plates for budgeted usage rate should be \$262,500 (35×7,500) for small air-blowers and \$228,000 (30.4×7,500).

There are still 2-ton steel plates used for repair workshop. Since the standard unit cost of steel plates is \$7,500/ton, total cost of those steel plates should be \$15,000.

Step 1 Analyze Transaction

Accounts Affected:

- For the first entry, there are three accounts affected. They are **Work-in-process–Small Air-blower, Material Quantity Variance** and **Steel Plates.**
- For the second entry, there are three accounts affected. They are **Work-in-process–Large Air-blower, Material Quantity Variance** and **Steel Plates.**
- For the third entry, there are two accounts affected. They are **Factory Overhead Incurred** and **Steel Plates.**

Increase/Decrease:

- **Work-in-process–Small Air-blower** is increased by \$259,875. **Material Quantity Variance** is increased by \$2,625. **Steel Plates** is decreased by \$262,500.
- **Work-in-process–Large Air-blower** is increased by \$226,125. **Material Quantity Variance** is increased by \$1,875. Steel Plates is decreased by \$228,000.
- **Factory Overhead Incurred** is increased by \$15,000. **Steel Plates** is decreased by \$15,000.

Account Category:

Work-in-process–Small Air-blower is an asset account.

Work-in-process–Large Air-blower is an asset account.

Material Quantity Variance is a contra-asset account. **Steel Plates** is an asset account.

Step 2 Determine Debit/Credit

–The normal balance of asset accounts is debit. **Work-in-process–Small Air-blower** is debited by $259,875. **Work-in-process–Large Air-blower** is debited by $226,125. **Steel Plates** is credited by $262,500, $228,000 and $15,000.

–The normal balance of contra-asset accounts is credit. **Material Quantity Variance** is debited by $2,625 and $1,875.

–The normal balance of expense accounts is debit. **Factory Overhead Incurred** is debited by $15,000.

Step 3 Record in T-accounts

Work-in-process–Small Air-blower

Debit	Credit
259,875	

Work-in-process–Large Air-blower

Debit	Credit
226,125	

Material Quantity Variance

Debit	Credit
2,625	
1,875	

Steel Plates

Debit	Credit
	262,500
	228,000
	15,000

Factory Overhead Incurred

Debit	Credit
15,000	

Step 4 Record in Journals

GENERAL JOURNAL PAGE 2

	DATE		DESCRIPTION	POST. REF.	DEBIT	CREDIT	
24	Dec.	28	Work-in-process–Small Air-blower		259 875 00		24
25			Material Quantity Variance		2 625 000		25
26			Steel Plates			262 500 00	26
27			*Memorandum 41*				27
28			Work-in-process–Large Air-blower		226 125 00		28
29			Material Quantity Variance		1 875 00		29
30			Steel Plates			228 000 00	30
31			*Memorandum 41*				31
32			Factory Overhead Incurred		15 000 00		32
33			Steel Plates			15 000 00	33
34			*Memorandum 41*				34
35							35

Allocation of Iron Castings

The standard usage rate of iron castings is 2.25kg/small air-blower and 2.75kg/large air-blower. The output of small air-blowers in December was 11,000 units. The output of large air-blowers in December was 9,000 units. The standard unit cost of iron castings is $4,500. Therefore, the standard deduction of iron castings for small air-blowers should be $111,375 (2.25×11,000/1,000×4,500). The standard deduction of iron castings for large air-blowers should be $111,375 (2.75×9,000/1,000×4,500). The actual usage of iron castings for small air-blowers was 25 tons and for large air-blowers was 24.8 tons. Deduction in iron castings for budgeted usage rate should be $112,500 (25×4,500) for small air-blowers and $111,600 (24.8×4,500).

There are still 5-ton iron castings used for repair workshop. Since the standard unit cost of iron castings is $4,500, total cost of those iron castings should be $22,500.

Step 1 Analyze Transaction

Accounts Affected:

- For the first entry, there are three accounts affected. They are **Work-in-process–Small Air-blower, Material Quantity Variance** and **Iron Castings.**
- For the second entry, there are three accounts affected. They are **Work-in-process–Large Air-blower, Material Quantity Variance** and **Iron Castings.**
- For the third entry, there are two accounts affected. They are **Factory Overhead Incurred** and **Iron Castings.**

Increase/Decrease:

- **Work-in-process–Small Air-blower** is increased by $111,375. **Material Quantity Variance** is increased by $1,125. **Iron Castings** is decreased by $112,500.
- **Work-in-process– Large Air-blower** is increased by $111,375. **Material Quantity Variance** is increased by $225. **Iron Castings** is decreased by $111,600.
- **Factory Overhead Incurred** is increased by $22,500. **Iron Castings** is decreased by $22,500.

Account Category:

Work-in-process–Small Air-blower is an asset account.

Work-in-process–Large Air-blower is an asset account.

Material Quantity Variance is a contra-asset account. **Iron Castings** is an asset account. **Factory Overhead Incurred** is an expense account.

Step 2 Determine Debit/Credit

- The normal balance of asset accounts is debit. **Work-in-process–Small Air-blower** is debited by $111,375. **Work-in-process–Large Air-blower** is debited by $111,375. **Iron Castings** is credited by $112,500, $111,600 and $22,500.

–The normal balance of contra-asset accounts is credit. **Material Quantity Variance** is debited by $1,125 and $225.

–The normal balance of expense accounts is debit. **Factory Overhead Incurred** is debited by $22,500

Step 3 Record in T-accounts

Work-in-process–Small Air-blower

Debit	Credit
111,375	

Work-in-process–Large Air-blower

Debit	Credit
111,375	

Material Quantity Variance

Debit	Credit
1,125	
225	

Iron Castings

Debit	Credit
	112,500
	111,600
	22,500

Factory Overhead Incurred

Debit	Credit
22,500	

Step 4 Record in Journals

GENERAL JOURNAL PAGE 2

	DATE		DESCRIPTION	POST. REF.	DEBIT	CREDIT	
35	Dec.	28	Work-in-process–Small Air-blower		111 3 7 500		35
36			Material Quantity Variance		1 1 2 500		36
37			Iron Castings			112 5 0 000	37
38			*Memorandum 41*				38
39			Work-in-process–Large Air-blower		111 3 7 500		39
40			Material Quantity Variance		2 2 500		40
41			Iron Castings			111 6 0 000	41
42			*Memorandum 41*				42
43			Factory Overhead Incurred		22 5 0 000		43
44			Iron Castings			22 5 0 000	44
45			*Memorandum 41*				45
46							46

Allocation of Copper Line

The standard usage rate of copper line is 0.90kg / small air-blower and 0.95kg / large air-blower. The output of small air-blowers in December was 11,000 units. The output of large air-blowers in December was 9, 000 units. The standard unit cost of copper line is $17, 500 / ton. Therefore, the standard deduction of copper line for small air-blowers should be $173,250 (0.90×11,000/1,000×17,500). The standard deduction of copper line for large air-blowers should be $149, 625 (0.95×9,000/1,000×17,500). The actual usage of copper line for small air-blowers was 10 tons and for large air-blowers was 8.8 tons. Deduction in copper line for budgeted usage rate should be $175,000 (10×17,500) for small air-blowers and $154,000 (8.8×17,500).

Step 1 Analyze Transaction

Accounts Affected:

- For the first entry, there are three accounts affected. They are **Work-in-process–Small Air-blower, Material Quantity Variance** and **Copper Line.**
- For the second entry, there are three accounts affected. They are **Work-in-process–Large Air-blower, Material Quantity Variance** and **Copper Line.**

Increase/Decrease:

- **Work-in-process–Small Air-blower** is increased by $173,250. **Material Quantity Variance** is increased by $1,750. **Copper Line** is decreased by $175,000.
- **Work-in-process–Large Air-blower** is increased by $149,625. **Material Quantity Variance** is increased by $4,375. **Copper Line** is decreased by $154,000.

Account Category:

Work-in-process–Small Air-blower is an asset account.

Work-in-process–Large Air-blower is an asset account.

Material Quantity Variance is a contra-asset account. **Copper Line** is an asset account.

Step 2 Determine Debit/Credit

- **The normal balance of asset accounts** is debit. **Work-in-process–Small Air-blower** is debited by $173,250. **Work-in-process–Large Air-blower** is debited by $149,625. **Copper Line** is credited by $175,000 and $154,000.

- The normal balance of contra-asset accounts is credit. **Material Quantity Variance** is debited by $1,750 and $4,375.

Step 3 Record in T-accounts

Work-in-process–Small Air-blower

Debit	Credit
173,250	

Work-in-process–Large Air-blower

Debit	Credit
149,625	

Material Quantity Variance

Debit	Credit
1,750	
4,375	

Copper Line

Debit	Credit
	175,000
	154,000

Step 4 Record in Journals

GENERAL JOURNAL PAGE 2

	DATE		DESCRIPTION	POST. REF.	DEBIT	CREDIT	
46	Dec.	28	Work-in-process–Small Air-blower		173 2 5 000		46
47			Material Quantity Variance		1 7 5 000		47
48			Copper Line			175 0 0 000	48
49			*Memorandum 41*				49
50			Work-in-process–Large Air-blower		149 6 2 500		50
51			Material Quantity Variance		4 3 7 500		51
52			Copper Line			154 0 0 000	52
53			*Memorandum 41*				53
54							54

Allocation of Refrigeration Oil

Since refrigeration oil is indirect material, the allocation of refrigeration oil is different from previous materials. The cost of refrigeration oil is $5,000/ton. The actual usage of refrigeration oil for small air-blowers was 6 tons and for large air-blowers was 7.5 tons. Therefore, the deduction of refrigeration oil for small air-blowers should be $30,000 (6×5,000). The deduction of refrigeration oil for large air-blowers should be $37,500 (7.5×5,000).

Step 1 Analyze Transaction

Accounts Affected:

- For the first entry, there are two accounts affected. They are **Factory Overhead Incurred** and **Refrigeration Oil**.
- For the second entry, there are two accounts affected. They are **Factory Overhead Incurred** and **Refrigeration Oil**.

Increase/Decrease:

- **Factory Overhead Incurred** is increased by $30,000. **Refrigeration Oil** is decreased by $30,000.
- **Factory Overhead Incurred** is increased by $37,500. **Refrigeration Oil** is decreased by $37,500.

Account Category:

Factory Overhead Incurred is an asset account. **Refrigeration Oil** is an asset account.

Step 2 Determine Debit/Credit

- The normal balance of asset accounts is debit. **Factory Overhead Incurred** is debited by $30,000 and $37,500. **Refrigeration Oil** is credited by $30,000 and $37,500.

Step 3 Record in T-accounts

Factory Overhead Incurred

Debit	Credit
30,000	
37,500	

Refrigeration Oil

Debit	Credit
	30,000
	37,500

Step 4 Record in Journals

GENERAL JOURNAL PAGE 2

	DATE		DESCRIPTION	POST. REF.	DEBIT	CREDIT	
54	Dec.	28	Factory Overhead Incurred		30 0 0 000		54
55			Refrigeration Oil			300 0 0 00	55
56			*Memorandum 41*				56
57			Factory Overhead Incurred		37 5 0 000		57
58			Refrigeration Oil			375 0 0 00	58
59			*Memorandum 41*				59
60							60

Allocation of Packing Box

Since packing box is indirect material, the allocation of packing box is different from previous materials. The unit cost of packing box is $40. The actual usage of packing box for small air-blowers was 100 and for large air-blowers was 80. Therefore, the deduction of packing box for small air-blowers should be $4,000 (100×40). The deduction of packing box for large air-blowers should be $3,200 (80×40).

Step 1 Analyze Transaction

Accounts Affected:

–For the first entry, there are two accounts affected. They are **Factory Overhead Incurred** and **Packing Boxes.**

–For the second entry, there are two accounts affected. They are **Factory Overhead Incurred** and **Packing Boxes.**

Increase/Decrease:

–**Factory Overhead Incurred** is increased by $4,000.

Packing Boxes is decreased by $4,000.

–**Factory Overhead Incurred** is increased by $3,200.

Packing Boxes is decreased by $3,200.

Account Category:

Factory Overhead Incurred is an asset account. **Packing Boxes** is an asset account.

Step 2 Determine Debit/Credit

–The normal balance of asset accounts is debit. **Factory Overhead Incurred** is debited by $4,000 and $3,200.

Packing Boxes is credited by $4,000 and $3,200.

Step 3 Record in T-accounts

Factory Overhead Incurred

Debit	Credit
4,000	
3,200	

Packing Boxes

Debit	Credit
	4,000
	3,200

Step 4 Record in Journals

GENERAL JOURNAL PAGE 3

	DATE		DESCRIPTION	POST. REF.	DEBIT	CREDIT	
1	Dec.	28	Factory Overhead Incurred		40 0 0 00		1
2			Packing Boxes			40 0 0 00	2
3			*Memorandum 41*				3
4			Factory Overhead Incurred		32 0 0 00		4
5			Packing Boxes			32 0 0 00	5
6			*Memorandum 41*				6
7							7

Allocation of Work Jackets, Work Shoes and Heat-resistant Gloves

Although items such as work jackets, work shoes and heat-resistant gloves do not belong to raw materials used for production. They are also materials called factory supplies and should also be allocated. Xinle purchased 300 work jackets at the unit price of $35, 300 work shoes at the unit price of $30, and 1,000 heat-resistant gloves at the unit price of $5. However, Xinle had already had those items in the warehouse. The actual usage of those factory supplies was 30 for work jackets, 60 for work shoes and 300 for heat-resistant gloves. Therefore, the deduction should be calculated as following table.

Items	Quantity	Amount	Average Unit Cost (AUC)	Period Cost
Work Jackets	Beg. 80 Add: 300 Total: 380	Beg. 2,400 Add: 10,500 Total: 12,900	12,900/380 =33.94736842	AUC×30 =1,018.42
Work Shoes	Beg. 46 Add: 300 Total: 346	Beg. 1,150 Add: 9,000 Total: 10,150	10,150/346 = 29.33526012	AUC×60 =1,760.12
Heat-resistant Gloves	Beg. 100 Add: 1,000 Total: 1,100	Beg. 450 Add: 5,000 Total: 5,450	5,450/1,100 = 4.954545455	AUC×300 =1,486.36

Step 1 Analyze Transaction

Accounts Affected:

- For the first entry, there are two accounts affected. They are **Factory Overhead Incurred** and **Work Jackets**.
- For the second entry, there are two accounts affected. They are **Factory Overhead Incurred** and **Work Shoes**.
- For the second entry, there are two accounts affected. They are **Factory Overhead Incurred** and **Heat-resistant Gloves**.

Increase/Decrease:

- **Factory Overhead Incurred** is increased by $1,018.42.
  Work Jackets is decreased by $1,018.42.
- **Factory Overhead Incurred** is increased by $1,760.12.
  Work Shoes is decreased by $1,760.12.
- **Factory Overhead Incurred** is increased by $1,486.36.
  Heat-resistant Gloves is decreased by $1,486.36.

Account Category:

Factory Overhead Incurred is an asset account. **Work Jackets** is an asset account. **Work Shoes** is an asset account.

Heat-resistant Gloves is an asset account.

Step 2 Determine Debit/Credit

The normal balance of asset accounts is debit. **Factory Overhead Incurred** is credited by $1,018.42, $1,760.12 and $1,486.36. **Work Jackets** is decreased by $1,018.42. **Work Shoes** is credited by $1,760.12. **Heat-resistant Gloves** is credited by $1,486.36.

Step 3 Record in T-accounts

Factory Overhead Incurred

Debit	Credit
1,018.42	
1,760.12	
1,486.36	

Work Jackets

Debit	Credit
	1,018.42

Work Shoes

Debit	Credit
	1,760.12

Heat-resistant Gloves

Debit	Credit
	1,486.36

Step 4 Record in Journals

GENERAL JOURNAL PAGE 3

	DATE		DESCRIPTION	POST. REF.	DEBIT	CREDIT	
7	Dec.	28	Factory Overhead Incurred		1 0 1 842		7
8			Work Jackets			1 0 1 842	8
9			*Memorandum 41*				9
10			Factory Overhead Incurred		1 7 6 012		10
11			Work Shoes			1 7 6 012	11
12			*Memorandum 41*				12
13			Factory Overhead Incurred		1 4 8 636		13
14			Heat-resistant Gloves			1 4 8 636	14
15			*Memorandum 41*				15
16							16

TRANSACTION 91

On December 29, amortization of intangible assets was recorded. The source document is MEMORANDUM 42. The amortization for patent was $2,000 during December. The amortization for trademark was $250 during December.

Xinle Air-blower Co., Ltd.
23 Tulan ST
Xiangshan, China 315700

MEMORANDUM 42

TO: Accounting Department
FROM: Sam Johvaska
DATE: December 29, 2016
SUBJECT: Amortization of Intangible Assets

I have made adjusting entries to record the amortization of intangible assets.

WHAT TO DO?

Step 1 Analyze Transaction

Accounts Affected:

- For the first entry, there are two accounts affected. They are **Amortization Expense–Patent** and **Accumulated Amortization–Patent**.
- For the second entry, there are two accounts affected. They are **Amortization Expense–Trademark** and **Accumulated Amortization–Trademark**.

Increase/Decrease:

–**Amortization Expense–Patent** is increased by $2,000.
Accumulated Amortization–Patent is decreased by $2,000.
–**Amortization Expense–Trademark** is increased by $250.
Accumulated Amortization–Trademark is decreased by $250.

Account Category:

Amortization Expense–Patent is an expense account.
Accumulated Amortization–Patent is a contra–asset account.
Amortization Expense–Trademark is an expense account.
Accumulated Amortization–Trademark is a contra–asset account.

Step 2 Determine Debit/Credit

–The normal balance of expense accounts is debit.
Amortization Expense–Patent is debited by $2,000.
Amortization Expense–Trademark is credited by $2,000.

–The normal balance of contra–asset accounts is credit.
Accumulated Amortization–Patent is credited by $250.
Accumulated Amortization–Trademark is credited by $250.

Step 3 Record in T-accounts

Amortization Expense–Patent

Debit	Credit
2,000	

Accumulated Amortization–Patent

Debit	Credit
	2,000

Amortization Expense–Trademark

Debit	Credit
250	

Accumulated Amortization–Trademark

Debit	Credit
	250

Step 4 Record in Journals

GENERAL JOURNAL PAGE 3

	DATE		DESCRIPTION	POST. REF.	DEBIT	CREDIT	
16	Dec.	29	Amortization Expense–Patent		2 0 0 0 00		16
17			Accum. Amortization–Patent			2 0 0 0 00	17
18			*Memorandum 42*				18
19			Amortization Expense–Trademark		2 5 0 00		19
20			Accum. Amortization–Trademark			2 5 0 00	20
21			*Memorandum 42*				21
22							22

TRANSACTION 92

On December 29, prepaid subscription and insurance were allocated. The source document is MEMORANDUM 43. The expired subscription was $9, 600 during December. The expired insurance was $90,000 during December.

Xinle Air-blower Co., Ltd. MEMORANDUM 43

23 Tulan ST

Xiangshan, China 315700

TO: Accounting Department

FROM: Sam Johvaska

DATE: December 29, 2016

SUBJECT: Amortization of Intangible Assets

I have made adjusting entries to record the allocation of prepaid subscription and insurance.

WHAT TO DO?

Step 1 Analyze Transaction

Accounts Affected:

–For the first entry, there are two accounts affected. They are **Subscription Expense** and **Prepaid Subscription.**

–For the second entry, there are two accounts affected. They are **Insurance Expense** and **Prepaid Insurance.**

Increase/Decrease:

–**Subscription Expense** is increased by $9,600. **Prepaid Subscription** is decreased by $9,600.

–**Insurance Expense** is increased by $90,000. **Prepaid Insurance** is decreased by $90,000.

Account Category:

Subscription Expense is an expense account. **Prepaid Subscription** is an asset account. **Insurance Expense** is an expense account. **Prepaid Insurance** is an asset account.

Step 2 Determine Debit/Credit

–The normal balance of expense accounts is debit.

Subscription Expense is debited by $9,600. **Insurance Expense** is debited by $90,000.

–The normal balance of asset accounts is debit. **A Prepaid Subscription** is credited by $9,600. **Prepaid Insurance** is credited by $90,000.

Step 3 Record in T-accounts

Subscription Expense

Debit	Credit
9,600	

Prepaid Subscription

Debit	Credit
	9,600

Insurance Expense

Debit	Credit
90,000	

Prepaid Insurance

Debit	Credit
	90,000

Step 4 Record in Journals

GENERAL JOURNAL							PAGE 3
	DATE		DESCRIPTION	POST. REF.	DEBIT	CREDIT	
22	Dec.	29	Subscription Expense		9 6 0 000		22
23			Prepaid Subscription			9 6 0 000	23
24			*Memorandum 43*				24
25			Insurance Expense		90 0 0 000		25
26			Prepaid Insurance			90 0 0 000	26
27			*Memorandum 43*				27
28							28

TRANSACTION 93

On December 29, prepaid broadband were allocated. The source document is MEMORANDUM 44. The expired broadband was $10,000 during December. Within the expired broadband, $2, 885.44 occurred due to production, while the rest $7, 114.56 occurred due to management process.

Xinle Air-blower Co., Ltd. MEMORANDUM 44
23 Tulan ST
Xiangshan, China 315700

TO: Accounting Department
FROM: Sam Johvaska
DATE: December 29, 2016
SUBJECT: Amortization of Prepaid Broadband

I have made adjusting entries to record the allocation of prepaid broadband.

WHAT TO DO?

Step 1 Analyze Transaction

Accounts Affected:

There are three accounts affected by this transaction. They are **Factory Overhead Incurred**, **M&A Broadband Expense** and **Prepaid Broadband**.

Increase/Decrease:

Factory Overhead Incurred is increased by $7,114.56. **M&A Broadband Expense** is increased by $2,885.44. **Prepaid Broadband** is decreased by $10,000.

Account Category:

Factory Overhead Incurred is an asset account. **M&A Broadband Expense** is an expense account. **Prepaid Broadband** is an asset account.

Step 2 Determine Debit/Credit

–The normal balance of asset accounts is debit. **Factory Overhead Incurred** is debited by $7,114.56. **Prepaid Broadband** is credited by $10,000.

–The normal balance of expense accounts is debit.
Broadband Expense is debited by $2,885.44.

Step 3 Record in T-accounts

Factory Overhead Incurred

Debit	Credit
7,114.56	

M&A Broadband Expense

Debit	Credit
2,885.44	

Prepaid Broadband

Debit	Credit
	10,000

Step 4 Record in Journals

GENERAL JOURNAL PAGE 3

	DATE		DESCRIPTION	POST. REF.	DEBIT	CREDIT	
28	Dec.	29	Factory Overhead Incurred		71 1 4 56		28
29			M&A Broadband Expense		28 8 5 44		29
30			Prepaid Broadband			100 0 0 00	30
31			*Memorandum 44*				31
32							32

TRANSACTION 94

On December 29, depreciation of Plant, Property & Equipment was recorded. The source document is MEMORANDUM 45. The amount was $103,287.26. Within the monthly depreciation, $15,984.70 occurred due to management process. The rest $87,302.56 occurred due to production.

Xinle Air-blower Co., Ltd. MEMORANDUM 45

23 Tulan ST
Xiangshan, China 315700

TO: Accounting Department
FROM: Sam Johvaska
DATE: December 29, 2016
SUBJECT: Depreciation of PP&E

I have made adjusting entries to record the depreciation of Plant, Property & Equipment.

WHAT TO DO?

Step 1 Analyze Transaction

Accounts Affected:

There are three accounts affected by this transaction. They are **Factory Overhead Incurred**, **M&A Depreciation Expense** and **Accumulated Depreciation**.

Increase/Decrease:

Factory Overhead Incurred is increased by \$87, 302.56. **M&A Depreciation Expense** is increased by \$15,984.70.

Accumulated Depreciation is decreased by \$103,287.26.

Account Category:

Factory Overhead Incurred is an asset account. **M&A Depreciation Expense** is an expense account. **Accumulated Depreciation** is a contra-asset account.

Step 2 Determine Debit/Credit

-The normal balance of asset accounts is debit. **Factory Overhead Incurred** is debited by \$87,302.56.

-The normal balance of expense accounts is debit. **M&A Depreciation Expense** is debited by \$15,984.70.

-The normal balance of contra-asset accounts is credit. **Accumulated Depreciation** is credited by \$103,287.26.

Step 3 Record in T-accounts

Factory Overhead Incurred

Debit	Credit
87,302.56	

M&A Depreciation Expense

Debit	Credit
15,984.70	

Accumulated Depreciation

Debit	Credit
	103,287.26

Step 4 Record in Journals

GENERAL JOURNAL PAGE 3

	DATE		DESCRIPTION	POST. REF.	DEBIT	CREDIT	
32	Dec.	29	Factory Overhead Incurred		87 3 0 256		32
33			M&A Depreciation Expense		15 9 8 470		33
34			Accumulated Depreciation			103 2 8 726	34
35			*Memorandum 45*				35
36							36

TRANSACTION 95

On December 30, material variance was allocated. The source document is MEMORANDUM 46.

Xinle Air-blower Co., Ltd. MEMORANDUM 46
23 Tulan ST
Xiangshan, China 315700

TO: Accounting Department
FROM: Sam Johvaska
DATE: December 30, 2016
SUBJECT: Allocation of Material Variance

I have made adjusting entries to record the allocation of material variance.

WHAT TO DO?

There are two types of material variance accounts. They are Material Price Variance and Material Quantity Variance. The current balance of Material Price Variance is $91, 000. The current balance of Material Price Variance is $91,000. The current balance of Material Quantity Variance is $11,975. In the United States, the amount of material variance is usually not very big for small and medium companies, and therefore the material variance is directly debited to Cost of Goods Sold. The allocation between small air-blowers and large air-blowers are decided by the balance of those two accounts.

Item	Balance	Percentage	Allocation of Material Price Variance
Small Air-blower	2,750,000	49.0196078%	44,607.84
Large Air-blower	2,860,000	50.9803922%	46,392.16
Total	5,610,000	100%	91,000.00

Item	Balance	Percentage	Allocation of Material Quantity Variance
Small Air-blower	2,750,000	49.0196078%	5,870.10
Large Air-blower	2,860,000	50.9803922%	6,104.90
Total	5,610,000	100%	11,975.00

Step 1 Analyze Transaction

Accounts Affected:

- For the first entry, there are three accounts affected. They are **Cost of Goods Sold–Small Air-blower, Cost of Goods Sold–Large Air-blower** and **Material Price Variance.**
- For the second entry, there are three accounts affected. They are **Cost of Goods Sold–Small Air-blower, Cost of Goods Sold–Large Air-blower** and **Material Quantity Variance.**

Increase/Decrease:

- **Cost of Goods Sold–Small Air-blower** is increased by $44,607.84. **Cost of Goods Sold–Large Air-blower** is increased by $46,392.16. **Material Price Variance** is decreased by $91,000.
- **Cost of Goods Sold–Small Air-blower** is increased by $5,870.10. **Cost of Goods Sold–Large Air-blower** is increased by $6, 104.90. **Material Quantity Variance** is decreased by $11,975.00.

Account Category:

Cost of Goods Sold–Small Air-blower is an expense account.

Cost of Goods Sold–Large Air-blower is an expense account.

Material Price Variance is an asset account. **Material Quantity Variance** is an asset account.

Step 2 Determine Debit/Credit

– The normal balance of expense accounts is debit. **Cost of Goods Sold–Small Air-blower** is debited by $44,607.84 and $5,870.10. **Cost of Goods Sold–Large Air-blower** is debited by $46,392.16 and $6,104.90.

– The normal balance of asset accounts is debit. **Material Price Variance** is credited by $91,000. **Material Quantity Variance** is credited by $11,975.00.

Step 3 Record in T-accounts

Cost of Goods Sold–Small Air-blower

Debit	Credit
44,607.84	
5,870.10	

Cost of Goods Sold–Large Air-blower

Debit	Credit
46,392.16	
6,104.90	

Material Price Variance

Debit	Credit
	91,000

Material Quantity Variance

Debit	Credit
	11,975

Step 4 Record in Journals

GENERAL JOURNAL PAGE 3

	DATE		DESCRIPTION	POST. REF.	DEBIT	CREDIT	
36	Dec.	30	COGS–Small Air-blower		44 6 0 784		36
37			COGS–Large Air-blower		46 3 9 216		37
38			Material Price Variance			91 0 0 000	38
39			*Memorandum 46*				39
40			COGS–Small Air-blower		5 8 7 010		40
41			COGS–Large Air-blower		6 1 0 490		41
42			Material Quantity Variance			11 9 7 500	42
43			*Memorandum 46*				43
44							44

TRANSACTION 96 & 97

On December 30, Xinle recorded payroll for December. On December 30, Xinle recorded insurance and welfare of employees. The source document is MEMORANDUM 47.

MEMORANDUM 47

Xinle Air-blower Co., Ltd.
23 Tulan ST
Xiangshan, China 315700

TO: Accounting Department
FROM: Sam Johvaska
DATE: December 30, 2016
SUBJECT: Employee Payroll

I have made adjusting entries to record employee payroll.

WHAT TO DO?

Just as mentioned before, employee payroll tax system in China is different from that in the United States, and therefore those employee payroll taxes should be adjusted to satisfy tax system in the United States. Xinle's payroll can be divided into three parts. They are manufacturing part, selling part and management part. The salaries payable for manufacturing part is $572,004. The salaries payable for selling part is $10,000. The salaries payable for management part is $140,015. Those can be described in following tables.

Employee Payroll–Production

Accounts	Amount	Adaption
Housing fund fee	$57,209.4	Social Security Tax Payable: $102,969.72
Pension fee	45,760.32	
Medical insurance fee	11,440.08	Medicare Tax Payable: $11,440.08
Unemployment insurance fee	5,720.04	–Federal Unemployment Tax Payable: $738.07 –State Unemployment Tax Payable: $4,981.97
Employee Income Tax	590	–Employee Federal Income Tax Payable: $196.67 –Employee State Income Tax Payable: $393.33

Employee Payroll–Selling

Accounts	Amount	Adaption
Housing fund fee	$1,000	Social Security Tax Payable: $1,800
Pension fee	800	
Medical insurance fee	200	Medicare Tax Payable: $200
Unemployment insurance fee	100	–Federal Unemployment Tax Payable: $12.90 –State Unemployment Tax Payable: $87.10
Employee Income Tax		–Employee Federal Income Tax Payable: $0 –Employee State Income Tax Payable: $0

Employee Payroll–Management		
Accounts	Amount	Adaption
Housing fund fee	$14,001.5	Social Security Tax Payable:
Pension fee	11,201.2	$25,202.70
Medical insurance fee	2,800.3	Medicare Tax Payable: $2,800.3
Unemployment insurance fee	1,400.15	–Federal Unemployment Tax Payable: $180.66 –State Unemployment Tax Payable: $1,219.49
Employee Income Tax	2,124	–Employee Federal Income Tax Payable: $708 –Employee State Income Tax Payable: $1,416

The standard rate of direct labor is $9.5/hr. The standard hour of direct labor for small air-blower is 2.55 hours and for large air-blower is 2.65 hours. The actual output of small air-blowers in December was 11,000 units. The output of large air-blowers in December was 9,000 units. Therefore, the standard increase of direct labor for small air-blowers should be $266,475 (2.55×9.5×11,000). The standard increase of direct labor for large air-blowers should be $226,575 (2.65×9.5×9,000). Total standard cost is $493,050. The total actual hour of direct labor for small air-blower is 28,500 hours and for large air-blower is 24,000 hours. The mixed increase of direct labor for small air-blowers should be $270,750 (9.5×28,500). The standard increase of direct labor for large air-blowers should be $228,000 (9.5×24,000). Total standard cost is $498,750. Therefore, Labor Efficiency Variance is $5,700. Labor Rate Variance is $1,002.

Step 1 Analyze Transaction

Accounts Affected:

There are ten accounts affected by this transaction. They are **Direct Labor, Labor Efficiency Variance, Labor Rate Variance, Factory Overhead Incurred, Sales Salaries Expense, M&A Salaries Expense, Social Security Tax Payable, Medicare Tax Payable, Federal Unemployment Tax Payable, State Unemployment Tax Payable, Employee Federal Income Tax Payable, Employee State Income Tax Payable** and **Salaries Payable.**

Increase/Decrease:

Direct Labor is increased by $493,050. **Labor Efficiency Variance** is increased by $5,700. **Labor Rate Variance** is increased by $1,002. **Factory Overhead Incurred** is increased by $72,252. **Sales Salaries Expense** is increased by $10,000. **M&A Salaries Expense** is increased by $140,015. **Social Security Tax Payable** is increased by $ 129,963.42. **Medicare Tax Payable** is increased by $14, 440.38. **Federal Unemployment Tax Payable** is increased by $931.64. **State Unemployment Tax Payable** is increased by $6,288.55. **Employee Federal Income Tax Payable** is increased by $904.67. **Employee State Income Tax Payable** is increased by $1,809.33. **Salaries Payable** is increased by $567,681.01.

Account Category:

Direct Labor is an asset account. **Labor Efficiency Variance** is an asset account. **Labor Rate Variance** is an asset account. **Factory Overhead Incurred** is an asset account. **Sales Salaries Expense** is an expense account. **M&A Salaries Expense** is an expense account. **Social Security Tax Payable** is a liability account. **Medicare Tax Payable** is a liability account. **Federal Unemployment Tax Payable** is a liability account. **State Unemployment Tax Payable** is a liability account. **Employee Federal Income Tax Payable** is a liability account. **Employee State Income Tax Payable** is a liability account. **Salaries Payable** is a liability account.

Step 2 Determine Debit/Credit

–The normal balance of asset accounts is debit. **Direct Labor** is debited by $493,050. **Labor Efficiency Variance** is debited by $5,700. **Labor Rate Variance** is debited by $1,002. **Factory Overhead Incurred** is debited by $72,252.

–The normal balance of expense accounts is debit. **Sales Salaries Expense** is debited by $10,000. **M&A Salaries Expense** is debited by $140,015.

–The normal balance of liability accounts is credit. **Social Security Tax Payable** is credited by $129,963.42. **Medicare Tax Payable** is credited by $14,440.38. **Federal Unemployment Tax Payable** is credited by $931.64. **State Unemployment Tax Payable** is credited by $6,288.55. **Employee Federal Income Tax Payable** is credited by $904.67. **Employee State Income Tax Payable** is credited by $1,809.33. **Salaries Payable** is credited by $567,681.01.

Step 3 Record in T-accounts

Direct Labor

Debit	Credit
493,050	

Labor Efficiency Variance

Debit	Credit
5,700	

Labor Rate Variance

Debit	Credit
1,002	

Factory Overhead Incurred

Debit	Credit
72,252	

Sales Salaries Expense

Debit	Credit
10,000	

M&A Salaries Expense

Debit	Credit
140,015	

Social Security Tax Payable

Debit	Credit
	129,963.42

Medicare Tax Payable

Debit	Credit
	14,440.38

Federal Unemployment Tax Payable

Debit	Credit
	931.64

State Unemployment Tax Payable

Debit	Credit
	6,288.55

Employee Federal Income Tax Payable

Debit	Credit
	904.67

Employee State Income Tax Payable

Debit	Credit
	1,809.33

Salaries Payable

Debit	Credit
	567,681.01

Step 4 Record in Journals

GENERAL JOURNAL PAGE 3

	DATE		DESCRIPTION	POST. REF.	DEBIT	CREDIT	
44	Dec.	30	Direct Labor		493 0 5 000		44
45			Labor Efficiency Variance		5 7 0 000		45
46			Labor Rate Variance		1 0 0 200		46
47			Factory Overhead Incurred		72 2 5 200		47
48			Sales Salaries Expense		10 0 0 000		48
49			M&A Salaries Expense		140 0 1 500		49
50			Social Security Tax Payable			129 9 6 342	50
51			Medicare Tax Payable			14 4 4 038	51
52			FUTP			9 3 164	52
53			SUTP			6 2 8 855	53
54			Employee FITP			9 0 467	54
55			Employee SITP			1 8 0 933	55
56			Salaries Payable			567 6 8 101	56
57			*Memorandum 47*				57
58							58

Besides employee side, employer should also pay for part of the payroll taxes. This can be illustrated in following table. Social Security Tax and Medicare Tax are just the same as employee side. Federal Unemployment Tax is approximately 0.6% of total payroll liabilities, while State Unemployment Tax Payable is approximately 4% of total payroll liabilities.

Item	Amount
Social Security Tax	129,963.42
Medicare Tax	14,440.38
Federal Unemployment Tax Payable	4,332.11
State Unemployment Tax Payable	28,880.76

Step 1 Analyze Transaction

Accounts Affected:

There are five accounts affected by this transaction. They are **Payroll Tax Expense, Social Security Tax Payable, Medicare Tax Payable, Federal Unemployment Tax Payable** and **State Unemployment Tax Payable.**

Increase/Decrease:

Payroll Tax Expense is increased by $177,616.67. **Social Security Tax Payable** is increased by $129,963.42. **Medicare Tax Payable** is increased by $14,440.38. **Federal Unemployment Tax Payable** is increased by $4,332.11. **State Unemployment Tax Payable** is increased by $28,880.76.

Account Category:

Payroll Tax Expense is an expense account. **Social Security Tax Payable** is a liability account. **Medicare Tax Payable** is a liability account. **Federal Unemployment Tax Payable** is a liability account. **State Unemployment Tax Payable** is a liability account.

Step 2 Determine Debit/Credit

-The normal balance of expense accounts is debit. **Payroll Tax Expense** is debited by $177,616.67.

-The normal balance of liability accounts is credit. **Social Security Tax Payable** is credited by $129,963.42. **Medicare Tax Payable** is credited by $14,440.38. **Federal Unemployment Tax Payable** is credited by $4,332.11. **State Unemployment Tax Payable** is credited by $28,880.76.

Step 3 Record in T-accounts

Payroll Tax Expense

Debit	Credit
177,616.67	

Social Security Tax Payable

Debit	Credit
	129,963.42

Medicare Tax Payable

Debit	Credit
	14,440.38

Federal Unemployment Tax Payable

Debit	Credit
	4,332.11

State Unemployment Tax Payable

Debit	Credit
	28,880.76

Step 4 Record in Journals

GENERAL JOURNAL PAGE 4

	DATE		DESCRIPTION	POST. REF.	DEBIT	CREDIT	
1	Dec.	30	Payroll Tax Expense		177 6 1 667		1
2			Social Security Tax Payable			129 9 6 342	2
3			Medicare Tax Payable			14 4 4 038	3
4			Federal Unemployment Tax Dayable			4 3 3 211	4
5			State Unemployment Tax Payable			28 8 8 076	5
6			*Memorandum 47*				6
7							7

Besides, Direct Labor is assigned to Work-in-process–Small Air-blower and Work-in-process–Large Air-blower.

Step 1 Analyze Transaction

Accounts Affected:

There are three accounts affected by this transaction. They are **Work-in-process–Small Air-blower, Work-in-process–Large Air-blower and Direct Labor.**

Increase/Decrease:

Work-in-process–Small Air-blower is increased by $266,475.

Work-in-process–Large Air-blower is increased by $226,575.

Direct Labor is decreased by $493,050.

Account Category:

Work-in-process–Small Air-blower is an asset account.

Work-in-process–Large Air-blower is an asset account. **Direct Labor** is an asset account.

Step 2 Determine Debit/Credit

–The normal balance of asset accounts is debit.

Work-in-process–Small Air-blower is debited by $266,475.

Work-in-process–Large Air-blower is debited by $226,575.

Direct Labor is credited by $493,050.

Step 3 Record in T-accounts

Work-in-process–Small Air-blower

Debit	Credit
266,475	

Work-in-process–Large Air-blower

Debit	Credit
226,575	

Direct Labor

Debit	Credit
	493,050

Step 4 Record in Journals

GENERAL JOURNAL PAGE 4

	DATE		DESCRIPTION	POST. REF.	DEBIT	CREDIT	
7	Dec.	30	Work-in-process–Small Air-blower		266 4 7 500		7
8			Work-in-process–Large Air-blower		226 5 7 500		8
9			Direct Labor			493 0 5 000	9
10			*Memorandum 47*				10
11							11

Labor variance should be allocated. There are two types of labor variance accounts. They are Labor Rate Variance and Labor Efficiency Variance. The current balance of Labor Rate Variance is $1,002. The current balance of Labor Efficiency Variance is $5,700. In the United States, the amount of labor variance is usually not very big for small and medium companies, and therefore the material variance is directly debited to Cost of Goods Sold. The allocation between small air-blowers and large air-blowers are decided by the balance of those two accounts.

Item	Balance	Percentage	Allocation of Labor Rate Variance
Small Air-blower	2,750,000	49.0196078%	491.18
Large Air-blower	2,860,000	50.9803922%	510.82
Total	5,610,000	100%	1,002

Item	Balance	Percentage	Allocation of Labor Efficiency Variance
Small Air-blower	2,750,000	49.0196078%	2,794.12
Large Air-blower	2,860,000	50.9803922%	2,905.88
Total	5,610,000	100%	5,700

Step 1 Analyze Transaction

Accounts Affected:

-For the first entry, there are three accounts affected. They are **Cost of Goods Sold–Small Air-blower, Cost of Goods Sold–Large Air-blower** and **Labor Rate Variance**.

-For the second entry, there are three accounts affected. They are **Cost of Goods Sold–Small Air-blower, Cost of Goods Sold–Large Air-blower** and **Labor Efficiency Variance**.

Increase/Decrease:

-**Cost of Goods Sold–Small Air-blower** is increased by $491.18. **Cost of Goods Sold–Large Air-blower** is increased by $510.82. **Labor Rate Variance** is decreased by $1,002.

-**Cost of Goods Sold–Small Air-blower** is increased by $2,794.12. **Cost of Goods Sold–Large Air-blower** is increased by $2,905.88. **Labor Efficiency Variance** is decreased by $5,700.

Account Category:

Cost of Goods Sold–Small Air-blower is an expense account. **Cost of Goods Sold–Large Air-blower** is an expense account. **Labor Rate Variance** is an asset account. **Labor Efficiency Variance** is an asset account.

Step 2 Determine Debit/Credit

-The normal balance of expense accounts is debit. **Cost of Goods Sold–Small Air-blower** is debited by $491.18 and $2,794.12. **Cost of Goods Sold–Large Air-blower** is debited by $510.82 and $2,905.88.

-The normal balance of asset accounts is debit. **Labor Rate Variance** is credited by $1,002. **Labor Efficiency Variance** is credited by $5,700.

Step 3 Record in T-accounts

Cost of Goods Sold–Small Air-blower

Debit	Credit
491.18	
2,794.12	

Cost of Goods Sold–Large Air-blower

Debit	Credit
510.82	
2,905.88	

Labor Rate Variance

Debit	Credit
	1,002

Labor Efficiency Variance

Debit	Credit
	5,700

Step 4 Record in Journals

GENERAL JOURNAL							PAGE 4
	DATE		DESCRIPTION	POST. REF.	DEBIT	CREDIT	
11	Dec.	30	Cost of Goods Sold–Small Air-blower		4 9 118		11
12			Cost of Goods Sold–Large Air-blower		5 1 082		12
13			Labor Rate Variance			1 0 0 200	13
14			*Memorandum 47*				14
15			Cost of Goods Sold–Small Air-blower		2 7 9 412		15
16			Cost of Goods Sold–Large Air-blower		2 9 0 588		16
17			Labor Efficiency Variance			5 7 0 000	17
18			*Memorandum 47*				18
19							19

TRANSACTION 98

On December 31, bad debt was recorded. The source document is MEMORANDUM 48. The balance of Accounts Receivable was $2,998,000. Total bad debt should be $29,980. The balance of Allowance for Doubtful Debts is $6,000. The rest amount is $23,980.

Xinle Air-blower Co., Ltd. MEMORANDUM 48
23 Tulan ST
Xiangshan, China 315700

TO: Accounting Department
FROM: Sam Johvaska
DATE: December 31, 2016
SUBJECT: Bad Debt

I have made adjusting entries to record the bad debt at the rate of 1%.

WHAT TO DO?

Step 1 Analyze Transaction

Accounts Affected:

There are three accounts affected by this transaction. They are **Bad Debt Expense** and **Allowance for Doubtful Debts**.

Increase/Decrease:

Bad Debt Expense is increased by \$23,980. **Allowance for Doubtful Debts** is increased by \$23,980.

Account Category:

Bad Debt Expense is an expense account. **Allowance for Doubtful Debts** is a contra-asset account.

Step 2 Determine Debit/Credit

–The normal balance of expense accounts is debit. **Bad Debt Expense** is debited by \$23,980.

–The normal balance of contra-asset accounts is credit. **Allowance for Doubtful Debts** is credited by \$23,980.

Step 3 Record in T-accounts

Bad Debt Expense	
Debit	Credit
23,980	

Allowance for Doubtful Debts	
Debit	Credit
	23,980

Step 4 Record in Journals

GENERAL JOURNAL PAGE 4

	DATE		DESCRIPTION	POST. REF.	DEBIT	CREDIT	
19	Dec.	31	Bad Debt Expense		23 9 8 000		19
20			Allowance for Doubtful Debts			23 9 8 000	20
21			*Memorandum 48*				21
22							22

TRANSACTION 99

On December 31, interests were recorded. The source document is MEMORANDUM 49.

There are two short-term borrowings. One was borrowed from China Construction Bank. The other was borrowed from Bank of China. The interest rate was 6.57%.

Xinle Air-blower Co., Ltd. MEMORANDUM 49

23 Tulan ST

Xiangshan, China 315700

TO: Accounting Department

FROM: Sam Johvaska

DATE: December 31, 2016

SUBJECT: Accrual Interests

I have made adjusting entries to record the accrual interests

WHAT TO DO?

Step 1 Analyze Transaction

Accounts Affected:

There are three accounts affected by this transaction. They are **Interest Expense and Interest Payable.**

Increase/Decrease:

Interest Expense is increased by $5,184. **Interest Payable** is increased by $5,184.

Account Category:

Interest Expense is an expense account. **Interest Payable** is a liability account.

Step 2 Determine Debit/Credit

–The normal balance of expense accounts is debit. **Interest Payable Expense** is debited by $5,184.

–The normal balance of liability accounts is credit. **Interest Payable** is credited by $5,184.

Step 3 Record in T-accounts

Interest Expense	
Debit	Credit
5,184	

Interest Payable	
Debit	Credit
	5,184

Step 4 Record in Journals

GENERAL JOURNAL						PAGE 4
	DATE	DESCRIPTION	POST. REF.	DEBIT	CREDIT	
22	Dec. 31	Interest Expense		5 1 8 400		22
23		Interest Payable			5 1 8 400	23
24		*Memorandum 49*				24
25						25

TRANSACTION 100

On December 31, factory overhead was applied to Auxiliary Workshop. The source document is MEMORANDUM 50.

Xinle Air-blower Co., Ltd. MEMORANDUM 50

23 Tulan ST

Xiangshan, China 315700

TO: Accounting Department

FROM: Sam Johvaska

DATE: December 31, 2016

SUBJECT: Application of Overhead

I have made adjusting entries to apply factory overhead.

WHAT TO DO?

In the United States, most small and medium companies apply their overhead cost by products. In other words, the factory overhead should be divided into two accounts. They are Work-in-process–Small Air-blower and Work-in-process–Large Air-blower. Those overhead will not be applied only to Auxiliary Workshop. Instead, overhead cost is applied to all workshops. The predetermined overhead rate is $10.12/direct labor hour. In the United States, this rate is set at the beginning of the year. The direct labor hour is 28,500 for small air-blowers and 24,000 for large air-blowers. Therefore, the total overhead applied to small air-blowers should be $288,420 and to large air-blowers should be $242,880. Total overhead applied should be $531,300.

Step 1 Analyze Transaction

Accounts Affected:

There are three accounts affected by this transaction. They are **Work-in-process–Small Air-blower, Work-in-process–Large Air-blower** and **Factory Overhead Applied.**

Increase/Decrease:

Work-in-process–Small Air-blower is increased by $288,420.

Work-in-process–Large Air-blower is increased by $242,880.

Factory Overhead Applied is increased by $531,300.

Account Category:

Work-in-process–Small Air-blower is an asset account.

Work-in-process–Large Air-blower is an asset account.

Factory Overhead Applied is a contra-asset account.

Step 2 Determine Debit/Credit

–The normal balance of asset accounts is debit.

Work-in-process–Small Air-blower is debited by $288,420.

Work-in-process–Large Air-blower is debited by $242,880.

–The normal balance of contra-asset accounts is credit.

Factory Overhead Applied is credited by $531,300.

Step 3 Record in T-accounts

Work-in-process–Small Air-blower

Debit	Credit
288,420	

Work-in-process–Large Air-blower

Debit	Credit
242,880	

Factory Overhead Applied

Debit	Credit
	531,300

Step 4 Record in Journals

GENERAL JOURNAL PAGE 4

	DATE		DESCRIPTION	POST. REF.	DEBIT	CREDIT	
25	Dec.	31	Work-in-process–Small Air-blower		288 4 2 000		25
26			Work-in-process–Large Air-blower		242 8 8 000		26
27			Factory Overhead Applied			531 3 0 000	27
28			*Memorandum 50*				28
29							29

TRANSACTION 101

On December 31, taxes on purchased of non-taxable items were transferred.

WHAT TO DO?

There is no record for this transaction since taxes on purchases are recorded as part of the cost of the assets or as overhead cost. Therefore, it is assumed that Xinle does not allow taxes on purchase to be measured in a separate account.

TRANSACTION 102

On December 31, factory overhead was applied to major workshops. The source document is MEMORANDUM 51. There is no record for this transaction since factory overhead had already been applied to all the workshops. However, this is an additional step necessary to complete the cycle. This step is not listed in the transactions.

Xinle Air-blower Co., Ltd. MEMORANDUM 51

23 Tulan ST

Xiangshan, China 315700

TO: Accounting Department

FROM: Sam Johvaska

DATE: December 31, 2016

SUBJECT: Overhead Difference

I have made adjusting entries to deal with the variance of overhead.

WHAT TO DO?

The difference between Factory Overhead Incurred and Factory Overhead Applied should be calculated and be transferred to Cost of Goods Sold. Based on previous transactions, the balance of Factory Overhead Incurred is $531,369.48. The balance of Factory Overhead Applied is $531,300. Therefore, the difference is $69.48.

Item	Balance	Percentage	Allocation of Material Price Variance
Small Air-blower	2,750,000	49.0196078%	34.06
Large Air-blower	2,860,000	50.9803922%	35.42
Total	5,610,000	100%	69.48

Step 1 Analyze Transaction

Accounts Affected:

There are three accounts affected by this transaction. They are **Cost of Goods Sold-Small Air-blower, Cost of Goods Sold-Large Air-blower** and **Factory Overhead.**

Increase/Decrease:

Cost of Goods Sold-Small Air-blower is increased by $34.06.

Cost of Goods Sold-Large Air-blower is increased by $35.42.

Factory Overhead is decreased by $69.48.

Account Category:

Cost of Goods Sold-Small Air-blower is an expense account.

Cost of Goods Sold-Large Air-blower is an expense account.

Factory Overhead is an asset account.

Step 2 Determine Debit/Credit

-The normal balance of asset accounts is debit. **Cost of Goods Sold-Small Air-blower** is debited by $34.06. **Cost of Goods Sold-Large Air-blower** is debited by $35.42.

-The normal balance of asset accounts is credit. **Factory Overhead** is credited by $69.48.

Step 3 Record in T-accounts

Cost of Goods Sold-Small Air-blower

Debit	Credit
34.06	

Cost of Goods Sold-Large Air-blower

Debit	Credit
35.42	

Factory Overhead

Debit	Credit
	69.48

Step 4 Record in Journals

GENERAL JOURNAL PAGE 4

	DATE		DESCRIPTION	POST. REF.	DEBIT	CREDIT	
29	Dec.	31	Cost of Goods Sold-Small Air-blower		3 406		29
30			Cost of Goods Sold-Large Air-blower		3 542		30
31			Factory Overhead			6 948	31
32			*Memorandum 51*				32
33							33

TRANSACTION 103

On December 31, products are moved to the warehouse. The source document is MEMORANDUM 52. The amount of transfer-in to finished goods is $1,161,416.42 for small air-blower and $961,716.37 for large air-blower.

Xinle Air-blower Co., Ltd.
23 Tulan ST
Xiangshan, China 315700

MEMORANDUM 52

TO: Warehouse
FROM: John Thompson
DATE: December 31, 2016
SUBJECT: Transfer finished goods to warehouse

I have ordered to transfer 11,000 small air-blowers and 9,000 large air-blowers to warehouse.

WHAT TO DO?

Step 1 Analyze Transaction

Accounts Affected:

There are two accounts affected by transactions. They are **Finished Goods–Small Air-blower and Work-in-process–Small Air-blower.**

Increase/Decrease:

Finished Goods–Small Air-blower is increased by $1,161,416.42. **Work-in-process–Small Air-blower** is increased by $1,161,416.42.

Account Category:

Finished Goods–Small Air-blower is an asset account.

Work-in-process–Small Air-blower is an asset account.

Step 2 Determine Debit/Credit

–The normal balance of asset accounts is debit. **Finished Goods–Small Air-blower** is debited by $1,161,416.42.

–The normal balance of asset accounts is debit. **Work-in-process–Small Air-blower** is credited by $1,161,416.42.

Step 3 Record in T-accounts

Finished Goods–Small Air-blower	
Debit	Credit
1,161,416.42	

Work-in-process–Small Air-blower	
Debit	Credit
	1,161,416.42

Step 4 Record in Journals

GENERAL JOURNAL						PAGE 4	
	DATE		DESCRIPTION	POST. REF.	DEBIT	CREDIT	
33	Dec.	31	Finished Goods–Small Air-blower		1161 4 1 642		33
34			WIP–Small Air-blower			1161 4 1 642	34
35			*Memorandum 52*				35
36							36

The amount of transfer-in to finished goods is $961,716.37 for large air-blower.

Step 1 Analyze Transaction

Accounts Affected:

There are two accounts affected by transactions. They are **Finished Goods–Large Air-blower and Work-in-process–Large Air-blower.**

Increase/Decrease:

Finished Goods–Large Air-blower is increased by $961,716.37.

Work-in-process–Large Air-blower is increased by $961,716.37.

Account Category:

Finished Goods–Large Air-blower is an asset account.

Work-in-process–Large Air-blower is an asset account.

Step 2 Determine Debit/Credit

–The normal balance of asset accounts is debit. **Finished Goods–Large Air-blower** is debited by $961,716.37.

–The normal balance of asset accounts is debit.

Work-in-process–Large Air-blower is credited by $961,716.37.

Step 3 Record in T-accounts

Finished Goods–Large Air-blower	
Debit	Credit
961,716.37	

Work-in-process–Large Air-blower	
Debit	Credit
	961,716.37

Step 4 Record in Journals

GENERAL JOURNAL PAGE 4

	DATE		DESCRIPTION	POST. REF.	DEBIT	CREDIT	
36	Dec.	31	Finished Goods–Large Air-blower		961 7 1 637		36
37			WIP–Large Air-blower			961 7 1 637	37
38			*Memorandum 52*				38
39							39

TRANSACTION 104

On December 31, cost of goods sold was transferred.

WHAT TO DO?

There is no record for this transaction since Xinle uses perpetual inventory system, and therefore the cost of goods sold has already been recorded when the company sold its products.

TRANSACTION 105

On December 31, Xinle recorded value-added taxes.

WHAT TO DO?

There is no record for this transaction. Since tax system in China is different from that in the United States, those taxes should be adjusted to satisfy tax system in the United States. Value-added tax is treated as a part of Income Tax and therefore will not be measured separately.

TRANSACTION 106

On December 31, Xinle recorded Construction and Maintenance Tax, Education Surcharge and Local Education Surcharge.

WHAT TO DO?

There is no record for this transaction. Since tax system in China is different from that in the

United States, those taxes should be adjusted to satisfy tax system in the United States. Construction and Maintenance Tax, Education Surcharge and Local Education Surcharge are treated as a part of Income Tax and therefore will not be measured separately.

TRANSACTION SUMMARY

Adjusting journal entries have been completed at this point. All entries have already been collected in General Journal. Updated General Journal is illustrated in following table.

GENERAL JOURNAL — PAGE 1

	DATE		DESCRIPTION	POST. REF.	DEBIT	CREDIT	
1	Dec.	4	Other Receivables–Fenghua Air-blower	1092	3000 00		1
2			Bank Deposit	102		3000 00	2
3			*Check Stub 34*	√			3
4	Dec.	4	Cost of Goods Sold–Small Air-blower	5011	250000 00		4
5			Finished Goods–Small Air-blower	11031		250000 00	5
6			*SALES SLIP 68*	√			6
7	Dec.	7	Cost of Goods Sold–Large Air-blower	5012	520000 00		7
8			Finished Goods–Large Air-blower	11032		520000 00	8
9			SALES SLIP 69	√			9
10	Dec.	7	Cost of Goods Sold–Small Air-blower	5011	250000 00		10
11			Finished Goods–Small Air-blower	11031		250000 00	11
12			SALES SLIP 70	√			12
13	Dec.	7	Cost of Goods Sold–Large Air-blower	5012	260000 00		13
14			Finished Goods–Large Air-blower	11032		260000 00	14
15			SALES SLIP 71	√			15
16	Dec.	9	Other Receivables–Ningbo Air-blower	1093	3000 00		16
17			Bank Deposit	102		3000 00	17
18			Check Stub 48	√			18
19	Dec.	9	Cost of Goods Sold–Small Air-blower	5011	250000 00		19
20			Finished Goods–Small Air-blower	11031		250000 00	20
21			SALES SLIP 72	√			21
22	Dec.	11	Cost of Goods Sold–Large Air-blower	5012	260000 00		22
23			Finished Goods–Large Air-blower	11032		260000 00	23
24			SALES SLIP 73	√			24
25	Dec.	11	Bank Deposit	102	10000 00		25
26			Loss on Disposal of Lathe	5061	5000 00		26
27			Accumulated Depreciation–Lathe	1161	135000 00		27

continued

	DATE		DESCRIPTION	POST. REF.	DEBIT	CREDIT	
28			Lathe	1151		150 0 0 0 00	28
29			Memorandum 32 & 33	√			29
30	Dec.	12	Cost of Goods Sold–Small Air-blower	5011	500 0 0 0 00		30
31			Finished Goods–Small Air-blower	11031		500 0 0 0 00	31
32			SALES SLIP 74	√			32
33	Dec.	15	Cost of Goods Sold–Large Air-blower	5012	520 0 0 0 00		33
34			Finished Goods–Large Air-blower	11032		520 0 0 0 00	34
35			SALES SLIP 75	√			35
36	Dec.	17	Other Receivables–Ningbo Air-blower	1093	2 0 0 0 00		36
37			Bank Deposit	102		2 0 0 0 00	37
38			Check Stub 168	√			38
39	Dec.	17	Cost of Goods Sold–Large Air-blower	5012	520 0 0 0 00		39
40			Finished Goods–Large Air-blower	11032		520 0 0 0 00	40
41			SALES SLIP 76	√			41
42	Dec.	17	Cost of Goods Sold–Small Air-blower	5011	250 0 0 0 00		42
43			Finished Goods–Small Air-blower	11031		250 0 0 0 00	43
44			SALES SLIP 77	√			44
45	Dec.	17	Cost of Goods Sold–Large Air-blower	5012	260 0 0 0 00		45
46			Finished Goods–Large Air-blower	11032		260 0 0 0 00	46
47			SALES SLIP 78	√			47
48	Dec.	17	Property Tax Expense	5052	54 0 9 0 00		48
49			Property Tax Payable	2062		54 0 9 0 00	49
50			Memorandum 36	√			50
51	Dec.	18	Bank Deposit	102	97 8 7 5 00		51
52			Discounts on N/R–Xiangshan AB	105	2 1 2 5 00		52
53			N/R–Xiangshan AB	1042		100 0 0 0 00	53
54			Check Stub 177	√			54
55	Dec.	19	Cost of Goods Sold–Small Air-blower	5011	750 0 0 0 00		55
56			Finished Goods–Small Air-blower	11031		750 0 0 0 00	56
57			SALES SLIP 79	√			57
58							
59							
60							

	GENERAL JOURNAL					PAGE 2	
	DATE		DESCRIPTION	POST. REF.	DEBIT	CREDIT	
1	Dec.	21	Grinder	1159	50000 00		1
2			Capital-Hefeng	301		50000 00	2
3			Memorandum 38	√			3
4	Dec.	22	Cost of Goods Sold-Small Air-blower	5011	500000 00		4
5			Finished Goods-Small Air-blower	11031		500000 00	5
6			SALES SLIP 80	√			6
7	Dec.	23	Steel Plates	110111	75000 00		7
8			Material Price Variance	111	5000 00		8
9			Factory Overhead Incurred	113	9200 00		9
10			Commercial Acceptance Bill Pay.	208		89200 00	10
11			Bill 117	√			11
12	Dec.	23	Bank Deposit	102	1500 00		12
13			Cash on Hand	101		1500 00	13
14			Receipt 926	√			14
15	Dec.	27	Cash Lost Expense	5038	50 00		15
16			Cash on Hand	101		50 00	16
17			Memorandum 39	√			17
18	Dec.	27	Cash on Hand	101	50 00		18
19			Cash Lost Expense	5038		50 00	19
20			Memorandum 40	√			20
21	Dec.	28	Cost of Goods Sold-Large Air-blower	5012	520000 00		21
22			Finished Goods-Large Air-blower	11032		520000 00	22
23			SALES SLIP 83	√			23
24	Dec.	28	Work-in-process-Small Air-blower		259875 00		24
25			Material Quantity Variance		2625 00		25
26			Steel Plates			262500 00	26
27			Memorandum 41				27
28			Work-in-process-Large Air-blower		226125 00		28
29			Material Quantity Variance		1875 00		29
30			Steel Plates			228000 00	30
31			Memorandum 41				31

continued

	DATE		DESCRIPTION	POST. REF.	DEBIT	CREDIT	
32			Factory Overhead Incurred		15 000 00		32
33			Steel Plates			15 000 00	33
34			Memorandum 41				34
35	Dec.	28	Work-in-process–Small Air-blower		111 375 00		35
36			Material Quantity Variance		1 125 00		36
37			Iron Castings			112 500 00	37
38			Memorandum 41				38
39			Work-in-process–Large Air-blower		111 375 00		39
40			Material Quantity Variance		225 00		40
41			Iron Castings			111 600 00	41
42			Memorandum 41				42
43			Factory Overhead Incurred		22 500 00		43
44			Iron Castings			22 500 00	44
45			Memorandum 41				45
46	Dec.	28	Work-in-process–Small Air-blower		173 250 00		46
47			Material Quantity Variance		1 750 00		47
48			Copper Line			175 000 00	48
49			Memorandum 41				49
50			Work-in-process–Large Air-blower		149 625 00		50
51			Material Quantity Variance		4 375 00		51
52			Copper Line			154 000 00	52
53			Memorandum 41				53
54	Dec.	28	Factory Overhead Incurred		30 000 00		54
55			Refrigeration Oil			30 000 00	55
56			Memorandum 41				56
57			Factory Overhead Incurred		37 500 00		57
58			Refrigeration Oil			37 500 00	58
59			Memorandum 41				59
60							60

GENERAL JOURNAL							PAGE 3
	DATE		DESCRIPTION	POST. REF.	DEBIT	CREDIT	
1	Dec.	28	Factory Overhead Incurred		4000 00		1
2			Packing Boxes			4000 00	2
3			Memorandum 41				3
4			Factory Overhead Incurred		3200 00		4
5			Packing Boxes			3200 00	5
6			Memorandum 41				6
7	Dec.	28	Factory Overhead Incurred		1018 42		7
8			Work Jackets			1018 42	8
9			Memorandum 41				9
10			Factory Overhead Incurred		1760 12		10
11			Work Shoes			1760 12	11
12			Memorandum 41				12
13			Factory Overhead Incurred		1486 36		13
14			Heat-resistant Gloves			1486 36	14
15			Memorandum 41				15
16	Dec.	29	Amortization Expense–Patent		2000 00		16
17			Accum. Amortization–Patent			2000 00	17
18			Memorandum 42				18
19			Amortization Expense–Trademark		250 00		19
20			Accum. Amortization–Trademark			250 00	20
21			Memorandum 42				21
22	Dec.	29	Subscription Expense		9600 00		22
23			Prepaid Subscription			9600 00	23
24			Memorandum 43				24
25			Insurance Expense		90000 00		25
26			Prepaid Insurance			90000 00	26
27			Memorandum 43				27
28	Dec.	29	Factory Overhead Incurred		7114 56		28
29			M&A Broadband Expense		2885 44		29
30			Prepaid Broadband			10000 00	30

continued

	DATE		DESCRIPTION	POST. REF.	DEBIT	CREDIT	
31			Memorandum 44				31
32	Dec.	29	Factory Overhead Incurred		87,302.56		32
33			M&A Depreciation Expense		15,984.70		33
34			Plant, Property & Equipment			103,287.26	34
35			Memorandum 45				35
36	Dec.	30	COGS–Small Air-blower		44,607.84		36
37			COGS–Large Air-blower		46,392.16		37
38			Material Price Variance			91,000.00	38
39			Memorandum 46				39
40			COGS–Small Air-blower		5,870.10		40
41			COGS–Large Air-blower		6,104.90		41
42			Material Quantity Variance			11,975.00	42
43			Memorandum 46				43
44	Dec.	30	Direct Labor		493,050.00		44
45			Labor Efficiency Variance		5,700.00		45
46			Labor Rate Variance		1,002.00		46
47			Factory Overhead Incurred		72,252.00		47
48			Sales Salaries Expense		10,000.00		48
49			M&A Salaries Expense		140,015.00		49
50			Social Security Tax Payable			129,963.42	50
51			Medicare Tax Payable			14,440.38	51
52			FUTP			931.64	52
53			SUTP			6,288.55	53
54			Employee FITP			904.67	54
55			Employee SITP			1,809.33	55
56			Salaries Payable			567,681.01	56
57			Memorandum 47				57
58							58
59							59
60							60

	GENERAL JOURNAL					PAGE 4	
	DATE		DESCRIPTION	POST. REF.	DEBIT	CREDIT	
1	Dec.	30	Payroll Tax Expense		177616 67		1
2			Social Security Tax Payable			129963 42	2
3			Medicare Tax Payable			14440 38	3
4			FUTP			4332 11	4
5			SUTP			28880 76	5
6			Memorandum 47				6
7	Dec.	30	Work-in-process–Small Air-blower		266475 00		7
8			Work-in-process–Large Air-blower		226575 00		8
9			Direct Labor			493050 00	9
10			Memorandum 47				10
11	Dec.	30	COGS–Small Air-blower		491 18		11
12			COGS–Large Air-blower		510 82		12
13			Labor Rate Variance			1002 00	13
14			Memorandum 47				14
15			COGS–Small Air-blower		2794 12		15
16			COGS–Large Air-blower		2905 88		16
17			Labor Efficiency Variance			5700 00	17
18			Memorandum 47				18
19	Dec.	31	Bad Debt Expense		23980 00		19
20			Allowance for Doubtful Debts			23980 00	20
21			Memorandum 48				21
22	Dec.	31	Interest Expense		5184 00		22
23			Interest Payable			5184 00	23
24			Memorandum 49				24
25	Dec.	31	Work-in-process–Small Air-blower		288420 00		25
26			Work-in-process–Large Air-blower		242880 00		26
27			Factory Overhead Applied			531300 00	27
28			Memorandum 50				28
29	Dec.	31	Cost of Goods Sold–Small Air-blower		34 06		29
30			Cost of Goods Sold–Large Air-blower		35 42		30
31			Factory Overhead			69 48	31
32			Memorandum 51				32
33	Dec.	31	Finished Goods–Small Air-blower		1161416 42		33
34			WIP–Small Air-blower			1161416 42	34
35			Memorandum 52				35
36	Dec.	31	Finished Goods–Large Air-blower		961716 37		36
37			WIP–Large Air-blower			961716 37	37
38			Memorandum 52				38

Updated T-accounts book is illustrated as follows. The highlighted red words mean several sub-accounts of this control account have not been listed. B means beginning balance. U means unadjusted ending balance. A means adjusted ending balance.

Cash on Hand*

	Debit	Credit
B	51,000	
		800
		1,200
		3,000
		2,000
		1,000
		4,500
		3,000
	3,000	
		1,500
		50
	50	
U	37,000.00	
A	37,000.00	

Bank Deposit*

	Debit	Credit
B	2,352,000	
		1,500
		30
		220,000
	100,000	
		178,400
		56,500
		2,180
		3,000
		2,000
		1,205,196
		90,000
	600,000	
		118,720
		32,700
		89,200
	872,000	
	381,500	
	436,000	
		1,000
		2,000
		2,180
	500,000	
		120,000
		3,000
		21,800
	436,000	
	10,000	
		1,500
		9,600
		56,500
	763,000	
		10,000
		1,000
		196,200
		3,000
		118,720
		535,184
		417,496
		56,500
	872,000	
		4,000
		26,705
		2,000
	381,500	
	436,000	
		2,180
		5,000
		240
		92,868
		6,722.46
		1,017,499
	97,875	
		10,000
		2,180
		2,000
	1,144,500	
		1,500
		21,800
		79,280
		56,500
		30,000
	1,500	
	436,000	
	381,500	
		2,000
		8,000
	872,000	
		54,090
U	6,093,704.54	
A	6,093,704.54	

Bank Draft*

	Debit	Credit
B	60,408	
U	60,408.00	
A	60,408.00	

Notes Receivable*

	Debit	Credit
B	302,125	
		100,000
U	202,125.00	
A	202,125.00	

Notes Receivable-Fenghua Air-blower**

	Debit	Credit
B	202,125	
U	202,125.00	
A	202,125.00	

Notes Receivable-Xiangshan Air-blower**

	Debit	Credit
B	100,000	
		100,000
U	0.00	
A	0.00	

Discounts on Notes Receivable*

Debit	Credit	
	2,125	B
2,125		
	0	U
	0	A

Debit	Credit

Debit	Credit

Accounts Receivable*

	Debit	Credit
B	700,000	
	1,044,500	
	1,253,500	
U	2,998,000.00	
A	2,998,000.00	

Accounts Receivable-Fenghua Air-blower**

	Debit	Credit
B	200,000	
		100,000
	381,500	
	763,000	
U	1,244,500.00	
A	1,244,500.00	

Accounts Receivable-Ningbo Air-blower**

	Debit	Credit
	381,500	
	872,000	
U	1,253,500.00	
A	1,253,500.00	

Accounts Receivable-Xiangshan Air-blower**

	Debit	Credit
B	500,000	
U	500,000.00	
A	500,000.00	

Debit	Credit

Debit	Credit

Allowance for Doubtful Debts*

Debit	Credit	
	6,000	B
	6,000	U
	23,980	
	29,980.00	A

Debit	Credit

Debit	Credit

Prepaid Expense*

	Debit	Credit
B	12,500	
	120,000	
	9,600	
	90,000	
U	232,100.00	
		10,000.00
		9,600.00
		90,000.00
A	122,500.00	

Prepaid Broadband**

	Debit	Credit
B	1,200	
	120,000	
U	121,200.00	
		10,000
A	111,200.00	

Prepaid Subscription**

	Debit	Credit
B	1,500	
	9,600	
U	11,100.00	
		9,600
A	1,500.00	

Prepaid Insurance**

	Debit	Credit
B	9,800	
	90,000	
U	99,800.00	
		90,000
A	9,800.00	

Debit	Credit

Debit	Credit

Other Receivables*

	Debit	Credit
	5,500	
	3,000	
	5,000	
U	13,500.00	
A	13,500.00	

Petty Cash**

	Debit	Credit
	1,500	
	2,000	
	2,000	
U	5,500.00	
A	5,500.00	

Other Receivables-Fenghua Air-blower**

	Debit	Credit
	3,000	
U	3,000.00	
A	3,000.00	

Other Receivables-Ningbo Air-blower**

	Debit	Credit
	2,000	
	3,000	
U	5,000.00	
A	5,000.00	

Debit	Credit

Debit	Credit

Inventory*

	Debit	Credit
B	5,612,121	
	1,123,000	
	-5,610,000	
U	1,125,121.00	
		1,155,800
		67,157.79
	2,123,132.79	
A	2,025,296.00	

Raw Material**

	Debit	Credit
B	516,200	
	1,045,000	
	78,000	
U	1,639,200.00	
		1,081,100
		74,700
A	483,400.00	

Direct Material***

	Debit	Credit
B	510,000	
	450,000	
	280,000	
	315,000	
U	1,555,000.00	
		505,500
		329,000
		246,600
A	473,900.00	

Indirect Material***

	Debit	Credit
B	6,200	
	70,000	
	8,000	
U	84,200.00	
		67,500
		7,200
A	9,500.00	

Steel Plates****

	Debit	Credit
B	230,000	
	150,000	
	75,000	
	150,000	
	75,000	
U	680,000.00	
		262,500
		228,000
		15,000
A	174,500.00	

Copper Line****

	Debit	Credit
B	180,000	
	105,000	
	105,000	
	70,000	
U	460,000.00	
		175,000
		154,000
A	131,000.00	

Iron Castings****

	Debit	Credit
B	100,000	
	45,000	
	45,000	
	45,000	
	45,000	
	45,000	
	45,000	
	45,000	
U	415,000.00	
		112,500
		111,600
		22,500
A	168,400.00	

Refrigeration Oil****

	Debit	Credit
B	5,000	
	30,000	
	20,000	
	20,000	
U	75,000.00	
		30,000
		37,500
A	7,500.00	

Packing Boxes****

	Debit	Credit
B	1,200	
	2,000	
	2,000	
	2,000	
	2,000	
U	9,200.00	
		4,000
		3,200
A	2,000.00	

Material Price Variance*

	Debit	Credit
B	18,000	
	10,000	
	5,000	
	3,000	
	5,000	
	5,000	
	5,000	
	3,000	
	5,000	
	10,000	
	5,000	
	2,000	
	5,000	
	5,000	
	5,000	
U	91,000.00	
		91,000
A	0.00	

Material Quantity Variance*

	Debit	Credit
	2,625	
	1,875	
	1,125	
	225	
	1,750	
	4,375	
		11,975
A	0.00	

Debit	Credit

Work-in-process**

	Debit	Credit
B	315,921	
U	315,921.00	
		62,021.42
		5,136
A	248,763.58	

Work-in-process-Small Air-blower***

	Debit	Credit
B	219,800	
U	219,800.00	
	259,875	
	111,375	
	173,250	
	266,475	
	288,420	
		1,161,416.42
A	157,778.58	

Work-in-process-Large Air-blower***

	Debit	Credit
B	96,121	
U	96,121.00	
	226,125	
	111,375	
	149,625	
	226,575	
	242,880	
		961,716.37
A	90,984.63	

Work-in-process-Small Air-blower-Stamping Workshop****

	Debit	Credit
B	75,760	
U	75,760.00	
	75,760.00	

Work-in-process-Small Air-blower-Machining Workshop****

	Debit	Credit
B	60,860	
U	60,860.00	
	60,860.00	

Work-in-process-Small Air-blower-Assembling Workshop****

	Debit	Credit
B	83,180	
U	83,180.00	
	83,180.00	

Work-in-process-Large Air-blower-Stamping Workshop****

	Debit	Credit
B	24,630	
U	24,630.00	
	24,630.00	

Work-in-process-Large Air-blower-Machining Workshop****

	Debit	Credit
B	32,210	
U	32,210.00	
	32,210.00	

Work-in-process-Large Air-blower-Assembling Workshop****

	Debit	Credit
B	39,281	
U	39,281.00	
	39,281.00	

Direct Labor*

	Debit	Credit
	493,050	
		493,050
A	0.00	

Labor Efficiency Variance*

	Debit	Credit
	5,700	
		5,700
A	0.00	

Labor Rate Variance*

	Debit	Credit
	1,002	
		1,002
A	0.00	

Factory Overhead*

	Debit	Credit
	18,400	
	6,500	
	180	
	10,720	
	2,700	
	9,200	
	6,500	
	180	
	1,800	
	6,500	
	10,720	
	6,500	
	18,400	
	2,205	
	180	
	92,868	
	6,722.46	
	10,000	
	180	
	6,500	
	1,800	
	7,280	
	9,200	
	6,500	
	6,500	
U	248,235.46	
	15,000	
	22,500	
	30,000	
	37,500	
	4,000	
	3,200	
	1,018.42	
	1,760.12	
	1,486.36	
	7,114.56	
	87,302.56	
	72,252	
		531,300
		69.48
A	0.00	

Debit	Credit

Debit	Credit

Finished Goods**

	Debit	Credit
B	4,780,000	
	-2,750,000	
	-2,860,000	
U	-830,000.00	
	1,161,416.42	
	961,716.37	
A	1,293,132.79	

Finished Goods-Small Air-blower***

	Debit	Credit
B	2,000,000	
		250,000
		250,000
		250,000
		500,000
		250,000
		750,000
		500,000
U	-750,000.00	
	1,161,416.42	
A	411,416.42	

Finished Goods-Large Air-blower***

	Debit	Credit
B	2,780,000	
		520,000
		260,000
		260,000
		520,000
		520,000
		260,000
		520,000
U	-80,000.00	
	961,716.37	
A	881,716.37	

Supplies*

	Debit	Credit
B	4,000	
	3,000	
	1,000	
	26,000	
U	34,000.00	
		4,264.90
A	29,735.10	

M&A Office Supplies**

	Debit	Credit
	2,000	
	1,000	
U	3,000.00	
A	3,000.00	

Sales Office Supplies**

	Debit	Credit
	1,000	
U	1,000.00	
A	1,000.00	

Factory Supplies**

	Debit	Credit
B	4,000	
	10,500	
	9,000	
	5,000	
	1,500	
U	30,000.00	
		1,018.42
		1,760.12
		1,486.36
A	25,735.10	

Work Jackets***

	Debit	Credit
B	2,400	
	10,500	
U	12,900.00	
		1018.42
A	11,881.58	

Work Shoes***

	Debit	Credit
B	1,150	
	9,000	
U	10,150.00	
		1,760.12
A	8,389.88	

Heat-resistant Gloves***

	Debit	Credit
B	450	
	5,000	
U	5,450.00	
		1,486.36
A	3,963.64	

Factory Office Supplies***

	Debit	Credit
	1500	
U	1,500.00	
A	1,500.00	

Debit	Credit

Plant, Property & Equipment*

	Debit	Credit
B	12,000,000	
		150,000
	220,000	
	199,200	
	50,000	
U	12,319,200.00	
A	12,319,200.00	

Lathe (Old)**

	Debit	Credit
B	150,000	
		150000
U	0.00	
	0.00	

Saw machine**

	Debit	Credit
	220,000	
U	220,000.00	
	220,000.00	

Lathe (New)**

	Debit	Credit
	196,200	
	3,000	
U	199,200.00	
	199,200.00	

Grinder**

	Debit	Credit
	50,000	
U	50,000.00	
	50,000.00	

Debit	Credit

Accumulated Depreciation*

Debit	Credit
	2,500,000 B
135,000	
	2,365,000 U
	103,287.26
	2,468,287.26 A

Accumulated Depreciation-Lathe**

Debit	Credit
	135,000 B
135,000	
U 0.00	
A 0.00	

Debit	Credit

Land

Debit	Credit
B 2,600,000	
U 2,600,000.00	
A 2,600,000.00	

Debit	Credit

Debit	Credit

Intangible Assets*

Debit	Credit
B 500,000	
30,000	
U 530,000.00	
A 530,000.00	

Patent**

Debit	Credit
B 500,000	
U 500,000.00	
A 500,000.00	

Trademark**

Debit	Credit
30000	
U 30,000.00	
A 30,000.00	

Accumulated Amortization*

Debit	Credit
	200,000 B
	200,000.00 U
	2,000
	250
	202,250.00 A

Accumulated Amortization-Patent**

Debit	Credit
B	200,000 B
	200,000.00 U
	2,000
	202,000.00 A

Accumulated Amortization-Trademark**

Debit	Credit
	250
	250 A

Short-term Borrowings*

Debit	Credit
	2,428,000 B
400,000	
	500,000
	2,528,000.00 U
	2,528,000.00 A

Short-term Borrowings-China Construction Bank**

Debit	Credit
	1,000,000 B
	600,000
1,000,000	
	600,000.00 U
	600,000.00 A

Short-term Borrowings-Bank of China**

Debit	Credit
	1,428,000 B
	500,000
	1,928,000.00 U
	1,928,000.00 A

Notes Payable*

Debit	Credit	
	110,000	B
	110,000.00	U
	110,000.00	A

Notes Payable–Beijing Steel**

Debit	Credit	
	68,000	B
	68,000.00	U
	68,000.00	A

Notes Payable–Hebei Steel**

Debit	Credit	
	42,000	B
	42,000.00	U
	42,000.00	A

Accounts Payable*

Debit	Credit	
	102,000	B
	339,900	
	441,900.00	U
	441,900.00	A

Accounts Payable–Beijing Steel**

Debit	Credit	
	60,000	B
	56,500	
	174,400	
	54,500	
	54,500	
	399,900.00	U
	399,900.00	A

Accounts Payable–Hebei Steel**

Debit	Credit	
	42,000	B
	42,000.00	U
	42,000.00	A

Unearned Revenue*

Debit	Credit	
	441,570	B
	400,000	
	350,000	
	1,191,570.00	U
	1,191,570.00	A

Unearned Revenue–Ningbo Air-blower**

Debit	Credit	
	290,047	B
	400,000	
	690,047.00	U
	690,047.00	A

Unearned Revenue–Xiangshan Air-blower**

Debit	Credit	
	151,523	B
	350,000	
	501,523.00	U
	501,523.00	A

Payroll Liabilities*

Debit	Credit	
	954,696	B
535,184		
335,896		
61,200		
2,632		
17,768		
672		
1,344		
	0.00	U
	567,681.01	
	259,926.84	
	28,880.76	
	5,263.75	
	35,169.31	
	904.67	
	1,809.33	
	899,635.67	A

Salaries Payable**

Debit	Credit	
	535,184	B
535,184		
	0.00	U
	567,681.01	
	567,681.01	A

Social Security Tax Payable**

Debit	Credit	
	335,896	B
335,896		
	0.00	U
	129,963.42	
	129,963.42	
	259,926.84	A

Medicare Tax Payable**

Debit	Credit	
	61,200	B
61,200		
	0.00	U
	14,440.38	
	14,440.38	
	28,880.76	A

Federal Unemployment Tax Payable**

Debit	Credit	
	2,632	B
2,632		
	0.00	U
	931.64	
	4,332.11	
	5,263.75	A

State Unemployment Tax Payable**

Debit	Credit	
	17,768	B
17,768		
	0.00	U
	6,288.55	
	28,880.76	
	35,169.31	A

Employee Federal Income Tax Payable**

Debit	Credit	
	672	B
672		
	0.00	U
	904.67	
	904.67	A

Employee State Income Tax Payable**

Debit	Credit	
	1,344	B
1,344		
	0	U
	1,809.33	
	1,809.33	A

Debit	Credit

Taxes Payable*

Debit	Credit	
	1,203,180	B
	810,000	
1,203,180		
	810,000.00	U
	810,000.00	A

Sales Tax Payable**

Debit	Credit	
	31,500	
	72,000	
	31,500	
	36,000	
	31,500	
	36,000	
	63,000	
	72,000	
	72,000	
	31,500	
	36,000	
	94,500	
	63,000	
	36,000	
	31,500	
	72,000	
	810,000.00	U
	810,000.00	A

Property Tax Payable**

Debit	Credit	
	54,090	
54,090		
	0.00	U
	0.00	A

Income Taxes Payable**

Debit	Credit	
	1,203,180	B
601,590		
601,590		
	0.00	U
	0.00	A

Federal Income Tax Payable***

Debit	Credit	
	601,590	B
601,590		
	0.00	U
	0.00	A

State Income Tax Payable***

Debit	Credit	
	601,590	B
601,590		
	0.00	U
	0.00	A

Interests Payable*

Debit	Credit	
	14,583	B
11,666		
	2,917.00	U
	5,184.00	
	8,101.00	A

Commercial Acceptance Bill Payable*

Debit	Credit	
	89,200	
	89,200.00	U
	89,200.00	A

Debit	Credit

Capital, Hefeng*

Debit	Credit	
	12,800,000	B
	50,000	
	12,850,000.00	U
	12,850,000.00	A

Capital Reserve*

Debit	Credit	
	550,000	B
	550,000.00	U
	550,000.00	A

Retained Earnings*

Debit	Credit	
	2,900,000	B
	2,900,000.00	U
	2,900,000.00	A

Sales Revenue*

Debit	Credit	
	3,850,000	
	4,400,000	
	8,250,000.00	U
	8,250,000.00	A

Sales Revenue-Small Air-blower**

Debit	Credit	
	350,000	
	350,000	
	350,000	
	700,000	
	350,000	
	1,050,000	
	700,000	
	3,850,000.00	U
	3,850,000.00	A

Sales Revenue-Large Air-blower**

Debit	Credit	
	800,000	
	400,000	
	400,000	
	800,000	
	800,000	
	400,000	
	800,000	
	4,400,000.00	U
	4,400,000.00	A

Other Revenue*

Debit	Credit	
	3,000	
	3,000.00	U
	3,000.00	A

Investment Earnings**

Debit	Credit	
	0.00	U
	0.00	A

Debit	Credit

Cost of Goods Sold*

	Debit	Credit
	2,750,000	
	2,860,000	
U	5,610,000	
	53,797.30	
	55,949.18	
A	5,719,746.48	

Cost of Goods Sold-Small Air-blower**

	Debit	Credit
	250,000	
	250,000	
	250,000	
	500,000	
	250,000	
	750,000	
	500,000	
U	2,750,000	
	44,607.84	
	5,870.10	
	34.06	
	491.18	
	2,794.12	
A	2,803,797.30	

Cost of Goods Sold-Large Air-blower**

	Debit	Credit
	520,000	
	260,000	
	260,000	
	520,000	
	520,000	
	260,000	
	520,000	
U	2,860,000	
	46,392.16	
	6,104.90	
	35.42	
	510.82	
	2,905.88	
A	2,915,949.18	

Selling Expense*

	Debit	Credit
	4,500	
	3,000	
	15,000	
	8,000	
U	30,500	
	10,000	
A	40,500	

Administrative & Managerial Expense*

	Debit	Credit
	800	
	3,000	
	30	
	1,200	
	2,500	
	240	
	5,833	
U	13,603	
	2,885.44	
	15,984.7	
	5,184	
	2,250	
	9,600	
	90,000	
	140,015	
	177,616.67	
	23,980	
A	481,118.81	

M&A Travel Expense**

	Debit	Credit
	800	
U	800	
A	800	

Sales Travel Expense**

	Debit	Credit
	4,500	
U	4,500	
A	4,500	

M&A Broadband Expense*

	Debit	Credit
	2,885.44	
A	2,885.44	

Sales Training Expense**

	Debit	Credit
	3,000	
U	3,000	
A	3,000	

A&M Training Expense**

	Debit	Credit
	3,000	
U	3,000	
A	3,000	

M&A Depreciation Expense*

	Debit	Credit
	15,984.70	
A	15,984.70	

Bank Fee Expense**

	Debit	Credit
	30	
U	30	
A	30	

Telecommunication Expense**

	Debit	Credit
	1,200	
U	1,200	
A	1,200	

Invitation Fee Expense**

	Debit	Credit
	1,000	
	1,500	
U	2,500	
A	2,500	

Advertising Expense**

	Debit	Credit
	10,000	
	5,000	
U	15,000	
A	15,000	

Television Expense**

	Debit	Credit
	240	
U	240	
A	240	

Interest Expense**

	Debit	Credit
	5,833	
U	5,833	
	5,184	
A	11,017	

Cash Lost Expense**

	Debit	Credit
	50	
		50
U	0	
A	0	

Telephone Expense**

	Debit	Credit
	8,000	
U	8,000	
A	8,000	

Sales Salaries Expense

	Debit	Credit
	10,000	
A	10,000	

Taxes Expense*

	Debit	Credit
	54,090	
U	54,090	
A	54,090	

Income Taxes Expense**

	Debit	Credit
U	0	
A	0	

Property Tax Expense**

	Debit	Credit
	54,090	
U	54,090	
A	54,090	

Loss on Disposal of PP&E*

	Debit	Credit
	5,000	
U	5,000	
A	5,000	

Loss on Disposal of Lathe**

	Debit	Credit
	5,000	
U	5,000	
A	5,000	

Debit	Credit

Amortization Expense*

	Debit	Credit
	2,000	
	250	
A	2,250	

Amortization Expense–Patent**

	Debit	Credit
	2,000	
A	2,000	

Amortization Expense–Trademark**

	Debit	Credit
	250	
A	250	

Subscription Expense*

	Debit	Credit
	9,600	
A	9,600	

Insurance Expense*

	Debit	Credit
	90,000	
A	90,000	

M&A Salaries Expense

	Debit	Credit
	140,015	
A	140,015	

Payroll Tax Expense

	Debit	Credit
	177,616.67	
A	177,616.67	

Bad Debt Expense

	Debit	Credit
	23,980	
A	23,980	

Debit	Credit

POST TO THE LEDGER

Initial recording of those adjusting entries have been finished. Those entries should be posted to the ledger. Both general ledger and subsidiary ledger should be used at this point. They are illustrated s following tables. In the following part of this section, general ledger and subsidiary ledgers will be recorded for all transactions of Xinle Air-blower Co., Ltd. Updated ledgers are illustrated in following tables.

ACCOUNT *Cash on Hand* ACCOUNT NO. 101

	DATE		DESCRIPTION	POST. REF.	DEBIT	CREDIT	BALANCE DEBIT	BALANCE CREDIT	
1	Dec.	1	Balance	√			5100000		1
2	Dec.	23	Deposit money	G2		150000	4950000		2
3	Dec.	27	Cash lost	G2		5000	4945000		3
4	Dec.	27	Reimbursement of cash lost	G2	5000		4950000		4
5	Dec.	28	Cash Receipts Journal	CRJ1	300000		5250000		5
6	Dec.	28	Cash Payments Journal	CPJ4		1550000	3700000		6
7									7
8									8
9									9
10									10

ACCOUNT *Bank Deposit* ACCOUNT NO. 102

	DATE		DESCRIPTION	POST. REF.	DEBIT	CREDIT	BALANCE DEBIT	BALANCE CREDIT	
1	Dec.	1	Balance	√			235200000		1
2	Dec.	4	Delivery fee	G1		300000	234900000		2
3	Dec.	9	Delivery fee	G1		300000	234600000		3
4	Dec.	11	Disposal of Lathe	G1	1000000		235600000		4
5	Dec.	17	Delivery fee	G1		200000	235400000		5
6	Dec.	18	Collection of the note	G1	9787500		245187500		6
7	Dec.	23	Deposit money	G2	150000		245337500		7
8	Dec.	31	Cash Receipts Journal	CRJ1	861200000		1106537500		8
9	Dec.	31	Cash Payments Journal	CPJ4		497167046	609370454		9
10									10

ACCOUNT *Bank Draft* ACCOUNT NO. 103

	DATE		DESCRIPTION	POST. REF.	DEBIT	CREDIT	BALANCE DEBIT	BALANCE CREDIT	
1	Dec.	1	Balance	√			6040800		1
2									2
3									3
4									4
5									5
6									6
7									7
8									8
9									9
10									10

ACCOUNT *Notes Receivable* ACCOUNT NO. 104

	DATE		DESCRIPTION	POST. REF.	DEBIT	CREDIT	BALANCE		
							DEBIT	CREDIT	
1	Dec.	1	Balance	√			302 1 2 500		1
2	Dec.	28	Xiangshan Air-blower	1042		100 0 0 000	202 1 2 500		2
3									3
4									4
5									5
6									6
7									7
8									8
9									9
10									10

ACCOUNT *Notes Receivable–Fenghua Air-blower* ACCOUNT NO. 1041

	DATE		DESCRIPTION	POST. REF.	DEBIT	CREDIT	BALANCE		
							DEBIT	CREDIT	
1	Dec.	1	Balance	√			202 1 2 500		1
2									2
3									3
4									4
5									5
6									6
7									7
8									8
9									9
10									10

ACCOUNT *Notes Receivable–Xiangshan Air-blower* ACCOUNT NO. 1042

	DATE		DESCRIPTION	POST. REF.	DEBIT	CREDIT	BALANCE		
							DEBIT	CREDIT	
1	Dec.	1	Balance	√			100 0 0 000		1
2	Dec.	18	Collection of the note	G1		100 0 0 000	~~0 0 0 000~~		2
3									3
4									4
5									5
6									6
7									7
8									8
9									9
10									10

ACCOUNT *Discounts on Notes Receivable* ACCOUNT NO. 105

DATE		DESCRIPTION	POST. REF.	DEBIT	CREDIT	BALANCE DEBIT	BALANCE CREDIT
Dec.	1	Balance	√				212500
Dec.	18	Collection of the note	G1	212500			~~000000~~

ACCOUNT *Accounts Receivable* ACCOUNT NO. 106

DATE		DESCRIPTION	POST. REF.	DEBIT	CREDIT	BALANCE DEBIT	BALANCE CREDIT
Dec.	1	Balance	√			70000000	
Dec.	28	Fenghua Air-blower	1061	104450000		174450000	
Dec.	28	Ningbo Air-blower	1062	125350000		299800000	

ACCOUNT *Accounts Receivable–Fenghua Air-blower* ACCOUNT NO. 1061

DATE		DESCRIPTION	POST. REF.	DEBIT	CREDIT	BALANCE DEBIT	BALANCE CREDIT
Dec.	1	Balance	√			20000000	
Dec.	28	Collect accounts receivable	CRJ1		10000000	10000000	
Dec.	28	Sales Journal	SJ1	114450000		124450000	

ACCOUNT *Accounts Receivable–Ningbo Air-blower* ACCOUNT NO. 1062

DATE		DESCRIPTION	POST. REF.	DEBIT	CREDIT	BALANCE DEBIT	BALANCE CREDIT
Dec.	28	Sales Journal	SJ1	125350000		125350000	

ACCOUNT *Accounts Receivable–Xiangshan Air-blower* ACCOUNT NO. 1063

DATE		DESCRIPTION	POST. REF.	DEBIT	CREDIT	BALANCE DEBIT	BALANCE CREDIT
Dec.	1	Balance	√			50000000	

ACCOUNT *Allowance for Doubtful Debts* ACCOUNT NO. 107

DATE		DESCRIPTION	POST. REF.	DEBIT	CREDIT	BALANCE DEBIT	BALANCE CREDIT
Dec.	1	Balance	√				600000
Dec.	31	Bad debt	GJ4		2398000		2998000

ACCOUNT *Prepaid Expense* ACCOUNT NO. 108

	DATE		DESCRIPTION	POST. REF.	DEBIT	CREDIT	BALANCE DEBIT	BALANCE CREDIT	
1	Dec.	1	Balance	√			1250000		1
2	Dec.	28	Prepaid Broadband	1081	12000000		13250000		2
3	Dec.	28	Prepaid Subscription	1082	960000		14210000		3
4	Dec.	28	Prepaid Insurance	1083	9000000		23210000		4
5	Dec.	29	Expired broadband	1081		1000000	22210000		5
6	Dec.	29	Expired subscription	1082		960000	21250000		6
7	Dec.	29	Expired insurance	1083		9000000	12250000		7
8									8
9									9
10									10

ACCOUNT *Prepaid Broadband* ACCOUNT NO. 1081

	DATE		DESCRIPTION	POST. REF.	DEBIT	CREDIT	BALANCE DEBIT	BALANCE CREDIT	
1	Dec.	1	Balance	√			1200 00		1
2	Dec.	28	Pay broadband fee	CPJ2	120000 00		121200 00		2
3	Dec.	29	Expired broadband	GJ3		10000 00	111200 00		3
4									4
5									5
6									6
7									7
8									8
9									9
10									10

ACCOUNT *Prepaid Subscription* ACCOUNT NO. 1082

	DATE		DESCRIPTION	POST. REF.	DEBIT	CREDIT	BALANCE DEBIT	BALANCE CREDIT	
1	Dec.	1	Balance	√			150000		1
2	Dec.	28	Pay subscription fee	CPJ2	960000		1110000		2
3	Dec.	29	Expired subscription	GJ3		960000	150000		3
4									4
5									5
6									6
7									7
8									8
9									9
10									10

ACCOUNT *Prepaid Insurance* ACCOUNT NO. 1083

	DATE		DESCRIPTION	POST. REF.	DEBIT	CREDIT	BALANCE		
							DEBIT	CREDIT	
1	Dec.	1	Balance	√			980000		1
2	Dec.	31	Pay insurance fee	CPJ1	9000000		9980000		2
3	Dec.	29	Expired insurance	GJ3		9000000	980000		3
4									4
5									5
6									6
7									7
8									8
9									9
10									10

ACCOUNT *Other Receivables* ACCOUNT NO. 109

	DATE		DESCRIPTION	POST. REF.	DEBIT	CREDIT	BALANCE		
							DEBIT	CREDIT	
1	Dec.	28	Petty Cash	1091	550000		550000		1
2	Dec.	28	Fenghua Air-blower	1092	300000		850000		2
3	Dec.	28	Ningbo Air-blower	1093	500000		1350000		3
4									4
5									5
6									6
7									7
8									8
9									9
10									10

ACCOUNT *Petty Cash* ACCOUNT NO. 1091

	DATE		DESCRIPTION	POST. REF.	DEBIT	CREDIT	BALANCE		
							DEBIT	CREDIT	
1	Dec.	28	Bank transfer	CPJ1	150000		150000		1
2	Dec.	28	Bank transfer	CPJ1	200000		350000		2
3	Dec.	28	Bank transfer	CPJ2	200000		550000		3
4									4
5									5
6									6
7									7
8									8
9									9
10									10

ACCOUNT *Other Receivables－Fenghua Air-blower* ACCOUNT NO. 1092

	DATE		DESCRIPTION	POST. REF.	DEBIT	CREDIT	BALANCE DEBIT	BALANCE CREDIT	
1	Dec.	4	Delivery fee	G1	300000		300000		1
2									2
3									3
4									4
5									5
6									6
7									7
8									8
9									9
10									10

ACCOUNT *Other Receivables－Ningbo Air-blower* ACCOUNT NO. 1093

	DATE		DESCRIPTION	POST. REF.	DEBIT	CREDIT	BALANCE DEBIT	BALANCE CREDIT	
1	Dec.	9	Delivery fee	G1	300000		300000		1
2	Dec.	17	Delivery fee	G1	200000		500000		2
3									3
4									4
5									5
6									6
7									7
8									8
9									9
10									10

ACCOUNT *Inventory* ACCOUNT NO. 110

	DATE		DESCRIPTION	POST. REF.	DEBIT	CREDIT	BALANCE DEBIT	BALANCE CREDIT	
1	Dec.	1	Balance	√			561212100		1
2	Dec.	28	Raw Material	1101	112300000		673512100		2
3	Dec.	28	Finished Goods	1103		561000000	112512100		3
4	Dec.	28	Raw Material	1101		115580000		3067900	4
5	Dec.	31	Work-in-process	1102		6715779		9783679	5
6	Dec.	31	Finished Goods	1103	212313279		202529600		6
7									7
8									8
9									9
10									10

ACCOUNT *Raw Material* ACCOUNT NO. 1101

	DATE		DESCRIPTION	POST. REF.	DEBIT	CREDIT	BALANCE DEBIT	BALANCE CREDIT	
1	Dec.	1	Balance	√			516200000		1
2	Dec.	28	Direct Material	11011	1045000000		1561200000		2
3	Dec.	28	Indirect Material	11012	78000000		1639200000		3
4	Dec.	28	Direct Material	11011		1081100000	558100000		4
5	Dec.	28	Indirect Material	11012		74700000	483400000		5
6									6
7									7
8									8
9									9
10									10

ACCOUNT *Direct Material* ACCOUNT NO. 11011

	DATE		DESCRIPTION	POST. REF.	DEBIT	CREDIT	BALANCE DEBIT	BALANCE CREDIT	
1	Dec.	1	Balance	√			510000000		1
2	Dec.	28	Steel Plates	110111	450000000		960000000		2
3	Dec.	28	Copper Line	110112	280000000		1240000000		3
4	Dec.	28	Iron Castings	110113	315000000		1555000000		4
5	Dec.	28	Steel Plates	110111		505500000	1049500000		5
6	Dec.	28	Copper Line	110112		329000000	720500000		6
7	Dec.	28	Iron Castings	110113		246600000	473900000		7
8									8
9									9
10									10

ACCOUNT *Steel Plates* ACCOUNT NO. 110111

	DATE		DESCRIPTION	POST. REF.	DEBIT	CREDIT	BALANCE DEBIT	BALANCE CREDIT	
1	Dec.	1	Balance	√			230000000		1
2	Dec.	23	Purchase steel plates	G2	75000000		305000000		2
3	Dec.	28	Purchase steel plates	CPJ1	150000000		455000000		3
4	Dec.	28	Purchase steel plates	CPJ2	75000000		530000000		4
5	Dec.	28	Purchases Journal	PJ1	150000000		680000000		5
6	Dec.	28	Assign steel plates	GJ2		262500000	417500000		6
7	Dec.	28	Assign steel plates	GJ2		228000000	189500000		7
8	Dec.	28	Assign steel plates	GJ2		15000000	174500000		8
9									9
10									10

ACCOUNT *Copper Line* ACCOUNT NO. 110112

	DATE		DESCRIPTION	POST. REF.	DEBIT	CREDIT	BALANCE DEBIT	BALANCE CREDIT	
1	Dec.	1	Balance	√			180000 00		1
2	Dec.	28	Purchase copper line	CPJ1	105000 00		285000 00		2
3	Dec.	28	Purchase copper line	CPJ3	105000 00		390000 00		3
4	Dec.	28	Purchase copper line	CPJ4	70000 00		460000 00		4
5	Dec.	28	Assign copper line	GJ2		175000 00	285000 00		5
6	Dec.	28	Assign copper line	GJ2		154000 00	131000 00		6
7									7
8									8
9									9
10									10

ACCOUNT *Iron Castings* ACCOUNT NO. 110113

	DATE		DESCRIPTION	POST. REF.	DEBIT	CREDIT	BALANCE DEBIT	BALANCE CREDIT	
1	Dec.	1	Balance	√			100000 00		1
2	Dec.	28	Purchase iron castings	CPJ1	45000 00		145000 00		2
3	Dec.	28	Purchase iron castings	CPJ2	45000 00		190000 00		3
4	Dec.	28	Purchase iron castings	CPJ3	45000 00		235000 00		4
5	Dec.	28	Purchase iron castings	CPJ4	45000 00		280000 00		5
6	Dec.	28	Purchases Journal	PJ1	135000 00		415000 00		6
7	Dec.	28	Assign iron castings	GJ2		112500 00	302500 00		7
8	Dec.	28	Assign iron castings	GJ2		111600 00	190900 00		8
9	Dec.	28	Assign iron castings	GJ2		22500 00	168400 00		9
10									10

ACCOUNT *Indirect Material* ACCOUNT NO. 11012

	DATE		DESCRIPTION	POST. REF.	DEBIT	CREDIT	BALANCE DEBIT	BALANCE CREDIT	
1	Dec.	1	Balance	√			6200 00		1
2	Dec.	28	Refrigeration Oil	110121	70000 00		76200 00		2
3	Dec.	28	Packing Boxes	110122	8000 00		84200 00		3
4	Dec.	28	Refrigeration Oil	110121		67500 00	16700 00		4
5	Dec.	28	Packing Boxes	110122		7200 00	9500 00		5
6									6
7									7
8									8
9									9
10									10

ACCOUNT *Refrigeration Oil* ACCOUNT NO. 110121

DATE		DESCRIPTION	POST. REF.	DEBIT	CREDIT	BALANCE	
						DEBIT	CREDIT
Dec.	1	Balance	√			500000	
Dec.	28	Purchase refrigeration oil	CPJ1	3000000		3500000	
Dec.	28	Purchase refrigeration oil	CPJ2	2000000		5500000	
Dec.	28	Purchase refrigeration oil	CPJ4	2000000		7500000	
Dec.	28	Assign refrigeration oil	GJ2		3000000	4500000	
Dec.	28	Assign refrigeration oil	GJ2		3750000	750000	

ACCOUNT *Packing Boxes* ACCOUNT NO. 110122

DATE		DESCRIPTION	POST. REF.	DEBIT	CREDIT	BALANCE	
						DEBIT	CREDIT
Dec.	1	Balance	√			120000	
Dec.	28	Purchase packing boxes	CPJ1	200000		320000	
Dec.	28	Purchase packing boxes	CPJ2	200000		520000	
Dec.	28	Purchase packing boxes	CPJ3	200000		720000	
Dec.	28	Purchase packing boxes	CPJ4	200000		920000	
Dec.	28	Assign packing boxes	GJ3		400000	520000	
Dec.	28	Assign packing boxes	GJ3		320000	200000	

ACCOUNT *Work-in-process* ACCOUNT NO. 1102

DATE		DESCRIPTION	POST. REF.	DEBIT	CREDIT	BALANCE	
						DEBIT	CREDIT
Dec.	1	Balance	√			31592100	
Dec.	31	Small Air-blower	11021		6202142	25389958	
Dec.	31	Large Air-blower	11022		513637	24876321	

ACCOUNT *Work-in-process–Small Air-blower* ACCOUNT NO. 11021

	DATE		DESCRIPTION	POST. REF.	DEBIT	CREDIT	BALANCE DEBIT	BALANCE CREDIT	
1	Dec.	1	Balance	√			219 8 0 000		1
2	Dec.	28	Assign steel plates	GJ2	259 8 7 500		479 6 7 500		2
3	Dec.	28	Assign iron castings	GJ2	111 3 7 500		591 0 5 000		3
4	Dec.	28	Assign copper line	GJ2	173 2 5 000		764 3 0 000		4
5	Dec.	30	Allocate direct labor	GJ4	266 4 7 500		1030 7 7 500		5
6	Dec.	31	Allocate factory overhead	GJ4	288 4 2 000		1319 1 9 500		6
7	Dec.	31	Transfer to F/G	GJ4		1161 4 1 642	157 7 7 858		7
8									8
9									9
10									10

ACCOUNT *Work-in-process–Large Air-blower* ACCOUNT NO. 11022

	DATE		DESCRIPTION	POST. REF.	DEBIT	CREDIT	BALANCE DEBIT	BALANCE CREDIT	
1	Dec.	1	Balance	√			96 1 2 1 00		1
2	Dec.	28	Assign steel plates	GJ2	226 1 2 5 00		322 2 4 6 00		2
3	Dec.	28	Assign iron castings	GJ2	111 3 7 5 00		433 6 2 1 00		3
4	Dec.	28	Assign copper line	GJ2	149 6 2 5 00		583 2 4 6 00		4
5	Dec.	30	Allocate direct labor	GJ4	226 5 7 5 00		809 8 2 1 00		5
6	Dec.	31	Allocate factory overhead	GJ4	242 8 8 0 00		1052 7 0 1 00		6
7	Dec.	31	Transfer to F/G	GJ4		961 7 1 6 37	90 9 8 4 63		7
8									8
9									9
10									10

ACCOUNT *Finished Goods* ACCOUNT NO. 1103

	DATE		DESCRIPTION	POST. REF.	DEBIT	CREDIT	BALANCE DEBIT	BALANCE CREDIT	
1	Dec.	1	Balance	√			4780 0 0 0 00		1
2	Dec.	28	Small Air-blower	11031		2750 0 0 0 00	2030 0 0 0 00		2
3	Dec.	28	Large Air-blower	11032		2860 0 0 0 00	−830 0 0 0 00		3
4	Dec.	31	Small Air-blower	11031	1161 4 1 6 42		331 4 1 6 42		4
5	Dec.	31	Large Air-blower	11032	961 7 1 6 37		1293 1 3 2 79		5
6									6
7									7
8									8
9									9
10									10

ACCOUNT *Finished Goods–Small Air-blower* ACCOUNT NO. 11031

	DATE		DESCRIPTION	POST. REF.	DEBIT	CREDIT	BALANCE DEBIT	BALANCE CREDIT	
1	Dec.	1	Balance	√			200000000		1
2	Dec.	4	Sold products	G1		25000000	175000000		2
3	Dec.	7	Sold products	G1		25000000	150000000		3
4	Dec.	9	Sold products	G1		25000000	125000000		4
5	Dec.	12	Sold products	G1		50000000	75000000		5
6	Dec.	17	Sold products	G1		25000000	50000000		6
7	Dec.	19	Sold products	G1		75000000	−25000000		7
8	Dec.	22	Sold products	G2		50000000	−75000000		8
9	Dec.	31	Transfer to F/G	GJ4	116141642		41141642		9
10									10

ACCOUNT *Finished Goods–Large Air-blower* ACCOUNT NO. 11032

	DATE		DESCRIPTION	POST. REF.	DEBIT	CREDIT	BALANCE DEBIT	BALANCE CREDIT	
1	Dec.	1	Balance	√			278000000		1
2	Dec.	7	Sold products	G1		52000000	226000000		2
3	Dec.	7	Sold products	G1		26000000	200000000		3
4	Dec.	11	Sold products	G1		26000000	174000000		4
5	Dec.	15	Sold products	G1		52000000	122000000		5
6	Dec.	17	Sold products	G1		52000000	70000000		6
7	Dec.	17	Sold products	G1		26000000	44000000		7
8	Dec.	28	Sold products	G2		52000000	−8000000		8
9	Dec.	31	Transfer to F/G	GJ4	96171637		88171637		9
10									10

ACCOUNT *Material Price Variance* ACCOUNT NO. 111

	DATE		DESCRIPTION	POST. REF.	DEBIT	CREDIT	BALANCE DEBIT	BALANCE CREDIT	
1	Dec.	1	Balance	√			1800000		1
2	Dec.	23	Purchase steel plates	G2	500000		2300000		2
3	Dec.	28	Purchase steel plates	CPJ1	1000000		3300000		3
4	Dec.	28	Purchase iron castings	CPJ1	500000		3800000		4
5	Dec.	28	Purchase copper line	CPJ1	300000		4100000		5
6	Dec.	28	Purchase steel plates	CPJ2	500000		4600000		6
7	Dec.	28	Purchase iron castings	CPJ2	500000		5100000		7
8	Dec.	28	Purchase copper line	CPJ3	300000		5400000		8
9	Dec.	28	Purchase iron castings	CPJ3	500000		5900000		9
10	Dec.	28	Purchase copper line	CPJ4	200000		6100000		10
11	Dec.	28	Purchase iron castings	CPJ4	500000		6600000		11
12	Dec.	28	Sales Journal	CJ1	2500000		9100000		12
13	Dec.	29	Allocate material price variance	GJ3		9100000	~~000000~~		13

ACCOUNT *Material Quantity Variance* ACCOUNT NO. 112

	DATE		DESCRIPTION	POST. REF.	DEBIT	CREDIT	BALANCE DEBIT	BALANCE CREDIT	
1	Dec.	28	Assign steel plates	GJ2	2625 00		2625 00		1
2	Dec.	28	Assign steel plates	GJ2	1875 00		4500 00		2
3	Dec.	28	Assign iron castings	GJ2	1125 00		5625 00		3
4	Dec.	28	Assign iron castings	GJ2	225 00		5850 00		4
5	Dec.	28	Assign copper line	GJ2	1750 00		7600 00		5
6	Dec.	28	Assign copper line	GJ2	4375 00		11975 00		6
7	Dec.	29	Allocate material quantity variance	GJ3		11975 00	~~0000 00~~		7
8									8
9									9
10									10

ACCOUNT *Factory Overhead* ACCOUNT NO. 113

	DATE		DESCRIPTION	POST. REF.	DEBIT	CREDIT	BALANCE DEBIT	BALANCE CREDIT	
1	Dec.	23	Purchase steel plates	G2	9200 00		9200 00		1
2	Dec.	28	Purchase steel plates	CPJ1	18400 00		27600 00		2
3	Dec.	28	Purchase iron castings	CPJ1	6500 00		34100 00		3
4	Dec.	28	Purchase packing boxes	CPJ1	180 00		34280 00		4
5	Dec.	28	Purchase copper line	CPJ1	10720 00		45000 00		5
6	Dec.	28	Purchase refrigeration oil	CPJ1	2700 00		47700 00		6
7	Dec.	28	Purchase steel plates	CPJ2	9200 00		56900 00		7
8	Dec.	28	Purchase packing boxes	CPJ1	180 00		57080 00		8
9	Dec.	28	Purchase refrigeration oil	CPJ2	1800 00		58880 00		9
10	Dec.	28	Purchase iron castings	CPJ2	6500 00		65380 00		10
11	Dec.	28	Purchase copper line	CPJ3	10720 00		76100 00		11
12	Dec.	28	Purchase iron castings	CPJ3	6500 00		82600 00		12
13	Dec.	28	Delivery fee	CPJ3	4000 00		86600 00		13
14	Dec.	28	Purchase factory supplies	CPJ3	2205 00		88805 00		14
15	Dec.	28	Purchase packing boxes	CPJ3	180 00		88985 00		15
16	Dec.	28	Pay electricity fee	CPJ3	92868 00		181853 00		16
17	Dec.	28	Pay water fee	CPJ4	6722 46		188575 46		17
18	Dec.	28	Pay repair and maintenance fee	CPJ4	10000 00		198575 46		18
19	Dec.	28	Purchase packing boxes	CPJ4	180 00		198755 46		19
20	Dec.	28	Delivery fee	CPJ4	2000 00		200755 46		20
21	Dec.	28	Purchase refrigeration oil	CPJ4	1800 00		202555 46		21
22	Dec.	28	Purchase copper line	CPJ4	7280 00		209835 46		22
23	Dec.	28	Purchase iron castings	CPJ4	6500 00		216335 46		23
24	Dec.	28	Delivery fee	CPJ4	2000 00		218335 46		24
25	Dec.	28	Sales Journal	CJ1	29900 00		248235 46		25
26	Dec.	28	Assign steel plates	GJ2	15000 00		263235 46		26
27	Dec.	28	Assign iron castings	GJ2	22500 00		285735 46		27
28	Dec.	28	Assign refrigeration oil	GJ2	30000 00		315735 46		28
29	Dec.	28	Assign refrigeration oil	GJ2	37500 00		353235 46		29
30	Dec.	28	Assign packing boxes	GJ3	4000 00		357235 46		30
31	Dec.	28	Assign packing boxes	GJ3	3200 00		360435 46		31
32	Dec.	28	Assign work jackets	GJ3	1018 42		361453 88		32
33	Dec.	28	Assign work shoes	GJ3	1760 12		363214 00		33
34	Dec.	28	Assign heat-resistant gloves	GJ3	1486 36		364700 36		34
35	Dec.	29	Expired broadband	GJ3	7114 56		371814 92		35
36	Dec.	29	Monthly depreciation	GJ3	87302 56		459117 48		36
37	Dec.	30	Monthly salaries	GJ3	72252 00		531369 48		37
38	Dec.	30	Allocate factory overhead	GJ4		531300 00	69 48		38
39	Dec.	31	Allocate difference for O/H	GJ4		69 48	~~0000 00~~		39

ACCOUNT *Supplies* ACCOUNT NO. 114

	DATE		DESCRIPTION	POST. REF.	DEBIT	CREDIT	BALANCE		
							DEBIT	CREDIT	
1	Dec.	1	Balance	√			400000		1
2	Dec.	28	M&A Office Supplies	1141	300000		700000		2
3	Dec.	28	Sales Office Supplies	1142	100000		800000		3
4	Dec.	28	Factory Supplies	1143	2600000		3400000		4
5									5
6									6
7									7
8									8
9									9
10									10

ACCOUNT *M&A Office Supplies* ACCOUNT NO. 1141

	DATE		DESCRIPTION	POST. REF.	DEBIT	CREDIT	BALANCE		
							DEBIT	CREDIT	
1	Dec.	28	Pay office supplies fee	CPJ2	200000		200000		1
2	Dec.	28	Pay office supplies fee	CPJ3	100000		300000		2
3									3
4									4
5									5
6									6
7									7
8									8
9									9
10									10

ACCOUNT *Sales Office Supplies* ACCOUNT NO. 1142

	DATE		DESCRIPTION	POST. REF.	DEBIT	CREDIT	BALANCE		
							DEBIT	CREDIT	
1	Dec.	31	Pay office supplies fee	CPJ2	100000		100000		1
2									2
3									3
4									4
5									5
6									6
7									7
8									8
9									9
10									10

ACCOUNT *Factory Supplies* ACCOUNT NO. 1143

	DATE		DESCRIPTION	POST. REF.	DEBIT	CREDIT	BALANCE DEBIT	BALANCE CREDIT	
1	Dec.	1	Balance	√			4000000		1
2	Dec.	28	Work Jackets	11431	10500000		14500000		2
3	Dec.	28	Work Shoes	11432	9000000		23500000		3
4	Dec.	28	Heat-resistant Gloves	11433	5000000		28500000		4
5	Dec.	28	Factory Office Supplies	11434	1500000		30000000		5
6	Dec.	28	Work Jackets	11431		101842	28981158		6
7	Dec.	28	Work Shoes	11432		176012	27222146		7
8	Dec.	28	Heat-resistant Gloves	11433		148636	25733510		8
9									9
10									10

ACCOUNT *Work Jackets* ACCOUNT NO. 11431

	DATE		DESCRIPTION	POST. REF.	DEBIT	CREDIT	BALANCE DEBIT	BALANCE CREDIT	
1	Dec.	1	Balance	√			2400000		1
2	Dec.	28	Pay work jackets	CPJ3	10500000		12900000		2
3	Dec.	28	Assign work jackets	GJ3		101842	11888158		3
4									4
5									5
6									6
7									7
8									8
9									9
10									10

ACCOUNT *Work Shoes* ACCOUNT NO. 11432

	DATE		DESCRIPTION	POST. REF.	DEBIT	CREDIT	BALANCE DEBIT	BALANCE CREDIT	
1	Dec.	1	Balance	√			115000		1
2	Dec.	28	Pay work shoes	CPJ3	9000000		10115000		2
3	Dec.	28	Assign work shoes	GJ3		176012	8388988		3
4									4
5									5
6									6
7									7
8									8
9									9
10									10

ACCOUNT *Heat-resistant Gloves* ACCOUNT NO. 11433

DATE		DESCRIPTION	POST. REF.	DEBIT	CREDIT	BALANCE DEBIT	BALANCE CREDIT
Dec.	1	Balance	√			4 5000	
Dec.	28	Pay heat-resistant gloves	CPJ3	5 0 0 000		5 4 5000	
Dec.	28	Assign heat-resistant gloves	GJ3		1 4 8 636	3 9 6364	

ACCOUNT *Factory Office Supplies* ACCOUNT NO. 11434

DATE		DESCRIPTION	POST. REF.	DEBIT	CREDIT	BALANCE DEBIT	BALANCE CREDIT
Dec.	28	Purchase factory office supplies	CPJ2	1 5 0 000		1 5 0000	

ACCOUNT *Plant, Property & Equipment* ACCOUNT NO. 115

DATE		DESCRIPTION	POST. REF.	DEBIT	CREDIT	BALANCE DEBIT	BALANCE CREDIT
Dec.	1	Balance	√			12000 0 0000	
Dec.	28	Lathe	1151		150 0 0 000	11850 0 0000	
Dec.	28	Saw Machine	1152	220 0 0 000		12070 0 0000	
Dec.	28	Lathe	1153	199 2 0 000		12269 2 0000	
Dec.	28	Grinder	1159	50 0 0 000		12319 2 0000	

ACCOUNT *Lathe (Old)* ACCOUNT NO. 1151

DATE		DESCRIPTION	POST. REF.	DEBIT	CREDIT	BALANCE	
						DEBIT	CREDIT
Dec.	1	Balance	√			150 00 000	
Dec.	11	Disposal of Lathe	G1		150 00 000	~~0 00 000~~	

ACCOUNT *Saw Machine* ACCOUNT NO. 1152

DATE		DESCRIPTION	POST. REF.	DEBIT	CREDIT	BALANCE	
						DEBIT	CREDIT
Dec.	31	Purchase of saw machine	CPJ1	220 00 000		220 00 000	

ACCOUNT *Lathe (New)* ACCOUNT NO. 1153

DATE		DESCRIPTION	POST. REF.	DEBIT	CREDIT	BALANCE	
						DEBIT	CREDIT
Dec.	28	Pay the lathe	CPJ2	196 20 000		196 20 000	
Dec.	28	Pay the lathe	CPJ2	3 00 000		199 20 000	

ACCOUNT *Grinder* ACCOUNT NO. 1159

	DATE		DESCRIPTION	POST. REF.	DEBIT	CREDIT	BALANCE		
							DEBIT	CREDIT	
1	Dec.	21	Donation of Grinder	G2	50 0 0 000		50 0 0 000		1
2									2
3									3
4									4
5									5
6									6
7									7
8									8
9									9
10									10

ACCOUNT *Accumulated Depreciation* ACCOUNT NO. 116

	DATE		DESCRIPTION	POST. REF.	DEBIT	CREDIT	BALANCE		
							DEBIT	CREDIT	
1	Dec.	1	Balance	√				2500 0 0 000	1
2	Dec.	28	Lathe	1161	135 0 0 000			2365 0 0 000	2
3	Dec.	29	Monthly depreciation	GJ3		103 2 8 726		2468 2 8 726	3
4									4
5									5
6									6
7									7
8									8
9									9
10									10

ACCOUNT *Accumulated Depreciation–Lathe* ACCOUNT NO. 1161

	DATE		DESCRIPTION	POST. REF.	DEBIT	CREDIT	BALANCE		
							DEBIT	CREDIT	
1	Dec.	1	Balance	√				135 0 0 000	1
2	Dec.	11	Disposal of Lathe	G1	135 0 0 000			-0 0 0 000-	2
3									3
4									4
5									5
6									6
7									7
8									8
9									9
10									10

ACCOUNT *Land* ACCOUNT NO. 117

	DATE		DESCRIPTION	POST. REF.	DEBIT	CREDIT	BALANCE DEBIT	BALANCE CREDIT	
1	Dec.	1	Balance	√			2600 0 0000		1
2									2
3									3
4									4
5									5
6									6
7									7
8									8
9									9
10									10

ACCOUNT *Intangible Assets* ACCOUNT NO. 118

	DATE		DESCRIPTION	POST. REF.	DEBIT	CREDIT	BALANCE DEBIT	BALANCE CREDIT	
1	Dec.	1	Balance	√			500 0 0 0 00		1
2	Dec.	28	Trademark	1182	30 0 0 0 00		530 0 0 0 00		2
3									3
4									4
5									5
6									6
7									7
8									8
9									9
10									10

ACCOUNT *Patent* ACCOUNT NO. 1181

	DATE		DESCRIPTION	POST. REF.	DEBIT	CREDIT	BALANCE DEBIT	BALANCE CREDIT	
1	Dec.	1	Balance	√			500 0 0000		1
2									2
3									3
4									4
5									5
6									6
7									7
8									8
9									9
10									10

ACCOUNT *Trademark* ACCOUNT NO. 1182

DATE		DESCRIPTION	POST. REF.	DEBIT	CREDIT	BALANCE DEBIT	BALANCE CREDIT
Dec.	28	Purchase patent	CPJ4	3000000		3000000	

ACCOUNT *Accumulated Amortization* ACCOUNT NO. 119

DATE		DESCRIPTION	POST. REF.	DEBIT	CREDIT	BALANCE DEBIT	BALANCE CREDIT
Dec.	1	Balance	√				20000000
Dec.	29	Patent	1191		200000		20200000
Dec.	29	Trademark	1192		25000		20225000

ACCOUNT *Accumulated Amortization–Patent* ACCOUNT NO. 1191

DATE		DESCRIPTION	POST. REF.	DEBIT	CREDIT	BALANCE DEBIT	BALANCE CREDIT
Dec.	1	Balance	√				20000000
Dec.	29	Monthly amortization	GJ3		200000		20200000

ACCOUNT *Accumulated Amortization–Trademark* ACCOUNT NO. 1192

DATE		DESCRIPTION	POST. REF.	DEBIT	CREDIT	BALANCE DEBIT	BALANCE CREDIT
Dec.	29	Monthly amortization	GJ3		25 000		25 000

ACCOUNT *Direct Labor* ACCOUNT NO. 120

DATE		DESCRIPTION	POST. REF.	DEBIT	CREDIT	BALANCE DEBIT	BALANCE CREDIT
Dec.	30	Monthly salaries	GJ3	493 05 000		493 05 000	
Dec.	30	Allocate direct labor	GJ4		493 05 000	~~0 0 0 000~~	

ACCOUNT *Labor Efficiency Variance* ACCOUNT NO. 121

DATE		DESCRIPTION	POST. REF.	DEBIT	CREDIT	BALANCE DEBIT	BALANCE CREDIT
Dec.	30	Monthly salaries	GJ3	5 70 000		5 70 000	
Dec.	30	Allocate labor rate variance	GJ4		5 70 000	~~0 0 0 000~~	

ACCOUNT *Labor Rate Variance* ACCOUNT NO. 122

	DATE		DESCRIPTION	POST. REF.	DEBIT	CREDIT	BALANCE DEBIT	BALANCE CREDIT	
1	Dec.	30	Monthly salaries	GJ3	100200		100200		1
2	Dec.	30	Allocate labor rate variance	GJ4		100200	~~000000~~		2
3									3
4									4
5									5
6									6
7									7
8									8
9									9
10									10

ACCOUNT *Short-term Borrowings* ACCOUNT NO. 201

	DATE		DESCRIPTION	POST. REF.	DEBIT	CREDIT	BALANCE DEBIT	BALANCE CREDIT	
1	Dec.	1	Balance	√				242800000	1
2	Dec.	28	China Construction Bank	2011	40000000				2
3	Dec.	28	Bank of China	2012		50000000		252800000	3
4									4
5									5
6									6
7									7
8									8
9									9
10									10

ACCOUNT *Short-term Borrowings–China Construction Bank* ACCOUNT NO. 2011

	DATE		DESCRIPTION	POST. REF.	DEBIT	CREDIT	BALANCE DEBIT	BALANCE CREDIT	
1	Dec.	1	Balance	√				100000000	1
2	Dec.	28	Bank loan	CRJ1		60000000		160000000	2
3	Dec.	28	Pay debt	CPJ3	100000000			60000000	3
4									4
5									5
6									6
7									7
8									8
9									9
10									10

ACCOUNT *Short-term Borrowings–Bank of China* ACCOUNT NO. 2012

	DATE		DESCRIPTION	POST. REF.	DEBIT	CREDIT	BALANCE DEBIT	BALANCE CREDIT	
1	Dec.	1	Balance	√				1428 0 0 000	1
2	Dec.	31	Bank loan	CRJ1		500 0 0 000		1928 0 0 000	2
3									3
4									4
5									5
6									6
7									7
8									8
9									9
10									10

ACCOUNT *Notes Payable* ACCOUNT NO. 202

	DATE		DESCRIPTION	POST. REF.	DEBIT	CREDIT	BALANCE DEBIT	BALANCE CREDIT	
1	Dec.	1	Balance	√				110 0 0 000	1
2									2
3									3
4									4
5									5
6									6
7									7
8									8
9									9
10									10

ACCOUNT *Notes Payable–Beijing Steel* ACCOUNT NO. 2021

	DATE		DESCRIPTION	POST. REF.	DEBIT	CREDIT	BALANCE DEBIT	BALANCE CREDIT	
1	Dec.	1	Balance	√				68 0 0 000	1
2									2
3									3
4									4
5									5
6									6
7									7
8									8
9									9
10									10

ACCOUNT *Notes Payable–Hebei Steel* ACCOUNT NO. 2022

	DATE		DESCRIPTION	POST. REF.	DEBIT	CREDIT	BALANCE DEBIT	BALANCE CREDIT	
1	Dec.	1	Balance	√				42 0 0000	1
2									2
3									3
4									4
5									5
6									6
7									7
8									8
9									9
10									10

ACCOUNT *Accounts Payable* ACCOUNT NO. 203

	DATE		DESCRIPTION	POST. REF.	DEBIT	CREDIT	BALANCE DEBIT	BALANCE CREDIT	
1	Dec.	1	Balance	√				102 0 0 000	1
2	Dec.	28	Beijing Steel	2031		339 9 0 000		441 9 0 000	2
3									3
4									4
5									5
6									6
7									7
8									8
9									9
10									10

ACCOUNT *Accounts Payable–Beijing Steel* ACCOUNT NO. 2031

	DATE		DESCRIPTION	POST. REF.	DEBIT	CREDIT	BALANCE DEBIT	BALANCE CREDIT	
1	Dec.	1	Balance	√				60 0 0 000	1
2	Dec.	28	Purchases Journal	PJ1		339 9 0 000		399 9 0 000	2
3									3
4									4
5									5
6									6
7									7
8									8
9									9
10									10

ACCOUNT *Accounts Payable–Hebei Steel* ACCOUNT NO. 2032

	DATE		DESCRIPTION	POST. REF.	DEBIT	CREDIT	BALANCE DEBIT	BALANCE CREDIT	
1	Dec.	1	Balance	√				42 000 00	1
2									2
3									3
4									4
5									5
6									6
7									7
8									8
9									9
10									10

ACCOUNT *Unearned Revenue* ACCOUNT NO. 204

	DATE		DESCRIPTION	POST. REF.	DEBIT	CREDIT	BALANCE DEBIT	BALANCE CREDIT	
1	Dec.	1	Balance	√				441 570 00	1
2	Dec.	28	Ningbo Air-blower			400 000 00		841 570 00	2
3	Dec.	28	Xiangshan Air-blower			350 000 00		1191 570 00	3
4									4
5									5
6									6
7									7
8									8
9									9
10									10

ACCOUNT *Unearned Revenue–Ningbo Air-blower* ACCOUNT NO. 2041

	DATE		DESCRIPTION	POST. REF.	DEBIT	CREDIT	BALANCE DEBIT	BALANCE CREDIT	
1	Dec.	1	Balance	√				290 047 00	1
2	Dec.	28	Prepaid sales	CRJ1		400 000 00		690 047 00	2
3									3
4									4
5									5
6									6
7									7
8									8
9									9
10									10

ACCOUNT *Unearned Revenue–Xiangshan Air-blower* ACCOUNT NO. 2042

	DATE		DESCRIPTION	POST. REF.	DEBIT	CREDIT	BALANCE		
							DEBIT	CREDIT	
1	Dec.	1	Balance	√				15152300	1
2	Dec.	28	Prepaid sales	CRJ1		35000000		50152300	2
3									3
4									4
5									5
6									6
7									7
8									8
9									9
10									10

ACCOUNT *Payroll Liabilities* ACCOUNT NO. 205

	DATE		DESCRIPTION	POST. REF.	DEBIT	CREDIT	BALANCE		
							DEBIT	CREDIT	
1	Dec.	1	Balance	√				95469600	1
2	Dec.	28	Salaries Payable	2051	53518400			41951200	2
3	Dec.	28	Social Security Tax Payable	2052	33589600			8361600	3
4	Dec.	28	Medicare Tax Payable	2053	6120000			2241600	4
5	Dec.	28	Federal Unemployment Tax Payable	2054	263200			1978400	5
6	Dec.	28	State Unemployment Tax Payable	2055	1776800			201600	6
7	Dec.	28	Employee FITP	2056	67200			134400	7
8	Dec.	28	Employee SITP	2057	134400			000000	8
9	Dec.	30	Salaries Payable	2051		56768101		56768101	9
10	Dec.	30	Social Security Tax Payable	2052		25992684		82760785	10
11	Dec.	30	Medicare Tax Payable	2053		2888076		85648861	11
12	Dec.	30	Federal Unemployment Tax Payable	2054		526375		86175236	12
13	Dec.	30	State Unemployment Tax Payable	2055		3516931		89692167	13
14	Dec.	30	Employee FITP	2056		90467		89782634	14
15	Dec.	30	Employee SITP	2057		180933		89963567	15

ACCOUNT *Salaries Payable* ACCOUNT NO. 2051

	DATE		DESCRIPTION	POST. REF.	DEBIT	CREDIT	BALANCE DEBIT	BALANCE CREDIT	
1	Dec.	1	Balance	√				535 1 8 400	1
2	Dec.	28	Pay salaries	CPJ3	535 1 8 400			~~0 0 0 000~~	2
3	Dec.	30	Monthly salaries	GJ3		567 6 8 101		567 6 8 101	3
4									4
5									5
6									6
7									7
8									8
9									9
10									10

ACCOUNT *Social Security Tax Payable* ACCOUNT NO. 2052

	DATE		DESCRIPTION	POST. REF.	DEBIT	CREDIT	BALANCE DEBIT	BALANCE CREDIT	
1	Dec.	1	Balance	√				335 8 9 600	1
2	Dec.	28	Pay social security tax	CPJ3	335 8 9 600			~~0 0 0 000~~	2
3	Dec.	30	Monthly salaries	GJ3		129 9 6 342		129 9 6 342	3
4	Dec.	30	Employer's part	GJ4		129 9 6 342		259 9 2 684	4
5									5
6									6
7									7
8									8
9									9
10									10

ACCOUNT *Medicare Tax Payable* ACCOUNT NO. 2053

	DATE		DESCRIPTION	POST. REF.	DEBIT	CREDIT	BALANCE DEBIT	BALANCE CREDIT	
1	Dec.	1	Balance	√				61 2 0 000	1
2	Dec.	28	Pay Medicare tax	CPJ3	61 2 0 000			~~0 0 0 000~~	2
3	Dec.	30	Monthly salaries	GJ3		14 4 4 038		14 4 4 038	3
4	Dec.	30	Employer's part	GJ4		14 4 4 038		28 8 8 076	4
5									5
6									6
7									7
8									8
9									9
10									10

ACCOUNT *Federal Unemployment Tax Payable* ACCOUNT NO. 2054

	DATE		DESCRIPTION	POST. REF.	DEBIT	CREDIT	BALANCE DEBIT	BALANCE CREDIT	
1	Dec.	1	Balance	√				2632 00	1
2	Dec.	28	Pay federal unemployment tax	CPJ3	2632 00			~~0000 00~~	2
3	Dec.	30	Monthly salaries	GJ3		931 64		931 64	3
4	Dec.	30	Employer's part	GJ4		4332 11		5263 75	4
5									5
6									6
7									7
8									8
9									9
10									10

ACCOUNT *State Unemployment Tax Payable* ACCOUNT NO. 2055

	DATE		DESCRIPTION	POST. REF.	DEBIT	CREDIT	BALANCE DEBIT	BALANCE CREDIT	
1	Dec.	1	Balance	√				17768 00	1
2	Dec.	28	Pay state unemployment tax	CPJ3	17768 00			~~0000 00~~	2
3	Dec.	30	Monthly salaries	GJ3		6288 55		6288 55	3
4	Dec.	30	Employer's part	GJ4		28880 76		35169 31	4
5									5
6									6
7									7
8									8
9									9
10									10

ACCOUNT *Employee Federal Income Tax Payable* ACCOUNT NO. 2056

	DATE		DESCRIPTION	POST. REF.	DEBIT	CREDIT	BALANCE DEBIT	BALANCE CREDIT	
1	Dec.	1	Balance	√				672 00	1
2	Dec.	31	Pay employee federal income tax	CPJ1	672 00			~~0000 00~~	2
3	Dec.	30	Monthly salaries	GJ3		904 67		904 67	3
4									4
5									5
6									6
7									7
8									8
9									9
10									10

ACCOUNT *Employee State Income Tax Payable* ACCOUNT NO. 2057

	DATE		DESCRIPTION	POST. REF.	DEBIT	CREDIT	BALANCE DEBIT	BALANCE CREDIT	
1	Dec.	1	Balance	√				134400	1
2	Dec.	28	Pay employee federal income tax	CPJ1	134400			~~000000~~	2
3	Dec.	30	Monthly salaries	GJ3		180933		180933	3
4									4
5									5
6									6
7									7
8									8
9									9
10									10

ACCOUNT *Taxes Payable* ACCOUNT NO. 206

	DATE		DESCRIPTION	POST. REF.	DEBIT	CREDIT	BALANCE DEBIT	BALANCE CREDIT	
1	Dec.	1	Balance	√				120318000	1
2	Dec.	28	Sales Tax Payable	2061		81000000		201318000	2
3	Dec.	28	Income Taxes Payable		120318000			81000000	3
4									4
5									5
6									6
7									7
8									8
9									9
10									10

ACCOUNT *Sales Tax Payable* ACCOUNT NO. 2061

	DATE		DESCRIPTION	POST. REF.	DEBIT	CREDIT	BALANCE DEBIT	BALANCE CREDIT	
1	Dec.	28	Collect sales tax	CRJ1		61200000		61200000	1
2	Dec.	28	Sales Journal	SJ1		19800000		81000000	2
3									3
4									4
5									5
6									6
7									7
8									8
9									9
10									10

ACCOUNT *Property Tax Payable* ACCOUNT NO. 2062

	DATE		DESCRIPTION	POST. REF.	DEBIT	CREDIT	BALANCE DEBIT	BALANCE CREDIT	
1	Dec.	17	Property Tax Submission	G1		54 0 9 000			1
2	Dec.	28	Pay property tax	CPJ4	54 0 9 000			~~0 0 0000~~	2
3									3
4									4
5									5
6									6
7									7
8									8
9									9
10									10

ACCOUNT *Income Taxes Payable* ACCOUNT NO. 2063

	DATE		DESCRIPTION	POST. REF.	DEBIT	CREDIT	BALANCE DEBIT	BALANCE CREDIT	
1	Dec.	1	Balance	√				1203 1 8000	1
2	Dec.	28	Federal Income Tax Payable	20631	601 5 9 000			601 5 9000	2
3	Dec.	28	State Income Tax Payable	20632	601 5 9 000			~~0 0 0000~~	3
4									4
5									5
6									6
7									7
8									8
9									9
10									10

ACCOUNT *Federal Income Tax Payable* ACCOUNT NO. 20631

	DATE		DESCRIPTION	POST. REF.	DEBIT	CREDIT	BALANCE DEBIT	BALANCE CREDIT	
1	Dec.	1	Balance	√				601 5 9000	1
2	Dec.	28	Payment of federal income tax	CPJ1	601 5 9 000			~~0 0 0000~~	2
3									3
4									4
5									5
6									6
7									7
8									8
9									9
10									10

ACCOUNT *State Income Tax Payable* ACCOUNT NO. 20632

DATE		DESCRIPTION	POST. REF.	DEBIT	CREDIT	BALANCE	
						DEBIT	CREDIT
Dec.	1	Balance	√				60159000
Dec.	28	Payment of federal income tax	CPJ1	60159000			~~000000~~

ACCOUNT *Interests Payable* ACCOUNT NO. 207

DATE		DESCRIPTION	POST. REF.	DEBIT	CREDIT	BALANCE	
						DEBIT	CREDIT
Dec.	1	Balance	√				1458300
Dec.	28	Pay debt	CPJ4	1166600			291700
Dec.	31	Accrual interest	GJ4		518400		810100

ACCOUNT *Commercial Acceptance Bill Payable* ACCOUNT NO. 208

DATE		DESCRIPTION	POST. REF.	DEBIT	CREDIT	BALANCE	
						DEBIT	CREDIT
Dec.	23	Purchase steel plates	G2		8920000		8920000

ACCOUNT *Capital, Hefeng* ACCOUNT NO. 301

	DATE		DESCRIPTION	POST. REF.	DEBIT	CREDIT	BALANCE DEBIT	BALANCE CREDIT	
1	Dec.	1	Balance	√				12800 0 0000	1
2	Dec.	21	Donation of grinder	G2		50 0 0 000		12850 0 0000	2
3									3
4									4
5									5
6									6
7									7
8									8
9									9
10									10

ACCOUNT *Capital Reserve* ACCOUNT NO. 302

	DATE		DESCRIPTION	POST. REF.	DEBIT	CREDIT	BALANCE DEBIT	BALANCE CREDIT	
1	Dec.	1	Balance	√				550 0 0000	1
2									2
3									3
4									4
5									5
6									6
7									7
8									8
9									9
10									10

ACCOUNT *Retained Earnings* ACCOUNT NO. 303

	DATE		DESCRIPTION	POST. REF.	DEBIT	CREDIT	BALANCE DEBIT	BALANCE CREDIT	
1	Dec.	1	Balance	√				2900 0 0000	1
2									2
3									3
4									4
5									5
6									6
7									7
8									8
9									9
10									10

ACCOUNT *Sales Revenue* ACCOUNT NO. 401

	DATE		DESCRIPTION	POST. REF.	DEBIT	CREDIT	BALANCE		
							DEBIT	CREDIT	
1	Dec.	28	Small Air-blower	4011		385000000		385000000	1
2	Dec.	28	Large Air-blower	4012		360000000		825000000	2
3									3
4									4
5									5
6									6
7									7
8									8
9									9
10									10

ACCOUNT *Sales Revenue-Small Air-blower* ACCOUNT NO. 4011

	DATE		DESCRIPTION	POST. REF.	DEBIT	CREDIT	BALANCE		
							DEBIT	CREDIT	
1	Dec.	28	Sold products	CRJ1	245000000			245000000	1
2	Dec.	28	Sales Journal	SJ1	140000000			385000000	2
3									3
4									4
5									5
6									6
7									7
8									8
9									9
10									10

ACCOUNT *Sales Revenue-Large Air-blower* ACCOUNT NO. 4012

	DATE		DESCRIPTION	POST. REF.	DEBIT	CREDIT	BALANCE		
							DEBIT	CREDIT	
1	Dec.	31	Sold products	CRJ1	360000000			360000000	1
2	Dec.	28	Sales Journal	SJ1	80000000			440000000	2
3									3
4									4
5									5
6									6
7									7
8									8
9									9
10									10

ACCOUNT *Other Revenue* ACCOUNT NO. 402

	DATE		DESCRIPTION	POST. REF.	DEBIT	CREDIT	BALANCE DEBIT	BALANCE CREDIT	
1	Dec.	31	Fine	CRJ1		300000		300000	1
2									2
3									3
4									4
5									5
6									6
7									7
8									8
9									9
10									10

ACCOUNT *Cost of Goods Sold* ACCOUNT NO. 501

	DATE		DESCRIPTION	POST. REF.	DEBIT	CREDIT	BALANCE DEBIT	BALANCE CREDIT	
1	Dec.	1	Balance	√					1
2	Dec.	28	Small Air-blower	5011	275000000		275000000		2
3	Dec.	28	Large Air-blower	5012	286000000		561000000		3
4	Dec.	31	Small Air-blower	5011	5379730		566379730		4
5	Dec.	31	Large Air-blower	5012	5594918		571974648		5
6									6
7									7
8									8
9									9
10									10

ACCOUNT *Cost of Goods Sold–Small Air-blower* ACCOUNT NO. 5011

	DATE		DESCRIPTION	POST. REF.	DEBIT	CREDIT	BALANCE DEBIT	BALANCE CREDIT	
1	Dec.	4	Sold products	G1	25000000		25000000		1
2	Dec.	7	Sold products	G1	25000000		50000000		2
3	Dec.	9	Sold products	G1	25000000		75000000		3
4	Dec.	12	Sold products	G1	50000000		125000000		4
5	Dec.	17	Sold products	G1	25000000		150000000		5
6	Dec.	19	Sold products	G1	75000000		225000000		6
7	Dec.	22	Sold products	G2	50000000		275000000		7
8	Dec.	29	Allocate material price variance	GJ3	4460784		279460784		8
9	Dec.	29	Allocate material quantity variance	GJ3	587010		280047794		9
10	Dec.	30	Allocate labor rate variance	GJ4	49118		280096912		10
11	Dec.	30	Allocate labor efficiency variance	GJ4	279412		280376324		11
12	Dec.	31	Allocate difference for O/H	GJ4	3406		280379730		12

ACCOUNT *Cost of Goods Sold–Large Air-blower* ACCOUNT NO. 5012

	DATE		DESCRIPTION	POST. REF.	DEBIT	CREDIT	BALANCE		
							DEBIT	CREDIT	
1	Dec.	7	Sold products	G1	52000000		52000000		1
2	Dec.	7	Sold products	G1	26000000		78000000		2
3	Dec.	11	Sold products	G1	26000000		104000000		3
4	Dec.	15	Sold products	G1	52000000		156000000		4
5	Dec.	17	Sold products	G1	52000000		208000000		5
6	Dec.	17	Sold products	G1	26000000		234000000		6
7	Dec.	28	Sold products	G2	52000000		286000000		7
8	Dec.	29	Allocate material price variance	GJ3	4639216		290639216		8
9	Dec.	29	Allocate material quantity variance	GJ3	610490		291249706		9
10	Dec.	30	Allocate labor rate variance	GJ4	51082		291300788		10
11	Dec.	30	Allocate labor efficiency variance	GJ4	290588		291591376		11
12	Dec.	31	Allocate difference for O/H	GJ4	3542		291594918		12

ACCOUNT *Selling Expense* ACCOUNT NO. 502

	DATE		DESCRIPTION	POST. REF.	DEBIT	CREDIT	BALANCE		
							DEBIT	CREDIT	
1	Dec.	28	Sales Travel Expense	5021	450000		450000		1
2	Dec.	28	Sales Training Expense	5022	300000		750000		2
3	Dec.	28	Advertising Expense	5023	1500000		2250000		3
4	Dec.	28	Telephone Expense	5024	800000		3050000		4
5	Dec.	30	Sales Salaries Expense	5025	1000000		4050000		5
6									6
7									7
8									8
9									9
10									10

ACCOUNT *Sales Travel Expense* ACCOUNT NO. 5021

	DATE		DESCRIPTION	POST. REF.	DEBIT	CREDIT	BALANCE		
							DEBIT	CREDIT	
1	Dec.	28	Pay travel fee	CPJ3	450000		450000		1
2									2
3									3
4									4
5									5
6									6
7									7
8									8
9									9
10									10

ACCOUNT *Sales Training Expense* ACCOUNT NO. 5022

	DATE		DESCRIPTION	POST. REF.	DEBIT	CREDIT	BALANCE	
							DEBIT	CREDIT
1	Dec.	28	Pay training fee	CPJ2	300000		300000	
2								
3								
4								
5								
6								
7								
8								
9								
10								

ACCOUNT *Advertising Expense* ACCOUNT NO. 5023

	DATE		DESCRIPTION	POST. REF.	DEBIT	CREDIT	BALANCE	
							DEBIT	CREDIT
1	Dec.	28	Pay advertising fee	CPJ2	1000000		1000000	
2	Dec.	28	Pay advertising fee	CPJ3	500000		1500000	
3								
4								
5								
6								
7								
8								
9								
10								

ACCOUNT *Telephone Expense* ACCOUNT NO. 5024

	DATE		DESCRIPTION	POST. REF.	DEBIT	CREDIT	BALANCE	
							DEBIT	CREDIT
1	Dec.	28	Pay telephone fee	CPJ4	800000		800000	
2								
3								
4								
5								
6								
7								
8								
9								
10								

ACCOUNT *Sales Salaries Expense* ACCOUNT NO. 5025

DATE		DESCRIPTION	POST. REF.	DEBIT	CREDIT	BALANCE DEBIT	BALANCE CREDIT
Dec.	30	Salaries expense	GJ3	1000000		1000000	

ACCOUNT *Administrative & Managerial Expense* ACCOUNT NO. 503

DATE		DESCRIPTION	POST. REF.	DEBIT	CREDIT	BALANCE DEBIT	BALANCE CREDIT
Dec.	28	M&A Travel Expense	5031	80000		80000	
Dec.	28	M&A Training Expense	5032	300000		380000	
Dec.	28	Bank Fee Expense	5033	3000		383000	
Dec.	28	Telecommunication Expense	5034	120000		503000	
Dec.	28	Invitation Fee Expense	5035	250000		753000	
Dec.	28	Television Expense	5036	24000		777000	
Dec.	28	Interest Expense	5037	583300		1360300	
Dec.	29	M&A Broadband Expense	5039	288544		1648844	
Dec.	29	M&A Depreciation Expense	50310	1598470		3247314	
Dec.	29	Amortization Expense	50311	225000		3472314	
Dec.	29	Subscription Expense	50312	960000		4432314	
Dec.	29	Insurance Expense	50313	9000000		13432314	
Dec.	30	M&A Salaries Expense	50314	14001500		27433814	
Dec.	30	Payroll Tax Expense	50315	17761667		45195481	
Dec.	31	Bad Debt Expense	50316	2398000		47593481	
Dec.	31	Interest Expense	5037	518400		48111881	

ACCOUNT *M&A Travel Expense* ACCOUNT NO. 5031

DATE		DESCRIPTION	POST. REF.	DEBIT	CREDIT	BALANCE DEBIT	BALANCE CREDIT
Dec.	31	Reimbursement of travel fee	CPJ1	80000		80000	

ACCOUNT *M&A Training Expense* ACCOUNT NO. 5032

	DATE		DESCRIPTION	POST. REF.	DEBIT	CREDIT	BALANCE		
							DEBIT	CREDIT	
1	Dec.	28	Pay training expense	CPJ4	300 000		300 000		1
2									2
3									3
4									4
5									5
6									6
7									7
8									8
9									9
10									10

ACCOUNT *Bank Fee Expense* ACCOUNT NO. 5033

	DATE		DESCRIPTION	POST. REF.	DEBIT	CREDIT	BALANCE		
							DEBIT	CREDIT	
1	Dec.	31	Payment of bank fee	CPJ1	3 000		3 000		1
2									2
3									3
4									4
5									5
6									6
7									7
8									8
9									9
10									10

ACCOUNT *Telecommunication Expense* ACCOUNT NO. 5034

	DATE		DESCRIPTION	POST. REF.	DEBIT	CREDIT	BALANCE		
							DEBIT	CREDIT	
1	Dec.	31	Payment of telecommunication fee	CPJ1	120 000		120 000		1
2									2
3									3
4									4
5									5
6									6
7									7
8									8
9									9
10									10

ACCOUNT *Invitation Fee Expense* ACCOUNT NO. 5035

	DATE		DESCRIPTION	POST. REF.	DEBIT	CREDIT	BALANCE DEBIT	BALANCE CREDIT	
1	Dec.	28	Pay invitation fee	CPJ2	1 000 00		1 000 00		1
2	Dec.	28	Pay invitation fee	CPJ4	1 500 00		2 500 00		2
3									3
4									4
5									5
6									6
7									7
8									8
9									9
10									10

ACCOUNT *Television Expense* ACCOUNT NO. 5036

	DATE		DESCRIPTION	POST. REF.	DEBIT	CREDIT	BALANCE DEBIT	BALANCE CREDIT	
1	Dec.	28	Pay television fee	CPJ3	240 00		240 00		1
2									2
3									3
4									4
5									5
6									6
7									7
8									8
9									9
10									10

ACCOUNT *Interest Expense* ACCOUNT NO. 5037

	DATE		DESCRIPTION	POST. REF.	DEBIT	CREDIT	BALANCE DEBIT	BALANCE CREDIT	
1	Dec.	28	Pay debt	CPJ4	5 833 00		5 833 00		1
2	Dec.	31	Accrual interest	GJ4	5 184 00		11 017 00		2
3									3
4									4
5									5
6									6
7									7
8									8
9									9
10									10

ACCOUNT *Cash Lost Expense* ACCOUNT NO. 5038

	DATE		DESCRIPTION	POST. REF.	DEBIT	CREDIT	BALANCE		
							DEBIT	CREDIT	
1	Dec.	27	Cash lost	G2	5000		5000		1
2	Dec.	27	Reimbursement of cash lost	G2		5000	000000		2
3									3
4									4
5									5
6									6
7									7
8									8
9									9
10									10

ACCOUNT *M&A Broadband Expense* ACCOUNT NO. 5039

	DATE		DESCRIPTION	POST. REF.	DEBIT	CREDIT	BALANCE		
							DEBIT	CREDIT	
1	Dec.	29	Expired broadband	GJ3	288544		288544		1
2									2
3									3
4									4
5									5
6									6
7									7
8									8
9									9
10									10

ACCOUNT *M&A Depreciation Expense* ACCOUNT NO. 50310

	DATE		DESCRIPTION	POST. REF.	DEBIT	CREDIT	BALANCE		
							DEBIT	CREDIT	
1	Dec.	29	Monthly depreciation	GJ3	1598470		1598470		1
2									2
3									3
4									4
5									5
6									6
7									7
8									8
9									9
10									10

ACCOUNT *Amortization Expense* ACCOUNT NO. 50311

	DATE		DESCRIPTION	POST. REF.	DEBIT	CREDIT	BALANCE DEBIT	BALANCE CREDIT	
1	Dec.	29	Patent	503111	200 000		200 000		1
2	Dec.	29	Trademark	503112	25 000		225 000		2
3									3
4									4
5									5
6									6
7									7
8									8
9									9
10									10

ACCOUNT *Amortization Expense-Patent* ACCOUNT NO. 503111

	DATE		DESCRIPTION	POST. REF.	DEBIT	CREDIT	BALANCE DEBIT	BALANCE CREDIT	
1	Dec.	29	Patent amortization	GJ3	200 000		200 000		1
2									2
3									3
4									4
5									5
6									6
7									7
8									8
9									9
10									10

ACCOUNT *Amortization Expense-Trademark* ACCOUNT NO. 503112

	DATE		DESCRIPTION	POST. REF.	DEBIT	CREDIT	BALANCE DEBIT	BALANCE CREDIT	
1	Dec.	29	Monthly amortization	GJ3	25 000		25 000		1
2									2
3									3
4									4
5									5
6									6
7									7
8									8
9									9
10									10

ACCOUNT *Subscription Expense* ACCOUNT NO. 50312

	DATE		DESCRIPTION	POST. REF.	DEBIT	CREDIT	BALANCE DEBIT	BALANCE CREDIT	
1	Dec.	29	Expired subscription	GJ3	9 6 0 000		9 6 0 000		1
2									2
3									3
4									4
5									5
6									6
7									7
8									8
9									9
10									10

ACCOUNT *Insurance Expense* ACCOUNT NO. 50313

	DATE		DESCRIPTION	POST. REF.	DEBIT	CREDIT	BALANCE DEBIT	BALANCE CREDIT	
1	Dec.	29	Expired insurance	GJ3	90 0 0 000		90 0 0 000		1
2									2
3									3
4									4
5									5
6									6
7									7
8									8
9									9
10									10

ACCOUNT *M&A Salaries Expense* ACCOUNT NO. 50314

	DATE		DESCRIPTION	POST. REF.	DEBIT	CREDIT	BALANCE DEBIT	BALANCE CREDIT	
1	Dec.	30	Monthly salaries	GJ3	140 0 1 500		140 0 1 500		1
2									2
3									3
4									4
5									5
6									6
7									7
8									8
9									9
10									10

ACCOUNT *Payroll Tax Expense* ACCOUNT NO. 50315

	DATE		DESCRIPTION	POST. REF.	DEBIT	CREDIT	BALANCE DEBIT	BALANCE CREDIT	
1	Dec.	30	Employer's part	GJ4	177 6 1 667		177 6 1 667		1
2									2
3									3
4									4
5									5
6									6
7									7
8									8
9									9
10									10

ACCOUNT *Bad Debt Expense* ACCOUNT NO. 50316

	DATE		DESCRIPTION	POST. REF.	DEBIT	CREDIT	BALANCE DEBIT	BALANCE CREDIT	
1	Dec.	31	Bad debt	GJ4	23 9 8 000		23 9 8 000		1
2									2
3									3
4									4
5									5
6									6
7									7
8									8
9									9
10									10

ACCOUNT *Taxes Expense* ACCOUNT NO. 505

	DATE		DESCRIPTION	POST. REF.	DEBIT	CREDIT	BALANCE DEBIT	BALANCE CREDIT	
1	Dec.	28	Property Tax Expense	5052	54 0 9 000		54 0 9 000		1
2									2
3									3
4									4
5									5
6									6
7									7
8									8
9									9
10									10

ACCOUNT *Property Tax Expense* ACCOUNT NO. 5052

	DATE		DESCRIPTION	POST. REF.	DEBIT	CREDIT	BALANCE DEBIT	BALANCE CREDIT	
1	Dec.	17	Property Document Submission	G1	5409000		5409000		1
2									2
3									3
4									4
5									5
6									6
7									7
8									8
9									9
10									10

ACCOUNT *Loss on Disposal of PP&E* ACCOUNT NO. 506

	DATE		DESCRIPTION	POST. REF.	DEBIT	CREDIT	BALANCE DEBIT	BALANCE CREDIT	
1	Dec.	11	Lathe	5061	500000		500000		1
2									2
3									3
4									4
5									5
6									6
7									7
8									8
9									9
10									10

ACCOUNT *Loss on Disposal of Lathe* ACCOUNT NO. 5061

	DATE		DESCRIPTION	POST. REF.	DEBIT	CREDIT	BALANCE DEBIT	BALANCE CREDIT	
1	Dec.	11	Disposal of Lathe	G1	500000		500000		1
2									2
3									3
4									4
5									5
6									6
7									7
8									8
9									9
10									10

All adjusting entries in General Journal have been posted to the ledger. Updated General Journal is illustrated in following table.

	GENERAL JOURNAL					PAGE 1	
	DATE		DESCRIPTION	POST. REF.	DEBIT	CREDIT	
1	Dec.	4	Other Receivables–Fenghua Air-blower	1092	3 0 0 000		1
2			Bank Deposit	102		3 0 0 000	2
3			Check Stub 34	√			3
4	Dec.	4	Cost of Goods Sold–Small Air-blower	5011	250 0 0 000		4
5			Finished Goods–Small Air-blower	11031		250 0 0 000	5
6			SALES SLIP 68	√			6
7	Dec.	7	Cost of Goods Sold–Large Air-blower	5012	520 0 0 000		7
8			Finished Goods–Large Air-blower	11032		520 0 0 000	8
9			SALES SLIP 69	√			9
10	Dec.	7	Cost of Goods Sold–Small Air-blower	5011	250 0 0 000		10
11			Finished Goods–Small Air-blower	11031		250 0 0 000	11
12			SALES SLIP 70	√			12
13	Dec.	7	Cost of Goods Sold–Large Air-blower	5012	260 0 0 000		13
14			Finished Goods–Large Air-blower	11032		260 0 0 000	14
15			SALES SLIP 71	√			15
16	Dec.	9	Other Receivables–Ningbo Air-blower	1093	3 0 0 000		16
17			Bank Deposit	102		3 0 0 000	17
18			Check Stub 48	√			18
19	Dec.	9	Cost of Goods Sold–Small Air-blower	5011	250 0 0 000		19
20			Finished Goods–Small Air-blower	11031		250 0 0 000	20
21			SALES SLIP 72	√			21
22	Dec.	11	Cost of Goods Sold–Large Air-blower	5012	260 0 0 000		22
23			Finished Goods–Large Air-blower	11032		260 0 0 000	23
24			SALES SLIP 73	√			24
25	Dec.	11	Bank Deposit	102	10 0 0 000		25
26			Loss on Disposal of Lathe	5061	5 0 0 000		26
27			Accumulated Depreciation–Lathe	1161	135 0 0 000		27
28			Lathe	1151		150 0 0 000	28
29			Memorandum 32 & 33	√			29
30	Dec.	12	Cost of Goods Sold–Small Air-blower	5011	500 0 0 000		30

continued

	DATE		DESCRIPTION	POST. REF.	DEBIT	CREDIT	
31			Finished Goods-Small Air-blower	11031		500 0 0 000	31
32			SALES SLIP 74	√			32
33	Dec.	15	Cost of Goods Sold-Large Air-blower	5012	520 0 0 000		33
34			Finished Goods-Large Air-blower	11032		520 0 0 000	34
35			SALES SLIP 75	√			35
36	Dec.	17	Other Receivables-Ningbo Air-blower	1093	2 0 0 000		36
37			Bank Deposit	102		2 0 0 000	37
38			Check Stub 168	√			38
39	Dec.	17	Cost of Goods Sold-Large Air-blower	5012	520 0 0 000		39
40			Finished Goods-Large Air-blower	11032		520 0 0 000	40
41			SALES SLIP 76	√			41
42	Dec.	17	Cost of Goods Sold-Small Air-blower	5011	250 0 0 000		42
43			Finished Goods-Small Air-blower	11031		250 0 0 000	43
44			SALES SLIP 77	√			44
45	Dec.	17	Cost of Goods Sold-Large Air-blower	5012	260 0 0 000		45
46			Finished Goods-Large Air-blower	11032		260 0 0 000	46
47			SALES SLIP 78	√			47
48	Dec.	17	Property Tax Expense	5052	54 0 9 000		48
49			Property Tax Payable	2062		54 0 9 000	49
50			Memorandum 36	√			50
51	Dec.	18	Bank Deposit	102	97 8 7 500		51
52			Discounts on N/R-Xiangshan AB	105	2 1 2 500		52
53			N/R-Xiangshan AB	1042		100 0 0 000	53
54			Check Stub 177	√			54
55	Dec.	19	Cost of Goods Sold-Small Air-blower	5011	750 0 0 000		55
56			Finished Goods-Small Air-blower	11031		750 0 0 000	56
57			SALES SLIP 79	√			57
58							
59							
60							

GENERAL JOURNAL							PAGE 2
	DATE		DESCRIPTION	POST. REF.	DEBIT	CREDIT	
1	Dec.	21	Grinder	1159	50 0 0 000		1
2			Capital-Hefeng	301		50 0 0 000	2
3			Memorandum 38	√			3
4	Dec.	22	Cost of Goods Sold-Small Air-blower	5011	500 0 0 000		4
5			Finished Goods-Small Air-blower	11031		500 0 0 000	5
6			SALES SLIP 80	√			6
7	Dec.	23	Steel Plates	110111	75 0 0 000		7
8			Material Price Variance	111	5 0 0 000		8
9			Factory Overhead Incurred	113	9 2 0 000		9
10			Commercial Acceptance Bill Pay	208		89 2 0 000	10
11			Bill 117	√			11
12	Dec.	23	Bank Deposit	102	1 5 0 000		12
13			Cash on Hand	101		1 5 0 000	13
14			Receipt 926	√			14
15	Dec.	27	Cash Lost Expense	5038	5 000		15
16			Cash on Hand	101		5 000	16
17			Memorandum 39	√			17
18	Dec.	27	Cash on Hand	101	5 000		18
19			Cash Lost Expense	5038		5 000	19
20			Memorandum 40	√			20
21	Dec.	28	Cost of Goods Sold-Large Air-blower	5012	520 0 0 000		21
22			Finished Goods-Large Air-blower	11032		520 0 0 000	22
23			SALES SLIP 83	√			23
24	Dec.	28	Work-in-process-Small Air-blower	11021	259 8 7 500		24
25			Material Quantity Variance	112	2 6 2 500		25
26			Steel Plates	110111		262 5 0 000	26
27			Memorandum 41	√			27
28			Work-in-process-Large Air-blower	11022	226 1 2 500		28
29			Material Quantity Variance	112	1 8 7 500		29

continued

	DATE		DESCRIPTION	POST. REF.	DEBIT	CREDIT	
30			Steel Plates	110111		228 0 0 000	30
31			Memorandum 41	√			31
32			Factory Overhead Incurred	113	15 0 0 000		32
33			Steel Plates	110111		15 0 0 000	33
34			Memorandum 41	√			34
35	Dec.	28	Work-in-process–Small Air-blower	11021	111 3 7 500		35
36			Material Quantity Variance	112	1 1 2 500		36
37			Iron Castings	110113		112 5 0 000	37
38			Memorandum 41	√			38
39			Work-in-process–Large Air-blower	11022	111 3 7 500		39
40			Material Quantity Variance	112	2 2 500		40
41			Iron Castings	110113		111 6 0 000	41
42			Memorandum 41	√			42
43			Factory Overhead Incurred	113	22 5 0 000		43
44			Iron Castings	110113		22 5 0 000	44
45			Memorandum 41	√			45
46	Dec.	28	Work-in-process–Small Air-blower	11021	173 2 5 000		46
47			Material Quantity Variance	112	1 7 5 000		47
48			Copper Line	110112		175 0 0 000	48
49			Memorandum 41	√			49
50			Work-in-process–Large Air-blower	11022	149 6 2 500		50
51			Material Quantity Variance	112	4 3 7 500		51
52			Copper Line	110112		154 0 0 000	52
53			Memorandum 41	√			53
54	Dec.	28	Factory Overhead Incurred	113	30 0 0 000		54
55			Refrigeration Oil	110121		30 0 0 000	55
56			Memorandum 41	√			56
57			Factory Overhead Incurred	113	37 5 0 000		57
58			Refrigeration Oil	110121		37 5 0 000	58
59			Memorandum 41	√			59
60							60

GENERAL JOURNAL PAGE 3

	DATE		DESCRIPTION	POST. REF.	DEBIT	CREDIT	
1	Dec.	28	Factory Overhead Incurred	113	4 0 0 000		1
2			Packing Boxes	110122		4 0 0 000	2
3			Memorandum 41	√			3
4			Factory Overhead Incurred	113	3 2 0 000		4
5			Packing Boxes	110122		3 2 0 000	5
6			Memorandum 41	√			6
7	Dec.	28	Factory Overhead Incurred	113	1 0 1 842		7
8			Work Jackets	11431		1 0 1 842	8
9			Memorandum 41	√			9
10			Factory Overhead Incurred	113	1 7 6 012		10
11			Work Shoes	11432		1 7 6 012	11
12			Memorandum 41	√			12
13			Factory Overhead Incurred	113	1 4 8 636		13
14			Heat-resistant Gloves	11433		1 4 8 636	14
15			Memorandum 41	√			15
16	Dec.	29	Amortization Expense–Patent	503111	2 0 0 000		16
17			Accum. Amortization–Patent	1191		2 0 0 000	17
18			Memorandum 42	√			18
19			Amortization Expense–Trademark	503112	2 5 000		19
20			Accum. Amortization–Trademark	1192		2 5 000	20
21			Memorandum 42	√			21
22	Dec.	29	Subscription Expense	50312	9 6 0 000		22
23			Prepaid Subscription	1082		9 6 0 000	23
24			Memorandum 43	√			24
25			Insurance Expense	50313	90 0 0 000		25
26			Prepaid Insurance	1083		90 0 0 000	26
27			Memorandum 43	√			27
28	Dec.	29	Factory Overhead Incurred	113	7 1 1 456		28
29			M&A Broadband Expense	5039	2 8 8 544		29

continued

	DATE		DESCRIPTION	POST. REF.	DEBIT	CREDIT	
30			Prepaid Broadband	1081		10 0 0 000	30
31			Memorandum 44	√			31
32	Dec.	29	Factory Overhead Incurred	113	87 3 0 256		32
33			M&A Depreciation Expense	50310	15 9 8 470		33
34			Accumulated Depreciation	116		103 2 8 726	34
35			Memorandum 45	√			35
36	Dec.	30	COGS–Small Air-blower	5011	44 6 0 784		36
37			COGS–Large Air-blower	5012	46 3 9 216		37
38			Material Price Variance	111		91 0 0 000	38
39			Memorandum 46	√			39
40			COGS–Small Air-blower	5011	5 8 7 010		40
41			COGS–Large Air-blower	5012	6 1 0 490		41
42			Material Quantity Variance	112		11 9 7 500	42
43			Memorandum 46	√			43
44	Dec.	30	Direct Labor	120	493 0 5 000		44
45			Labor Efficiency Variance	121	5 7 0 000		45
46			Labor Rate Variance	122	1 0 0 200		46
47			Factory Overhead Incurred	113	72 2 5 200		47
48			Sales Salaries Expense	5025	10 0 0 000		48
49			M&A Salaries Expense	50314	140 0 1 500		49
50			Social Security Tax Payable	2052		129 9 6 342	50
51			Medicare Tax Payable	2053		14 4 4 038	51
52			FUTP	2054		9 3 164	52
53			SUTP	2055		6 2 8 855	53
54			Employee FITP	2056		9 0 467	54
55			Employee SITP	2057		1 8 0 933	55
56			Salaries Payable	2051		567 6 8 101	56
57			Memorandum 47	√			57
58							58
59							59
60							60

GENERAL JOURNAL					PAGE 4
DATE		DESCRIPTION	POST. REF.	DEBIT	CREDIT
Dec.	30	Payroll Tax Expense	50315	177 6 1 667	
		Social Security Tax Payable	2052		129 9 6 342
		Medicare Tax Payable	2053		14 4 4 038
		FUTP	2054		4 3 3 211
		SUTP	2055		28 8 8 076
		Memorandum 47	√		
Dec.	30	Work-in-process–Small Air-blower	11021	266 4 7 500	
		Work-in-process–Large Air-blower	11022	226 5 7 500	
		Direct Labor	120		493 0 5 000
		Memorandum 47	√		
Dec.	30	COGS–Small Air-blower	5011	4 9 118	
		COGS–Large Air-blower	5012	5 1 082	
		Labor Rate Variance	122		1 0 0 200
		Memorandum 47	√		
		COGS–Small Air-blower	5011	2 7 9 412	
		COGS–Large Air-blower	5012	2 9 0 588	
		Labor Efficiency Variance	121		5 7 0 000
		Memorandum 47	√		
Dec.	31	Bad Debt Expense	50316	23 9 8 000	
		Allowance for Doubtful Debts	107		23 9 8 000
		Memorandum 48	√		
Dec.	31	Interest Expense	5037	5 1 8 400	
		Interest Payable	207		5 1 8 400
		Memorandum 49	√		
Dec.	31	Work-in-process–Small Air-blower	11021	288 4 2 000	
		Work-in-process–Large Air-blower	11022	242 8 8 000	
		Factory Overhead Applied	113		531 3 0 000
		Memorandum 50	√		
Dec.	31	Cost of Goods Sold–Small Air-blower	5011	3 406	
		Cost of Goods Sold–Large Air-blower	5012	3 542	
		Factory Overhead	113		6 948
		Memorandum 51	√		
Dec.	31	Finished Goods–Small Air-blower	11031	1161 4 1 642	
		WIP–Small Air-blower	11021		1161 4 1 642
		Memorandum 52	√		
Dec.	31	Finished Goods–Large Air-blower	11032	961 7 1 637	
		WIP–Large Air-blower	11022		961 7 1 637
		Memorandum 52	√		

CHAPTER 6 PREPARE ADJUSTED TRIAL BALANCE

The fifth step of accounting cycle is to prepare adjusted trial balance. The purpose of worksheet adjusted trials balance is to make sure that all debits equals to all credits before income statement is made. This reduces the time that accountants spend in searching for errors and therefore improves the efficiency. This is illustrated in following table.

Adjusted Trial Balance		
Account Name	Debit	Credit
Cash on Hand	37,000.00	
Bank Deposit	6,093,704.54	
Bank Draft	60,408.00	
Notes Receivable	202,125.00	
Discounts on Notes Receivable		
Accounts Receivable	2,998,000.00	
Allowance for Doubtful Debts		29,980.00
Prepaid Expense	122,500.00	
Other Receivables	13,500.00	
Inventory	2,025,296.00	
Material Price Variance	0.00	
Direct Labor	0.00	
Labor Efficiency Variance	0.00	
Labor Rate Variance	0.00	
Factory Overhead	0.00	
Supplies	29,735.10	
Plant, Property & Equipment	12,319,200.00	
Accumulated Depreciation		2,468,287.26
Land	2,600,000.00	
Intangible Assets	530,000.00	
Accumulated Amortization		202250
Short-term Borrowings		2,528,000.00
Notes Payable		110,000.00
Accounts Payable		441,900.00
Unearned Revenue		1,191,570.00
Payroll Liabilities		899,635.67
Taxes Payable		810,000.00
Interests Payable		8,101.00
Commercial Acceptance Bill Payable		89,200.00
Capital, Hefeng		12,850,000.00
Capital Reserve		550,000.00
Retained Earnings		2,900,000.00
Sales Revenue		8,250,000.00
Other Revenue		3,000.00
Cost of Goods Sold	5,719,746.48	
Selling Expense	40,500.00	
Administrative & Managerial Expense	481,118.81	
Taxes Expense	54,090.00	
Loss on Disposal of PP&E	5,000.00	
Total	33,331,923.93	33,331,923.93

CHAPTER 7 PREPARE CLOSING ENTRIES AND POST TO THE LEDGER

The sixth step of accounting cycle is to make closing journal entries and record those transactions in T-accounts. At this moment, there are no longer two types of journals. Only one journal book should be used, which is General Journal Book. The recording and posting methods are similar to the ones for period transactions. Those entries should also be posted to the ledger. When journal entries are posted to the ledger, post reference should be recorded.

In the following part of this section, closing entries will be made for of Xinle Air-blower Co., Ltd. in December. Those adjusting entries will also be recorded in T-accounts book. These will be illustrated in following transaction.

TRANSACTION 107

On December 31, Income Statement accounts are closed. The source document is MEMORANDUM 53.

Xinle Air-blower Co., Ltd. MEMORANDUM 53

23 Tulan ST

Xiangshan, China 315700

TO: Warehouse

FROM: John Thompson

DATE: December 31, 2016

SUBJECT: Close Income Statement Accounts

Please make closing entries to close Income Statement accounts.

WHAT TO DO?

STEP 1 Analyze Transaction

Accounts Affected:

There are eight accounts affected by transactions. They are **Sales Revenue, Other Revenue, Cost of Goods Sold, Selling Expense, Administrative & Managerial Expense, Taxes Expense, Loss on Disposal of PP&E and Income Summary.**

Increase/Decrease:

Sales Revenue is decreased by $8,250,000. **Other Revenue** is decreased by $3,000. **Cost of Goods Sold** is decreased by $5, 719, 746.48. **Selling Expense** is decreased by $40, 500. **Administrative & Managerial Expense** is decreased by $481,118.81. **Taxes Expense** is decreased by $54,090. **Loss on Disposal of PP&E** is decreased by $5,000. **Income Summary** is increased by $1,952,544.71.

Account Category:

Sales Revenue is a revenue account. **Other Revenue** is a revenue account. **Cost of Goods Sold** is an expense account. **Selling Expense** is an expense account. **Administrative & Managerial Expense** is an expense account. **Taxes Expense** is an expense account. **Loss on Disposal of PP&E** is a loss account. **Income Summary** is a revenue account.

STEP 2 Determine Debit/Credit

-The normal balance of revenue accounts is credit. **Sales Revenue** is debited by $8,250,000.

Other Revenue is debited by $3,000. **Income Summary** is credited by $1,952,544.71.

–The normal balance of expense accounts is debit. **Cost of Goods Sold** is credited by $5,719,746.48. **Selling Expense** is credited by $40,500. **Administrative & Managerial Expense** is credited by $481,118.81. **Taxes Expense** is credited by $54,090.

–The normal balance of loss accounts is credit. **Loss on Disposal of PP&E** is credited by $5,000.

Step 3 Record in T-accounts

Sales Revenue	
Debit	Credit
8,250,000	

Other Revenue	
Debit	Credit
3,000	

Cost of Goods Sold	
Debit	Credit
	5,719,746.48

Selling Expense	
Debit	Credit
	40,500

Administrative & Managerial Expense	
Debit	Credit
	481,118.81

Taxes Expense	
Debit	Credit
	54,090

Loss on Disposal of PP&E	
Debit	Credit
	5,000

Income Summary	
Debit	Credit
	1,952,544.71

Step 4 Record in Journals

GENERAL JOURNAL PAGE 4

	DATE		DESCRIPTION	POST. REF.	DEBIT	CREDIT	
39	Dec.	31	Sales Revenue		8250000 00		39
40			Other Revenue		3000 00		40
41			Cost of Goods Sold			5719746 48	41
42			Selling Expense			40500 00	42
43			M&A Expense			481118 81	43
44			Taxes Expense			54090 00	44
45			Loss on Disposal of PP&E			5000 00	45
46			Income Summary			1952544 71	46
47			*Memorandum 53*				47
48							48

TRANSACTION 108

On December 31, income taxes were calculated and closed. The source document is MEMORANDUM 54.

Xinle Air-blower Co., Ltd. MEMORANDUM 54

23 Tulan ST

Xiangshan, China 315700

TO: Warehouse

FROM: John Thompson

DATE: December 31, 2016

SUBJECT: Calculate Income Tax

Please make closing entries for Income Tax.

WHAT TO DO?

Since tax system in China is different from that in the United States, income taxes should be adjusted to satisfy tax system in the United States. There are two types of income tax in the United States. They are federal income tax and state income tax. In previous cases, it is assumed that California is adopted. In California, state income tax rate is 8.840%. State income tax should be \$172,604.95 (1,952,544.71×8.840%). The federal income tax rate is illustrated in following table.

Tax Bracket (\$)	Marginal Corporate Income Tax Rate
\$0 to \$50,000	15%
\$50,000 to \$75,000	\$7,500 + 25% of the amount over 50,000
\$75,000 to \$100,000	\$13,750 + 34% of the amount over 75,000
\$100,000 to \$335,000	\$22,250 + 39% of the amount over 100,000
\$335,000 to \$10,000,000	\$113,900 + 34% of the amount over 335,000
\$10,000,000 to \$15,000,000	\$3,400,000 + 35% of the amount over 10,000,000
\$15,000,000 to \$18,333,333	\$5,150,000 + 38% of the amount over \$15,000,000
\$18,333,333 and up	\$6,416,667 + 35% of the amount over \$18,333,333

The current balance of Income Summary is $1,952,544.71, and therefore the tax bracket adopted should be the one from $335,000 to $10,000,000. The amount over $335,000 is $1,617,544.71. Federal income tax should be $663,865.20 (113,900+34%×1,617,544.71).

Step 1 Analyze Transaction

Accounts Affected:

–For the first entry, there are three accounts affected. They are **Income Tax Expense, Federal Income Tax Payable** and **State Income Tax Payable.**

– For the second entry, there are two accounts affected. They are **Income Summary** and **Income Tax Expense.**

Increase/Decrease:

– **Income Tax Expense** is increased by $836, 470.15. **Federal Income Tax Payable** is increased by $663,865.20. **State Income Tax Payable** is increased by $172,604.95.

–**Income Summary** is decreased by $836,470.15. **Income Tax Expense** is decreased by $836,470.15.

Account Category:

Income Tax Expense is an expense account. **Federal Income Tax Payable** is a liability account. **State Income Tax Payable** is a liability account. **Income Summary** is a revenue account.

Step 2 Determine Debit/Credit

–The normal balance of expense accounts is debit. **Income Tax Expense** is debited by $836,470.15.

–The normal balance of liability accounts is credit. **Federal Income Tax Payable** is credited by $663,865.20. **State Income Tax Payable** is credited by $172,604.95.

–The normal balance of revenue accounts is credit. **Income Summary** is debited by $836,470.15.

–The normal balance of expense accounts is debit. **Income Tax Expense** is credited by $836,470.15.

Step 3 Record in T-accounts

Income Tax Expense

Debit	Credit
836,470.15	
	836,470.15

Federal Income Tax Payable

Debit	Credit
	663,865.20

State Income Tax Payable

Debit	Credit
	172,604.95

Income Summary

Debit	Credit
836,470.15	

Step 4 Record in Journals

GENERAL JOURNAL							PAGE 4
	DATE		DESCRIPTION	POST. REF.	DEBIT	CREDIT	
48	Dec.	31	Income Tax Expense		836 470 15		48
49			Federal Income Tax Payable			663 865 20	49
50			State Income Tax Payable			172 604 95	50
51			*Memorandum 54*				51
52			Income Summary		836 470 15		52
53			Income Tax Expense			836 470 15	53
54			*Memorandum 54*				54
55							55

TRANSACTION 109

On December 31, net income was transferred. The source document is MEMORANDUM 55. The current balance of Income Summary is $1,116,074.56.

Xinle Air-blower Co., Ltd. MEMORANDUM 55

23 Tulan ST

Xiangshan, China 315700

TO: Warehouse

FROM: John Thompson

DATE: December 31, 2016

SUBJECT: Close Income Summary

Please make closing entries to close income summary account.

WHAT TO DO?

Step 1 Analyze Transaction

Accounts Affected:

There are two accounts affected by this transaction. They are **Income Summary** and **Retained Earnings.**

Increase/Decrease:

Income Summary is decreased by $1,116,074.56. **Retained Earnings** is increased by $1,116,

074.56.

Account Category:

Income Summary is a revenue account. **Retained Earnings** is an equity account.

Step 2 Determine Debit/Credit

–The normal balance of revenue accounts is credit. **Income Summary** is debited by $1,116,074.56.

–The normal balance of equity accounts is credit. **Retained Earnings** is credited by $1,116,074.56.

Step 3 Record in T-accounts

Income Summary

Debit	Credit
1,116,074.56	

Retained Earnings

Debit	Credit
	1,116,074.56

Step 4 Record in Journals

GENERAL JOURNAL PAGE 4

	DATE		DESCRIPTION	POST. REF.	DEBIT	CREDIT	
55	Dec.	31	Income Summary		1116 074 56		55
56			Retained Earnings			1116 074 56	56
57			*Memorandum 55*				57
58							58

TRANSACTION 110

On December 31, Xinle distributed net income.

WHAT TO DO?

There is no record for this transaction. Income Summary has already been closed, and the balance of Income Summary has been transferred to Retained Earnings. There is no sub-accounts for Retained Earnings, and therefore it is not necessary to allocate earnings among those sub-accounts.

TRANSACTION 111

On December 31, Xinle closed distributed income.

WHAT TO DO?

There is no record for this transaction. Since there is no record for last transaction, close of distributed income is also not necessary.

TRANSACTION SUMMARY

Closing journal entries have been completed at this point. All entries have already been collected in General Journal. Updated General Journal is illustrated in following table.

GENERAL JOURNAL							PAGE 1
	DATE		DESCRIPTION	POST. REF.	DEBIT	CREDIT	
1	Dec.	4	Other Receivables-Fenghua Air-blower	1092	3 0 0 0 00		1
2			Bank Deposit	102		3 0 0 0 00	2
3			Check Stub 34	√			3
4	Dec.	4	Cost of Goods Sold-Small Air-blower	5011	250 0 0 0 00		4
5			Finished Goods-Small Air-blower	11031		250 0 0 0 00	5
6			SALES SLIP 68	√			6
7	Dec.	7	Cost of Goods Sold-Large Air-blower	5012	520 0 0 0 00		7
8			Finished Goods-Large Air-blower	11032		520 0 0 0 00	8
9			SALES SLIP 69	√			9
10	Dec.	7	Cost of Goods Sold-Small Air-blower	5011	250 0 0 0 00		10
11			Finished Goods-Small Air-blower	11031		250 0 0 0 00	11
12			SALES SLIP 70	√			12
13	Dec.	7	Cost of Goods Sold-Large Air-blower	5012	260 0 0 0 00		13
14			Finished Goods-Large Air-blower	11032		260 0 0 0 00	14
15			SALES SLIP 71	√			15
16	Dec.	9	Other Receivables-Ningbo Air-blower	1093	3 0 0 0 00		16
17			Bank Deposit	102		3 0 0 0 00	17
18			Check Stub 48	√			18
19	Dec.	9	Cost of Goods Sold-Small Air-blower	5011	250 0 0 0 00		19
20			Finished Goods-Small Air-blower	11031		250 0 0 0 00	20
21			SALES SLIP 72	√			21
22	Dec.	11	Cost of Goods Sold-Large Air-blower	5012	260 0 0 0 00		22
23			Finished Goods-Large Air-blower	11032		260 0 0 0 00	23
24			SALES SLIP 73	√			24
25	Dec.	11	Bank Deposit	102	10 0 0 0 00		25
26			Loss on Disposal of Lathe	5061	5 0 0 0 00		26

continued

GENERAL JOURNAL							PAGE 1
	DATE		DESCRIPTION	POST. REF.	DEBIT	CREDIT	
27			Accumulated Depreciation-Lathe	1161	1350000 00		27
28			Lathe	1151		1500000 00	28
29			Memorandum 32 & 33	√			29
30	Dec.	12	Cost of Goods Sold-Small Air-blower	5011	5000000 00		30
31			Finished Goods-Small Air-blower	11031		5000000 00	31
32			SALES SLIP 74	√			32
33	Dec.	15	Cost of Goods Sold-Large Air-blower	5012	5200000 00		33
34			Finished Goods-Large Air-blower	11032		5200000 00	34
35			SALES SLIP 75	√			35
36	Dec.	17	Other Receivables-Ningbo Air-blower	1093	20000 00		36
37			Bank Deposit	102		20000 00	37
38			Check Stub 168	√			38
39	Dec.	17	Cost of Goods Sold-Large Air-blower	5012	5200000 00		39
40			Finished Goods-Large Air-blower	11032		5200000 00	40
41			SALES SLIP 76	√			41
42	Dec.	17	Cost of Goods Sold-Small Air-blower	5011	2500000 00		42
43			Finished Goods-Small Air-blower	11031		2500000 00	43
44			SALES SLIP 77	√			44
45	Dec.	17	Cost of Goods Sold-Large Air-blower	5012	2600000 00		45
46			Finished Goods-Large Air-blower	11032		2600000 00	46
47			SALES SLIP 78	√			47
48	Dec.	17	Property Tax Expense	5052	540900 00		48
49			Property Tax Payable	2062		540900 00	49
50			Memorandum 36	√			50
51	Dec.	18	Bank Deposit	102	978750 00		51
52			Discounts on N/R-Xiangshan AB	105	21250 00		52
53			N/R-Xiangshan AB	1042		1000000 00	53
54			Check Stub 177	√			54
55	Dec.	19	Cost of Goods Sold-Small Air-blower	5011	7500000 00		55
56			Finished Goods-Small Air-blower	11031		7500000 00	56
57			SALES SLIP 79	√			57
58							58
59							59
60							60

GENERAL JOURNAL PAGE 2

	DATE		DESCRIPTION	POST. REF.	DEBIT	CREDIT	
1	Dec.	21	Grinder	1159	50000 00		1
2			Capital, Hefeng	301		50000 00	2
3			Memorandum 38	√			3
4	Dec.	22	Cost of Goods Sold–Small Air-blower	5011	500000 00		4
5			Finished Goods–Small Air-blower	11031		500000 00	5
6			SALES SLIP 80	√			6
7	Dec.	23	Steel Plates	110111	75000 00		7
8			Material Price Variance	111	5000 00		8
9			Factory Overhead Incurred	113	9200 00		9
10			Commercial Acceptance Bill Pay.	208		89200 00	10
11			Bill 117	√			11
12	Dec.	23	Bank Deposit	102	1500 00		12
13			Cash on Hand	101		1500 00	13
14			Receipt 926	√			14
15	Dec.	27	Cash Lost Expense	5038	50 00		15
16			Cash on Hand	101		50 00	16
17			Memorandum 39	√			17
18	Dec.	27	Cash on Hand	101	50 00		18
19			Cash Lost Expense	5038		50 00	19
20			Memorandum 40	√			20
21	Dec.	28	Cost of Goods Sold–Large Air-blower	5012	520000 00		21
22			Finished Goods-Large Air-blower	11032		520000 00	22
23			SALES SLIP 83	√			23
24	Dec.	28	Work-in-process–Small Air-blower		259875 00		24
25			Material Quantity Variance		2625 00		25
26			Steel Plates			262500 00	26
27			Memorandum 41				27
28			Work-in-process–Large Air-blower		226125 00		28
29			Material Quantity Variance		1875 00		29
30			Steel Plates			228000 00	30
31			Memorandum 41				31
32			Factory Overhead Incurred		15000 00		32
33			Steel Plates			15000 00	33
34			Memorandum 41				34
35	Dec.	28	Work-in-process–Small Air-blower		111375 00		35
36			Material Quantity Variance		1125 00		36
37			Iron Castings			112500 00	37
38			Memorandum 41				38
39			Work-in-process–Large Air-blower		111375 00		39
40			Material Quantity Variance		225 00		40
41			Iron Castings			111600 00	41
42			Memorandum 41				42
43			Factory Overhead Incurred		22500 00		43
44			Iron Castings			22500 00	44
45			Memorandum 41				45
46	Dec.	28	Work-in-process–Small Air-blower		173250 00		46
47			Material Quantity Variance		1750 00		47
48			Copper Line			175000 00	48
49			Memorandum 41				49
50			Work-in-process–Large Air-blower		149625 00		50
51			Material Quantity Variance		4375 00		51
52			Copper Line			154000 00	52
53			Memorandum 41				53
54	Dec.	28	Factory Overhead Incurred		30000 00		54
55			Refrigeration Oil			30000 00	55
56			Memorandum 41				56
57			Factory Overhead Incurred		37500 00		57
58			Refrigeration Oil			37500 00	58
59			Memorandum 41				59
60							60

GENERAL JOURNAL PAGE 3

DATE		DESCRIPTION	POST. REF.	DEBIT	CREDIT
Dec.	28	Factory Overhead Incurred		4000 00	
		Packing Boxes			4000 00
		Memorandum 41			
		Factory Overhead Incurred		3200 00	
		Packing Boxes			3200 00
		Memorandum 41			
Dec.	28	Factory Overhead Incurred		1018 42	
		Work Jackets			1018 42
		Memorandum 41			
		Factory Overhead Incurred		1760 12	
		Work Shoes			1760 12
		Memorandum 41			
		Factory Overhead Incurred		1486 36	
		Heat-resistant Gloves			1486 36
		Memorandum 41			
Dec.	29	Amortization Expense-Patent		2000 00	
		Accum. Amortization-Patent			2000 00
		Memorandum 42			
		Amortization Expense-Trademark		250 00	
		Accum. Amortization-Trademark			250 00
		Memorandum 42			
Dec.	29	Subscription Expense		9600 00	
		Prepaid Subscription			9600 00
		Memorandum 43			
		Insurance Expense		90000 00	
		Prepaid Insurance			90000 00
		Memorandum 43			
Dec.	29	Factory Overhead Incurred		7114 56	
		M&A Broadband Expense		2885 44	
		Prepaid Broadband			10000 00
		Memorandum 44			
Dec.	29	Factory Overhead Incurred		87302 56	
		M&A Depreciation Expense		15984 70	
		Plant, Property & Equipment			103287 26
		Memorandum 45			
Dec.	30	COGS–Small Air-blower		44607 84	
		COGS–Large Air-blower		46392 16	
		Material Price Variance			91000 00
		Memorandum 46			
		COGS–Small Air-blower		5870 10	
		COGS–Large Air-blower		6104 90	
		Material Quantity Variance			11975 00
		Memorandum 46			
Dec.	30	Direct Labor		493050 00	
		Labor Efficiency Variance		5700 00	
		Labor Rate Variance		1002 00	
		Factory Overhead Incurred		72252 00	
		Sales Salaries Expense		100000 00	
		M&A Salaries Expense		140015 00	
		Social Security Tax Payable			129963 42
		Medicare Tax Payable			14440 38
		FUTP			931 64
		SUTP			6288 55
		Employee FITP			904 67
		Employee SITP			1809 33
		Salaries Payable			567681 01
		Memorandum 47			

GENERAL JOURNAL PAGE 4

	DATE		DESCRIPTION	POST. REF.	DEBIT	CREDIT	
1	Dec.	30	Payroll Tax Expense	50315	177616 67		1
2			Social Security Tax Payable	2052		129963 42	2
3			Medicare Tax Payable	2053		14440 38	3
4			FUTP	2054		4332 11	4
5			SUTP	2055		28880 76	5
6			Memorandum 47	√			6
7	Dec.	30	Work-in-process–Small Air-blower	11021	266475 00		7
8			Work-in-process–Large Air-blower	11022	226575 00		8
9			Direct Labor	120		493050 00	9
10			Memorandum 47	√			10
11	Dec.	30	COGS–Small Air-blower	5011	491 18		11
12			COGS–Large Air-blower	5012	510 82		12
13			Labor Rate Variance	122		1002 00	13
14			Memorandum 47	√			14
15			COGS–Small Air-blower	5011	2794 12		15
16			COGS–Large Air-blower	5012	2905 88		16
17			Labor Efficiency Variance	121		5700 00	17
18			Memorandum 47	√			18
19	Dec.	31	Bad Debt Expense	50316	23980 00		19
20			Allowance for Doubtful Debts	107		23980 00	20
21			Memorandum 48	√			21
22	Dec.	31	Interest Expense	5037	5184 00		22
23			Interest Payable	207		5184 00	23
24			Memorandum 49	√			24
25	Dec.	31	Work-in-process–Small Air-blower	11021	288420 00		25
26			Work-in-process–Large Air-blower	11022	242880 00		26
27			Factory Overhead Applied	113		531300 00	27
28			Memorandum 50	√			28
29	Dec.	31	Cost of Goods Sold–Small Air-blower	5011	34 06		29
30			Cost of Goods Sold–Large Air-blower	5012	35 42		30
31			Factory Overhead	113		69 48	31
32			Memorandum 51	√			32
33	Dec.	31	Finished Goods–Small Air-blower	11031	1161416 42		33
34			WIP-Small Air-blower	11021		1161416 42	34
35			Memorandum 52	√			35
36	Dec.	31	Finished Goods–Large Air-blower	11032	961716 37		36
37			WIP-Large Air-blower	11022		961716 37	37
38			Memorandum 52	√			38
39	Dec.	31	Sales Revenue		8250000 00		39
40			Other Revenue		3000 00		40
41			Cost of Goods Sold			5719746 48	41
42			Selling Expense			40500 00	42
43			M&A Expense			481118 81	43
44			Taxes Expense			54090 00	44
45			Loss on Disposal of PP&E			5000 00	45
46			Income Summary			1952544 71	46
47			Memorandum 53				47
48	Dec.	31	Income Tax Expense		836470 15		48
49			Federal Income Tax Payable			663865 20	49
50			State Income Tax Payable			172604 95	50
51			Memorandum 54				51
52			Income Summary		836470 15		52
53			Income Tax Expense			836470 15	53
54			Memorandum 54				54
55	Dec.	31	Income Summary		1116074 56		55
56			Retained Earnings			1116074 56	56
57			Memorandum 55				57
58							58
59							59
60							60

Updated T - accounts book is illustrated as follows. Since only temporary accounts are affected, those accounts are illustrated alone. B means beginning balance. U means unadjusted ending balance. A means adjusted ending balance. C means closed ending balance.

Sales Revenue*

Debit	Credit	
	3,850,000	
	4,400,000	
	8,250,000.00	U
	8,250,000.00	A
3,850,000.00		
4,400,000.00		
	0.00	C

Sales Revenue-Small Air-blower**

Debit	Credit	
	350,000	
	350,000	
	350,000	
	700,000	
	350,000	
	1,050,000	
	700,000	
	3,850,000.00	U
	3,850,000.00	A
3,850,000.00		
	0.00	C

Sales Revenue-Large Air-blower**

Debit	Credit	
	800,000	
	400,000	
	400,000	
	800,000	
	800,000	
	400,000	
	800,000	
	4,400,000.00	U
	4,400,000.00	A
4,400,000.00		
	0.00	C

Other Revenue*

Debit	Credit	
	3,000	
	3,000.00	U
	3,000.00	A
3,000		
	0.00	C

Investment Earnings**

Debit	Credit	
	0.00	U
	0.00	A
	0.00	C

Cost of Goods Sold*

	Debit	Credit
	2,750,000	
	2,860,000	
U	5,610,000	
	53,797.30	
	55,949.18	
A	5,719,746.48	
		2,803,797.30
		2,915,949.18
C	0.00	

Cost of Goods Sold-Small Air-blower**

	Debit	Credit
	250,000	
	250,000	
	250,000	
	500,000	
	250,000	
	750,000	
	500,000	
U	2,750,000	
	44,607.84	
	5,870.10	
	34.06	
	491.18	
	2,794.12	
A	2,803,797.30	
		2,803,797.30
C	0.00	

Cost of Goods Sold-Large Air-blower**

	Debit	Credit
	520,000	
	260,000	
	260,000	
	520,000	
	520,000	
	260,000	
	520,000	
U	2,860,000	
	46,392.16	
	6,104.90	
	35.42	
	510.82	
	2,905.88	
A	2,915,949.18	
		2,915,949.18
C	0.00	

Selling Expense*

	Debit	Credit
	4,500	
	3,000	
	15,000	
	8,000	
U	30,500	
	10,000	
A	40,500	
		4,500
		3,000
		15,000
		8,000
		10,000
C	0.00	

Administrative & Managerial Expense*

	Debit	Credit
	800	
	3,000	
	30	
	1,200	
	2,500	
	240	
	5,833	
U	13,603	
	2,885.44	
	15,984.70	
	5,184	
	2,250	
	9,600	
	90,000	
	140,015	
	177,616.67	
	23,980	
A	481,118.81	
		800
		2,885.44
		3,000
		15,984.70
		30
		1,200
		2,500
		240
		11,017
		2,250
		9,600
		90,000
		140,015
		177,616.67
		23,980
C	0.00	

M&A Travel Expense**

	Debit	Credit
	800	
U	800	
A	800	
		800
C	0.00	

Sales Travel Expense**

	Debit	Credit
	4,500	
U	4,500	
A	4,500	
		4,500
C	0.00	

M&A Broadband Expense*

	Debit	Credit
	2,885.44	
A	2,885.44	
		2,885.44
C	0.00	

Sales Training Expense**

	Debit	Credit
	3,000	
U	3,000	
A	3,000	
		3,000
C	0.00	

M&A Training Expense**

	Debit	Credit
	3,000	
U	3,000	
A	3,000	
		3,000
C	0.00	

M&A Depreciation Expense*

	Debit	Credit
	15,984.70	
A	15,984.70	
		15,984.70
C	0.00	

Bank Fee Expense**

	Debit	Credit
	30	
U	30	
A	30	
		30
C	0.00	

Telecommunication Expense**

	Debit	Credit
	1,200	
U	1,200	
A	1,200	
		1,200
C	0.00	

Invitation Fee Expense**

	Debit	Credit
	1,000	
	1,500	
U	2,500	
A	2,500	
		2,500
C	0.00	

Advertising Expense**

	Debit	Credit
	10,000	
	5,000	
U	15,000	
A	15,000	
		15,000
C	0.00	

Television Expense**

	Debit	Credit
	240	
U	240	
A	240	
		240
C	0.00	

Interest Expense**

	Debit	Credit
	5,833	
U	5,833	
	5,184	
A	11,017	
		11,017
C	0.00	

Cash Lost Expense**

	Debit	Credit
	50	
		50
U	0	
A	0	
C	0.00	

Telephone Expense**

	Debit	Credit
	8,000	
U	8,000	
A	8,000	
		8,000
C	0.00	

Sales Salaries Expense

	Debit	Credit
	10,000	
A	10,000	
		10,000
C	0.00	

Taxes Expense*

	Debit	Credit
	54,090	
U	54,090	
A	54,090	
		54,090
C	0.00	

Income Taxes Expense**

	Debit	Credit
U	0.00	
A	0.00	
	836,470.15	
		836,470.15
C	0.00	

Property Tax Expense**

	Debit	Credit
	54,090	
U	54,090	
A	54,090	
		54,090
C	0.00	

Loss on Disposal of PP&E*

	Debit	Credit
	5,000	
U	5,000	
A	5,000	
		5,000
C	0.00	

Loss on Disposal of Lathe**

	Debit	Credit
	5,000	
U	5,000	
A	5,000	
		5,000
C	0.00	

Amortization Expense*

	Debit	Credit
	2,000	
	250	
A	2,250	
		2,250
C	0.00	

Amortization Expense–Patent**

	Debit	Credit
	2,000	
A	2,000	
		2,000
C	0.00	

Amortization Expense–Trademark**

	Debit	Credit
	250	
A	250	
		250
C	0.00	

Subscription Expense*

	Debit	Credit
	9,600	
A	9,600	
		9,600
C	0.00	

Insurance Expense*

	Debit	Credit
	90,000	
A	90,000	
		90,000
C	0.00	

M&A Salaries Expense

	Debit	Credit
	140,015	
A	140,015	
		140,015
C	0.00	

Payroll Tax Expense

	Debit	Credit
	177,616.67	
A	177,616.67	
		177,616.67
C	0.00	

Bad Debt Expense

	Debit	Credit
	23,980	
A	23,980	
		23,980
C	0.00	

Income Summary

Debit	Credit	
	8,250,000	
	3,000	
5,719,746.48		
40,500		
481,118.81		
54,090		
5,000		
836,470.15		
1,116,074.56		
	0.00	C

POST TO THE LEDGER

Initial recording of those closing entries have been finished. Those entries should be posted to the ledger. Both general ledger and subsidiary ledger should be used at this point. They are illustrated as following tables. In the following part of this section, general ledger and subsidiary ledgers will be recorded for all transactions of Xinle Air-blower Co., Ltd. Updated part of the ledgers are illustrated in following tables.

ACCOUNT *Income Taxes Payable* ACCOUNT NO. 2063

	DATE		DESCRIPTION	POST. REF.	DEBIT	CREDIT	BALANCE		
							DEBIT	CREDIT	
1	Dec.	1	Balance	√				1203 18000	1
2	Dec.	28	Federal Income Tax Payable	20631	601 590 00			601 59000	2
3	Dec.	28	State Income Tax Payable	20632	601 590 00			~~000000~~	3
4	Dec.	31	Closing entries	GJ4		836 470 15		836 47015	4
5									5
6									6
7									7
8									8
9									9
10									10

ACCOUNT *Federal Income Tax Payable* ACCOUNT NO. 20631

	DATE		DESCRIPTION	POST. REF.	DEBIT	CREDIT	BALANCE		
							DEBIT	CREDIT	
1	Dec.	1	Balance	√				601 59000	1
2	Dec.	28	Payment of federal income tax	CPJ1	601 590 00			~~000000~~	2
3	Dec.	31	Closing entries	GJ4		663 865 20		663 86520	3
4									4
5									5
6									6
7									7
8									8
9									9
10									10

ACCOUNT *State Income Tax Payable* ACCOUNT NO. 20632

	DATE		DESCRIPTION	POST. REF.	DEBIT	CREDIT	BALANCE		
							DEBIT	CREDIT	
1	Dec.	1	Balance	√				601 59000	1
2	Dec.	28	Payment of federal income tax	CPJ1	601 590 00			~~000000~~	2
3	Dec.	31	Closing entries	GJ4		172 604 95		172 60495	3
4									4
5									5
6									6
7									7
8									8
9									9
10									10

ACCOUNT *Retained Earnings* ACCOUNT NO. 303

	DATE		DESCRIPTION	POST. REF.	DEBIT	CREDIT	BALANCE		
							DEBIT	CREDIT	
1	Dec.	1	Balance	√				2900 0 0 000	1
2	Dec.	31	Closing entries	GJ4		1116 0 7 4 56		4016 0 7 456	2
3									3
4									4
5									5
6									6
7									7
8									8
9									9
10									10

ACCOUNT *Sales Revenue* ACCOUNT NO. 401

	DATE		DESCRIPTION	POST. REF.	DEBIT	CREDIT	BALANCE		
							DEBIT	CREDIT	
1	Dec.	28	Small Air-blower	4011		3850 0 0 0 00		3850 0 0 000	1
2	Dec.	28	Large Air-blower	4012		3600 0 0 0 00		8250 0 0 000	2
3	Dec.	31	Closing entries	GJ4	8250 0 0 0 00			~~00 0 000~~	3
4									4
5									5
6									6
7									7
8									8
9									9
10									10

ACCOUNT *Sales Revenue-Small Air-blower* ACCOUNT NO. 4011

	DATE		DESCRIPTION	POST. REF.	DEBIT	CREDIT	BALANCE		
							DEBIT	CREDIT	
1	Dec.	28	Sold products	CRJ1	2450 0 0 0 00			2450 0 0 000	1
2	Dec.	28	Sales Journal	SJ1	1400 0 0 0 00			3850 0 0 000	2
3	Dec.	31	Closing entries	G4	3850 0 0 0 00			~~00 0 000~~	3
4									4
5									5
6									6
7									7
8									8
9									9
10									10

ACCOUNT Sales *Revenue-Large Air-blower* ACCOUNT NO. 4012

DATE		DESCRIPTION	POST. REF.	DEBIT	CREDIT	BALANCE	
						DEBIT	CREDIT
Dec.	31	Sold products	CRJ1	36000 0 0 00			3600 0 0 000
Dec.	28	Sales Journal	SJ1	8000 0 0 00			4400 0 0 000
Dec.	31	Closing entries	G4	44000 0 0 00			~~00 0 000~~

ACCOUNT *Other Revenue* ACCOUNT NO. 402

DATE		DESCRIPTION	POST. REF.	DEBIT	CREDIT	BALANCE	
						DEBIT	CREDIT
Dec.	31	Fine	CRJ1		3 0 0 000		3 0 0 000
Dec.	31	Closing entries	G4	3 0 0 000			~~00 0 000~~

ACCOUNT *Cost of Goods Sold* ACCOUNT NO. 501

DATE		DESCRIPTION	POST. REF.	DEBIT	CREDIT	BALANCE	
						DEBIT	CREDIT
Dec.	1	Balance	√				
Dec.	28	Small Air-blower	5011	2750 0 0 0 00		2750 0 0 0 00	
Dec.	28	Large Air-blower	5012	2860 0 0 0 00		5610 0 0 0 00	
Dec.	31	Small Air-blower	5011	53 7 9 7 30		5663 7 9 7 30	
Dec.	31	Large Air-blower	5012	55 9 4 9 18		5719 7 4 6 48	
Dec.	31	Closing entries	GJ4		5719 7 4 6 48	~~00 0 000~~	

ACCOUNT *Cost of Goods Sold-Small Air-blower* ACCOUNT NO. 5011

	DATE		DESCRIPTION	POST. REF.	DEBIT	CREDIT	BALANCE DEBIT	BALANCE CREDIT	
1	Dec.	4	Sold products	G1	25000000		25000000		1
2	Dec.	7	Sold products	G1	25000000		50000000		2
3	Dec.	9	Sold products	G1	25000000		75000000		3
4	Dec.	12	Sold products	G1	50000000		125000000		4
5	Dec.	17	Sold products	G1	25000000		150000000		5
6	Dec.	19	Sold products	G1	75000000		225000000		6
7	Dec.	22	Sold products	G2	50000000		275000000		7
8	Dec.	29	Allocate material price variance	GJ3	4460784		279460784		8
9	Dec.	29	Allocate material quantity variance	GJ3	587010		280047794		9
10	Dec.	30	Allocate labor rate variance	GJ4	49118		280096912		10
11	Dec.	30	Allocate labor efficiency variance	GJ4	279412		280376324		11
12	Dec.	31	Allocate difference for O/H	GJ4	3406		280379730		12
13	Dec	31	Closing entries	GJ4		280379730	~~000000~~		13

ACCOUNT *Cost of Goods Sold-Large Air-blower* ACCOUNT NO. 5012

	DATE		DESCRIPTION	POST. REF.	DEBIT	CREDIT	BALANCE DEBIT	BALANCE CREDIT	
1	Dec.	7	Sold products	G1	52000000		52000000		1
2	Dec.	7	Sold products	G1	26000000		78000000		2
3	Dec.	11	Sold products	G1	26000000		104000000		3
4	Dec.	15	Sold products	G1	52000000		156000000		4
5	Dec.	17	Sold products	G1	52000000		208000000		5
6	Dec.	17	Sold products	G1	26000000		234000000		6
7	Dec.	28	Sold products	G2	52000000		286000000		7
8	Dec.	29	Allocate material price variance	GJ3	4639216		290639216		8
9	Dec.	29	Allocate material quantity variance	GJ3	610490		291249706		9
10	Dec.	30	Allocate labor rate variance	GJ4	51082		291300788		10
11	Dec.	30	Allocate labor efficiency variance	GJ4	290588		291591376		11
12	Dec.	31	Allocate difference for O/H	GJ4	3542		291594918		12
	Dec.	31	Closing entries	GJ4		291594918	~~000000~~		

ACCOUNT *Selling Expense* ACCOUNT NO. 502

	DATE		DESCRIPTION	POST. REF.	DEBIT	CREDIT	BALANCE DEBIT	BALANCE CREDIT	
1	Dec.	28	Sales Travel Expense	5021	450000		450000		1
2	Dec.	28	Sales Training Expense	5022	300000		750000		2
3	Dec.	28	Advertising Expense	5023	1500000		2250000		3
4	Dec.	28	Telephone Expense	5024	800000		3050000		4
5	Dec.	30	Sales Salaries Expense	5025	1000000		4050000		5
6	Dec.	31	Closing entries	GJ4		4050000	~~000000~~		6
7									7
8									8
9									9
10									10

ACCOUNT *Sales Travel Expense* ACCOUNT NO. 5021

DATE		DESCRIPTION	POST. REF.	DEBIT	CREDIT	BALANCE	
						DEBIT	CREDIT
Dec.	28	Pay travel fee	CPJ3	4 500 00		450000	
Dec.	31	Closing entries	GJ4		4 500 00	~~000000~~	

ACCOUNT *Sales Training Expense* ACCOUNT NO. 5022

DATE		DESCRIPTION	POST. REF.	DEBIT	CREDIT	BALANCE	
						DEBIT	CREDIT
Dec.	28	Pay training fee	CPJ2	3 000 00		300000	
Dec.	31	Closing entries	GJ4		3 000 00	~~000000~~	

ACCOUNT *Advertising Expense* ACCOUNT NO. 5023

DATE		DESCRIPTION	POST. REF.	DEBIT	CREDIT	BALANCE	
						DEBIT	CREDIT
Dec.	28	Pay advertising fee	CPJ2	10 000 00		1000000	
Dec.	28	Pay advertising fee	CPJ3	5 000 00		1500000	
Dec.	31	Closing entries	GJ4		15 000 00	~~000000~~	

ACCOUNT *Telephone Expense* ACCOUNT NO. 5024

	DATE		DESCRIPTION	POST. REF.	DEBIT	CREDIT	BALANCE DEBIT	BALANCE CREDIT	
1	Dec.	28	Pay telephone fee	CPJ4	8 000 00		8 000 00		1
2	Dec.	31	Closing entries	GJ4		8 000 00	0 000 00		2
3									3
4									4
5									5
6									6
7									7
8									8
9									9
10									10

ACCOUNT *Sales Salaries Expense* ACCOUNT NO. 5025

	DATE		DESCRIPTION	POST. REF.	DEBIT	CREDIT	BALANCE DEBIT	BALANCE CREDIT	
1	Dec.	30	Salaries expense	GJ3	10 000 00		10 000 00		1
2	Dec.	31	Closing entries	GJ4		10 000 00	0 000 00		2
3									3
4									4
5									5
6									6
7									7
8									8
9									9
10									10

ACCOUNT *Administrative & Managerial Expense* ACCOUNT NO. 503

	DATE		DESCRIPTION	POST. REF.	DEBIT	CREDIT	BALANCE DEBIT	BALANCE CREDIT	
1	Dec.	28	M&A Travel Expense	5031	800 00		800 00		1
2	Dec.	28	M&A Training Expense	5032	3 000 00		3 800 00		2
3	Dec.	28	Bank Fee Expense	5033	30 00		3 830 00		3
4	Dec.	28	Telecommunication Expense	5034	1 200 00		5 030 00		4
5	Dec.	28	Invitation Fee Expense	5035	2 500 00		7 530 00		5
6	Dec.	28	Television Expense	5036	240 00		7 770 00		6
7	Dec.	28	Interest Expense	5037	5 833 00		13 603 00		7
8	Dec.	29	M&A Broadband Expense	5039	2 885 44		16 488 44		8
9	Dec.	29	M&A Depreciation Expense	50310	15 984 70		32 473 14		9
10	Dec.	29	Amortization Expense	50311	2 250 00		34 723 14		10
11	Dec.	29	Subscription Expense	50312	9 600 00		44 323 14		11
12	Dec.	29	Insurance Expense	50313	90 000 00		134 323 14		12
13	Dec.	30	M&A Salaries Expense	50314	140 015 00		274 338 14		13
14	Dec.	30	Payroll Tax Expense	50315	177 616 67		451 954 81		14
15	Dec.	31	Bad Debt Expense	50316	23 980 00		475 934 81		15
16	Dec.	31	Interest Expense	5037	5 184 00		481 118 81		16
	Dec.	31	Closing entries	GJ4		481 118 81	0 000 00		

ACCOUNT *M&A Travel Expense* ACCOUNT NO. 5031

DATE		DESCRIPTION	POST. REF.	DEBIT	CREDIT	BALANCE DEBIT	BALANCE CREDIT
Dec.	31	Reimbursement of travel fee	CPJ1	800 00		800 00	
Dec.	31	Closing entries	GJ4		800 00	~~000000~~	

ACCOUNT *M&A Training Expense* ACCOUNT NO. 5032

DATE		DESCRIPTION	POST. REF.	DEBIT	CREDIT	BALANCE DEBIT	BALANCE CREDIT
Dec.	28	Pay training expense	CPJ4	3 000 00		3 000 00	
Dec.	31	Closing entries	GJ4		3 000 00	~~000000~~	

ACCOUNT *Bank Fee Expense* ACCOUNT NO. 5033

DATE		DESCRIPTION	POST. REF.	DEBIT	CREDIT	BALANCE DEBIT	BALANCE CREDIT
Dec.	31	Payment of bank fee	CPJ1	30 00		30 00	
Dec.	31	Closing entries	GJ4		30 00	~~000000~~	

ACCOUNT *Telecommunication Expense* ACCOUNT NO. 5034

	DATE		DESCRIPTION	POST. REF.	DEBIT	CREDIT	BALANCE		
							DEBIT	CREDIT	
1	Dec.	31	Payment of telecommunication fee	CPJ1	1 200 00		1 200 00		1
2	Dec.	31	Closing entries	GJ4		1 200 00	~~0 000 00~~		2
3									3
4									4
5									5
6									6
7									7
8									8
9									9
10									10

ACCOUNT *Invitation Fee Expense* ACCOUNT NO. 5035

	DATE		DESCRIPTION	POST. REF.	DEBIT	CREDIT	BALANCE		
							DEBIT	CREDIT	
1	Dec.	28	Pay invitation fee	CPJ2	1 000 00		1 000 00		1
2	Dec.	28	Pay invitation fee	CPJ4	1 500 00		2 500 00		2
3	Dec.	31	Closing entries	GJ4		2 500 00	~~0 000 00~~		3
4									4
5									5
6									6
7									7
8									8
9									9
10									10

ACCOUNT *Television Expense* ACCOUNT NO. 5036

	DATE		DESCRIPTION	POST. REF.	DEBIT	CREDIT	BALANCE		
							DEBIT	CREDIT	
1	Dec.	28	Pay television fee	CPJ3	240 00		240 00		1
2	Dec.	31	Closing entries	GJ4		240 00	~~0 000 00~~		2
3									3
4									4
5									5
6									6
7									7
8									8
9									9
10									10

ACCOUNT *Interest Expense* ACCOUNT NO. 5037

	DATE		DESCRIPTION	POST. REF.	DEBIT	CREDIT	BALANCE DEBIT	BALANCE CREDIT	
1	Dec.	28	Pay debt	CPJ4	5 833 00		5 833 00		1
2	Dec.	31	Accrual interest	GJ4	5 184 00		11 017 00		2
3	Dec.	31	Closing entries	GJ4		11 017 00	000000		3
4									4
5									5
6									6
7									7
8									8
9									9
10									10

ACCOUNT *Cash Lost Expense* ACCOUNT NO. 5038

	DATE		DESCRIPTION	POST. REF.	DEBIT	CREDIT	BALANCE DEBIT	BALANCE CREDIT	
1	Dec.	27	Cash lost	G2	50 00		50 00		1
2	Dec.	27	Reimbursement of cash lost	G2		50 00	000000		2
3									3
4									4
5									5
6									6
7									7
8									8
9									9
10									10

ACCOUNT *M&A Broadband Expense* ACCOUNT NO. 5039

	DATE		DESCRIPTION	POST. REF.	DEBIT	CREDIT	BALANCE DEBIT	BALANCE CREDIT	
1	Dec.	29	Expired broadband	GJ3	2 885 44		2 885 44		1
2	Dec.	31	Closing entries	GJ4		2 885 44	000000		2
3									3
4									4
5									5
6									6
7									7
8									8
9									9
10									10

ACCOUNT *M&A Depreciation Expense* ACCOUNT NO. 50310

	DATE		DESCRIPTION	POST. REF.	DEBIT	CREDIT	BALANCE		
							DEBIT	CREDIT	
1	Dec.	29	Monthly depreciation	GJ3	15 984 70		1598470		1
2	Dec.	31	Closing entries	GJ4		15 984 70	000000		2
3									3
4									4
5									5
6									6
7									7
8									8
9									9
10									10

ACCOUNT *Amortization Expense* ACCOUNT NO. 50311

	DATE		DESCRIPTION	POST. REF.	DEBIT	CREDIT	BALANCE		
							DEBIT	CREDIT	
1	Dec.	29	Patent	503111	2 000 00		200000		1
2	Dec.	29	Trademark	503112	250 00		225000		2
3	Dec.	31	Closing entries	GJ4		2 250 00	000000		3
4									4
5									5
6									6
7									7
8									8
9									9
10									10

ACCOUNT *Amortization Expense—Patent* ACCOUNT NO. 503111

	DATE		DESCRIPTION	POST. REF.	DEBIT	CREDIT	BALANCE		
							DEBIT	CREDIT	
1	Dec.	29	Patent amortization	GJ3	2 000 00		200000		1
2	Dec.	31	Closing entries	GJ4		2 000 00	000000		2
3									3
4									4
5									5
6									6
7									7
8									8
9									9
10									10

ACCOUNT *Amortization Expense–Trademark* ACCOUNT NO. 503112

	DATE		DESCRIPTION	POST. REF.	DEBIT	CREDIT	BALANCE DEBIT	BALANCE CREDIT	
1	Dec.	29	Monthly amortization	GJ3	250 00		250 00		1
2	Dec.	31	Closing entries	GJ4		250 00	000000		2
3									3
4									4
5									5
6									6
7									7
8									8
9									9
10									10

ACCOUNT *Subscription Expense* ACCOUNT NO. 50312

	DATE		DESCRIPTION	POST. REF.	DEBIT	CREDIT	BALANCE DEBIT	BALANCE CREDIT	
1	Dec.	29	Expired subscription	GJ3	9 600 00		9 600 00		1
2	Dec.	31	Closing entries	GJ4		9 600 00	000000		2
3									3
4									4
5									5
6									6
7									7
8									8
9									9
10									10

ACCOUNT *Insurance Expense* ACCOUNT NO. 50313

	DATE		DESCRIPTION	POST. REF.	DEBIT	CREDIT	BALANCE DEBIT	BALANCE CREDIT	
1	Dec.	29	Expired insurance	GJ3	90 000 00		90 000 00		1
2	Dec.	31	Closing entries	GJ4		90 000 00	000000		2
3									3
4									4
5									5
6									6
7									7
8									8
9									9
10									10

ACCOUNT *M&A Salaries Expense* ACCOUNT NO. 50314

	DATE		DESCRIPTION	POST. REF.	DEBIT	CREDIT	BALANCE		
							DEBIT	CREDIT	
1	Dec.	30	Monthly salaries	GJ3	140015 00		140015 00		1
2	Dec.	31	Closing entries	GJ4		140015 00	~~0000 00~~		2
3									3
4									4
5									5
6									6
7									7
8									8
9									9
10									10

ACCOUNT *Payroll Tax Expense* ACCOUNT NO. 50315

	DATE		DESCRIPTION	POST. REF.	DEBIT	CREDIT	BALANCE		
							DEBIT	CREDIT	
1	Dec.	30	Employer's part	GJ4	177616 67		177616 67		1
2	Dec.	31	Closing entries	GJ4		177616 67	~~0000 00~~		2
3									3
4									4
5									5
6									6
7									7
8									8
9									9
10									10

ACCOUNT *Bad Debt Expense* ACCOUNT NO. 50316

	DATE		DESCRIPTION	POST. REF.	DEBIT	CREDIT	BALANCE		
							DEBIT	CREDIT	
1	Dec.	31	Bad debt	GJ4	23980 00		23980 00		1
2	Dec.	31	Closing entries	GJ4		23980 00	~~0000 00~~		2
3									3
4									4
5									5
6									6
7									7
8									8
9									9
10									10

ACCOUNT *Taxes Expense* ACCOUNT NO. 505

	DATE		DESCRIPTION	POST. REF.	DEBIT	CREDIT	BALANCE		
							DEBIT	CREDIT	
1	Dec.	28	Property Tax Expense	5052	54 090 00		54 090 00		1
2	Dec.	31	Closing entries	GJ4		54 090 00	000000		2
3	Dec.	31	Closing entries	GJ4	836 470 15		836 470 15		3
4	Dec.	31	Closing entries	GJ4		836 470 15	000000		4
5									5
6									6
7									7
8									8
9									9
10									10

ACCOUNT *Income Taxes Expense* ACCOUNT NO. 5051

	DATE		DESCRIPTION	POST. REF.	DEBIT	CREDIT	BALANCE		
							DEBIT	CREDIT	
1	Dec.	31	Closing entries	GJ4	836 470 15		836 470 15		1
2	Dec.	31	Closing entries	GJ4		836 470 15	000000		2
3									3
4									4
5									5
6									6
7									7
8									8
9									9
10									10

ACCOUNT *Property Tax Expense* ACCOUNT NO. 5052

	DATE		DESCRIPTION	POST. REF.	DEBIT	CREDIT	BALANCE		
							DEBIT	CREDIT	
1	Dec.	17	Property Document Submission	G1	54 090 00		54 090 00		1
2	Dec.	31	Closing entries	GJ4		54 090 00	000000		2
3									3
4									4
5									5
6									6
7									7
8									8
9									9
10									10

ACCOUNT *Loss on Disposal of PP&E* ACCOUNT NO. 506

DATE		DESCRIPTION	POST. REF.	DEBIT	CREDIT	BALANCE	
						DEBIT	CREDIT
Dec.	11	Lathe	5061	5 000 00		5 000 00	
Dec.	31	Closing entries	GJ4		5 000 00	~~0 000 00~~	

ACCOUNT *Loss on Disposal of Lathe* ACCOUNT NO. 5061

DATE		DESCRIPTION	POST. REF.	DEBIT	CREDIT	BALANCE	
						DEBIT	CREDIT
Dec.	11	Disposal of Lathe	G1	5 000 00		5 000 00	
Dec.	31	Closing entries	GJ4		5 000 00	~~0 000 00~~	

ACCOUNT *Income Summary* ACCOUNT NO. 601

DATE		DESCRIPTION	POST. REF.	DEBIT	CREDIT	BALANCE	
						DEBIT	CREDIT
Dec.	31	Closing entries	GJ4		1952 544 71		1952 544 71
Dec.	31	Closing entries	GJ4	836 470 15			1116 074 56
Dec.	31	Closing entries	GJ4	1116 074 56			~~0 000 00~~

All closing entries in General Journal have been posted to the ledger. Updated General Journal is illustrated in following table.

GENERAL JOURNAL						PAGE 1	
	DATE		DESCRIPTION	POST. REF.	DEBIT	CREDIT	
1	Dec.	4	Other Receivables-Fenghua Air-blower	1092	3000 00		1
2			Bank Deposit	102		3000 00	2
3			Check Stub 34	√			3
4	Dec.	4	Cost of Goods Sold-Small Air-blower	5011	2500000 00		4
5			Finished Goods-Small Air-blower	11031		2500000 00	5
6			SALES SLIP 68	√			6
7	Dec.	7	Cost of Goods Sold-Large Air-blower	5012	5200000 00		7
8			Finished Goods-Large Air-blower	11032		5200000 00	8
9			SALES SLIP 69	√			9
10	Dec.	7	Cost of Goods Sold-Small Air-blower	5011	2500000 00		10
11			Finished Goods-Small Air-blower	11031		2500000 00	11
12			SALES SLIP 70	√			12
13	Dec.	7	Cost of Goods Sold-Large Air-blower	5012	2600000 00		13
14			Finished Goods-Large Air-blower	11032		2600000 00	14
15			SALES SLIP 71	√			15
16	Dec.	9	Other Receivables-Ningbo Air-blower	1093	3000 00		16
17			Bank Deposit	102		3000 00	17
18			Check Stub 48	√			18
19	Dec.	9	Cost of Goods Sold-Small Air-blower	5011	2500000 00		19
20			Finished Goods-Small Air-blower	11031		2500000 00	20
21			SALES SLIP 72	√			21
22	Dec.	11	Cost of Goods Sold-Large Air-blower	5012	2600000 00		22
23			Finished Goods-Large Air-blower	11032		2600000 00	23
24			SALES SLIP 73	√			24
25	Dec.	11	Bank Deposit	102	100000 00		25
26			Loss on Disposal of Lathe	5061	50000 00		26
27			Accumulated Depreciation-Lathe	1161	1350000 00		27
28			Lathe	1151		1500000 00	28
29			Memorandum 32 & 33	√			29
30	Dec.	12	Cost of Goods Sold-Small Air-blower	5011	5000000 00		30
31			Finished Goods-Small Air-blower	11031		5000000 00	31
32			SALES SLIP 74	√			32
33	Dec.	15	Cost of Goods Sold-Large Air-blower	5012	5200000 00		33
34			Finished Goods-Large Air-blower	11032		5200000 00	34
35			SALES SLIP 75	√			35
36	Dec.	17	Other Receivables-Ningbo Air-blower	1093	2000 00		36
37			Bank Deposit	102		2000 00	37
38			Check Stub 168	√			38
39	Dec.	17	Cost of Goods Sold-Large Air-blower	5012	5200000 00		39
40			Finished Goods-Large Air-blower	11032		5200000 00	40
41			SALES SLIP 76	√			41
42	Dec.	17	Cost of Goods Sold-Small Air-blower	5011	2500000 00		42
43			Finished Goods-Small Air-blower	11031		2500000 00	43
44			SALES SLIP 77	√			44
45	Dec.	17	Cost of Goods Sold-Large Air-blower	5012	2600000 00		45
46			Finished Goods-Large Air-blower	11032		2600000 00	46
47			SALES SLIP 78	√			47
48	Dec.	17	Property Tax Expense	5052	54090 00		48
49			Property Tax Payable	2062		54090 00	49
50			Memorandum 36	√			50
51	Dec.	18	Bank Deposit	102	97875 00		51
52			Discounts on N/R-Xiangshan AB	105	2125 00		52
53			N/R-Xiangshan AB	1042		100000 00	53
54			Check Stub 177	√			54
55	Dec.	19	Cost of Goods Sold-Small Air-blower	5011	7500000 00		55
56			Finished Goods-Small Air-blower	11031		7500000 00	56
57			SALES SLIP 79	√			57
58							
59							
60							

GENERAL JOURNAL PAGE 2

	DATE		DESCRIPTION	POST. REF.	DEBIT	CREDIT	
1	Dec.	21	Grinder	1159	5000000		1
2			Capital, Hefeng	301		5000000	2
3			Memorandum 38	√			3
4	Dec.	22	Cost of Goods Sold-Small Air-blower	5011	50000000		4
5			Finished Goods-Small Air-blower	11031		50000000	5
6			SALES SLIP 80	√			6
7	Dec.	23	Steel Plates	110111	7500000		7
8			Material Price Variance	111	500000		8
9			Factory Overhead Incurred	113	920000		9
10			Commercial Acceptance Bill Pay	208		8920000	10
11			Bill 117	√			11
12	Dec.	23	Bank Deposit	102	150000		12
13			Cash on Hand	101		150000	13
14			Receipt 926	√			14
15	Dec.	27	Cash Lost Expense	5038	5000		15
16			Cash on Hand	101		5000	16
17			Memorandum 39	√			17
18	Dec.	27	Cash on Hand	101	5000		18
19			Cash Lost Expense	5038		5000	19
20			Memorandum 40	√			20
21	Dec.	28	Cost of Goods Sold-Large Air-blower	5012	52000000		21
22			Finished Goods-Large Air-blower	11032		52000000	22
23			SALES SLIP 83	√			23
24	Dec.	28	Work-in-process-Small Air-blower	11021	25987500		24
25			Material Quantity Variance	112	262500		25
26			Steel Plates	110111		26250000	26
27			Memorandum 41	√			27
28			Work-in-process-Large Air-blower	11022	22612500		28
29			Material Quantity Variance	112	187500		29
30			Steel Plates	110111		22800000	30
31			Memorandum 41	√			31
32			Factory Overhead Incurred	113	1500000		32
33			Steel Plates	110111		1500000	33
34			Memorandum 41	√			34
35	Dec.	28	Work-in-process-Small Air-blower	11021	11137500		35
36			Material Quantity Variance	112	112500		36
37			Iron Castings	110113		11250000	37
38			Memorandum 41	√			38
39			Work-in-process-Large Air-blower	11022	11137500		39
40			Material Quantity Variance	112	22500		40
41			Iron Castings	110113		11160000	41
42			Memorandum 41	√			42
43			Factory Overhead Incurred	113	2250000		43
44			Iron Castings	110113		2250000	44
45			Memorandum 41	√			45
46	Dec.	28	Work-in-process-Small Air-blower	11021	17325000		46
47			Material Quantity Variance	112	175000		47
48			Copper Line	110112		17500000	48
49			Memorandum 41	√			49
50			Work-in-process-Large Air-blower	11022	14962500		50
51			Material Quantity Variance	112	437500		51
52			Copper Line	110112		15400000	52
53			Memorandum 41	√			53
54	Dec.	28	Factory Overhead Incurred	113	3000000		54
55			Refrigeration Oil	110121		3000000	55
56			Memorandum 41	√			56
57			Factory Overhead Incurred	113	3750000		57
58			Refrigeration Oil	110121		3750000	58
59			Memorandum 41	√			59
60							60

GENERAL JOURNAL PAGE 3

DATE		DESCRIPTION	POST. REF.	DEBIT	CREDIT
Dec.	28	Factory Overhead Incurred	113	4000 00	
		Packing Boxes	110122		4000 00
		Memorandum 41	√		
		Factory Overhead Incurred	113	3200 00	
		Packing Boxes	110122		3200 00
		Memorandum 41	√		
Dec.	28	Factory Overhead Incurred	113	1018 42	
		Work Jackets	11431		1018 42
		Memorandum 41	√		
		Factory Overhead Incurred	113	1760 12	
		Work Shoes	11432		1760 12
		Memorandum 41	√		
		Factory Overhead Incurred	113	1486 36	
		Heat-resistant Gloves	11433		1486 36
		Memorandum 41	√		
Dec.	29	Amortization Expense-Patent	503111	2000 00	
		Accum. Amortization-Patent	1191		2000 00
		Memorandum 42	√		
		Amortization Expense-Trademark	503112	250 00	
		Accum. Amortization-Trademark	1192		250 00
		Memorandum 42	√		
Dec.	29	Subscription Expense	50312	9600 00	
		Prepaid Subscription	1082		9600 00
		Memorandum 43	√		
		Insurance Expense	50313	90000 00	
		Prepaid Insurance	1083		90000 00
		Memorandum 43	√		
Dec.	29	Factory Overhead Incurred	113	7114 56	
		M&A Broadband Expense	5039	2885 44	
		Prepaid Broadband	1081		10000 00
		Memorandum 44	√		
Dec.	29	Factory Overhead Incurred	113	87302 56	
		M&A Depreciation Expense	50310	15984 70	
		Accumulated Depreciation	116		103287 26
		Memorandum 45	√		
Dec.	30	COGS–Small Air-blower	5011	44607 84	
		COGS–Large Air-blower	5012	46392 16	
		Material Price Variance	111		91000 00
		Memorandum 46	√		
		COGS–Small Air-blower	5011	5870 10	
		COGS–Large Air-blower	5012	6104 90	
		Material Quantity Variance	112		11975 00
		Memorandum 46	√		
Dec.	30	Direct Labor	120	493050 00	
		Labor Efficiency Variance	121	5700 00	
		Labor Rate Variance	122	1002 00	
		Factory Overhead Incurred	113	72252 00	
		Sales Salaries Expense	5025	10000 00	
		M&A Salaries Expense	50314	140015 00	
		Social Security Tax Payable	2052		129963 42
		Medicare Tax Payable	2053		14440 38
		FUTP	2054		931 64
		SUTP	2055		6288 55
		Employee FITP	2056		904 67
		Employee SITP	2057		1809 33
		Salaries Payable	2051		567681 01
		Memorandum 47	√		

GENERAL JOURNAL PAGE 4

	DATE		DESCRIPTION	POST. REF.	DEBIT	CREDIT	
1	Dec.	30	Payroll Tax Expense	50315	177616 67		1
2			Social Security Tax Payable	2052		129963 42	2
3			Medicare Tax Payable	2053		14440 38	3
4			FUTP	2054		4332 11	4
5			SUTP	2055		28880 76	5
6			Memorandum 47	√			6
7	Dec.	30	Work-in-process–Small Air-blower	11021	266475 00		7
8			Work-in-process–Large Air-blower	11022	226575 00		8
9			Direct Labor	120		493050 00	9
10			Memorandum 47	√			10
11	Dec.	30	COGS–Small Air-blower	5011	491 18		11
12			COGS–Large Air-blower	5012	510 82		12
13			Labor Rate Variance	122		1002 00	13
14			Memorandum 47	√			14
15			COGS–Small Air-blower	5011	2794 12		15
16			COGS–Large Air-blower	5012	2905 88		16
17			Labor Efficiency Variance	121		5700 00	17
18			Memorandum 47	√			18
19	Dec.	31	Bad Debt Expense	50316	23980 00		19
20			Allowance for Doubtful Debts	107		23980 00	20
21			Memorandum 48	√			21
22	Dec.	31	Interest Expense	5037	5184 00		22
23			Interest Payable	207		5184 00	23
24			Memorandum 49	√			24
25	Dec.	31	Work-in-process–Small Air-blower	11021	288420 00		25
26			Work-in-process–Large Air-blower	11022	242880 00		26
27			Factory Overhead Applied	113		531300 00	27
28			Memorandum 50	√			28
29	Dec.	31	Cost of Goods Sold–Small Air-blower	5011	34 06		29
30			Cost of Goods Sold–Large Air-blower	5012	35 42		30
31			Factory Overhead	113		69 48	31
32			Memorandum 51	√			32
33	Dec.	31	Finished Goods–Small Air-blower	11031	1161416 42		33
34			WIP–Small Air-blower	11021		1161416 42	34
35			Memorandum 52	√			35
36	Dec.	31	Finished Goods–Large Air-blower	11032	961716 37		36
37			WIP–Large Air-blower	11022		961716 37	37
38			Memorandum 52	√			38
39	Dec.	31	Sales Revenue	401	8250000 00		39
40			Other Revenue Other Revenue	402	30000 00		40
41			Cost of Goods Sold	501		5719746 48	41
42			Selling Expense	502		40500 00	42
43			M&A Expense	503		481118 81	43
44			Taxes Expense	505		54090 00	44
45			Loss on Disposal of PP&E	506		5000 00	45
46			Income Summary	601		1952544 71	46
47			Memorandum 53	√			47
48	Dec.	31	Income Tax Expense	5051	836470 15		48
49			Federal Income Tax Payable	20631		663865 20	49
50			State Income Tax Payable	20632		172604 95	50
51			Memorandum 54	√			51
52			Income Summary	601	836470 15		52
53			Income Tax Expense	5051		836470 15	53
54			Memorandum 54	√			54
55	Dec.	31	Income Summary	601	1116074 56		55
56			Retained Earnings	303		1116074 56	56
57			Memorandum 55	√			57
58							58
59							59
60							60

CHAPTER 8 PREPARE FINANCIAL STATEMENTS

The seventh step of accounting cycle is to prepare financial statements. There are three types of financial statements. They are Income Statement, Balance Sheet and Cash Flow Statement. Statement of Owners' Equity will also be prepared. The first two types of financial statements will be prepared for Xinle Air-blower Co., Ltd. The balances of each account in the ledgers will be used to prepare those two statements. Those two statements are illustrated in following tables.

Income Statement

For Year 2016

Revenue	
Sales Revenue, Net	$ 8,250,000.00
Cost of Goods Sold	(5,719,746.48)
Gross Profit	2,530,253.52
Expense	
Selling Expense	(40,500.00)
Administrative & Managerial Expense	(481,118.81)
Operating Income	2,008,634.71
Other Revenue & Expense	
Other Revenue	3,000.00
Loss on Disposal of PP&E	(5,000.00)
Income Before Taxes	2,006,634.71
Taxes	(890,560.15)
Net Income	$ 1,116,074.56

Balance Sheet

For the Year Ended on December 31, 2016

Assets	12/31/2016
Cash on Hand	$ 37,000.00
Bank Deposit	6,093,704.54
Bank Draft	60,408.00
Notes Receivable	202,125.00
Acccounts Receivable, Net	2,968,020.00
Prepaid Expense	122,500.00
Inventory	2,025,296.00
Supplies	29,735.10
Other Receivables	13,500.00
Total Current Assets	11,552,288.64
Plant, Property & Equipment, Net	9,850,912.74
Land	2,600,000.00
Intangible Assets, Net	327,750.00
Total Non-current Assets	12,778,662.74
Total Assets	24,330,951.38
Liabilities	
Short-term Borrowings	2,528,000.00
Notes Payable	110,000.00
Accounts Payable	441,900.00
Unearned Revenue	1,191,570.00
Payroll Liabilities	899,635.67
Taxes Payable	1,646,470.15
Interests Payable	8,101.00
Commercial Acceptance Bill Payable	89,200.00
Total Current Liabilities	6,914,876.82
Total Liabilities	6,914,876.82
Owner's Equity	
Capital, Hefeng	12,850,000.00
Capital Reserve	550,000.00
Retained Earnings	4,016,074.56
Total Owner's Equity	17,416,074.56
Total Liabilities and Owner's Equity	$ 24,330,951.38

后　记

中美合作办学会计学专业是浙江省首批中外合作办学示范建设项目，进入示范项目建设期以来，宁波工程学院中外合作办学教育呈现出前所未有的发展势头。本教材是宁波工程学院中外合作办学的系列成果之一，也是宁波工程学院中外合作办学在坚持引进、吸收融通和逐步本土化方面作出的一点探索。

国际交流学院是宁波工程学院承办中外合作办学项目的实体学院，拥有一支教学经验和实践经验都很丰富的资深教师队伍。教材的编写工作由中美双方教师共同承担，写作目的是满足中外合作办学需求，现由东北财经大学出版社陆续向广大读者推出，希望对中外合作办学领域的会计学专业教学及实务有所裨益。

宁波工程学院国际交流学院

院长　聂利亚